# Frommer's

# Alaska Cruises
## & Ports of Call

## 2005

### by Jerry Brown & Fran Wenograd Golden

Here's what the critics say about F

"Amazingly easy to use. Very portable, very complete."

—*Booklist*

"Detailed, accurate, and easy-to-read information for all price ranges."
—*Glamour Magazine*

"Hotel information is close to encyclopedic."

—*Des Moines Sunday Register*

"Frommer's Guides have a way of giving you a real feel for a place."
—*Knight Ridder Newspapers*

**WILEY**

Wiley Publishing, Inc.

## About the Authors

**Jerry Brown** was born in Edinburgh, Scotland, and worked as a reporter for Scottish newspapers before joining the news department of the *London Daily Mail.* Later, for 31 years, he was the West Coast Bureau Chief of a leading travel trade newspaper. He and Margaret, his wife and best editor, have two grown sons, a granddaughter, Victoria Rose, and a grandson, Mason Patrick. **Fran Wenograd Golden** is travel editor of the *Boston Herald,* and a well-established travel writer. She is also author of *TV Vacations: A Fun Guide to the Sites, the Stars, and the Inside Stories Behind Your Favorite TV Shows,* and co-author (with Jerry) of *Cruise Vacations For Dummies* and *Frommer's European Cruises & Ports of Call.* She lives north of Boston with her husband, Ed, and is the proud parent of Erin and Eli.

Published by:

## Wiley Publishing, Inc.

111 River St.
Hoboken, NJ 07030-5774

ISBN 0-7645-7579-1

Editor: Risa Weinreb Wyatt, Naomi Kraus
Production Editor: Heather Wilcox
Cartographer: Roberta Stockwell
Photo Editor: Richard Fox
Production by Wiley Indianapolis Composition Services

For information on our other products and services or to obtain technical support, please contact our Customer Care Department within the U.S. at 800/762-2974, outside the U.S. at 317/572-3993 or fax 317/572-4002.

Wiley also publishes its books in a variety of electronic formats. Some content that appears in print may not be available in electronic formats.

Manufactured in the United States of America

5   4   3   2   1

# Contents

# List of Maps

## An Invitation to the Reader

In researching this book, we discovered many wonderful places—hotels, restaurants, shops, and more. We're sure you'll find others. Please tell us about them, so we can share the information with your fellow travelers in upcoming editions. If you were disappointed with a recommendation, we'd love to know that, too. Please write to:

*Frommer's Alaska Cruises & Ports of Call 2005*
Wiley Publishing, Inc. • 111 River St. • Hoboken, NJ 07030-5774

## An Additional Note

Please be advised that travel information is subject to change at any time—and this is especially true of prices. We therefore suggest that you write or call ahead for confirmation when making your travel plans. The authors, editors, and publisher cannot be held responsible for the experiences of readers while traveling. Your safety is important to us, however, so we encourage you to stay alert and be aware of your surroundings. Keep a close eye on cameras, purses, and wallets, all favorite targets of thieves and pickpockets.

## Frommer's Icons & Abbreviations

We use **a feature icon** that points you to the great deals, in-the-know advice, and unique experiences that separate travelers from tourists. Throughout the book, look for:

**Tips**        Insider tips—great ways to save time and money

The following **abbreviations** are used for credit cards:

| | | | |
|---|---|---|---|
| AE | American Express | DISC Discover | V Visa |
| DC | Diners Club | MC MasterCard | |

## Frommers.com

Now that you have the guidebook to a great trip, visit our website at **www.frommers.com** for travel information on more than 3,000 destinations. With features updated regularly, we give you instant access to the most current trip-planning information available. At Frommers.com, you'll also find the best prices on airfares, accommodations, and car rentals—and you can even book travel online through our travel booking partners. At Frommers.com, you'll also find the following:

- Online updates to our most popular guidebooks
- Vacation sweepstakes and contest giveaways
- Newsletter highlighting the hottest travel trends
- Online travel message boards with featured travel discussions

# What's New in Alaska Cruising in 2005

Just like the glaciers, the world of Alaska travel is always changing. New ships come, and others go—in some years more so than in others, as you will see. Cruise lines add new shore excursions and land packages and enhance their onboard offerings. Embarkation ports suddenly get very popular. And in our travels, we constantly find interesting new changes in the tourism industry of the 49th state. In writing this book, we've tried to keep track of the latest and greatest developments.

**THE CRUISE INDUSTRY IN GENERAL** 2004 was a very good year for cruise companies in Alaska. There were more ships in the market (an 11% increase in bed capacity over 2003), yet they were surprisingly full. We expect the trend to continue in 2005 (with only a 6% capacity increase). What this means for consumers is there may not be as many of those big discount last-minute deals as there were in 2002 and 2003 (years when the aftereffects of the Sept 11, 2001, terrorist attacks were still being felt big time). We believe your best bet for getting a good deal on a cruise in 2005 is to book early, by mid-February 2005—earlier if possible—for the best selection and biggest early-bird savings. If you take your chances and wait, be prepared to take leftovers. Alaska is hot, hot, hot.

**SHIPS** As we indicated above, some years see greater increases in capacity than in others. Just last year in this space, we wrote, "This is where it's all happening in 2004. More ships, bigger ships—and brand-new ships. There are half a dozen vessels in the market this year that weren't there before."

Guess what? There's not a single brand-new ship in the market in 2005 and none that hasn't been there before. One, **Silversea**'s *Silver Shadow,* has departed for other destinations, but the total complement of ships remains the same because of the return of the *Norwegian Dream.* This lack of expansion makes it an unusual summer for an Alaska market in which the number—and certainly the size—of ships has risen steadily in recent years. Last year was a year of spectacular growth in the number of berths being offered, with the arrival of two huge new vessels right out of the builder's yard, **Princess Cruises'** *Diamond Princess* and the *Sapphire Princess,* as well as the *Oosterdam* of **Holland America (HAL).** These three, and two dozen others, are back in 2005.

**Norwegian Cruise Line,** a relatively young and innovative company in the Alaska market, does have a ship with a new name there in 2005—the *Norwegian Spirit.* But don't be fooled; it's not a new ship in the truest sense of the word. Rather, it is the renamed *SuperStar Leo,* joining three fleetmates in the Pacific Northwest. The strengthening demand for Alaska cruising, of course, makes life easier for cruise-line marketers and reduces the downward pressure on prices. So be alert. If you see a bargain, don't hesitate to grab it. You may not get a second chance.

## PORTS OF EMBARKATION

Seattle has suddenly become the hottest port in the market. Seattle had been used for years as a port of embarkation for smaller ships, most notably by **Cruise West** (whose biggest ship holds fewer than 140 passengers), but 5 years ago **Norwegian Cruise Line (NCL)** pioneered the use of Seattle as a big-ship port, placing its ship *Norwegian Sky* (now departed for Hawaii) there for the Alaska season. Some competitors predicted that this plan was rash, would never succeed. Then came 9/11, and overnight, every line started looking for U.S. ports to use. In 2005, **NCL** is sending the *Norwegian Spirit* and *Norwegian Dream* to Seattle to join the *Norwegian Star* out of that port.

**Princess** will again have its two newest and biggest vessels (the *Diamond* and *Sapphire*) in Seattle for the summer season, and **Holland America** will again position its *Oosterdam* and *Amsterdam* in the Washington State port.

To top it all off, **Celebrity** is deploying the *Mercury* out of that city as well. If you're keeping score, that means Seattle has gone from having one large ship in 2000 to no fewer than eight in 2005, a solid indication that the industry doesn't believe NCL is so crazy any more!

An interesting thing we're hearing from cruise-line executives is the demographic of cruisers from Seattle is younger than from other Alaska ports, with more families on board the ships sailing from Washington State.

Last year, **Princess** opted to replace Seward with the rather colorless port of Whittier as the northern terminus of its Gulf of Alaska cruises. The reason is that, nondescript as it may be,

Whittier is closer to Anchorage. This year, **Carnival** will use that township as its northern terminus as well.

Another port that looks to be on the rise is Prince Rupert, B.C. Local authorities there are upgrading the Northland Dock, at Cow Bay where the cruise ships tie up, by building a complex of 12 retail stores that are scheduled to open by the start of the 2005 season. Last year Prince Rupert had a couple of visits a week by one ship of **Norwegian Cruise Line** and one of Silversea Cruises (now gone) and has been working feverishly to attract more business. The town's cause is greatly aided by the need for cruise lines to find new ports of call in a market where destinations and port facilities are being stretched to the limit. Truly, the battle for the minds (and pocketbooks) of cruisers now is being fought not so much with hardware—new ships, fancier staterooms, more restaurants—but with itineraries, shore excursions, onboard activities, cruisetours, and the like.

## ONBOARD CHANGES

Cruise lines are constantly tweaking their onboard products and services, with the aim of making life easier for passengers and reducing regimentation, especially at meal times. All of the new ships have scads of alternative dining opportunities, some for a price, some gratis. Perhaps the most flexible of all is **Princess,** which offers seven dining options on both the *Diamond* and *Sapphire.* And now, the line is offering a program under which passengers may buy a soft drinks sticker that attaches to the cruise card/door key and allows unlimited Cokes and other carbonated soft drinks for the duration of the cruise without having to sign a chit each time. The program will be fleetwide in all destination areas this summer.

## CRUISETOURS

A lot of the emphasis here is on the Denali Corridor (Anchorage to Fairbanks, through

Denali), where rail tours hold sway. **Holland America, Princess,** and **Royal Celebrity Tours** (the tour operation for **Royal Caribbean** and **Celebrity**) will all have new domed glass rail cars in service this year. They will be billed as "the most luxurious," with "the easiest viewing windows" and will serve "gourmet meals." Suffice it to say that these new cars are uniformly spectacular. And, incidentally, a tribute to the power of market forces. This year, both **HAL** and **Princess** will make it easier to get to the Denali corridor. Each is instituting a "direct to the wilderness" service that will allow passengers to disembark in Seward (in HAL's case) or in Whittier (in the case of Princess) and step onto domed rail cars right on the pier. The train ride will take them through Anchorage and into the Denali Park area without change of train and with no layover in Anchorage.

**SHORE EXCURSIONS** Cruise lines are increasingly looking at Alaskan ports as just the starting point for exploration. They have to. How else to disperse crowds of thousands? Toward that end, the lines have beefed up their offerings. **Carnival,** for instance, has a brochure that lists over 100 shore excursions, and **Princess** has a couple dozen in Juneau alone. A new name appearing more frequently in listings this year is Icy Strait Point, an area (it can hardly be called a town) between Juneau and Glacier Bay. It is, in essence, nothing more than a single dock, an old cannery unit strategically placed for entry on foot to some of Alaska's most pristine and hitherto inaccessible wilderness areas. Both **Royal Caribbean** and **Celebrity** experimented with occasional stops there last year; they'll make more in 2005. And the developers of the dock, a Tlingit Indian corporation, are lobbying hard for others to follow suit. There will, however, never be more than one ship in Icy Strait Point at any given time, for ecological (and purely practical) reasons.

**CRUISE ITINERARIES** Alaska is somewhat limited in the itinerary variations it can offer. It is essentially either the Inside Passage (through the part of Alaska known as Southeast or the Panhandle), or the popular one-way cruises across the Gulf of Alaska between Vancouver and Anchorage (with embarkation or disembarkation in Seward or Whittier, the ports for Anchorage). Other alternative routes include all-Alaska cruises beginning and ending in places like Juneau and Ketchikan, cruises to remote Indian villages, and cruises embarking and disembarking at San Francisco and Seattle. One interesting Inside Passage itinerary not often offered is the *Norwegian Dream*'s 10-day cruise out of Seattle. All other Seattle-originating Inside Passage voyages are of 1-week duration; this innovative longer version allows the *Dream* to cover more ports and wilderness areas in greater depth.

**THE GLACIER BAY ACCESS DEBATE** Environmental issues involving passenger-ship entry into Glacier Bay continue to pit conservationists (who want to limit the number of cruise ships allowed into the bay) against the cruise lines. The subject of how many ships can safely enter the vast wilderness area without upsetting the whales and other forms of aquatic life that inhabit it in the summer has been hotly debated—and disputed—for more than a decade. The environmentalists would like to prohibit all big cruise ships from visiting Glacier Bay in June, July, and August; the cruise lines, naturally, feel that more ships should be granted access during those peak travel months. The U.S. government has given some indications that not only will access *not* be cut from the current 107 cruise ship visitations allowed throughout the 3 peak summer months (June, July,

Aug), but it might eventually be raised. None of the cruise lines, though, expects that to occur in time for the 2005 season. If, by some chance, it should happen, look for the cruise giants—**HAL, Princess,** and **Royal Caribbean/Celebrity,** to rework their itineraries to take advantage of the extra entry authorizations.

An environmental impact study now underway to determine exactly how much damage ships do to the aquatic population of the bay will be the determinant.

In 2005, **Holland America** will offer more ships that have access to the park than any other line in the market, and **Princess** will have the most berths visiting the area because the company has larger ships. There are many other ships with a varying number of authorizations to enter the park in 2005 (check chapters 5 and 6).

Don't worry if your cruise doesn't include a visit to Glacier Bay because there are plenty of other equally delightful and—in our opinion, sometimes even more attractive—glacier areas to visit. The cruise lines have found ways to live with the Glacier Bay entry restrictions by substituting visits to Hubbard Glacier, Icy Bay, Misty Fjords, or Tracy Arm. And, as a matter of fact, we would rather visit Hubbard Glacier any day of the week!

**ENVIRONMENTAL CONCERNS**
The state legislature has enacted a series of pollution-mitigating restrictions on cruise lines, including increased environmental-reporting requirements and stricter rules about where cruise ships may legally discard treated waste. And the legislature is likely to continue to turn up the heat to keep the cruise lines honest.

Some cruise executives believe that environmental concerns, serious though they are, are being overplayed and used as an "excuse" to make cruise lines and their passengers pay to

reduce Alaska's budget shortfall. Whether this is true or not, Alaskans' perception of cruising and their efforts to make cruise passengers pay more are matters that concern ship operators greatly. Cruise lines have done their part to alleviate the locals' fears. They've staggered their shore excursion vehicle traffic to cut down on crowds in the streets. They've hooked up to city power supplies while in port rather than continuing to operate their own generators in order to minimize the outflow of pollutants from their smokestacks. They've installed sophisticated garbage disposal equipment and new procedures to do away with unclean dumping at sea. They've done all kinds of things to respond positively to the concerns of Alaska citizens. It's an uneasy truce—but it's holding.

**THE ISSUE OF TAXATION** An unfortunate result of the rising visitor volume is increasing impact on the environment of some Alaska communities and on the psyches of some of the state's residents. The combination of increased visitor volume and the state's declining oil revenues, which have left Alaska with an estimated $3-billion-plus budget shortfall through 2006, has led to a rush to tax cruise passengers. Juneau, the state's beautiful capital, imposes a $5-per-passenger head tax, ostensibly to pay for the essential services (police, sewage, roadways, and so on) used by the estimated 600,000 cruisers who visit the city annually. In addition, some communities, such as Haines, have responded to the rise in cruise passengers by putting a limit on the volume of cruise-tour traffic it will allow to dock.

The vexing issue of cruise-ship taxation in Alaska—at both local and state levels—is one that is not likely to go away in a hurry. For years, legislators and residents have opted to tax the cruise industry, the theory being that cruise businesses absolutely must have Alaska as a summer product, and thus will be forced to pay the taxes. In recent years, one energetic lawmaker went so far as to introduce a bill that would have imposed a $50-per-person head tax on all cruise passengers. Half of the money collected was to have been divided among the first five ports on any itinerary, and the remaining $25 was to have gone into the treasury. That tax would have superseded all local cruise passenger fees. The bill never got out of committee, and so never came to a vote of the legislature. In another attempt to levy high taxes on the cruise industry, a group of private citizens in Anchorage pushed hard for a $75-a-head tax-ballot initiative that would no doubt seriously impact pricing, were it to be adopted. The lines can absorb a few bucks here and there, but there would be no way they could underwrite a $75 tax without passing it on to customers.

Alaska's then-new governor, Frank Murkowski, got into the act late in 2003, proposing a rather subtle tax on the tourism industry in general—which he called a summer-season sales tax (the state has no state sales tax right now). Alaska residents would have had to pay it during the summer as well, of course, but the clear intent was to make money from visitors, the majority of whom are cruise passengers. The legislature did not take Murkowski up on his suggestion during the 2004 session. But anybody who doesn't believe that taxation is going to remain a threat to the cruise industry is a Pollyanna. It will. And the tax-the-passengers merry-go-round is likely to start spinning again during the 2005 session of the Alaska state legislature, starting January 2 and running through May.

***A word to the wise:*** Don't let all this legislative wrangling frighten you off. On the whole, you'll find the residents of Alaska remain warm to visitors, whether they come from cruise ships or travel independently.

# 1

# The Best of Alaska Cruising

Alaska is one of the top cruise destinations in the world, and when you're sailing through the calm waters of the Inside Passage or across the Gulf of Alaska, it's easy to see why. The scenery is simply breathtaking.

Much of the coastline is wilderness, with snowcapped mountain peaks, immense glaciers that create a thunderous noise as they calve into the sea, emerald rainforests, fjords, icebergs, soaring eagles, lumbering bears, and majestic whales all easily visible from the comfort of your ship.

Visit the towns and you'll find people who retain the spirit of frontier independence that brought them here in the first place. Add Alaska's colorful history and heritage, with its European influences, its spirit of discovery, and its rich Native cultures, and you have a destination that is utterly and endlessly fascinating.

The fact that approximately 700,000 cruise passengers—give or take a few—arrive annually in this last great frontier has had its impact, of course. In the summer some towns turn into tourist malls populated by seasonal vendors and imported souvenirs. However, the port towns you'll visit—from Juneau, the most remote state capital in the country, to Sitka, with its proud reminders of Native and Russian culture—retain much of their rustic charm and historical allure. Sure, you may have to jostle for a seat in Juneau's popular Red Dog Saloon (a must-do beer stop) or ask other visitors to step out of the way as you try to snap a picture of Skagway's historic gold-rush buildings, but these are minor hassles for cruise ship passengers. And if you want to get away from the crowds by taking a small-ship cruise or an organized shore excursion, or touring on your own, there's opportunity for that, too. In addition, by signing up for the cruise lines' pre- or post-cruise land-tour packages (known as "cruisetours"), you can also visit such inland destinations as Denali National Park, Fairbanks, the Yukon Territory, or the Canadian Rockies.

Even before you cruise, we can predict you'll want to visit again. Jerry first visited 32 years ago and claims he's never been the same—the place put such a spell on him that he's gone back every year since, sometimes two or three times. Fran's first visit to the state wasn't quite that long ago, but she also noticed that her view of the world was forever changed, and she quickly put the state at the top of her list of cruise destinations. Alaska is like that. It grabs you by the scruff of the neck and won't let you go.

Whether you're looking for pampering and resort amenities or a you-and-the-sea adventure experience, you'll find it offered by cruise ships in Alaska. Here are some of our favorites, along with our picks of the best ports, shore excursions, and sights.

## 1 The Best of Alaska's Ships

- **The Best Ships for Luxury:** Crystal Cruises' 940-passenger *Crystal Harmony* is the big luxury ship in the Alaska market. We're talking superb cuisine, elegant service, lovely surroundings, great cabins, and sparkling entertainment. It also has what we consider to be the prettiest public room afloat—the Palm Court. If you want a more casual kind of luxury (a really nice ship with a no-tie-required policy), Radisson Seven Seas Cruises' *Seven Seas Mariner* offers just that, with plush all-suite cabins (most with private balconies) and excellent cuisine (plus, you get complimentary wine with dinner). And for the ultimate Alaska small-ship experience, check out the yachts of **American Safari Cruises,** where soft adventure comes with luxury accoutrements.

- **The Best of the Mainstream Ships:** Every line's most recent ships are beautiful, but Celebrity's *Infinity* is a true stunner, as is sister ship *Summit.* These modern vessels, with their extensive art collections, cushy public rooms, and expanded spa areas, give Celebrity a formidable presence in Alaska. And the late model *Sapphire Princess* and *Diamond Princess* (which debuted last year) have raised the art of building big ships to new heights.

- **The Best of the Small Ships:** Clipper Cruise Line's newest vessel, the *Clipper Odyssey,* is a really gorgeous little ship, offering a higher level of comfort than most of the other small ships in this category. The most adventurous small-ship itineraries in Alaska are offered by Glacier Bay Cruiseline, whose *Wilderness Adventurer* and *Wilderness Explorer* both concentrate on kayaking, hiking, and wildlife, hardly visiting any ports at all over the course of their itineraries.

- **The Best Ships for Families:** All the major lines have well-established kids' programs. Holland America and Norwegian Cruise Line win points in Alaska for their special shore excursions for kids and teens, and Carnival gets a nod for offering special shore excursions for teens.

- **The Best Ships for Pampering:** It's a tossup—Celebrity's *Infinity* and **Summit** offer wonderful AquaSpas complete with thalassotherapy pools and a wealth of soothing and beautifying treatments, while *Crystal Harmony* pampers all around, and the solariums on Royal Caribbean's *Vision of the Seas, Serenade of the Seas,* and *Radiance of the Seas* offer relaxing indoor-pool retreats.

- **The Best Shipboard Cuisine:** Radisson and Crystal (in that order) are tops. Of the mainstream lines, Celebrity is the best, with its cuisine overseen by renowned French chef Michel Roux. Dinner in the reservations-only specialty restaurants on the *Infinity* or *Summit* ($25-per-person service charge) is a world-class dining experience. And there are signs of a new and rather surprising challenger for the cuisine award: Carnival, which has upgraded both its main dining room and buffet offerings. And the line's *Carnival Spirit* in Alaska boasts the Nouveau Supper Club ($25-per-person service charge), where you can enjoy just about as fine a meal as you're likely to find anywhere.

- **The Best Ships for Onboard Activities:** The ships operated by Carnival and Royal Caribbean offer a very full roster of onboard activities that range from the sublime (such as lectures) to the ridiculous (such as contests designed to get passengers to do or say outrageous things). Princess' ScholarShip@Sea program is a real winner, with excitingly packaged classes in such diverse subjects as photography, personal computers, cooking, and even pottery.

# Alaska

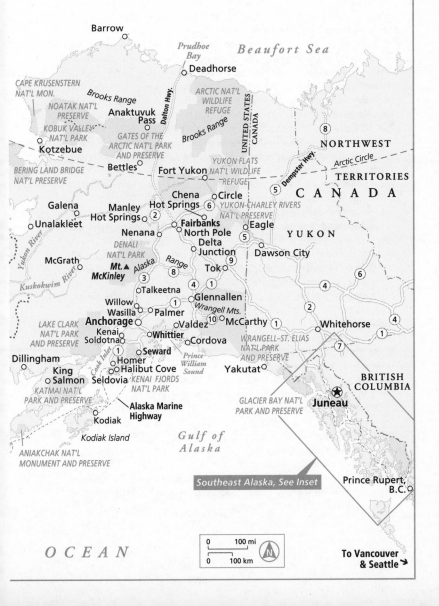

Paved Road
State or Provincial Route
Dirt Road

ARCTIC OCEAN

Barrow

*Prudhoe Bay*

*Beaufort Sea*

Deadhorse

CAPE KRUSENSTERN NAT'L MON.

*Brooks Range*

ARCTIC NAT'L WILDLIFE REFUGE

NOATAK NAT'L PRESERVE

Anaktuvuk Pass

Dalton Hwy.

KOBUK VALLEY NAT'L PARK

GATES OF THE ARCTIC NAT'L PARK AND PRESERVE

*Brooks Range*

UNITED STATES
CANADA

NORTHWEST

Kotzebue

BERING LAND BRIDGE NAT'L PRESERVE

Bettles

Fort Yukon

YUKON FLATS NAT'L WILDLIFE REFUGE

Dempster Hwy.

Arctic Circle

TERRITORIES
CANADA

Galena

Manley Hot Springs ②

Chena Hot Springs ⑥

Circle

YUKON-CHARLEY RIVERS NAT'L PRESERVE

⑤

Unalakleet

*Yukon River*

Nenana

Fairbanks
North Pole

Eagle

⑤

YUKON

McGrath

DENALI NAT'L PARK

*Kuskokwim River*

Mt. ▲ McKinley

Alaska Range

Delta Junction

⑨

Tok

Dawson City

⑥

③

Talkeetna

④ ①

Glennallen

*Wrangell Mts.*

④

Willow
Wasilla Palmer ①

②

⑥

Anchorage
Kenai Soldotna

Valdez ⑩ McCarthy ①

Whitehorse

④

LAKE CLARK NAT'L PARK AND PRESERVE

Whittier

Cordova

WRANGELL-ST. ELIAS NAT'L PARK AND PRESERVE

①

Dillingham

*Cook Inlet*

① Seward

Homer

*Prince William Sound*

⑦

King Salmon

Halibut Cove
Seldovia

KENAI FJORDS NAT'L PARK

Yakutat

BRITISH COLUMBIA

KATMAI NAT'L PARK AND PRESERVE

**Alaska Marine Highway**

GLACIER BAY NAT'L PARK AND PRESERVE

★ Juneau

Kodiak

*Kodiak Island*

*Gulf of Alaska*

ANIAKCHAK NAT'L MONUMENT AND PRESERVE

Southeast Alaska, See Inset

Prince Rupert, B.C.

OCEAN

0    100 mi
0    100 km
N

**To Vancouver & Seattle** →

## Personal Reminiscence

One of the great delights of Alaska is that you're never quite certain what to expect. It constantly surprises you. Just when you think you've seen it all—there's more! Never was that point more vividly illustrated than on a recent trip to the 49th state. Both during the cruise portion, on Celebrity's magnificent *Infinity,* and on land, during a Denali Park rail ride in Royal Celebrity's plush domed cars, one wonder followed another.

You should know upfront that I have cruised in Alaskan waters at least once a year since the early 1970s and have done the Denali trip umpteen times—often by rail, sometimes by coach. Yet on this particular trip I saw things I had never seen before.

I was with a small group of people, some of whom were visiting Alaska for the first time. My wife, Margaret, was with me, and although she's most decidedly not new to Alaska cruising, she had somehow missed out on Denali all these years. A few in the group regretted that *Infinity's* itinerary did not include Glacier Bay but featured, instead, Hubbard Glacier. I offered the opinion that I'd rather visit Hubbard any day of the week. I'm not sure many of them believed me, but it's true. The approaches to the mouth of Yakutat Bay and Hubbard, I told them, are scenically spectacular, with the St. Elias Mountain Range stretching as far as the eye can see in either direction. And I added that, in my experience, Hubbard was more active in calving huge chunks off its ice wall than other glaciers I had seen.

"Be on deck early and don't forget your cameras" was my sage advice.

Fortune smiled on us on the day of our visit. The air was chilly, but the sun was bright, and the peaks—Mount Vancouver, Mount Logan, Mount Hubbard, Mount St. Elias, and the other snowcapped sentinels by the bay—stood out in sharp relief against a clear blue sky. It was a dream day to be in such a place. When we got into Enchantment Bay, at the top of Yakutat, in which Hubbard is located, the glacier was every bit as active as I had predicted. In fact, I had to admit that its calving— both in the size of the falls and the accompanying thunderous sounds— was even more impressive than I had seen in the past.

At dinner that night, my advice to the group was validated by their reactions to what they had seen. There was so much activity on the ice wall, one of my companions complained, that he wore himself out running from one side of the deck to the other trying to capture the perfect picture. His wife, a sun lover, admitted that she didn't expect to stay on deck for long once she realized how cold it was. "But I didn't dare leave," she said. "There was so much going on." Hubbard Glacier had been, in every respect, a success.

And then came the whales!

In my 3 decades of savoring Alaska, I had seen whales—hundreds of them. But until a few years ago, I had never seen one breaching. When a whale breaches, it hurls itself clear out of the water and drops in again on its back with a mighty crash and a mountainous splash. Scientists aren't sure exactly why whales do it. According to one theory, it could be a form of communication. Another theory proposes that the creatures are trying to dislodge barnacles and parasites clinging to their bellies. Or it might be that they're just playing. Or warning off their enemies. I had seen pictures of this activity but never experienced it firsthand. Until this voyage!

On a wildlife cruise (a shore excursion) out of Juneau, we watched not one but two whales breach in rapid succession. Each must have been 6 feet clear of the water. It seemed almost orchestrated—like something from a Samuel Goldwyn extravaganza. I sort of expected Esther Williams to put in an appearance. It was, in every way, an awesome sight, made all the more awesome by the fact that it was my first personal experience of the phenomenon.

But it was left to Denali Park to put on the biggest show of all. I eyed that segment of the cruisetour with some trepidation. Margaret had never been there before and was so excited at the prospect that I worried that perhaps the weather would disappoint her. I cautioned her and the others that I had been in that area for days on end on some previous trips without getting so much as a glimpse of Mount McKinley. Its 20,320-foot summit—and for that matter, its entire bulk—is often shrouded in clouds and impossible to see. For Margaret's sake, and for the sake of the others, I didn't want that to happen on this occasion.

I needn't have worried. The hugely photogenic mountain was visible the whole time. And the best was yet to come.

I've taken wildlife tours of the park before—and seen precious little wildlife! If you see Mount McKinley, a moose, a caribou, a Dall sheep, and a grizzly bear on the same day, you are said to have seen "the Grand Slam." I never had. I had seen four of the five and three of the five and, on a really bad day, just two of the five. But this time—bingo!

Not only did we see all components of the Grand Slam, we saw them at close range. A mother grizzly and her cub foraged, unconcerned, along the side of the road as our bus stopped not 10 feet from them, with passengers' cameras clicking and whirring. The caribou and moose were just 40 or 50 yards from us, and the Dall sheep were everywhere. And Mount McKinley stood out as clear as day, outlined against a high, blue sky. As a bonus, we also had a very clear sighting of a red fox and numerous brushes with the state's national bird, the willow ptarmigan.

So there we were, one old Alaska/Denali hand and a number of neophytes. And the neophytes had seen on their first cruisetour what it took me 30 years to see! It's stuff like that that keeps me going back to Alaska.

—by Jerry Brown

- **The Best Ships for Entertainment:** Look to the big ships here. Carnival and Royal Caribbean are tops when it comes to an overall package of show productions, nightclub acts, lounge performances, and audience-participation entertainment. Princess also offers particularly well-done—if somewhat less lavishly staged—shows.
- **The Best Ship for Nostalgia:** No contest. It's American West Steamboat Company's *Empress of the North,* a paddle-wheeler, the likes of which hasn't been seen in Alaska in almost a century. The vessel defies characterization. It's clearly not a mainstream ship, it's not absolutely a luxury ship, and it really isn't a small ship (it holds 235 passengers). Warmly decorated with rich brocade wall coverings, the vessel features velvet booths in the dining room and a wonderful bar aft in which passengers can listen to live music while watching the paddle wheel throw spray against the floor-to-ceiling window. Sailing on the *Empress* is to take a step back in time to the golden age of steamboat travel.
- **The Best Ships for Whale-Watching:** If the whales come close enough, you can see them from all the ships in Alaska. Smaller ships, though—such as those operated by Glacier Bay Cruiseline and Cruise West— might actually change course to follow a whale. Get your cameras ready!
- **The Best Ships for Cruisetours:** Princess and Holland America are the entrenched market leaders in getting you into the Interior, either before or after your cruise. They own their own hotels, deluxe motorcoaches, and rail cars; and after many years in the business, they both really know what they're doing. Some of the other lines actually buy their land products from Princess or HAL. Holland America's strengths are its 3- and 4-night cruises combined with an Alaska/Yukon land package. In addition, the company's exclusive entry into the Yukon's Kluane National Park last year proved extremely popular. Not only will it continue in the Kluane area this year, HAL has added yet another Yukon gem—Tombstone Territorial Park, about 90 minutes drive up the Dempster Highway from Dawson City. Tombstone is a region of staggering wilderness beauty, Native architecture, stunning vistas, and wildlife. Princess is arguably stronger in 7-day Gulf of Alaska cruises in conjunction with Denali/Fairbanks or Kenai Peninsula land arrangements. In 2002, Princess also introduced its fifth wilderness lodge—the Copper River Lodge, by the entry to hitherto difficult-to-access Wrangell–St. Elias National Park. Its addition gave Princess an attractive new cruisetour component, which has become more popular each year with the growing public awareness. This year, getting to the company's wilderness lodges in Denali will be easier and faster than ever before with the inauguration of a "Direct to the Wilderness" rail link. Passengers will board trains right on the dock in Whittier and whisk through some of Alaska's most scenic areas to Denali.

## 2 The Best Ports

**Juneau** and **Skagway** are our favorites. Juneau is one of the most visually pleasing small cities anywhere and certainly the prettiest capital city in America. It's fronted by the Gastineau Channel and backed by

Mount Juneau and Mount Roberts, offers the very accessible Mendenhall Glacier, and is otherwise surrounded by wilderness—and it's a really fun city to visit, too. As for Skagway, no town in Alaska is more historically significant, and the old buildings are so perfect you might think you stepped into a Disney version of what a gold-rush town should look like. If, that is, you can get over the decidedly turn-of-the-millennium Starbucks coffee vendor in the Mercantile Center, the pizza parlor at the bottom of Broadway, and all the upscale jewelry shops that have followed cruise passengers from the Caribbean. There are people who will tell you that Skagway is hokey, touristy. Yes, it's all of that. But if you can get yourself into the right frame of mind, if you can recall the history of the place, the gold-rush frenzy that literally put the town on the map, it's easier to capture the true spirit of Skagway. The residents have made every effort to retain as much as possible of the architecture and historic significance of their community, and they don't mind sharing it with visitors during the cruise season. For a more low-key Alaska experience, take the ferry from Skagway to **Haines,** which reminds us of the folksy, frontier Alaska depicted on the TV show *Northern Exposure,* and is a great place to spot eagles and other wildlife. Some ships also stop at Haines as a port of call.

## 3 The Best Shore Excursions

Flightseeing and helicopter trips in Alaska are absolutely unforgettable ways to check out the scenery if you can afford them. But airborne tours tend to be pretty pricey—sometimes $400 or more. A helicopter trip to a dog-sled camp at the top of a glacier (usually the priciest of the offerings) affords both incredibly pretty views and a chance to try your hand at the truly Alaskan sport of dog sledding. (Yes, even in summer: The sleds are fitted with wheels.) It's a great way to earn bragging rights with the folks back home. For a less extravagant excursion, nothing beats a ride on a clear day on the White Pass and Yukon Route Railway out of Skagway to the Canadian border at Fraser—the route followed by the gold stampeders of '98. And we also like to get active with kayak and mountain-biking excursions offered by most lines at most ports. In addition to affording a chance to work off those shipboard calories, these excursions typically provide optimum opportunities for spotting eagles, bears, seals, and other wildlife.

Another, less hectic shore excursion that goes down well with many passengers is a float ride down one of the more placid stretches of Alaska's myriad rivers, such as the Kenai, the Mendenhall, or the Chilkat. These outings don't involve a lot of paddling—which can be hard work—but instead use the natural flow of the river to propel the four- to six-person rubber raft downstream. And they involve *no* white water. Generally, the group will stop for a picnic lunch en route and return to the staging area by motorcoach or automobile.

# 2

# Choosing Your Ideal Cruise

Just like clothes, cars, and gourmet coffee, Alaska cruises come in all different styles to suit all different tastes, so the first step in assuring that you have the best possible vacation is to match your expectations to the appropriate itinerary and ship.

In this chapter we explore the advantages of the two main Alaska itineraries, examine the differences between big-ship cruising and small-ship cruising, pose some questions you should ask yourself to determine which cruise is right for you, and give you the skinny on cruisetours, which combine a cruise with a land tour that gets you into the Alaskan Interior.

## 1 The Alaska Cruise Season

Alaska is a seasonal, as opposed to year-round, cruise destination, with the season generally running from May through September, although some smaller ships start up in April. May and September are considered the shoulder seasons, and lower brochure rates and more aggressive discounts are offered during these months. We particularly like cruising in May, before the crowds arrive, when we've generally found locals to be friendlier than they are later in the season, when they're pretty much ready to see the tourists go home for the winter. There is also the statistical fact that in the Inside Passage ports, May is one of the driest months in the season. Late September, though, also offers the advantage of fewer fellow cruise passengers clogging the ports. The warmest months are June, July, and August, with temperatures generally around 50°F to 80°F (10°C–27°C) during the day and cooler at night. You may not need a parka, but you will need to bring along some outerwear. June 21 is the longest day of the year, with the sky lit virtually all night. June tends to be drier than July and August (we have experienced trips in July when it rained nearly every day). April and May are drier than September, although in early April you may encounter freezing rain and other vestiges of winter. If you are considering traveling in a shoulder month, keep in mind that some shops don't open until Memorial Day, and the visitor season is generally considered over on Labor Day (although cruise lines operate well into Sept).

## 2 The Inside Passage or the Gulf of Alaska?

For the purposes of cruising, Alaska comprises essentially two separate and distinct areas, known generically as "the Inside Passage" and "the Gulf."

### THE INSIDE PASSAGE

The Inside Passage runs through the area of Alaska known as Southeast (which the locals also call "the Panhandle"), that narrow strip of the state—islands, mainland coastal communities, and mountains—that runs from the Canadian

## Shore Excursions: The What, When & Why

Shore excursions offered by the cruise lines provide a chance for you to get off the ship and explore the sights close up, taking in the history, nature, and culture of the region, from exploring gold-rush-era streets to experiencing Native Alaskan traditions such as totem carving.

Some excursions are of the walking-tour or bus-tour variety, but many others are activity oriented: Cruise passengers have the opportunity to go sea kayaking, mountain biking, horseback riding, salmon fishing, and even rock climbing, and to see the sights by seaplane or helicopter—and maybe even to land on a glacier and go for a walk. Occasionally, with some of the smaller cruise lines, you'll find quirky excursions, such as a visit with local artists in their studios. Some lines even offer scuba diving and snorkeling.

With some lines, shore excursions are included in your cruise fare, but with most lines they are an added (though very worthwhile) expense. See chapters 8 and 9 for details on the excursions available at the various ports. For more information, see "Cruisetours: The Best of Land & Sea," later in this chapter, and chapter 10.

border in the south to the start of the Gulf in the north, just above the Juneau/Haines/Skagway area. The islands on the western side of the area afford cruise ships a welcome degree of protection from the sea and its attendant rough waters (hence the name "Inside Passage"). Because of that shelter, such ports as Ketchikan, Wrangell, Petersburg, and others are reached with less rocking and rolling, and thus less risk of seasickness. Sitka is not on the Inside Passage (it's on the ocean side of Baranof Island) but is included in most Inside Passage cruise itineraries.

Southeast encompasses the capital city, **Juneau,** and townships influenced by the former Russian presence in the state (**Sitka,** for instance), the Tlingit and Haida Native cultures (**Ketchikan**), and the great gold rush of 1898 (**Skagway**). It is a land of rainforests, mountains, inlets, and glaciers (including Margerie, Johns Hopkins, Muir, and the others contained within the boundaries of **Glacier Bay National Park**). The region is rich in wildlife, especially of the marine variety. It is a scenic delight. But then, what part of Alaska isn't?

## THE GULF OF ALASKA

The other major cruising area is the **Southcentral** region's Gulf of Alaska, usually referred to by the cruise lines as the "Glacier Discovery Route" or the "Voyage of the Glaciers," or some such catchy title. "Gulf of Alaska," after all, sounds pretty bland.

The coastline of the Gulf is that arc of land from just north of Glacier Bay to the Kenai Peninsula. Southcentral also takes in **Prince William Sound;** the **Cook Inlet,** on the northern side of the peninsula; **Anchorage,** Alaska's biggest city; the year-round **Alyeska Resort** at Girdwood, 40 miles from Anchorage; the **Matanuska** and **Susitna valleys** (the "Mat/Su"), a fertile agricultural region renowned for the record size of some of its produce; and part of the Alaska Mountain Range.

The principal Southcentral terminus ports are **Seward** or **Whittier** for **Anchorage.** Few ships actually head for Anchorage proper, instead carrying passengers from Seward or Whittier to Anchorage by bus or train. However, let us stress that going on a Gulf cruise does not mean that you don't visit any of the Inside Passage. The big difference is that, whereas the more popular Inside Passage cruise itineraries run round-trip to and from Vancouver or Seattle, the Gulf routing is one-way—northbound and southbound—between Vancouver and Seward or Vancouver and Whittier. A typical Gulf itinerary also visits such Inside Passage ports as **Ketchikan, Juneau, Sitka,** and/or **Skagway.**

The Gulf's glaciers are quite dazzling and every bit as spectacular as their counterparts to the south. **College Fjord,** for instance, is lined with glaciers—16 of them, each one grander than the last. Our favorite part of a Gulf cruise, though, is not College Fjord. It's the visit to the gigantic **Hubbard Glacier**—at 6 miles, Alaska's longest—at the head of **Yakutat Bay.** A few years back we saw the ice face at its best on a bright, sunny day during a *Crystal Harmony* cruise. As we stood on the deck in shirt-sleeves, the glacier was hyperactive, popping and cracking and shedding tons of ice into the bay. The ship got so close to the face that passengers began speculating about just how near we might be. One awestruck golf enthusiast assured all within hearing, "It's not more than a nine-iron shot away." Now that's close!

We should mention, however, that on a recent visit we couldn't even get into the bay because another ship was blocking our path (and hogging the optimum views). Our fear is that, with so many new ships in Alaska, glacier viewing could become a blood sport.

## WHICH ITINERARY IS BETTER?

It's a matter of personal taste. Some people don't like open-jaw flights (flying into one city and out of another)—which can add to the ticket price—and prefer the round-trip Inside Passage route. Others don't mind splitting up the air travel because they want to enjoy the additional glacier visits on the Gulf cruise itineraries. It's entirely up to you.

It wasn't so long ago that you wouldn't have had a choice. A few years back, there were practically no Gulf crossings. Then Princess and its tour-operating affiliate decided to accelerate the development of its land components (lodges, rail cars, motorcoaches, and so on), particularly in the Kenai Peninsula and Denali National Park areas, for which Anchorage is a logical springboard. To feed these land services with cruisetour passengers, Princess beefed up the number of Gulf sailings it offered. In 2005, it will deploy four of its seven Alaska ships on that route, while also having a formidable Inside Passage capacity. Two of the line's newest and most amenity-filled ships, the *Diamond Princess* and the *Sapphire Princess,* each carrying 2,670 passengers, will do Inside Passage duty this year. The other cruisetour giant, Holland America Line, will have four of its seven vessels in the Inside Passage, including the *Amsterdam* round-trip from Seattle, and three vessels cruising across the Gulf. HAL tends to go more heavily into the Inside Passage than Princess because it is arguably stronger in Yukon Territory land services, and the Yukon Territory is most accessible from Juneau or Skagway.

## 3 Big Ship or Small Ship?

Picking the right ship is the most important factor in ensuring that you get the vacation you're looking for. Cruise ships in Alaska range from **small adventure–type vessels** to really **big resortlike megaships,** with the cruise experience

## SHIP SIZE COMPARISONS

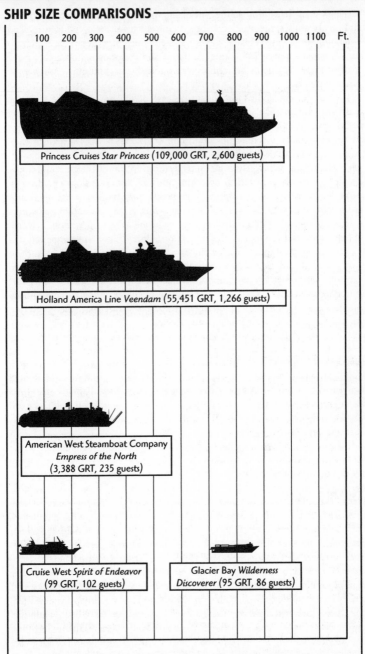

| | 100 | 200 | 300 | 400 | 500 | 600 | 700 | 800 | 900 | 1000 | 1100 | Ft. |

Princess Cruises *Star Princess* (109,000 GRT, 2,600 guests)

Holland America Line *Veendam* (55,451 GRT, 1,266 guests)

American West Steamboat Company
*Empress of the North*
(3,388 GRT, 235 guests)

Cruise West *Spirit of Endeavor*
(99 GRT, 102 guests)

Glacier Bay *Wilderness
Discoverer* (95 GRT, 86 guests)

Ships in this chart represent the various size vessels sailing in Alaska. See ship reviews in chapters 5 and 6 for comparative sizes of ships not shown here. (GRT = gross register tons, which is not literally a measure of weight, but rather a measure of interior space on ships.)

varying widely depending on the type of ship you select. There are casual cruises and luxury cruises; there are educational cruises where you attend lectures, and entertainment-focused cruises where you attend musical revues; there are adventure-oriented cruises where hiking, kayaking, and exploring remote areas are the main activities, and resortlike cruises where aquatherapy and mud baths are the order of the day.

Besides the availability (or nonavailability) of the programs, the spas, the activities, and the like, there is another question you have to answer before deciding on a ship. Do you want, or do you need, to be with people and, if so, in an intimate daily setting or only on an occasional basis? On a small ship, there's no escape. The people you meet on a 12-passenger or even a 100-passenger vessel are the ones you're going to be seeing every day of the cruise. And woe betide you if they turn out to be boring, or bombastic, or slow-witted, or in some other way not to your taste. Some people may think that the megaships are too big, but they do have at least one saving grace. On a 2,000-passenger ship, there's plenty of room to steer clear of people who turn you off. Personal chemistry plays a big part in the success or failure of any cruise experience—especially a small-ship cruise experience.

You'll need to decide what overall cruise experience you want. Itinerary and type of cruise are even more important than price. After all, what kind of bargain is a party cruise if what you're looking for is a quiet time? Or an adventure-oriented cruise if you're not physically in the best of shape? Your fantasy vacation may be someone else's nightmare, and vice versa.

Unlike the Caribbean, which generally attracts people looking to relax in the sun, people who want to spend all their time scuba diving and snorkeling, and people who want to party till the cows come home, Alaska attracts visitors with a different goal: They want to experience Alaska's glaciers, forests, wildlife, and other natural wonders. All the cruise lines recognize this, so almost any cruise you choose will give you opportunities to see what you've come for. The main question, then, is how you want to see those sights. Do you want to be down at the waterline, seeing them from the deck of an adventure vessel, or do you want to see them from a warm lounge or from your own private veranda?

In this section, we'll run through the pros and cons of the big ships and the small and alternative ships.

## THE BIG SHIPS

Big ships operating in Alaska vary in size, amenities, and activities, and include really, really big and really, really new megaships (the *Diamond Princess* and the *Sapphire Princess* are the biggest and newest). All the big ships offer a comfortable cruising experience, with virtual armies of service employees overseeing your well-being and ship stabilizers assuring smooth sailing.

The size of these ships may keep Alaska's wildlife at a distance (you'll probably need binoculars to see the whales), but these ships offer plenty of deck space and comfy lounge chairs to sit in as you take in the gorgeous mountain and glacier views, and sip a cup of coffee or cocoa. Due to their deeper drafts (the amount of ship below the waterline), the big ships can't get as close to the sights as the smaller ships, and they can't visit the more pristine fjords, inlets, and narrows. However, the more powerful engines on these ships do allow them to visit more ports during each trip—generally popular ports where your ship may be one of several, and where shopping for souvenirs is a main attraction. Some of the less massive ships in this category may also visit alternative ports, away from the cruise crowds.

The big-ship cruise lines put a lot of emphasis on **shore excursions,** which often take you beyond the port city to explore different aspects of Alaska—nature, Native culture, and so on (see the shore excursion listings in chapters 8 and 9 for more information). Dispersing passengers to different locales on these shore trips is a must. When 6,000 passengers from three or four ships disembark on a small Alaska town, much of the ambience goes out the window—on particularly busy days there may actually be more cruise passengers in the port than locals. Also, due to the number of people involved, disembarkation from the big ships can be a lengthy process.

The big ships in the Alaska market fall generally into two categories: midsize ships and megaships.

Carrying as many as 2,670 passengers, the **megaships** look and feel like floating resorts. Big on glitz, they offer loads of activities, attract many families and (especially in Alaska) seniors, offer many public rooms (including fancy casinos and fully equipped gyms), and provide a wide variety of meal and entertainment options. And though they may feature 1 or 2 formal nights per trip, the ambience is generally casual. The Alaska vessels of the Carnival, Celebrity, Princess, and Royal Caribbean fleets all fit in this category, as do Norwegian Cruise Line's *Spirit, Sun,* and *Star,* and Holland America's *Oosterdam.*

**Midsize ships** in Alaska for 2005 fall into two segments: the ultraluxury ships of Crystal and Radisson Seven Seas and the modern midsize *Veendam, Ryndam, Volendam, Amsterdam, Zaandam,* and *Statendam* of the Holland America Line, and the *Norwegian Dream* of Norwegian Cruise Line. In general, the size of these ships is less significant than the general onboard atmosphere: Holland America's midsize ships all have a similar calm, adult-oriented feel, while Norwegian's vessels all share the same ultracasual, activities-oriented approach. The vessels of Crystal and Radisson Seven Seas have a luxurious ambience (though the atmosphere on Radisson's ships is more casually luxurious).

Both the midsize ships and the megaships have a great range of **facilities** for passengers. There are swimming pools, health clubs, spas (of various sizes), nightclubs, movie theaters, shops, casinos, bars, and special kids' playrooms. In some cases, especially on the megaships, you'll also find sports decks, virtual golf, computer rooms, and cigar clubs, as well as quiet spaces where you can get away from it all. There are so many public rooms that you more than likely won't feel claustrophobic. **Cabins** range from cubbyholes to large suites, depending on the ship and the type of accommodations you book. They offer TVs and telephones, and some have minibars, picture windows, and private verandas.

These ships have big dining rooms and buffet areas and serve a tremendous variety of **cuisine** throughout the day, often offering food service until midnight. There may also be additional dining venues, such as pizzerias, hamburger grills, ice-cream parlors, alternative restaurants, wine bars, cigar bars, champagne bars, caviar bars, and patisseries.

In most cases, these ships have lots of **onboard activities** to keep you occupied when you're not whale- or glacier-watching, including games, contests, and classes and lectures (sometimes by naturalists, park rangers, or wildlife experts; sometimes on topics such as line dancing and napkin folding). These ships also offer a variety of entertainment options that may even include celebrity headline acts and usually include stage-show productions, some very extravagant (those of Princess and Carnival come to mind). These ships carry a lot of people and, as such, can at times feel crowded—there may be lines at the buffets and in other public areas, and it may take a while to disembark in port.

## Weighing the Dining Options on Various Cruises

**Smaller ships** usually serve dinner at a certain time, with open seating, allowing you to sit at any table you want. **Large ships** may offer only two, fairly rigid set seating times, especially for dinner. This means that your table will be preassigned and remain the same for the duration of the cruise. However, increasingly, there are some exceptions to the rule in the large-ship category. The ships of Norwegian Cruise Line and *Seven Seas Mariner* now serve all meals with open seating—dine when you want and sit with whom you want (within the restaurants' open hours). Princess has its own version of this system (introduced last year), allowing guests to choose between traditional early or late seating, or open restaurant-style seating, before the cruise. Most large ships today also offer multiple **alternative dining options,** featuring casual buffets and specialty restaurants, some with an additional charge of anything from $6.95 (as a gratuity) to $25. See "Choosing Your Dining Options" in chapter 3 for more information on dining choices, and see the individual ship reviews in chapters 5 and 6 for ship-specific dining information.

## THE SMALL & ALTERNATIVE SHIPS

While big cruise ships are mostly for people who want every resort amenity, small or alternative ships are best suited for people who prefer a casual, crowd-free cruise experience that gives passengers a chance to get up close and personal with Alaska's **natural surroundings** and **wildlife.**

Thanks to their smaller size, these ships, carrying fewer than 150 passengers (American Safari Cruises' *Safari Spirit* carries only 12), can go places that larger ships can't, such as narrow fjords, uninhabited islands, and smaller ports that cater mostly to small fishing vessels. Due to their shallow draft, they can nose right up to sheer cliff faces, bird rookeries, bobbing icebergs, and cascading waterfalls that you can literally reach out and touch. Also, sea animals are not as intimidated by these ships, so you might find yourself having a rather close encounter with a humpback whale, or watching other sea mammals bobbing in the ship's wake. The decks on these ships are closer to the waterline, too, giving passengers a more intimate view than they would get from the high decks of the large cruise ships. Some of these ships stop at ports on a daily basis, like the larger ships, while some avoid ports almost entirely, exploring natural areas instead. Small ships also have the flexibility to change direction as opportunities arise—say, to go where whales have been sighted and to linger awhile once a sighting's been made.

The alternative ship experience is all about a sense of adventure (it's usually adventure of a soft rather than a rugged sort) and offers a generally casual cruise experience: There are no dress-up nights and food may be rather simply prepared. Because there are so few public areas to choose from—usually only one or two small lounges—camaraderie tends to develop more quickly between passengers on these ships than aboard larger vessels, which can be as anonymous as a big city. **Cabins** on these ships don't usually offer TVs or telephones and tend to be very small and, in some cases, downright spartan. Meals are generally served in a single open seating (meaning seats are not assigned), and dress codes are usually nonexistent.

None of these ships offer the kind of significant exercise or spa facilities that you'll find on the big ships—your best exercise bet is usually a brisk walk around the deck after dinner—but many compensate by offering **more active off-ship opportunities,** such as hiking or kayaking. (On Glacier Bay Cruiseline's ships, stern launch platforms actually allow you to kayak right from the ship.) The alternative ships are also more likely to feature **expert lectures** on Alaska-specific topics, such as marine biology, history, and Native culture.

There are no stabilizers on most of these smaller ships, and the ride can be bumpy in open water—which isn't much of a problem on Inside Passage itineraries, since most of the cruising area is protected from sea waves. They are also difficult for travelers with disabilities, as only four (American West Steamboat Company's *Empress of the North,* Cruise West's *Spirit of '98* and *Spirit of Oceanus,* and Clipper's *Clipper Odyssey*) have elevators. And the alternative ship lines do not offer specific activities or facilities for children, although you will find a few families on some of these vessels.

## 4 Cruisetours: The Best of Land & Sea

Most folks who go to the trouble of getting to a place as far off the beaten path as Alaska try to stick around for a while once they're there rather than jetting home as soon as they hop off the boat. Knowing this, the cruise lines have set themselves up in the land-tour business as well, offering a number of great land-based excursions that can be tacked on to your cruise experience.

We're not just talking about an overnight stay in Anchorage or Juneau before or after your cruise. Almost any cruise line will arrange an extra night's hotel accommodation for you, but, enjoyable as that may be, it doesn't begin to hint at the real opportunities available in Alaska. No, the subject here is **cruisetours,** a total package with a cruise and a structured, prearranged, multiple-day land itinerary already programmed in—for instance, a 7-day cruise with a 5-day land package. There are any number of combinations between 9 and 21 days in length.

In this section we'll discuss the various cruisetour itineraries that are available through the lines. See chapter 10 for details on the various cruisetour destinations.

### CRUISETOUR ITINERARIES

Many parts of inland Alaska can be visited on cruisetour programs, including Denali National Park, Fairbanks, Wrangell–St. Elias, Nome, and Kotzebue. If you've a mind to, you can even go all the way to the oil fields of the North Slope of Prudhoe Bay, hundreds of miles north of the Arctic Circle.

Three tour destination areas are combinable with your Inside Passage or Gulf of Alaska cruise—two major ones, which we'll call the **Anchorage/Denali/Fairbanks** corridor and the **Yukon Territory,** and one less-traveled route that we'll call the **Canadian Rockies Route,** which is an option due to Vancouver's position as an Alaska cruise hub.

### ANCHORAGE/DENALI/FAIRBANKS CRUISETOUR

A typical Anchorage/Denali/Fairbanks cruisetour package (we'll use Princess as an example, since it is heavily involved in the Denali sector) might include a 7-day Vancouver-Anchorage cruise, followed by 2 nights in Anchorage, and a scenic ride in a private rail car into **Denali National Park** for 2 more nights at Princess's Denali Lodge or Mount McKinley Lodge (or 1 night at each) before heading on to Fairbanks. On a clear day, the McKinley property affords a panoramic view of the Alaska Mountain Range and its centerpiece, **Mount**

**McKinley,** which at 20,320 feet is North America's highest peak. A full day in the park allows guests to explore the staggeringly beautiful wilderness expanse and its wildlife before reboarding the train and heading into the Interior of Alaska, to **Fairbanks,** for 2 more nights. Fairbanks itself isn't much to look at, but the activities available in outlying areas are fantastic—the riverboat *Discovery* paddle-wheel day cruise on the Chena and Tanana rivers and an excursion to a gold mine are two excellent activity options in the area. Passengers on that particular cruisetour fly home from Fairbanks.

A shorter variation of that itinerary might be a cruise combined with an overnight (or 2-night) stay in Anchorage along with the Denali portion, perhaps with rail transportation into the park and a motorcoach back to Anchorage, skipping Fairbanks. Princess also recently introduced cruisetours that include visits to a hitherto largely inaccessible area, **Wrangell–St. Elias National Park,** where they have built the Cooper River Princess Wilderness Lodge, the fifth hotel in the company's lodging network.

## YUKON TERRITORY CRUISETOUR

Another popular land itinerary offered along with Alaska cruises typically involves a 3- or 4-day cruise between Vancouver and Juneau/Skagway (you either join a 7-day sailing late or get off early), combined with a land program into the **Klondike,** in Canada's Yukon Territory, then through the Interior of Alaska to Anchorage. En route, passengers experience a variety of transportation modes, which may include rail, riverboat, motorcoach, and possibly air. There are a number of variations.

The Yukon, although located in Canada, is nevertheless an integral part of the overall Alaska cruisetour picture, due to its intimate ties to Alaska's gold-rush history. The overnight stops are **Whitehorse,** the territorial capital, and **Dawson City,** a remote, picture-perfect gold-rush town near the site where gold was found in 1896. Last year, Holland America added a drive through Canada's **Kluane National Park,** a Yukon Territory wilderness area designated a UNESCO World Heritage Site. The park contains five of North America's tallest peaks. And if it's wilderness scenery you want, you'll be hard-pressed to find any that's more awesome. This year, HAL has added yet another magnificent Yukon Territory wilderness area to its brochure—Tombstone Territorial Park, about 90 minutes drive up the Dempster Highway from Dawson City, with stunning scenery, native architectural beauty, and wildlife.

After heading north through the Yukon, cruisetour passengers cross the Alaska border near Beaver Creek, travel to **Fairbanks,** and from there go through **Denali** to **Anchorage.** Again, the tour can be taken in either direction and on a pre- or post-cruise basis.

## CANADIAN ROCKIES CRUISETOUR

A Canadian Rockies tour is easily combined with a Vancouver-originating (or terminating) Inside Passage or Gulf cruise. In 5-, 6-, or 7-day chunks, you can visit such scenic wonders as **Banff, Lake Louise,** and **Jasper National Park** in conjunction with an Alaska sailing.

The Canadian Rockies offer some of the finest **mountain scenery** on earth. It's not just that the glacier-carved mountains are astonishingly dramatic and beautiful; it's also that there are hundreds and hundreds of miles of this wonderful wilderness high country. Between them, **Banff National Park** and **Jasper National Park** preserve much of this mountain beauty. Other national and provincial parks make accessible other vast and equally spectacular regions of the

Rockies, as well as portions of the nearby Columbia and Selkirk mountain ranges. The beautiful **Lake Louise,** colored deep green from its mineral content, is located 35 miles north of Banff.

## SHOULD YOU TAKE YOUR CRUISETOUR BEFORE OR AFTER YOUR CRUISE?

Though the land portion of both the Denali and the Yukon itineraries can be taken either before or after the cruise, we feel that it's better to take the land portion pre-cruise rather than post-cruise. Why? After several days of traveling around in the wilderness, it's nice to be able to get aboard a ship to relax and be pampered for a while.

Because of the distances that must be covered on some wilderness cruisetour itineraries, passengers often have to be rousted out of bed and ready to board the motorcoach by, say, 7:30 a.m. And the day may seem to go on forever, with a stop to view this waterfall, or that river or mountain. Then, upon arrival at the next stop—in the early evening usually—the request is "Hurry and get cleaned up for dinner." By the time you've crawled into your new bed often quite late at night, you're beat. It's a nice kind of tired, as the saying goes, but it's tired nevertheless. After a few days of that, it's great to get on a luxurious cruise ship, unpack just once and rise when you feel like it, comfortable in the knowledge that you haven't missed your transportation and that you'll still be in time to have a leisurely breakfast.

That, at any rate, is the conventional wisdom, and there's more of a demand for pre-cruise land packages than for post-cruise. Since the lines obviously can't always accommodate everybody on a land itinerary *before* the cruise (they're hoping to even out the traffic flow by having a like number of requests to go touring after the voyage), it's smart to get your bid in early.

## BATTLE OF THE TOP PLAYERS

If we talk in this section more about **Princess** and **Holland America** than we do about other lines, it's because they, by investing tens of millions of dollars in land tourism, have become the 800-pound gorillas duking it out for dominance in Alaska. Other lines offer some of the same cruisetours as these two, but many of them buy at least some of their cruisetour components from Princess and/or Holland America's land operations. It may seem odd to have companies buying from (or selling to) competitors, but with tourism in Alaska, there's practically no other way. As recently as the 1980s, when Holland America–Westours owned the bulk of the land-tour components, Princess, its number-one rival, was also its number-one customer! Hey, a 4-month season makes for strange bedfellows.

It was to carve out a niche for itself and to lessen its reliance on the services of a competitor that Princess plunged heavily into the lodging and transportation sectors. Princess is arguably stronger in the Denali corridor than any other line, while Holland America clearly has the upper hand in the Yukon/Klondike market. But each line offers both of these tour areas among other options.

Princess owns rail cars (called the *Midnight Sun Express*) in the Denali corridor. Holland America also owns rail cars there (called the *McKinley Explorer*). Both, incidentally, rely on the Alaska Railroad to pull them. Princess owns wilderness lodges; Holland America owns primarily city hotels. Princess has a fleet of motorcoaches; so does Holland America, including a number of wonderfully comfortable, double-length Alaska Yukon Explorer flexi-vehicles with a cozy lounge at the rear for snacking and schmoozing.

The fast-growing baby gorilla is **Royal Caribbean.** With its Royal Caribbean International and Celebrity Cruises brands, Royal Caribbean is on its way to becoming a major player in its own right. The company will have three Royal Caribbean ships and three Celebrity ships in the 49th state this summer. A few years ago the company formed **Royal Celebrity Tours** to operate its own land packages. Its first investment was in luxury motorcoaches and truly state-of-the-art domed rail carriages for the Denali Park run. The first of the carriages (the *Wilderness Express*) debuted in 2001 in competition with those of Holland America and Princess. By 2003, Royal Celebrity had increased to four wagons in service and this year will have six. The rail cars have comfortable, airline-style leather seats at least on a par with the business-class seating of most major airlines, huge expanses of glass that make for excellent sightseeing, a fine kitchen on the lower level (lunch is about $7–$13 and dinner is $18–$22), and a friendly, knowledgeable staff. Plus, the carriages are more accessible for travelers with disabilities than those run by Princess or Holland America (each of Royal Caribbean's is equipped with a mechanical lift that can carry two wheelchairs at a time to the second level from the station platform).

## 5 Quiz Time: Questions to Ask When Choosing Your Cruise

After you've decided which itinerary and what kind of ship appeal to you, we suggest you ask yourself some questions about the kind of experience you want, then read through the cruise-line and ship reviews in chapters 5 and 6 to see which ones match your vision of the perfect Alaska cruise vessel.

When looking at the attributes of the various ships to make your choice, some determining factors will be no-brainers. For instance, if you're traveling with kids, you'll want a ship with a good kids' program. If you're a foodie, you'll want a ship with gourmet cuisine. If you're used to staying at a Ritz-Carlton hotel when you travel, you'll probably want to cruise on a luxury ship. If you usually stay at B&Bs, you'll probably prefer one of the small ships.

Also ask yourself whether you require resortlike amenities, such as a heated swimming pool, spa, casino, aerobics classes, and state-of-the-art gym. Or do you care more about having an adventure or an educational experience? If you want the former, choose a large cruise ship; if you prefer the latter, a small ship may be more your speed.

Here are some more pertinent questions to help you narrow down the field:

**How do you get a deal and what's not included?**    The best way to get a deal on a cruise in Alaska is to book early. Virtually all the lines (with the exception of some of the small-ship lines) offer early-booking discounts. The numbers and dates may vary a bit, but the formula has been fairly standard: You get about 25% to 30% off and your best choice of ship, cabin, and itinerary if you book by mid-February and 20% off if you book by mid-April. In the 2005 Princess brochure, starting prices are $649 to $949, while Holland America's are $799 to $949, depending on the sailing. Because 2004 was a very popular year for Alaska (the best year since 2000) and because there won't be a great increase in capacity in 2005, we suggest you book your Alaska cruise and particularly your Alaska cruisetour (because these are increasingly popular) as early as possible. Sure, there will always be last-minute discounts (you may be able to snag a cruise for $599 or even as low as $499), but we expect these to be for a limited number of cabins and on a limited number of sailings in 2005.

Cruise fares cover onboard accommodations, meals, entertainment, and activities. There are, however, a number of expenses not covered in the typical cruise package, and you should factor these in when planning your vacation budget. Airfare to and from your port of embarkation and debarkation is usually extra (though cruise lines sometimes offer reduced rates). Necessary hotel stays before or after the cruise are also usually not included. Gratuities, taxes, and trip insurance are typically extra as well. Shore excursions are rarely included in the cruise fare, and if you opt for pricey ones like flightseeing, you can easily add $500 to $1,000 to your total. Alcoholic beverages and soda are typically extra also, as are such incidentals as laundry, telephone calls from the ship, beauty and spa services, photos taken by ship photographers, and babysitting.

Because travel agents constantly keep abreast of the latest bargains, we believe they are best equipped to advise you on the best Alaska cruise deals.

See chapter 3 for more information on when to book for the best prices.

**How much time is spent in port and how much at sea?**   Generally, ships on 7-night itineraries spend 3 days in port and cruise in natural areas like Glacier Bay, College Fjord, or Tracy Arm during the other 3.

Coming into port, ships generally dock right after breakfast, allowing you the morning and afternoon to take a shore excursion or explore on your own. They usually depart in the early evening, giving you an hour or two to rest up before dinner. On rare occasions, a ship might cruise through a glacier area in the morning and dock at the next port in the early afternoon, not leaving until 10pm or 11pm.

On days at sea, the emphasis will be on exploring natural areas, viewing glaciers, and scanning for wildlife. Big ships stick to prearranged schedules on these days, but on small-ship, soft adventure–type cruises, days at sea can be very unstructured, with the captain choosing a destination based on reports of whale sightings, for example. Some itineraries (notably those sailed by some of Glacier Bay Cruiseline's ships) visit almost no ports, sticking instead to isolated natural areas that passengers explore by kayak, by Zodiac boat, or on foot.

**Is the cruise formal or casual?**   If you don't care to get dressed up, select a less formal cruise, such as those offered by many of the small ships, by Radisson's luxurious but country club–casual *Seven Seas Mariner,* and by the Norwegian Cruise Line ships, which do not have official formal nights (there's 1 night when you can dress up if you want to). If, on the other hand, having the chance to put on your finery appeals to you, select one of the more elegant ships, such as the ultraluxurious Crystal or premium lines such as Princess, Celebrity, or Holland America (and, to a lesser extent, mass-market lines like Royal Caribbean and Carnival). These ships will offer casual, semiformal, and formal nights, meaning women can show off everything from a sundress to an evening gown over the course of a week, and men will go from shirt-sleeves one night to jacket and tie the next to full-on tuxedo (or dark suit) the next.

**What are the other passengers usually like?**   Each ship attracts a fairly predictable type of passenger. On small ships, you'll find a more physically active bunch that's highly interested in nature, but you'll find fewer families and single travelers. Larger ships cater to a more diverse group—singles, newlyweds, families, and couples over 55. Alaska sailings from Seattle, we're told by cruise executives, are attracting a younger, more family-oriented crowd. We've included information on typical passengers in all the cruise line reviews in chapters 5 and 6.

**I'll be traveling alone. Will I have fun? And does it cost more?**    A nice thing about cruises is that you needn't worry about dining alone because you'll be seated with other guests. (If you don't want to be, seek a ship with alternative dining options.) You also needn't worry much about finding people to talk to because the general atmosphere on nearly all ships is very congenial and allows you to find conversation easily, especially during group activities. Some ships host a party to give singles a chance to get to know one another, and some ships offer social hosts as dance partners.

The downside is that you may have to pay more for the cruise experience than do passengers who are sharing a cabin. Because their rates are based on two people per cabin, some lines charge a "single supplement" rate (aka an extra charge) that ranges from 110% to an outrageous 200% of the per-person, double-occupancy fare. As a single person, you have two choices: Find a line with a reasonable single supplement rate (Radisson is a good bet) or ask if the line has a cabin-share program, under which the line will pair you with another single so you can get a lower fare. Some lines also offer a single-guarantee program, which means if they can't find you a roommate, they'll book you in a cabin alone but still honor the shared rate. Singles seeking real savings have the option on some ships of cramming into a shared quad (a room for four). Some older ships and a few small ships have special cabins designed for singles, but these tend to sell out fast and are not necessarily offered at bargain prices.

**Is shipboard life heavily scheduled?**    That depends to a certain extent on you and the ship you choose. Meals are generally served during set hours only, though on larger ships you'll have plenty of alternative options if those hours don't suit you. On smaller ships you may be out of luck if you miss a meal—unless you can charm the cook. On both large and small ships, times for disembarking and reboarding at the ports are strict—if you miss the boat, you miss the boat. (See chapter 4 for tips on what to do in this situation.) Other than these two considerations, the only schedule you'll have to follow on board is your own. It all depends on how busy you want to be.

**What are the cabins like?**    Cabins come in all sizes and configurations. See "Choosing Your Cabin" in chapter 3 for a detailed discussion.

**What are meals like?**    Meals are a big part of the cruise experience. The larger the ship, the more dining options you'll find. When booking your cruise on a larger vessel, you'll be asked ahead of time to decide on your preferred dinner hour since most large ships feature two dining-room seatings each evening, with tables assigned. Norwegian, Princess, and Radisson ships are the exceptions to this rule, offering open, restaurant-style seating, meaning that you can dine when you prefer and with whomever you choose. (On Princess ships, you choose in advance of your cruise whether to dine traditional- or restaurant-style; Norwegian and Radisson ships offer open seating at all times.) On smaller ships, dining is also usually open seating. In the reviews in chapters 5 and 6, we discuss dining options for each line.

If you have any **special dietary requirements** (vegetarian, kosher, low salt, low fat), be sure the line is informed well in advance—preferably at the time you book your cruise. Some ships have vegetarian and health-conscious options available at every meal, and those that don't can usually meet your needs with some advance warning.

**What activities and entertainment does the ship offer?**    On small ships, activities are limited by the available public space but often include recent-release videos, group-oriented games (bingo, Trivial Pursuit, and the like), and perhaps an informal evening dance party or social hour. The small ships typically offer a lecture series dealing with the flora, fauna, and geography of Alaska, usually conducted by a trained naturalist. These lectures are also becoming more popular on the larger ships.

The big ships offer activities such as fitness, personal finance, photography, and art classes; Ping-Pong and bingo tournaments; audience-participation games; and parties. Glitzy floor shows at night are almost de rigueur. (See the general big-ship and small-ship descriptions earlier in this chapter for more information on activities and entertainment.)

**Does the ship have a children's program?**    More and more parents are taking their kids with them on vacation, and cruises to Alaska are no exception. The lines are responding by adding youth counselors and supervised programs, fancy playrooms, teen centers, and even video-game rooms to keep kids entertained while their parents relax. Some lines offer special shore excursions for children and teens, and most ships offer babysitting (for an extra charge). Some lines have reduced rates for kids. Most lines discourage parents from bringing infants.

It's important to ask whether a supervised program will be offered on your specific cruise, as sometimes the programs only operate if there are a certain number of kids on board. If your kids are TV addicts, you may want to make sure that your cabin will have a TV and VCR. Even if it does, though, channel selection will be very limited.

**I have a disability; will I have any trouble taking a cruise?**    It's important to let the cruise line know about your special needs when you make your booking. If you use a wheelchair, you'll need to know if wheelchair-accessible cabins are available (and how they're equipped), as well as whether public rooms are accessible and can be reached by elevator, and whether the cruise line has any special policy regarding travelers with disabilities. For instance, some lines require that you be accompanied by a fully mobile companion. We've noted all this information in the cabin sections of the ship reviews in chapters 5 and 6. Note that newer ships tend to have the largest number of wheelchair-accessible cabins, and that of the small ships in Alaska, only the four we mentioned earlier—the *Empress of the North,* the *Spirit of '98* and *Spirit of Oceanus,* and the *Clipper Odyssey*—are even moderately wheelchair friendly.

Travelers with disabilities should inquire when they're booking whether the ship docks at ports or uses tenders (small boats) to go ashore. Tenders cannot always accommodate passengers with wheelchairs—in most cases you can't wheel yourself but, rather, will need crew assistance. One exception is Holland America, which uses a special lift system to get passengers into the tenders without requiring them to leave their wheelchairs. Once on board the ship, travelers with disabilities will want to seek the advice of the tour staff before choosing shore excursions, as not all will be wheelchair friendly.

If you have a chronic health problem, we advise you to check with your doctor before booking the cruise and, if you have any specific needs, to notify the cruise line in advance. This will ensure that the medical team on the ship is properly prepared to offer assistance.

**What if I want to take a cruise for my honeymoon?**    One-week Alaska cruises start not only on Saturdays and Sundays, but also on Mondays, Thursdays, and Fridays, which should help you find an appropriate departure date so that you won't have to run out of your wedding reception to catch a plane. You will want to make sure that the ship you choose offers double, queen-, or king-size beds; and you may want to also request a cabin with a tub or Jacuzzi. Rooms with private verandas are particularly romantic. You can take in the sights in privacy and even enjoy a quiet meal, assuming that the veranda is big enough for a table and chairs (some are not), and that the weather doesn't turn chilly. If you want to dine alone each night, make sure the dining room offers tables for two or that the ship offers room service. Your travel agent can fill you in on these matters. You may also want to inquire as to the likelihood that there will be other honeymooners your age on the ship. Some ships—among them those of Princess, Royal Caribbean, Carnival, Celebrity, and Holland America—offer special honeymoon packages, and there might even be honeymoon suites. Most lines offer special perks such as champagne and chocolates if you let them know in advance that you will be celebrating your honeymoon on the ship.

**Can I get married on board?**    The answer is yes. On Princess's *Coral Princess* and *Island Princess,* you can get married at sea in the chapel, with the nuptials conducted by the ship's captain. And your friends at home can even watch the ceremony on the Internet, thanks to a special wedding cam. You can also get married at sea on the *Carnival Spirit,* which boasts a nice wedding chapel. The ceremony is conducted by a designated crewmember who is a notary (not the captain). You can, in fact, get married on many big ships—but only if you're willing to bring your own clergyman along with you at full price.

**Will I get seasick?**    On Inside Passage itineraries, most of your time will be spent in protected waters where there are islands between you and the open sea, making for generally smooth sailing. However, there are certain points, such as around Sitka and at the entrance to Queen Charlotte Strait, where there's nothing between you and Japan but a lot of wind, water, and choppy seas. Ships with sailing itineraries on the Gulf of Alaska and those sailing from San Francisco will of necessity spend more time in rough, open waters. Although ships that ply these routes tend to be very stable, you'll probably notice some rocking and rolling.

Unless you're particularly prone to seasickness, you probably don't need to worry much. But if you are, there are medications that can help, including Dramamine, Bonine, and Marezine, which are available over the counter and also stocked by most ships—the purser's office may even give them out free. Another option is the Transderm patch, available by prescription only, which goes behind your ear and time-releases medication. The patch can be worn for up to 3 days but comes with a slew of side-effect warnings. Some people have also had success in curbing seasickness by using ginger capsules, which are available at health-food stores, or acupressure wristbands, which are available at most pharmacies.

# 3

# Booking Your Cruise & Getting the Best Price

Okay, you've thought about what type of cruise vacation experience you're looking for. You've decided when and for how long you'd like to travel. You know what sort of itinerary interests you. And after reading through our ship reviews in chapters 5 and 6, and narrowing your focus down to a couple of cruise lines that appeal to you, you'll be ready to get down to brass tacks and make your booking.

## 1 Booking a Cruise: The Short Explanation

Every cruise line has a brochure, or sometimes many different brochures, full of beautiful glossy photos of beautiful glossy people enjoying beautiful glossy vacations. They're colorful! They're gorgeous! They're enticing! They're confusing!

You'll see low starting rates on the charts, but look further and you'll realize those are for tiny inside cubicles; most of the cabins sell for much more. Sometimes the brochures feature published rates that are nothing more than the pie-in-the-sky wish of cruise lines for what they'd like to sell the cruise (most customers will pay less). We strongly suggest you look at the early-bird savings column and book your cruise early (by mid-Feb for average savings of 25%–30%). In reality, you may be able to get the cruise for less at the last minute. But here's the problem with waiting: Alaska right now is hot, hot, hot. Sure, you may be able to save as much as 50% by taking your chances, but if you don't reserve space early, you may also be left out in the cold (cold in Alaska, get it?). Keep in mind the most expensive and cheapest cabins tend to sell out first. As they say in the cruise business, ships sell out from the top and from the bottom first.

So how do you book your cruise? Traditionally (meaning over the past 30 years or so) people have booked their cruises through **travel agents.** But you may be wondering, hasn't the traditional travel agent gone the way of typewriters and eight-track tapes and been replaced by the **Internet?** Not exactly. Travel agents are alive and kicking, though the Internet has indeed staked its claim alongside them and knocked some of them out of business. In an effort to keep pace, some traditional travel agencies have created their own websites.

So which is the better way to book a cruise these days? Good question. The answer can be both. If you're computer savvy, have a good handle on all the elements that go into a cruise, and have narrowed down the choices to a few cruise lines that appeal to you, websites are a great way to trawl the seas at your own pace and check out last-minute deals, which can be dramatic. On the other hand, you'll barely get a stitch of personalized service searching for and booking a cruise online. If you need help getting a refund or arranging special meals or other matters, or deciding which cabin to choose, you're on your own. In addition, agents usually know about cruise and airfare discounts that the lines don't publicize on their websites.

However you arrange to buy your cruise, what you basically have in hand at the end is a contract for transportation, lodging, dining, entertainment, housekeeping, and assorted other miscellaneous services that will be provided to you over the course of your vacation. That's a lot of services, involving a lot of people. It's complex, and like any complex thing, it pays (and saves) to study up. That's why it's important that you read the rest of this chapter.

## 2 Booking Through a Travel Agent

The large majority of cruise passengers book through agents. The cruise lines are happy with this system, and have only small reservations staffs themselves (unlike airlines). In some cases, if you try to call a cruise line to book your own passage, you may be advised by the line to contact an agent in your area. The cruise line may even offer you a name from its list of preferred agencies, and there are often links to preferred agencies on some of the lines' websites.

A good travel agent can save you both time and money. If you're reluctant to use an agent, consider this: Would you represent yourself in court? Perform surgery on your own abdomen? Tackle complicated IRS forms without seeking help? You may be the rare type that doesn't need a travel agent, but most of us are better off working with one.

A good agent can offer you expert advice, save you time, and (best of all) will usually work for you for free or for a nominal fee—the bulk of their fees are paid by the cruise lines. In addition to advising you about the different ships, the agent can also help you make decisions about the type of cabin you will need, your dining room–seating choices, any special airfare offerings from the cruise lines, pre- and post-cruise land offerings, and travel insurance.

It's important to realize that not all agents represent all cruise lines. In order to be experts on what they sell, and to maximize the commissions the lines pay them (they're often paid more based on volume of sales), some agents may limit their offerings to, say, one luxury line, one midprice line, one mass-market line, and so on. If you have your sights set on a particular line or have narrowed down your preferences to a couple of lines, you'll have to find an agent who handles your choices. As we mentioned above, you can call the lines themselves to get the name of an agent near you.

Most bargains are offered by agents rather than the cruise lines themselves. In cases where the lines do post Internet specials, the same deals are usually also available through travel agents. The lines don't want to upset their travel agent partners and generally try not to compete against them.

Agents, especially those who specialize in cruises, are in frequent contact with the cruise lines and are continually alerted by the lines about the latest and best deals and special offers. The cruise lines tend to communicate such deals and offers to their top agents first, before they offer them to the general public, and some of these deals will never appear in your local newspaper, on bargain travel websites, or even on the websites of the cruise lines themselves.

Experienced agents know how to play the cruise lines' game and get you the best deals. As an example, the lines run promotions that allow you to book a category of cabin, rather than a specific cabin, and guarantees that you'll be placed in that category or better. An informed agent will not only know about these offers, but may be able to direct you to a category on a specific ship in which your chances of an upgrade are better. The cruise lines will also sometimes upgrade passengers as a favor to their top-producing agents or agencies.

To keep their clients alert to specials, agencies may offer newsletters or communicate through other means, such as postcards or e-mail, or post specials on their websites. Depending on the agency you choose, you may run across other incentives for booking through an agent. Some agencies buy big blocks of space on a ship in advance and offer it to their clients at a group price only available through that agency. These are called group rates, although "group" in this case means savings, not that you have to hang out with the other people booking through the agency. In addition, some agencies are willing to negotiate, especially if you've found a better deal somewhere else. It never hurts to ask. Finally, some agencies are willing to give back to the client a portion of their commissions from the cruise line in order to close a sale. This percent may be monetary, or it might take the form of a perk such as a free bottle of champagne or a limo ride to the ship (hardly reasons to book in and of themselves, but nice perks nevertheless).

## FINDING A GREAT AGENT

If you don't know a good travel agent already, try to find one through your friends, preferably those who have cruised before. For the most personal service, look for an agent in your area, and for the most knowledgeable service, look for an agent who has cruising experience. It's perfectly okay to ask an agent questions about his or her personal knowledge of the product, such as whether he or she has ever cruised in Alaska or with one of the lines you're considering. The easiest way to be sure that the agent is experienced in booking cruises is to work with an agent at a **cruise-only agency** (meaning that the whole agency specializes in cruises) or to find an agent who is a **cruise specialist** (meaning he or she specializes in booking cruises) within a full-service agency. If you are calling a full-service travel agency, ask for the **cruise desk.** A good and easy rule of thumb to maximize your chances of finding an agent who has cruise experience and who won't rip you off is to book with agencies that are members of the **Cruise Lines International Association** (CLIA; ✆ 212/921-0066; www.cruising.org) or the **National Association of Cruise Oriented Agencies** (NACOA; ✆ 305/663-5626; www.nacoaonline.com). Members of both groups are cruise specialists. Membership in the **American Society of Travel Agents** (ASTA; ✆ 800/275-2782; www.astanet.com) assures that the agency is monitored for ethical practices, although it does not designate cruise experience. You can tap into the Internet sites of these organizations to find reliable agents in your area.

## BOOKING WITH DISCOUNTERS

Keep in mind that discounters, who specialize in great-sounding last-minute offers (usually without airfare) and whose ads you can find in Sunday papers and all over the Internet, don't necessarily offer service that matches their prices. Their staffs are more likely to be order takers than advice givers. Go to these companies to compare prices only when you are really sure what it is you want.

## WATCHING OUT FOR SCAMS

The travel business tends to attract more than its share of scam operators trying to lure consumers with incredible come-ons. If you get a solicitation by phone, fax, mail, or e-mail that just doesn't sound right, or if you are uneasy about an agent you are dealing with, call your state consumer protection agency or the local office of the Better Business Bureau. Or you can check with the cruise line to see whether they have heard of the agency in question. Be wary of working

## Watch Out for Scams

It can be difficult to know if the travel agency you're dealing with to make your Alaska cruise booking is or isn't reliable, legit, or, for that matter, stable. It pays to be on your guard against fly-by-night operators and agents who may lead you astray.

- **Get a referral.** A recommendation from a trusted friend or colleague is one of the best ways to hook up with a reputable agent.
- **Use the cruise lines' agent lists.** Many cruise line websites include agency locator lists, naming agencies around the country with whom they do business. These are by no means comprehensive lists of all good or bad agencies, but an agent's presence on these lists is usually another good sign of experience.
- **Beware of snap recommendations.** If an agent suggests a cruise line without asking you a single question first about your tastes, beware. Because agents work on commissions from the lines, some may try to shanghai you into cruising with a company that pays them the highest rates, even though that line may not be right for you.
- **Always use a credit card to pay for your cruise.** It gives you more protection in the event the agency or cruise line fails. When your credit card statement arrives, make sure the payment was made to the cruise line, not the travel agency. If you find that payment was actually made to the agency, it's a big red flag that something's wrong. If you insist on paying by check, you'll be making it out to the agency, so it may be wise to ask if the agency has default protection. Many do.
- **Always follow the cruise line's payment schedule.** Never agree to a different schedule the travel agency comes up with. The lines' terms are always clearly printed in their brochures and usually require an initial deposit, with the balance due no later than 45 to 75 days before departure, depending on the cruise line. If you're booking 2 months or less before departure, the full payment is usually required at the time of booking.
- **Keep on top of your booking.** If you ever fail to receive a document or ticket on the date it's been promised, inquire about it immediately. If you're told that your cruise reservation was canceled because of overbooking and that you must pay extra for a confirmed and rescheduled sailing, demand a full refund and/or contact your credit card company to stop payment.

with any company, be it on the phone or Internet, that won't give you its street address. You can find more advice on how to avoid scams at the **ASTA** site, **www.astanet.com**.

## BOOKING A SMALL-SHIP CRUISE

The small-ship companies in Alaska—American Safari Cruises, American West Steamboat Company, Clipper, Cruise West, Glacier Bay Cruiseline, and Lindblad Expeditions—all offer real niche-oriented cruise experiences, attracting passengers who have a very good idea of the kind of experience they want (usually educational or adventurous, and always casual and small scale). In many cases, a large percentage of passengers on any given cruise will have sailed with the line before. Because of all this, and because the passenger capacity of these small ships is so low (12–235), in general you don't find the kind of deep discounts that you do with the large ships. For the most part, these lines rely on agents to handle their bookings, taking very few reservations directly. (Clipper is the exception to this rule, taking most of its Alaska bookings directly rather than through agents.) All of the lines have a list of agents with whom they do considerable business, and they can hook you up with one of them if you call or e-mail the cruise line and ask for an agent near you.

## 3 Cruising on the Internet

For those who know exactly what they want (we don't recommend Internet shopping for first-time cruisers), there are deals to be had on the Internet. Those sites that sell cruises include top online travel agencies (Travelocity.com, Expedia.com), agencies that specialize in cruises (icruise.com, Uniglobe.com, Cruise.com, Cruise411.com), travel discounters (Bestfares.com, OneTravel.com, Lowestfare.com), and auction sites (Allcruiseauction.com, Priceline.com).

There are also some good sites on the Internet that specialize in providing cruise information rather than selling cruises. Two terrific sites that are dedicated to cruising in general (rather than linked with one line) are **Cruisemates.com** and **Cruisecritic.com.** On these sites, there are reviews by professional writers as well as ratings by cruise passengers, plus useful tips, frequent chat opportunities, and message boards. In addition, nearly all the cruise lines have their own sites, which are chock-full of information—some even offer virtual tours of specific ships. You will find the website addresses for the various cruise companies in our cruise-line reviews in chapters 5 and 6.

## 4 Cruise Costs

In chapters 5 and 6, we've included the brochure rates for every ship reviewed, but as noted above, these prices may actually be higher than any passenger will pay. Prices constantly fluctuate based on any special deals the cruise lines (and the travel agents) are running. The volume of travelers interested in cruising Alaska heavily influences rates. If the sales season (Sept–Jan are the key months) fails to achieve certain predetermined passenger volume goals, the lines are very quick to start slashing rates to goose the market. The prices we've noted are for the following three basic types of accommodations: inside cabins (without windows), outside cabins (with windows), and suites. Remember that cruise ships generally have several different categories of cabins within each of these three basic divisions, all priced differently. That's why we give a range. See "Choosing Your Cabin," later in the chapter, for more information on cabin types.

The price you pay for your cabin represents the bulk of your cruise vacation cost, but there are other costs to consider. Whether you're working with an agent or booking online, be sure that you really understand what's included in the fare you're being quoted. Are you getting a price that includes the cruise fare, port charges, taxes, fees, and insurance, or are you getting a cruise-only fare? Are airfare and airport transfers included, or do you have to book them separately (either as an add-on to the cruise fare or on your own)? One agent might break down the charges in a price quote, while another might bundle them all together. Make sure you're comparing apples with apples when making price comparisons. Read the fine print!

It's important when figuring out what your cruise will cost to remember what extras are not included in your cruise fare. The items discussed in the section below are not included in most cruise prices and will add to the cost of your trip.

## SHORE EXCURSIONS

The priciest additions to your cruise fare, particularly in Alaska, will likely be shore excursions. Rates range from about $35 to $50 for a sightseeing tour by bus, to $290 and up (sometimes as high as $430) for a lengthy helicopter or seaplane flightseeing excursion. Although these sightseeing tours are designed to help cruise passengers make the most of their time at the ports the ship visits, they can add a hefty sum to your vacation costs, so be sure to factor these expenses into your budget. Of course, whether or not you take the excursions is a personal choice, but we suggest you set aside at least $400 per person for trips in port, which might just about cover a short flightseeing trip, a kayak or jeep safari, and a bus tour.

See p. 55 for more information on shore excursions.

## TIPS

You'll want to add tips for the ship's crew to your budget calculations. Crewmembers are usually paid low base wages with the expectation that they'll make up the difference in gratuities. An exception is Radisson, which is the only line in Alaska that includes tips in the cruise fare (but you can still leave a few bucks for your favorite crew members if you want to).

Because some people find the whole tipping process confusing, a couple of years ago some lines began automatically adding tips to guests' shipboard accounts. Carnival, for instance, adds a standard tip of $9.75 per passenger, per day. Norwegian Cruise Line, Holland America, and Princess automatically add tips of $10 per day. In all these cases you are free to adjust the amount up or down as you see fit, based on the service you received.

Tips are given at the end of the cruise, and passengers should set aside at least $9 per passenger per day ($10 on some ships) for tips for the room steward, waiter, and busperson. In practice, we find that most people tend to give a little more. Additional tips to other personnel, such as the headwaiter or maitre d', are at your discretion. If you have a fancy room with a butler, slip him or her about $3 a day. Most lines automatically add 15% to bar bills, so you don't have to tip your bartender.

Most lines suggest you tip in cash, but some also have a means to allow you to tip via your shipboard account. On small ships, tips are typically pooled among the crew: You hand over a lump sum, and they divide it up. Since tipping etiquette on small ships varies, we include information on tipping specifics for each small-ship line on p. 119.

## BOOZE & SODA

Most ships charge extra for alcoholic beverages (including wine at dinner) and for soda. Nonbubbly soft drinks, such as lemonade and iced tea, are included in your cruise fare. Soda will cost $1.50 to $2.50, beer $3.25 and up, and mixed drinks $3.95 and up. A bottle of wine with dinner will run anywhere from $15 to upwards of $300.

## PORT CHARGES, LOCAL TAXES & FEES

Every ship has to pay docking fees at each port. It also has to pay some local taxes per passenger in some places. Juneau, for instance, imposes a $5-a-head tax on arriving cruise passengers. Port charges, taxes, and other fees are sometimes included in your cruise fare but not always, and these charges can add as much as $210 per person onto the price of a 7-day Alaska cruise. Make sure you know whether these fees are included in the cruise fare when you are comparing rates.

## 5 Money-Saving Strategies

### EARLY-BIRD & LAST-MINUTE DISCOUNTS

As we said earlier, the best way to save on an Alaska cruise is to **book in advance.** In a typical year, lines offer early-bird rates, usually 25% to 30% off the brochure rate, to those who book their Alaska cruise by mid-February of the year of the cruise. If the cabins do not fill up by the cutoff date, the early-bird rate may be extended, but it may be lowered slightly—say, a 15% or 20% savings. In the past couple of years, the lines have been getting even more aggressive with early-booking discounts, hoping to encourage passengers to make their Alaska cruise plans months in advance (cruise-line executives like their ships filled up as early as possible). Princess's lowest early-booking price for Alaska cruises for 2005, for instance, is $649; Holland America's is $799. If the cabins are still not full as the cruise season begins, cruise lines typically start marketing special deals, usually through their top-producing travel agents. Again, it's our feeling that in 2005, these discounts, which can run as high as 50% or more, will be less common. And keep in mind last-minute deals are usually for a very limited selection of cabins. Planning your Alaska cruise vacation well in advance and taking advantage of early-booking discounts is still the best way to go.

### SHOULDER-SEASON DISCOUNTS

You can also save by booking a cruise in the **shoulder months of May or September,** when cruise pricing is lower than during the high-season summer months. Typically, Alaska cruises are divided into budget, low, economy, value, standard, and peak seasons, but since these overlap quite a bit from cruise line to cruise line, we can lump them into three basic periods:

1. **Budget/Low/Economy Season:** May and September
2. **Value/Standard Season:** Early June and late August
3. **Peak Season:** Late June, July, and early to mid-August

### THIRD- & FOURTH-PASSENGER DISCOUNTS

Most ships offer highly discounted rates for third and fourth passengers sharing a cabin with two full-fare passengers, even if those two have booked at a discounted rate. You can add the four rates together and then divide by four to get your per-person rate. This is a good option for families (or *very* good friends) on a budget, but remember that it'll be a tight fit, since most cabins aren't all that big. Some lines also offer **special rates for kids,** usually on a seasonal or select-sailing basis, that may include free or discounted airfare.

### GROUP DISCOUNTS

One of the best ways to get a cruise deal is to book as a group, so you may want to gather family together for a reunion or convince your friends or colleagues they need a vacation, too. A "group," as defined by the cruise lines, is generally at least 16 people in at least eight cabins. The savings include not only a discounted rate, but at least the cruise portion of the 16th ticket will be free. On some upscale ships, you can negotiate a free ticket for groups of eight or more. The gang can split the proceeds from the free ticket or hold a drawing for the ticket, maybe at a cocktail party on the first night. If your group is large enough, you may even be able to get that cocktail party for free, and perhaps some other onboard perks as well.

Some travel agencies buy big blocks of space on a ship in advance and offer it to their clients at a group price only available through that agency. These are called group rates, although, as we mention earlier in the chapter, "group" in this case means savings, not that you have to hang out with (or even know) the other people booking through the agency.

## SENIOR CITIZEN DISCOUNTS

Senior citizens might be able to get extra savings on their cruise. Some lines will take 5% off the top for those 55 and up, and the senior rate applies even if the second person in the cabin is younger. Membership in groups such as AARP is not required, but such membership may bring additional savings.

## OTHER DEALS

Check each line's website for the latest savings schemes.

If you like your Alaska cruise so much you that decide you want to vacation here again, consider booking your next cruise on the spot. Cruise lines have become smart about the fact that when you're on a ship, you're a captive audience, so they may propose that you make your future vacation plans on board. *Before you sign on the dotted line, though, make sure the on-the-spot discount can be combined with other offers you might find later.* Keep in mind that if you do choose to book on board, you can still do the reconfirmation and ticketing through your travel agent by giving the cruise line his or her name.

Lines tend to offer cut rates when they are introducing a new ship or moving into a new market. So it pays to keep track of what's happening in the cruise industry—or have your agent do so—when you're looking for a deal.

## 6 Airfares & Pre-/Post-Cruise Hotel Offerings

Also see the information on cruisetours in chapter 10.

## AIR ADD-ONS

Unless you live within driving distance of your port of embarkation, you'll probably be flying to Vancouver, Anchorage, Seattle, or one of the other ports to join your ship. Your cruise package may include airfare, but if not, you'll have to make other arrangements. You can book air travel separately, but remember that those attractive discount fares you see in the newspapers may not apply, especially if your cruise departs on the peak travel days of Friday or Saturday. A better option is usually to take advantage of the cruise lines' air **add-ons.** Why? First of all, as frequent customers of the airlines, cruise lines tend to get decent (if not the best) discounts on airfare, which they pass on to their customers. Second, booking air with the cruise line also allows the line to keep track of you. If your plane is late, for instance, they may hold the boat, though not always. When you book air travel with your cruise line, most lines will include **transfers** from the airport to the ship, saving you the hassle of getting a cab. (If you do book the air travel on your own, you may still be able to get the transfers separately—ask your agent about this.) Be aware that once the air ticket is issued by the cruise line, you usually aren't allowed to make changes.

The only times it may pay to book your own air transportation is if you are using frequent-flier miles and can get your air travel for free, or if you are fussy about which carrier you fly or which route you take. You are more or less at the mercy of the cruise line in terms of carrier and route if you take their air offers, and you may even end up on chartered aircraft. Some lines offer special **deviation programs** that allow you to request specific airlines and routing for an extra fee. The deadline for these requests is usually 60 days before the sailing date, or if you book later, on the day your cruise reservations are made.

If airfare is part of the cruise package, but you choose not to book your air transportation with the cruise line, you will be refunded the air portion of the fare.

## PRE- & POST-CRUISE HOTEL OFFERINGS

Even if you don't take a cruisetour, you may want to consider spending a day or two in your port of embarkation or debarkation either before or after your cruise (see details on exploring the port cities in chapters 8 and 9). An advantage to coming in a day or two early is that you don't have to worry if your flight is running late. Plus, Vancouver, Anchorage, and Seattle, cities into which most passengers fly, happen to be great cities to explore.

Just as with airfare, you need to decide whether you want to buy your hotel stay from the cruise line or make arrangements on your own. The cruise lines negotiate **special deals with hotels** at port cities, so you will often get a bargain by booking through the cruise line.

When evaluating a cruise line's hotel package, make sure that you review it carefully to see what's included. See whether the line offers a transfer from the airport to the hotel and from the hotel to the cruise ship (or vice versa); make sure that the line offers a hotel that you will be happy with in terms of type of property and location; and inquire if any escorted tours, car-rental deals, or meals are included. You'll also want to compare the price of booking on your own (see chapter 7 for information on hotels in the various ports). Keep in mind that cruise lines usually list rates for hotels on a per-person basis, whereas hotels post their rates on a per-room basis.

### 7 Choosing Your Cabin

Once you've looked at the ship descriptions in chapters 5 and 6, talked over your options with your travel agent, and selected an itinerary and ship, you're going to have to choose your cabin. The cruise lines have improved things a bit since Charles Dickens declared that his stateroom reminded him of a coffin, but cramped, windowless spaces can still be found. On the other hand, so can penthouse-size suites with expansive verandas, Jacuzzis, and butler service. Most cabins on cruise ships today have twin beds that are convertible to queen-size (you can request which configuration you want), plus a private bathroom with a shower. Some cabins have bunk beds, which are obviously not convertible. Most ships also offer cabins designed for three or four people that will include two twin beds plus one or two bunks that fold down from the wall in some way. In some cases, it is possible to add a fifth bed to the room. Some lines offer special cabins designed for families, with "regular" twin beds that can be pushed together to create a double bed, plus fold-down bunks. Families may also be able to book connecting cabins (although they'll have to pay for two cabins to do so).

Most cabins, but not all, have televisions. Some also have extra amenities, such as safes, minifridges, VCRs, bathrobes, and hair dryers. A bathtub is considered a luxury on ships and will usually only be offered in more expensive rooms.

## CABIN TYPES

What kind of cabin is right for you? Price will likely be a big factor here, but so should the vacation style you prefer. The typical ship offers several types of cabins, which are illustrated by floor plans in the cruise line's brochure. The cabins are usually described by price (highest to lowest), category (suite, deluxe, superior, standard, economy, and other types), and furniture configuration ("sitting area with two lower beds," for example—"lower bed" meaning that the bed is a standard floor bed rather than a bunk that pulls out from the wall). The cabins will also be described as being **inside** or **outside.** Simply put, inside cabins do not have windows (or even portholes) and outside cabins do. However, views from some outside cabins may be obstructed—usually by a lifeboat—or look out onto a public area; an experienced travel agent should be able to advise you on which cabin to choose if full views and privacy are important. On the big ships, the more deluxe outside cabins may also come with **verandas** that give you a private outdoor space to enjoy the sea breezes. Remember that the verandas vary in size, so if you're looking to do more than stand on your balcony, make sure the space is big enough to accommodate deck chairs, a table, or whatever else you require. Also keep in mind that these verandas are not completely isolated—your neighbors may be able to see you and vice versa. With few exceptions, veranda cabins will not have obstructed views.

**Noise** can be a factor that may influence your cabin choice. If you take a cabin on a lower deck, you may hear engine noises; in the front of the ship, anchor noises; and in the back of the ship, thruster noises. A cabin near an elevator may bring door-opening and -closing sounds. And a cabin above or below the disco may pulse until all hours of the night. The loudest areas of a ship vary depending on how well insulated the different areas are, so if noise will be a problem for you, ask what the quietest part of the ship is when you are booking your cabin. We would say that, generally, midships on a higher deck will be the quietest part of the ship (unless, of course, you're above a disco).

If you plan to spend a lot of quiet time in your cabin, you should probably consider booking the biggest room you can afford, and you should also consider taking a cabin with a picture window or a private veranda. If, conversely, you plan to be off on shore excursions or on deck checking out the glaciers and wildlife and will only be using your cabin to change clothes and collapse in at the end of the day, you might be happy with a smaller (and cheaper) cabin. Usually, cabins on the higher decks are more expensive and much nicer, with plusher amenities and superior decor, even if they are the same size as cabins on lower decks. **Luxury suites** are usually on upper decks. The top suites on some ships are actually apartment-size, and you'll get lots of space to stretch out. A quirky thing about cabin pricing is that the most stable cabins during rough seas are those in the middle and lower parts of the ship.

On the small ships, cabins can be truly tiny and spartan, though some give the big-ship cabins a run for their money. Generally, the difference lies in the orientation of the cruise line: Those promising a real adventure experience tend to feature somewhat utilitarian cabins.

---

### Bed Lingo

On cruise ships, "lower beds" refer to standard twin beds, while "bunks" (or less commonly "upper beds") refer to beds that passengers pull out from the wall to sleep in.

## MODEL CABIN LAYOUTS

### Typical Outside Cabins

- Twin beds (can usually be pushed together)
- Some have sofa bed or bunk for third passenger
- Shower (tubs are rare)
- TV and music
- Window or porthole, or veranda

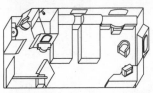

Outside Cabin

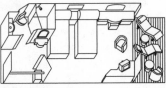

Outside Cabin with Veranda

### Typical Suites

- King, queen, or double beds
- Sitting areas (often with sofa beds)
- Large bathrooms, usually with tub, sometimes with Jacuzzi
- Refrigerators, sometimes stocked
- TVs w/VCR and stereo
- Large closets
- Large veranda

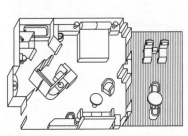

Suite with Veranda

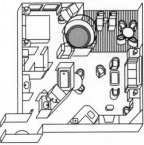

Grand Suite with Veranda

*Thanks to Princess Cruises for all photos and diagrams.*

Aboard both large and small ships, keep in mind that the most expensive and least expensive cabins tend to sell out fast. Also keep in mind that, just as with real estate, it's sometimes better to take a smaller cabin in a nicer ship than a bigger cabin in a less pleasant ship.

## READING A SHIP'S DECK PLAN

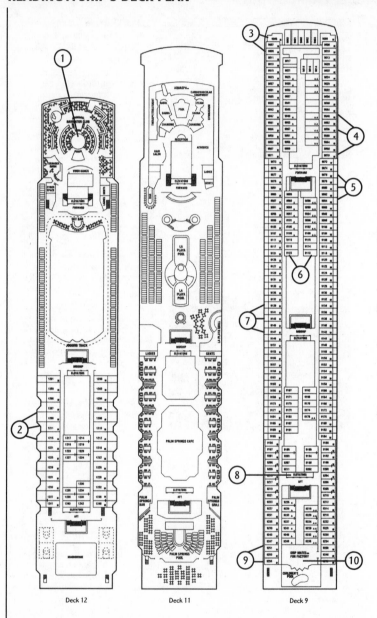

Deck 12          Deck 11          Deck 9

## CABIN SIZES

The size of a cabin is described in terms of square feet. This number may not mean a lot unless you want to mark it out on your floor at home. But to give

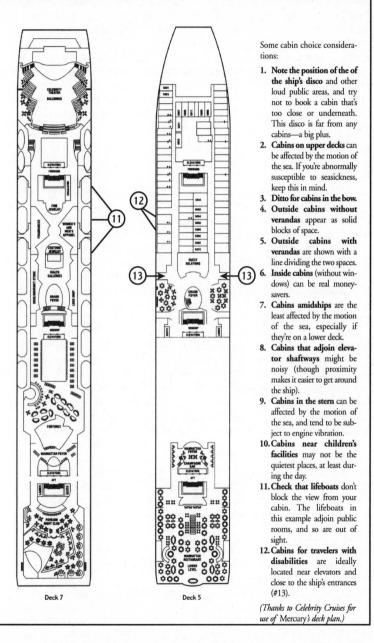

Some cabin choice considerations:

1. **Note the position of the of the ship's disco** and other loud public areas, and try not to book a cabin that's too close or underneath. This disco is far from any cabins—a big plus.
2. **Cabins on upper decks** can be affected by the motion of the sea. If you're abnormally susceptible to seasickness, keep this in mind.
3. **Ditto for cabins in the bow.**
4. **Outside cabins without verandas** appear as solid blocks of space.
5. **Outside cabins with verandas** are shown with a line dividing the two spaces.
6. **Inside cabins** (without windows) can be real money-savers.
7. **Cabins amidships** are the least affected by the motion of the sea, especially if they're on a lower deck.
8. **Cabins that adjoin elevator shaftways** might be noisy (though proximity makes it easier to get around the ship).
9. **Cabins in the stern** can be affected by the motion of the sea, and tend to be subject to engine vibration.
10. **Cabins near children's facilities** may not be the quietest places, at least during the day.
11. **Check that lifeboats** don't block the view from your cabin. The lifeboats in this example adjoin public rooms, and so are out of sight.
12. **Cabins for travelers with disabilities** are ideally located near elevators and close to the ship's entrances (#13).

*(Thanks to Celebrity Cruises for use of* Mercury's *deck plan.)*

you an idea: 120 square feet and under is low-end and cramped, 180 square feet is midrange (and the minimum for people with claustrophobia), and 250 square feet and up is suite size.

## 8 Choosing Your Dining Options

**Smaller ships** usually serve dinner at a certain time, with unassigned seating, allowing you to sit at any table you want. So if you plan to sail on one of the smaller lines, you don't have to read this section at all. Because most dining rooms on **larger ships** are not large enough to accommodate all passengers at once, large ships typically offer two different seating times, especially for dinner. In this case, your table will be preassigned and remain the same for the duration of the cruise. You will generally make your choice of seating time and table size when you book your cruise. Exceptions to the reserved seating approaches are noted in the "Open Seating" portion of this section.

### MEAL TIMES

If you are on a ship with set dinner times, early or main seating is typically at 6pm and late seating is at 8:30pm. There are advantages and disadvantages to both times, and it basically comes down to personal choice. **Early seating** is usually less crowded and the preferred time for families and seniors. The dining experience can be a bit more rushed (the staff needs to make way for the next wave of guests), but food items may be fresher. You can see a show right after dinner and have first dibs on other nighttime venues as well. And you just may be hungry again in time for the midnight buffet.

**Late seating,** on the other hand, allows you time for a good long nap or late spa appointment before dining. Dinner is not rushed at all. You can sit as long as you want, enjoying after-dinner drinks—unless, that is, you choose to go catch a show, which will usually start at 10 or 10:15pm.

If you also choose to eat **breakfast** and **lunch** in the dining room as opposed to at the more casual venues on the ship, you are theoretically supposed to eat at assigned times as well—typical meal times for breakfast are 7 or 8am for the early seating and 8:30 or 9am for the late; for lunch, it's usually noon for the early seating and 1:30pm or so for the late. We've found, though, that most ships aren't hard and fast on this. Crowds in the dining room are typically only an issue at dinner. If you show up outside of your assigned time for breakfast or lunch and your assigned table is full, the staff will probably just seat you elsewhere.

Most large ships today also offer **alternative dining options.** Most have a casual, buffet-style cafe restaurant, usually located on the Lido Deck, with indoor and outdoor poolside seating and an extensive spread of both hot and cold food items at breakfast, lunch, and dinner. Some ships also have **reservations-only restaurants,** seating fewer than 100, where—except on some luxury ships—a small fee is charged, mainly to cover gratuities.

### TABLE SIZE

Do you mind sitting with strangers? Are you looking to make new friends? Your dinner companions can make or break your cruise experience. Most ships offer tables configured for two to eight people. For singles or couples who want to socialize, a table of eight seats generally provides enough variety so that you don't get bored, and also allows you to steer clear of any individual you don't particularly care for (tables are assigned, not seats). Couples may choose to sit on their own, but singles may find it hard to secure a table for one. A family of four may want to choose a table for four, or request to sit with another family at a table for eight.

You need to state your table size preference in advance, unless you are on a ship with an open-seating policy, but don't worry if you change your mind once you're on board. You'll probably be able to move around. Just tell the dining-room maitre d' and he or she will review the seating charts for an opening.

## OPEN SEATING

Put off by all this formality? Want guaranteed casual all the way? Norwegian Cruise Line and Radisson's *Seven Seas Mariner* now serve all meals with open seating—dine when you want and sit with whom you want (within the restaurants' open hours). Princess has its own version of this system (introduced last year), allowing guests to choose traditional early or late seating, or open restaurant-style seating, before the cruise.

## SPECIAL MENU REQUESTS

The cruise line should be informed at the time you make your reservations about any special dietary requirements you have. Some lines offer kosher menus, and all will have vegetarian, low-fat, low-salt, and sugar-free options available.

## SMOKE-FREE DINING

Many ships now feature smoke-free dining rooms, but if smoking is a particular concern to you, check this out with your travel agent. If the room isn't nonsmoking, you can request a nonsmoking table. On the other hand, smokers can request a smoking table.

## 9 Deposits & Cancellation Policies

You'll be asked by your travel agent to make a **deposit,** either of a fixed amount or of some percentage of your total cruise cost. You'll then receive a receipt in the mail from the cruise line. You'll be asked to pay the remaining fare usually no later than 2 months before your departure date.

Cruise lines have varying policies regarding **cancellations,** and it's important to look at the fine print in the line's brochure to make sure you understand the policy. Most lines allow you to cancel for a full refund on your deposit and payment anytime up to 76 days before the sailing, after which you have to pay a penalty. If you cancel at the last minute, you will typically be refunded only 75% of what you've paid (although post-9/11, some lines have introduced more lenient policies).

## 10 Travel Insurance

There are three kinds of travel insurance: trip-cancellation, medical, and lost-luggage coverage. Rule number one: Check your existing policies before you buy any additional coverage. **Trip-cancellation insurance** is a good idea if you have paid a large portion of your vacation expenses up front—as is the case with cruises. It offers protection if, for some reason, you're not able to take your cruise or your trip is interrupted. For trip-cancellation insurance information, contact one of the following insurers: **Access America** (✆ 866/807-3982; www.access america.com), **Travel Guard International** (✆ 800/826-4919; www.travelguard. com), **Travel Insured International** (✆ 800/243-3174; www.travelinsured.com), or **Travelex Insurance Services** (✆ 888/457-4602; www.travelex-insurance.com).

Health insurance doesn't make sense for most travelers. Your existing health insurance should cover you if you get sick while on vacation (though if you belong to an HMO, you should check to see whether you are fully covered when away from home). If you require additional medical insurance, try **MEDEX International** (✆ **800/527-0218** or 410/453-6300; www.medexassist.com) or

## Onboard Medical Care

Large ships usually have a fully equipped medical facility and staff (a doctor and a nurse or two) on board to handle any emergency. They work from a medical center that typically offers set office hours but is also open on an emergency basis 24 hours a day. A fee (sometimes a steep one) is charged. They're equipped to do some surgery, but in cases of major medical emergencies, passengers may be airlifted off the ship by helicopter to the nearest hospital.

**Travel Assistance International** (℡ 800/821-2828; www.travelassistance.com; for general information on services, call the company's Worldwide Assistance Services, Inc., at ℡ 800/777-8710).

Small ships may have someone on staff with nursing skills, though they rarely have a doctor, but such ships in Alaska never get so far from civilization that a plane couldn't be summoned by radio to airlift a sick passenger to a hospital.

Lost-luggage insurance doesn't make much sense for most travelers either. On domestic flights, checked baggage is covered up to $2,500 per ticketed passenger. On international flights (including U.S. portions of international trips), baggage is limited to approximately $9.05 per pound, up to approximately $635 per checked bag. If you plan to check items more valuable than the standard liability, see if your valuables are covered by your homeowner's policy, get baggage insurance as part of your comprehensive travel-insurance package (contact one of the travel insurance providers listed above), or buy Travel Guard's "BagTrak" product. Don't buy insurance at the airport, as it's usually overpriced. Be sure to take any valuables or irreplaceable items with you in your carry-on luggage, as many valuables (including books, money, and electronics) aren't covered by airline policies.

If your luggage is lost, immediately file a lost-luggage claim at the airport, detailing the luggage contents. For most airlines, you must report delayed, damaged, or lost baggage within 4 hours of arrival. The airlines are required to deliver luggage, once found, directly to your house or destination free of charge.

The cruise line may also offer its own insurance policies, including trip-cancellation insurance, lost-baggage insurance, and death and dismemberment insurance. It may pay to compare these policies with the plans offered by insurance companies (this is another area where your travel agent can be of assistance).

## *FAST FACTS:* Alaska

*Area Code*   All of Alaska is in area code **907**. Well, *almost* all. The tiny community of Hyder, about 90 miles northeast of Ketchikan, lies on the Alaska/British Columbia border, almost a suburb of the larger town of Stewart, B.C. For practical and technical reasons, Hyder uses the same area code as Stewart: **250**. In the Yukon Territory, the area code is **867**. When placing a toll call within the state, you must dial 1, the area code, and the number. See "Telephone," below, for an important tip on phone cards.

*Banks & ATMs*   There are banks and automated teller machines in all but the tiniest towns.

*Business Hours* In the larger cities, major **grocery stores** are open 24 hours a day and carry a wide range of products (even fishing gear) in addition to food. At a minimum, **stores** are open Monday through Friday from 10am to 6pm, are open on Saturday afternoon, and are closed on Sunday, but many are open for much longer hours, especially during summer. **Banks** may close an hour earlier and, if they're open on Saturday, it's only in the morning. Under state law, **bars** don't have to close until 5am, but many communities have an earlier closing time, generally around 2am.

*Cellular Phone Coverage* Most of the populated portion of the state has cellular coverage. The largest provider is an Alaska company called ACS, which posts maps of its coverage area at **www.acsalaska.com**. AT&T has the second-best network. We've found that usable coverage is often less than what the companies claim, so don't bet your life on being able to make a call. Your cellphone provider should be able to give you a brochure detailing roaming charges, which can be steep.

*Emergencies* Generally, you can call ⓒ **911** for medical, police, or fire emergencies. On remote highways there sometimes are gaps in 911 coverage, but dialing 0 will generally get an operator, who can connect you to emergency services. Citizens band channels 9 and 11 are monitored for emergencies on most highways, as are channels 14 and 19 in some areas.

*Holidays* Besides the normal national holidays, banks and state and local government offices close on two state holidays: Seward's Day (the last Mon in Mar) and Alaska Day (Oct 18, or the nearest Fri or Mon if it falls on a weekend).

*Liquor Laws* The minimum drinking age in Alaska is 21. Most restaurants sell beer and wine, and a minority have full bars that serve hard liquor as well. Packaged alcohol, beer, and wine are sold only in licensed stores, not in grocery stores, but these are common and are open long hours every day. More than 100 rural communities have laws prohibiting the importation and possession of alcohol (this is known as being "dry") or only the sale but not possession of alcohol (known as being "damp"). With a few exceptions, these are tiny bush communities off the road network; urban areas are all "wet." Of the communities featured in this book, Kotzebue and Barrow are damp, and the rest are wet. Before flying into a Native village with alcohol, ask about the law—bootlegging is a serious crime (and serious bad manners), or check a list online (go to **www.dps.state.ak.us/abc/Index.asp** and click on "Local Option Restrictions").

*Lost or Stolen Credit Cards* Be sure to tell all of your credit card companies the minute you discover your wallet has been lost or stolen and file a report at the nearest police precinct. Your credit card company or insurer may require a police report number or record of the loss. Most credit card companies have an emergency toll-free number to call if your card is lost or stolen; they may be able to wire you a cash advance immediately or deliver an emergency credit card in a day or two. Visa's U.S. emergency number is ⓒ **800/847-2911** or 410/581-9994. American Express cardholders and traveler's check holders should call ⓒ **800/221-7282.** MasterCard holders should call ⓒ **800/307-7309** or 636/722-7111. For other credit cards, call the toll-free number directory at ⓒ **800/555-1212.**

If you need emergency cash over the weekend when all banks and American Express offices are closed, you can have money wired to you via **Western Union** (℃ 800/325-6000; www.westernunion.com).

Identity theft or fraud are potential complications of losing your wallet, especially if you've lost your driver's license along with your cash and credit cards. Notify the major credit-reporting bureaus immediately; placing a fraud alert on your records may protect you against liability for criminal activity. The three major U.S. credit-reporting agencies are **Equifax** (℃ 800/766-0008; www.equifax.com), **Experian** (℃ 888/397-3742; www.experian.com), and **TransUnion** (℃ 800/680-7289; www.transunion.com). Finally, if you've lost all forms of photo ID, call your airline and explain the situation; they might allow you to board the plane if you have a copy of your passport or birth certificate and a copy of the police report you've filed.

*Newspapers* The state's dominant newspaper is the *Anchorage Daily News* (www.adn.com); it's available everywhere but is not always easy to find in Southeast Alaska. Seattle newspapers and *USA Today* are often available, and in Anchorage you can get virtually any newspaper.

*Taxes* There is no state sales tax, but most local governments have a sales tax and a bed tax on accommodations. The state is considering imposing a sales tax, so this information may change.

*Telephone* We have been assured that all major calling cards will work in Alaska, but this certainly hasn't been the case in the past. To make sure, contact your long-distance company, or buy a by-the-minute card.

*Time Zone* Although the state naturally spans five time zones, in the 1980s Alaska's middle time zone was stretched so almost the entire state would lie all in one zone, known as Alaska Time. It's 1 hour earlier than the U.S. West Coast's Pacific Standard Time and 4 hours earlier than Eastern Standard Time. Crossing over the border from Alaska to Canada adds an hour and puts you at the same time as the West Coast. As with almost everywhere else in the United States, daylight saving time is in effect from 1am on the first Sunday in April (turn your clocks ahead 1 hr.) until 2am on the last Sunday in October (turn clocks back again).

*Water* Unpurified river or lake water may not be safe to drink. Hand-held filters available from sporting-goods stores for around $75 are the most practical way of dealing with the problem. Iodine kits and boiling also work.

# 4

# The Cruise Experience

Now that you've made most of the hard decisions—choosing and booking your cruise—the rest of your vacation planning should be relatively easy because the cruise lines take over much of the work, particularly if you've booked a package that includes air travel.

You should carefully read the brochure of your chosen cruise line—make sure that your agent gives you one or that you get one directly from the cruise line—because most lines' brochures include sections that address commonly asked questions. In this chapter, we'll add our own two cents' worth on these matters, and provide some practical hints that'll help you get underway glitch-free and be prepared for all you'll find in the 49th state, both aboard ship and in the ports of call.

## 1 Packing for Your Cruise

### PREPARING FOR THE WEATHER

The sometimes extreme and always unpredictable Alaska weather will be a big factor in the success of your vacation. During your summertime cruise, you may experience temperature variations from the 40s to the 80s (single digits to 20s Celsius). The days will be long, with the sun all but refusing to set, and people will be energized by the extra daylight hours. You'll likely encounter some rain, but there could also be weeks of sunny skies with no rain at all. You're less likely to encounter snow, but it is a remote possibility, especially in the spring.

Weather plays a factor in what you need to pack, with the must-haves on an Alaska cruise including a raincoat, an umbrella, and comfortable walking shoes that you don't mind getting wet or muddy. A swimsuit is also a must if your ship has a pool (sometimes covered, sometimes heated) or hot tubs.

Even in the summer, temperatures in Alaska may not go much higher than the 50s or 60s (low or high teens Celsius), although they also may go into the 70s or 80s (low to high 20s Celsius). Having **layers of clothing** that you can peel off if the weather is hot and add if the weather is cold is the most convenient approach.

### ESSENTIALS

What you choose to pack obviously involves a lot of personal choice, but here's a checklist of some items that everyone should bring along:

- A lightweight, waterproof coat or jacket
- Two sweaters or fleece pullovers, or substitute a warm vest for one
- A warm hat and gloves
- Two to four pairs of pants or jeans
- Two pairs walking shoes (preferably waterproof)
- Sunscreen (SPF 15 or higher)
- Bug spray (Alaska has 55 different kinds of mosquitoes)

- Sunglasses
- Binoculars (some small ships stock them for guest use, but none of the big ships do)
- A camera, preferably with a telephoto or zoom lens
- Film (bring more than you think you'll need)
- Formal wear (with accessories) if your ship has formal nights (not all do)
- Semidressy wear for informal nights
- Long underwear if you're on a shoulder-season cruise

## ALASKA'S CLIMATE, BY MONTHS & REGIONS

### Anchorage: Southcentral Alaska

|  | May | June | July | Aug | Sept |
|---|---|---|---|---|---|
| Average high/low (°F) | 54/39 | 62/47 | 65/52 | 63/50 | 55/42 |
| Average high/low (°C) | 12/4 | 17/8 | 18/11 | 17/10 | 13/6 |
| Hours of light | 17:45 | 19:30 | 18:15 | 15:30 | 12 |
| Sunny days | 11 | 10 | 9 | 9 | 9 |
| Rainy days | 7 | 8 | 11 | 13 | 14 |
| Precipitation | .7 | 1.1 | 1.7 | 2.4 | 2.7 |

### Juneau: Southeast Alaska

|  | May | June | July | Aug | Sept |
|---|---|---|---|---|---|
| Average high/low (°F) | 55/39 | 61/45 | 64/48 | 63/47 | 56/43 |
| Average high/low (°C) | 13/4 | 16/7 | 18/9 | 17/8 | 13/6 |
| Hours of light | 17 | 18:15 | 17:30 | 15:30 | 12:30 |
| Sunny days | 8 | 8 | 8 | 9 | 6 |
| Rainy days | 17 | 15 | 17 | 17 | 20 |
| Precipitation | 3.4 | 3.1 | 4.2 | 5.3 | 6.7 |

## PACKING FOR FORMAL, INFORMAL & CASUAL EVENTS

Some people agonize over what to pack for a cruise vacation, but there's no reason to fret. Except for the addition of a formal night or two, a cruise vacation is really no different from any resort vacation. And in some cases, it's much more casual.

Don't feel you have to go out and buy "cruise wear." Sweatshirts, jeans, and jogging outfits are the norm during the day. Dinner is dress-up time on most ships, although several have begun to offer more casual alternatives. And the small adventure-type ships are all-casual all the time.

Generally, ships describe proper dinner attire as formal, informal or semiformal (the two terms mean the same thing in this case), or casual. There are usually 2 formal nights and 2 informal (or semiformal) nights during a weeklong cruise, with the rest casual; check with your line for specifics. **Formal,** although the term has gotten somewhat more relaxed recently, generally means a tux or dark suit with tie for men, and a nice cocktail dress, long dress, gown, or dressy pantsuit for women. **Informal** (or semiformal) is a jacket, tie, and dress slacks, or a light suit, for men (jeans are frowned upon), and a dress, skirt and blouse, or pants outfit for women (the ubiquitous little black dress is appropriate here). **Casual** at dinner means a sports shirt or open-collar dress shirt with slacks for men (some will also wear a jacket), and a casual dress, pants outfit, or skirt and blouse for women. Recently, a new term—country-club casual—has developed; in our experience, this is pretty much the same as informal without the tie. For country-club casual nights, dress as you would to go out to dinner at a midrange restaurant.

> ## Tips   Cleaned & Pressed
>
> Many ships offer dry cleaning and laundry services (for a fee, of course), and some offer coin-operated laundry facilities. Check your line's brochures for details. Using these services can save you a lot of packing.

Men who don't own a **tuxedo** may be able to rent one in advance through the cruise line's preferred supplier, who will deliver the tux right to the ship. In some cases the ship will keep a limited supply of tuxes on board. But if you attend a formal evening wearing a dark business suit instead of a tuxedo, you won't be alone.

## 2 Money Matters

There are few forms of travel that are as easy as a cruise, at least as far as money is concerned. That's because you've already paid the lion's share of your all-inclusive vacation by the time you board the ship.

When you check in at the cruise terminal for a large-ship cruise, the cruise-line folks will ask for a major credit card to which you will charge your onboard expenses, unless you've established that you will be paying your onboard expenses by cash or check. On some ships you must report to the purser's office once on board to establish your onboard credit account. On all cruises you also have the option of paying your account with cash, traveler's checks, or, in some cases, a personal check. Check the cruise line's brochure for specific rules on this. You may be asked to leave a deposit if you are paying with cash, usually $250 for a 1-week sailing. You should let the cruise line know as early as possible if you wish to pay with cash or checks (some lines like to know at the time you make your cruise reservations).

The staff at the check-in counter will give you a special **ship charge card** (sometimes called a "signature card") that you will use for the length of your cruise. From this point on, on most ships, your time aboard is virtually cashless, except for any gambling you do in the casino. On many ships you can even put your crew tips on your credit card, though on some you're expected to use cash (more on tipping later in this chapter).

On most small ships, things aren't so formal—since there are so few passengers, and since the only places to spend money aboard are at the bar and the small gift counters, the staff will just mark down your purchases and you'll settle your account at the end of the week.

In all cases you will need some cash on hand for when you stop at a port, in order to pay for cabs, make small purchases, buy sodas and snacks, tip your tour guides, and so on. Having bills smaller than $20 is useful for these purposes. At all the ports described in this book (even the Canadian ones), U.S. dollars are accepted, as are major credit cards. If you prefer to deal in Canadian currency in Canada, there are exchange counters, banks, and ATMs at most ports you will visit. Ships in Alaska do not usually offer currency-conversion services.

Some ships have their own ATMs aboard, most often located, not surprisingly, in the casino. These give out U.S. dollars.

It's recommended that you not leave large amounts of cash in your room. All ships have some sort of safes available, either in-room or at the purser's desk, and passengers are wise to use them. You should also store your plane ticket and passport or ID papers there.

| The Cost of Common Cruise Incidentals | US$ |
|---|---|
| Alternative dining (service charge) | 5.00–25.00 |
| Babysitting (per hour, for two children) | |
|    Private | 10.00 |
|    Group | 6.00–8.00 |
| Beverages | |
|    Beer (domestic) | 3.25 |
|    Beer (imported) | 4.50 |
|    Mineral water | 2.00 |
|    Mixed drinks | 3.75–6.75 (more for fine liquors) |
|    Soft drinks | 1.50–2.50 |
|    Wine with dinner | 15.00–300.00 per bottle |
| Cruise-line logo souvenirs | 3.00–50.00 |
| Dry cleaning (per item) | 2.50–7.50 |
| E-mail (per minute) | 0.50–1.50 |
| Haircuts | |
|    Men's | 32.00 |
|    Women's | 57.00–77.00 |
| Massage (50 min.) | 89.00–109.00 |
| Phone calls (per minute) | 6.95–16.95 |
| Photos (5×7) | 6.95–8.95 |

## BUDGETING

Before your trip you may want to make a tentative budget. You should set aside money for shore excursions ($400 per person or more if you plan to do several) and tips (about $70 per passenger for a 1-week cruise).

Areas that should also be included in your planning are bar drinks, dry cleaning, phone calls, massage and other spa services, beauty parlor services, babysitting, photos taken by the ship's photographer, wine at dinner, souvenirs, and costs for any other special splurges your particular ship might offer (items at the caviar bars or cigar bars, time on the golf simulator, and so on). Above are some rough prices for the more common incidentals.

We suggest that you keep careful track of your onboard expenses to avoid an unpleasant surprise at the end of your cruise.

On big ships, a final bill will be slipped under your door on the last night of your cruise. If everything is okay and you're paying by credit card, you don't have to do anything but keep the copy. If there's a problem on the bill, or if you are paying by cash, traveler's check, or personal check, you will have to go down to the purser's or guest-relations desk and wait in what will likely be a very long line. On small ships you usually have to settle up directly with the purser on the last full day of the cruise.

## 3 Your Very Important Papers

About 1 month (and no later than 1 week) before your cruise, you should receive in the mail your **cruise documents,** including your airline tickets (if you purchased them from the cruise line), a boarding document with your cabin and dining choices on it, boarding forms to fill out, luggage tags, and your pre-arranged bus-transfer vouchers from the airport to the port (if applicable). Also included will likely be a description of shore excursions available for purchase either on board or, in some cases, in advance, as well as additional material detailing things you need to know before you sail.

All this information is important. Read it carefully. Make sure that your cabin category and dining preference are as you requested and also check your airline tickets to make sure everything is okay in terms of flights and arrival times. Make sure that there is enough time to arrive at the port no later than half an hour before departure time, and preferably a lot earlier. Be sure to carry these documents in your carry-on rather than in your luggage, since you can't board without them.

## PASSPORTS & NECESSARY IDENTIFICATION

If you are embarking or disembarking your Alaska cruise in Vancouver, you will be required to show either a **passport** or a photo ID and proof of citizenship (such as a birth certificate with a raised seal). A driver's license is not considered sufficient ID. If you are not a U.S. citizen but live in the United States, you will have to carry your alien registration card and passport. Foreign-born travelers who do not reside in the U.S. will be required to show a valid visa to enter the U.S. through Canada. For more information about passports and to find your regional passport office, consult the State Department website (http://travel. state.gov) or call the **National Passport Information Center**'s automated service at ✆ **877/487-2778.**

Even if your cruise does not visit Canada, you will still be required to show a photo ID when boarding the ship; in this case, however, a driver's license is sufficient.

### 4  Getting to the Ship & Checking In

Before you leave for the airport, put one of the luggage tags sent by the cruise line on each of your bags. Make sure that you correctly fill in the tags with your departure date, port, cabin number, and so forth. You can find all this information in your cruise documents. Put a luggage tag on your carry-on as well.

## AIRPORT ARRIVAL

If you booked your air travel and/or transfers with the cruise line, you should see a **cruise-line representative** holding a card with the name of the line, either when you get off the plane or at the baggage area. (If you're arriving on a flight from the United States to Vancouver, you will need to clear Customs and Immigration. Follow the appropriate signs. The cruise-line rep will be waiting to greet you after you've cleared.) Check in with this person. If you are on a pre-cruise package, the details of what to do at the airport will be described in the cruise line's brochure.

When you arrive at your gateway airport, you will be asked by a cruise-line representative to identify your luggage, which will then go straight to the ship for delivery to your cabin. It won't necessarily go in the same bus as you, and it may not (almost certainly will not) be waiting for you when you board, but it'll arrive eventually, have no fear. Make certain that your bags have the cruise line's tags on them, properly filled out, before you leave the airport for the ship. The tags will be in the package of documents sent to you by the cruise line along with your cruise tickets.

You will have to turn over the **transportation voucher** you received with your cruise documents to the bus driver, so you'll want to have it handy.

---

*Tips* **Where's My Luggage?!**

Don't panic if your bags aren't in your cabin when you arrive: Getting all the bags on board is a rather slow process—on big ships, as many as 6,000 bags need to be loaded and distributed. If it gets close to sailing time and you're concerned, call guest relations or the purser's office. They'll probably advise you that it's on the way. If your luggage really is lost rather than just late, the cruise line's customer-relations folks will track it down and arrange for it to be delivered to the ship's first port of call.

---

If you're flying independent of the cruise line, claim your luggage at the baggage area and proceed to the pier by cab, by rental car, or by whatever other arrangements you have made. And again, remember to put the luggage tags provided by the cruise lines on your bags at this point if you haven't already because when you get to the pier, your bags will be taken from you by a porter for loading onto the ship. The porter who takes your bags may expect a tip of $1 per bag (some will be more aggressive than others in asking for it).

Also, if you're taking non-cruise-line-operated transportation to the cruise dock, make sure you get to the right ship at the right pier. That may sound silly, but in cities with multiple piers, it can get confusing. And cab drivers don't always know their way around the docks. Know your pier number!

## WHAT TO DO IF YOUR FLIGHT IS DELAYED

First of all, tell the airline personnel at the airport that you are a cruise passenger and that you're sailing that day. They may be able to put you on a different flight. Second, have the airline folks call the cruise line to advise them of your delay. There should be an emergency number included in your cruise documents. Keep in mind that you may not be the only person delayed, and the line just may hold the ship until your arrival. (Jerry, however, remembers one embarrassing occasion on which several passengers bound for Vancouver through Los Angeles to join a Holland America ship had had the first leg of their trip from Dallas delayed by an aircraft mechanical problem and were now running late. "Don't worry," Jerry assured them. "You'll only be half an hour late in Vancouver. Holland America will wait for you." Bad advice. The group arrived at Canada Place just in time to see their ship disappear in the distance. Jerry has never offered encouragement in such a situation since!)

## WHAT TO DO IF YOU MISS THE BOAT

Don't panic. Go directly to the cruise line's port agent at the pier. You may be able to get to your ship via a chartered boat or tug, assuming that the vessel isn't too far out at sea by that time. (Be aware that if you do follow in a small boat, you'll have to transfer from it to a moving ship at sea—not an exercise to be taken lightly!) Or you may be put up in a hotel for the night and flown or provided with other transportation to the next port the next day. If you booked your flight on your own, you will likely be charged for this service.

## CHECKING IN

Most ships start embarkation in the early afternoon, and depart between 4 and 6pm. You will not be able to board the ship before the scheduled embarkation time, usually about 2 or 3 hours before sailing, and even then it's likely that you'll have to wait in line unless you're sailing on a small ship carrying very few passengers. If you've booked a suite, you may get priority boarding at a special desk. Special-needs passengers may also be processed separately. Ship personnel will check your boarding tickets and ID and collect any documents you've been sent to fill out in advance. You will then be given a boarding card and your cabin key. (On some lines, your key may be waiting in your cabin.) Be prepared for increased security measures that will include an X-ray of your hand luggage and possibly a search with a metal-detecting wand.

## Safety at Sea in the New World (Dis)Order

Traditionally, safety-at-sea issues have included the occasional hurricane, fire, gastrointestinal bug, petty theft, and rogue iceberg. But in the wake of the September 11, 2001, terrorist attacks, the threat of terrorism immediately assumed a high place on that list, prompting the cruise lines, port authorities, and the U.S. Coast Guard to implement a number of new security measures throughout their destination areas—including Alaska.

Logistically, ships are more difficult to protect than planes because of their larger passenger loads; their numerous labyrinthine public and "crew only" areas; their regular presence at public port facilities; the access they offer to the numerous contractors who come aboard on turnaround days to refresh flowers, service machinery, and perform other needed functions; and their multicountry itineraries—Alaska cruises usually include Canadian ports as well. For these reasons, all the major cruise lines have their own dedicated onboard security forces, and events over the years have periodically forced enhancements to security procedures. These have included the hiring of ex–Navy SEALs as top-level security consultants, the drilling of deck officers in how to react to takeover attempts, and a mandate that ships have alternative onboard command sites, making it difficult for a small number of terrorists to take and maintain control of a ship. Following 9/11, all cruise ships went to Security Level III, the highest dictated by the Coast Guard, but because stringent security measures were already in place, onboard changes have been relatively few. The cruise lines already were using metal detectors at the gangways, requiring that anyone boarding be on a preapproved list, and employing computerized systems that could tell instantly who was aboard at any given time. Recent additions to these regulations dictate a no-visitors policy; a 300-foot (or more) security zone around all cruise ships; the use of sniffer dogs, concrete barriers, patrol boats, and other security measures at some ports; and the screening of all luggage, ship's stores, mail, and cargo. Many cruise lines have begun photographing passengers digitally at embarkation and matching face to picture every time travelers get back aboard in port.

Because Level III guidelines apply only to U.S. ports, the cruise lines have been working diligently with foreign port officials to beef up security around the ships and protect passengers on shore excursions that the cruise lines sell. Measures include tightening access to ports and increasing local law enforcement patrols in the water around the vessels.

You have up until a half-hour (on some ships, it's 1 hr.) before departure to board, but there are some advantages to boarding earlier, like getting first dibs on spa-treatment times. Plus, if you get on early enough, you can eat lunch on the ship.

Protocol for establishing your **dining-room table assignment,** if one is required (some ships have open seating), varies by ship. You may be given your assignment in advance of your sailing (on your tickets), you may be advised of your table number as you check in, or a card with your table number may be waiting for you in your cabin. If you do not receive an assignment by the time you get to your cabin, you will be directed to a maitre d's desk, set up in a convenient spot on board. This is also the place to make any changes if your assignment does not meet with your approval.

## 5 Keeping in Touch with the Outside World

### SENDING MAIL

If you want to send mail from the ship, you should be able to find both stamps and a mailbox at the purser's office. The purser's office should have the appropriate postage available.

### GETTING THE NEWS & KEEPING IN TOUCH

Newshounds don't have to feel out of touch on a cruise ship. Most newer cruise ships offer CNN on in-room TVs, and nearly every ship will post the latest news from the wire services outside the purser's office. Some lines excerpt information from leading newspapers each day and deliver the news to your room.

Every ship will offer the opportunity to make satellite phone calls, but these can be exorbitantly expensive—usually anywhere from $6.95 to $17 per minute. A cheaper alternative is e-mail, offered by an increasing number of ships, including most of the large ships reviewed in this book. Rates range from 50¢ to $1.50 per minute. Some of the small ships also offer e-mail access. And many of the port cities in Alaska now have Internet cafes.

You may also be able to use your cellular phone in some of the more populated areas of Alaska. Check with your cellular provider for details.

## 6 Visiting the Ports of Call

### VISITING THE PORTS OF CALL

Here's where the kind of ship you chose for your cruise, and the itinerary, comes into play. On a big ship, you will likely visit the popular ports of Skagway, Juneau, and Ketchikan (and possibly Sitka, Victoria, or Valdez, depending on your itinerary) and will have several days at sea to enjoy the glorious glaciers, fjords, and wildlife, as well as participate in shipboard activities and relax. On a

---

### *Tips* Religion on the High Seas

Religious services depend, of course, on the ship and the clergy on board. Some ships offer Catholic Mass every day. Most ships offer a nondenominational service on Sunday and a Friday-night Jewish Sabbath service, usually run by a passenger. On Jewish and Christian holidays, clergy are typically aboard on large ships to lead services, which are usually held in the library or conference room.

smaller ship, you may also visit several smaller ports of call and head into wilderness areas that cannot accommodate larger vessels.

On **days in port,** you will want to have a plan of what you want to see on land—more on that in this section. On **days at sea,** you will probably want to be out on deck much of the time looking for whales and listening to the commentary of glacier and wildlife experts. There will be plenty of activities offered, but these may be reduced at certain times—for instance, when the ship is scheduled to pass one of the famous glaciers.

Nearly every ship in Alaska has **naturalists and other Alaska experts** on board to share their expertise on glaciers, geography, plant life, and wildlife. Sometimes these experts are on for the entire cruise and offer lectures complete with slides or films. Other times they are Forest Service rangers who come on board at glacier sites (particularly in Glacier Bay) to offer commentary, usually over the ship's PA system. Depending on the ship, local fishermen, Native Alaskans, teachers, photographers, librarians, historians, or anthropologists may come on board to teach about local history and culture.

Cruise lines carefully arrange their itineraries to visit places that offer a little something for everyone, whether your thing is nature, museum hopping, barhopping, or no hopping at all. You can take in the location's ambience and natural beauty, learn a little something about the local culture and history, eat local foods, and enjoy sports activities. And you'll have the opportunity to shop to your heart's content.

## SHORE EXCURSIONS

When the ship gets into port, you'll have the choice of going on a shore excursion organized by the cruise line or going off on your own. The shore excursions are designed to help you make the most of your limited time at each port of call, to get you to the top natural or historical attractions, and to make sure you get back to the ship on time. But shore excursions are also a moneymaking area for the cruise line, and the offerings can add a hefty sum to your vacation costs. Whether or not you choose to take one of these prearranged sightseeing trips is a matter of both personal preference and pocketbook concerns; you should in no way feel that you need to do an excursion in every port. Our picks of some of the best shore-excursion offerings in Alaska's Southeast and Southcentral, as well as in Vancouver and Victoria, are included with all the port listings in chapters 8 and 9, along with advice on exploring on your own.

At most ports, the cruise lines offer **guided tours** to the top sights, usually by bus. The most worthwhile tours take you outside the downtown area, or include a meal, a dance or music performance, or a crafts demonstration (or sometimes all of the above). There's a guide on each bus, and the excursion price includes all incidental admission costs. The commentary is sometimes hokey, other times educational.

In most Alaska ports, it's easy to explore the downtown area on your own. The advantages to independent exploration are that walking around is often the best way to see the sights, and you can plan your itinerary to steer clear of the crowds. In some ports, however, there's not much within walking distance of the docks, and it's difficult to find a cab or other transportation. In these cases the cruise line's excursion program may be your best and most cost-effective option. For instance, a typical $40 to $45 **historical tour** in Sitka will take in the Russian St. Michael's Cathedral in the downtown area plus two great sights a little ways out of downtown: Sitka National Historic Park, with its totem poles and forest trails; and the Alaska Raptor Rehabilitation Center, where injured bald eagles and other birds of prey are nursed back to health. The tour may also include a Russian dance performance by the New Archangel Dancers. Although you could visit the church on your own, it's a long walk to the park, and the bus is the best way to get to see the eagles.

There are plenty of shore excursions in Alaska for those who want to get active, such as **mountain-bike trips, fishing, snorkeling,** and **kayak voyages,** all of which get you close to nature and allow you to experience stunning views. These trips are generally worth taking. They usually involve small groups of passengers, and by booking your activity through the cruise line, you have the advantage of knowing that the vendors having been prescreened: Their prices may be slightly higher than those offered by the outfitters that you'll find once you disembark at the port, but you can be assured that those outfitters that the cruise lines work with are reputable.

For those who enjoy trips in small planes or helicopters, and are willing to pay for the experience (they are on the pricey side), **flightseeing trips,** offered as shore excursions at many of the ports of call, are a fascinating way to see the Alaska landscape. Again, the ship's offerings may be priced slightly higher than the tours offered at the port, but by booking the ship's package, you should be able to avoid touring with Reckless Mike and His Barely Flying Machine. The extra few bucks you pay will be worth it.

Per person, shore excursions usually range in price from about $40 to $50 for a bus tour, to $200 and up (sometimes as high as $350) for an elaborate offering such as helicopter sightseeing.

You may be in port long enough to book more than one option or to take an excursion and still have several hours to explore the port on your own. And you may very well find that you want to do a prearranged shore excursion at one port and go it on your own at the next.

The best way to decide which shore excursions you want to take is to do some research in advance of your trip. In addition to our descriptions in chapters 8 and 9, which detail the most common and popular excursions offered in the various ports, your cruise line will probably send you a booklet listing its shore excursions with your cruise tickets. You can compare and contrast. On board your ship, a shore-excursion order form should either be in your cabin, available at the purser's desk or shore-excursion desk, or at the shore-excursion lecture that will be offered the first day of your cruise. To make your reservations, check off the appropriate places on the shore-excursion order form, sign the form (make sure to include your cabin number), and drop it off as directed, probably at the ship's shore-excursion desk or at the purser's office. Your account will be automatically charged, and tickets will be sent to your cabin before your first scheduled tour. The tickets will include such information as where and when to meet for the tour. Carefully note the time: If you are not at the right place at the right time, the tour will probably leave without you.

Remember, the most popular excursions (such as flightseeing trips) sell out fast. For that reason, you're best off booking your shore excursions the first or second day of your cruise. Some lines, including Holland America, Princess, Royal Caribbean, and Celebrity, offer the option of booking shore excursions in advance of your trip, which we recommend that you do in order to assure yourself a spot.

## ARRIVING IN PORT

When the ship arrives in port, it will either dock at the pier or anchor slightly offshore. You may think that when the ship docks right at the pier you can walk right off, but you can't. Before the gangway is open to the public, lots of papers must be signed, and local authorities must give their clearance, a process that can take as long as 2 hours. Don't bother going down to the gangplank until you hear an announcement saying the ship has been cleared.

If your ship anchors rather than docks (which ships usually will do in Alaska), you will go ashore in a small boat called a **launch** or **tender,** which ties up next to your ship and shuttles passengers back and forth all day. Getting on the tender may require a helping hand from crew members, and the waves may keep the tender swaying, sometimes requiring passengers to literally jump to get aboard.

Whether the ship is docked or anchored, you are in no way required to get off at every port of call. The ship's restaurants will remain open, and there will be activities offered, though usually on a limited basis.

If you do get off, before you reboard you may want to use the phones at the docks to call home. This is much cheaper than making calls from the ship. But be prepared to wait for a phone. No matter how many telephones there are on the pier, you will invariably find that off-duty members of the crew, who generally get off the ship earlier than passengers, have beaten you to them. It's an interesting exercise to stand near a dozen public telephones and listen to the Filipino, cockney, French, Norwegian, and other languages and dialects being spoken by the users.

## TIPS FOR YOUR PORT VISITS
### THE ESSENTIALS: DON'T LEAVE THE SHIP WITHOUT 'EM
You must bring your **ship boarding pass** (or shipboard ID) with you when you disembark or you will have trouble getting back on board. You may also be required to show a photo ID or driver's license (the ship will let you know if you have to carry this as well). And also don't forget to bring a little **cash**—although your ship operates on a cashless system, the ports do not. Many passengers get so used to carrying no cash or credit cards while aboard ship that they forget them when going ashore.

### WATCH THE CLOCK
If you're going off on your own, whether on foot or on one of the alternate tours or transportation options that we've listed, remember to be very careful about timing. Cruise lines are very strict about sailing times, which will be posted around the ship. You're generally required to be back at the dock at least a half-hour before the ship's scheduled departure. Passengers running late on one of the line's shore excursions needn't worry: If an excursion runs late, the ship accepts responsibility and won't leave without the late passengers.

If you're on your own and do miss the boat, immediately contact the cruise-line representative at the port. You'll probably be able to catch your ship at the next port of call, but you'll have to pay your own way to get there.

## 7 Tipping, Packing for Disembarkation & Other End-of-Cruise Concerns

Here are a few hints that should save you some time and aggravation at the end of your cruise.

## TIPS ON TIPPING
Tipping is a subject that some people find confusing. First, let's establish that you are expected to tip the crew at the end of the cruise, in particular your cabin steward, server, and busperson; not to do so is bad form. The cruise line will give

suggested tip amounts in the daily bulletin and in the cruise director's disembarkation briefing, but these are just suggestions—you can tip more or less, at your own discretion. Keep in mind, though, that stewards, servers, and buspersons are often extremely underpaid (some lines pay their waiters $1 a day base pay), and that their salaries are largely dependent on tips. Many of these crewmembers support families back home on their earnings.

We think the **minimum tip** you should consider is $4 per passenger per day for your room steward and your waiter, and $2 per passenger per day for your busperson. That totals up to $70 per passenger for a 7-night cruise (you don't have to include disembarkation day). We also recommend leaving about half of these amounts on behalf of child passengers 12 and under. Some lines recommend more, some a little less. Of course, you can always tip more for good service or simply to round out the number. You'll also be encouraged to tip the dining room maitre d', the headwaiter, and other better-salaried employees. Whether to tip these folks or not is your decision. If you have a cabin with butler service, tip the butler about $3 per person, per day. Most lines suggest that you tip in cash, but some also allow you to tip via your shipboard account. And recently, lines including Carnival, Holland America, Princess, and Norwegian Cruise Line have begun automatically adding tips of about $10 per passenger, per day, to your shipboard account. Even if the cruise line automatically adds the tips to your shipboard account, you can visit the purser's office and ask them to increase or decrease the amount depending on your opinion of the service you received. Bar bills automatically include the tip (usually 15%), but if the dining-room wine steward, for instance, has served you exceptionally well, you can slip him or her a few bucks, too. The captain and his officers should not be tipped—it'd be like tipping your doctor.

Usually, when ships operate on a no-tipping-required basis (Holland America is one such case), the staff will still accept a tip. Radisson Seven Seas Cruises includes tips in the cruise fare, although some people choose to tip key personnel anyway—it's really up to you.

If you have spa or beauty treatments, you can tip that person at the time of the service (just add it to your shipboard account), and you can hand a bartender a buck if you like, but otherwise tips are usually given on the last night of your cruise. On some ships (especially small ships) you may be asked to submit your tips in a single sum that the crew will divide among itself after the cruise, but generally you reward people individually, usually in little preprinted envelopes that the ship distributes.

If a staff member is particularly great, a written letter to a superior is always good form and may earn that person an employee-of-the-month honor, and maybe even a bonus.

## SETTLING YOUR SHIPBOARD ACCOUNT

On big ships, your shipboard account will close just before the end of your cruise, but before that time you will receive a preliminary bill in your cabin. If you are using a credit card, just make sure the charges are correct. If there is a problem, you will have to go to the purser's office, where you will likely encounter long lines. If you're paying by cash or traveler's check, you'll be asked to settle your account during either the day or night before you leave the ship. This will also require you to go to the purser's office. A final invoice will be delivered to your room before departure.

On small ships, the procedure will be simpler. Often, you can just mosey over to the purser's desk on the last evening, check to see that the bill they give you looks right, and sign your name.

## LUGGAGE PROCEDURES

With thousands of suitcases to deal with, big ships have established the routine of requiring guests to pack the night before they disembark. You will be asked to leave your bags in the hallway before you retire for the night (you must usually leave them in the hallway by midnight). The bags will be picked up overnight and placed in the cruise terminal before passengers are allowed to disembark. It's important to make sure that your bags are tagged with the luggage tags given to you by the cruise line toward the end of your cruise. These are not the same tags you arrived with; rather, they're color-coded to indicate deck number and disembarkation order—the order in which they'll likely be arranged on the dock. If you need more tags, alert your cabin steward or the purser's staff.

If you booked your air travel through the cruise line, you may be able to check-in your luggage for your flight right at the cruise terminal. You will collect your bags—there should be porters to help—turn them over to an airline representative, and receive your claim checks. You may even be able to get your flight boarding passes at the cruise terminal. You will then proceed to a bus that will take you to the airport.

If you're on a **post-cruise tour,** special instructions will be given by the cruise line.

## DISEMBARKATION

You won't be able to get off the ship until it is cleared by Customs and other authorities, a process that usually takes 90 minutes or more. In most cases you'll be asked to vacate your cabin by 8am and wait in one of the ship's lounges. If you have a flight home on the same day, you will disembark based on your flight departure time. Passengers with mobility problems, those who booked suites, and travelers who will be staying on in the port will often be debarked early. If you have booked a land package through the cruise line, they will have transportation waiting to take you from the ship to your hotel.

## CUSTOMS & IMMIGRATION

If your cruise begins or ends in Canada, you'll have to clear Canadian Customs and Immigration, which usually means that your name goes on a list that is reviewed by authorities. You must fill out a Customs declaration form, and you may be required to show your passport or ID.

When disembarking in U.S. ports after starting out from Vancouver, non-U.S. citizens (including green-card holders) will be required to meet with U.S. Immigration authorities, usually in a lounge or theater, when the ship arrives at the port. You will have to bring your passport receipt with you, and all family members must attend.

If you're flying home from Vancouver, you'll have to pay an **airport improvement fee** at the Vancouver Airport. The tax is C$10 (US$7.50) and can be paid in Canadian or U.S. dollars.

The U.S. Customs Service has a preclearance program in Vancouver that allows cruise passengers to go through Customs there before boarding their flights home. The procedure in Vancouver—purely because of the lower number of travelers to be processed—is generally a lot faster than it is at LAX, JFK, or other U.S. airport facilities, where half a dozen flights arrive close together.

# 5

# The Cruise Lines, Part 1: The Big Ships

**H**ere's where the rudder hits the road: It's time to choose the ship that will be your home away from home for the duration of your Alaska cruise.

As we said earlier, your biggest decision is whether you want to sail on a big ship or a small ship. So that you can more easily compare like with like, in this chapter we'll deal only with the big ships; in chapter 6, we'll discuss the small ships.

The ships in Alaska are bigger than ever, and Princess holds the title of heavyweight champ. The company's *Diamond Princess* and *Sapphire Princess,* which both debuted in 2004, will again be plying Alaska's waters from Seattle this year. The ships weigh in at 116,000 tons and carry 2,670 passengers. Another impressive statistic: Among the seven Princess ships in the Alaska fleet this year, there will be about 15,000 berths available each week! And there are other megaships that don't sport the Princess colors: Celebrity Cruises' returning *Summit* and *Infinity* each weigh 91,000 tons and carry 1,950 passengers. In addition, Royal Caribbean's 90,000-ton *Radiance of the Seas,* spending a third year in Alaska and offering 2,100 berths, is joined for the second successive year by a newer sister ship, the similarly dimensioned *Serenade of the Seas.* Carnival Cruise Lines' returning *Carnival Spirit* weighs 86,000 tons and carries 2,124 passengers. The list of massive vessels is a long one. (If you're wondering why Holland America Line—which has seven ships in Alaska this year—isn't included in the megaship list, it's because the company doesn't have one. Megaship, that is. Its biggest, *Oosterdam,* is "only" 85,000 tons and carries 1,840 passengers. By today's standards, that's positively midsize!)

The beauty of these latter-day megaships is that they are designed so that it doesn't seem as though you're sharing your vacation with thousands of others. There are lots of nooks and crannies in which to relax and hide far from the maddening crowd, so to speak.

The evolution of cruise ships is almost worth a chapter all by itself. Two decades ago, major cruise lines operated ships that ranged from about 20,000 to 40,000 gross registered tons. These were considered "big" ships. Their cabins had portholes or, at best, picture windows that didn't open. The ships had one dining room, with two seatings for lunch and dinner, and a snack bar/buffet as pretty much the only alternative. Many of them had large numbers of inside cabins and all of their cabins, inside and outside, tended to be rather basic (in some cases downright spartan). Only the very best half-dozen or so suites on some of them had private verandas. The ship that set industry standards for the number of verandas was the *Royal Princess* of Princess Cruises, which debuted in 1984. Of its 600 staterooms, no fewer than 150 of them came balcony-equipped. And the elegant ship had *no* inside rooms. At 45,000 tons it was getting up there in size and was proving to the industry that extra luxury could be provided at the prevailing rate. Its builder, the Wartsila Yard in Helsinki, Finland, trumpeted the message that *Royal Princess* was "the most advanced cruise ship ever built."

Whether that claim was strictly accurate or not, other cruise lines sat up and took notice. Suddenly, verandas were included on their new builds. In some cases inside rooms were greatly reduced in number. As the demand for cruises grew—stoked by the popular TV show, *The Love Boat*—the lines began to look for bigger and better ways to make life at sea enjoyable for their passengers. Advances in shipbuilding technology allowed them to move up from 45,000 GRT, as in the case of the *Royal Princess,* to 65,000 GRT, to 90,000 GRT, and now to 130,000 GRT. The additional space made possible more technologically advanced showrooms, million-dollar collections of original art, better trained and higher paid entertainment directors, flashy and extensive children's and teens' centers—and alternative dining facilities. Lots and lots of alternative dining facilities! Nowadays, the roster of available food choices on cruise ships would do credit to the Manhattan telephone directory. Depending on your ship, you can have Italian, Chinese, Tex-Mex, Cajun, Asian fusion, French, even good old British fish and chips. And more and more cruise ships are going to an open seating (come when you like, eat with whom you like) policy. On some ships it is literally possible nowadays to eat dinner every night and never enter the same restaurant twice.

The *Royal Princess* didn't make all that happen. In fact, the ship has virtually no alternative dining sites. But there can be no question that it raised the standards for cruising, so Princess's rivals had to get a little more creative. Improvements in marine architecture and building techniques did the rest.

The ships featured in this chapter vary in size, age, and offerings, but share the common thread of having scads of activities and entertainment offerings. You will not be roughing it. On these ships you'll find swimming pools, health clubs, spas, nightclubs, movie theaters, shops, casinos, multiple restaurants, bars, and special kids' playrooms, and in some cases sports decks, virtual golf, computer rooms, martini bars, and cigar clubs, as well as the aforementioned quiet spaces where you can get away from it all. Onboard activities generally include games, contests, classes, and lectures, plus a variety of entertainment options and show productions, some very sophisticated. An array of shore excursions is offered, for which you will have to pay extra. Cabins vary in size and amenities but are usually roomy enough for the time you'll be spending aboard. And with all the public rooms, you won't be spending much time in your cabin anyway.

## 1 Some Components of the Cruise-Line Reviews

Each cruise line's review begins with a quick word about the line in general and a short summation of the kind of cruise experience you can expect to have aboard that line. The text that follows fleshes out the review, providing all the details you need to get a feel for what kind of vacation the cruise line will give you.

The individual ship reviews that follow the general cruise-line description get into the nitty-gritty, giving you all the details on the ships' accommodations, facilities, amenities, comfort levels, and upkeep.

People feel very strongly about ships. For centuries, mariners have imbued their vessels with human personalities, usually referring to an individual ship as "her." In fact, an old (really old) seafaring superstition holds that women should never be allowed aboard a ship because the ship, being a woman herself, will get jealous. (That could make Fran's job just a teeny bit difficult! And Jerry's wife wouldn't like it much either.) It's a fact that people bond with the ships aboard which they sail. They find themselves in the gift shop loading up on T-shirts with the ship's name emblazoned on the front. They get to port and the first question they ask other cruisers they meet is "Which ship are you sailing on?" They engage in a (usually) friendly comparison, and both parties walk away knowing in their hearts that their ship is the best. We know people who have sailed the same ship a dozen times or more and feel as warmly about it as though it were their own summer cottage. That's why, when looking at the reviews, you want to look for a ship that says "you."

We've listed some of the ships' vital statistics—ship size, years built and most recently refurbished, number of cabins, number of crew—to help you compare. Size is listed in tons. Note that these are not actual measures of weight but gross register tons (GRTs), which is a measure of the interior space used to produce revenue on a ship. One GRT equals 100 cubic feet of enclosed, revenue-generating space. Among the crew/officers statistics, an important one is the **passenger/crew ratio,** which tells you, in theory, how many passengers each crewmember is expected to serve and, thus, how much personal service you can expect.

*New cruisers please note:* There is a saying in the industry that nobody should cruise just once. On any voyage, a ship could encounter bad weather. On any given day at sea, the only seat left in the show lounge might be behind an unforgiving pillar. Or a technical problem might affect the enjoyment of the onboard experience. Jerry remembers vividly one occasion on which the air-conditioning on a ship on which he was traveling—which shall remain nameless to spare the line blushes—went out for half a day. It was an uncomfortable time and could have turned a neophyte off cruising forever. That would have been a mistake. In travel, there is liable to be an occasional snafu. Your hotel room is not available, even though you have a valid confirmation number. Your flight is canceled. The luxury car you thought you rented is not on the lot and all that's available is a minisubcompact. But you don't stop flying, you don't refuse to stay in a hotel ever again, and you don't stop renting cars. Nor should one unforeseen problem on a cruise ship cause you to swear off the product forever. Give it another go. On a different cruise line, if you prefer. If you still haven't had the enjoyable experience that millions of others have discovered, then, and only then, maybe it's time to abandon hope of becoming a cruise aficionado.

## ITINERARIES

Each cruise line review includes a chart showing itineraries for each ship the line has assigned to Alaska for 2005. Often, a ship sails on alternating itineraries—for instance, sailing southbound from Seward (or, in the case of Princess and Carnival this year, Whittier) to Vancouver one week and doing the same route in reverse the next. When this is the case, we've listed both and noted that they alternate. These cruises represent the Gulf of Alaska routing, as opposed to the Inside Passage itinerary, which is generally round-trip from Seattle or Vancouver. (Some longer round-trip cruises depart San Francisco.) All itineraries are subject to change. Consult your travel agent for exact sailing dates.

The variety of cruise itineraries and of ports of embarkation (and disembarkation, for that matter) also demonstrates the maturing of the cruise industry and the growth in demand for the product. Not so long ago, just about the only thing you could do in Alaska cruising was a Vancouver-Vancouver Inside Passage loop. Very few lines had Gulf itineraries. It was simply easier for the ship operators to stick with the tried and true. People wanted it. Ships' crews got into a rhythm—arrive Vancouver at 8 a.m., discharge passengers, take on a fresh complement, and start all over again. But demand began to outstrip the available berths. San Francisco became an attractive alternative, then Seattle. And people who had done the Inside Passage round-trip began to demand a new experience—a cruise across the Gulf. Princess and Holland America, who had invested heavily in physical plant in Alaska (hotels/lodges, motorcoaches, rail cars for land tour add-ons in the Denali Park corridor between Anchorage and Fairbanks), began to see that route as the way to go. Princess and Carnival, sister companies in the Carnival Corp. family, have further tweaked the itinerary by using Whittier, rather than Seward, as the northern terminal of the Gulf

## Weddings at Sea

Lovers have long known that there is nothing as romantic as cruising. Luxury cruise ships have been vastly popular honeymoon vehicles for decades. And recently, with the growing popularity of cruises, they have assumed new significance in the marriage business. Now ship operators are making it easier than ever to tie the knot either in a port of call during the voyage or even right on board the vessel. Most lines will help you set it all up—if you give them enough advance notice. They will provide the music, the photographer, the bouquets, the champagne, hors d'oeuvres, the cake, and other frills and fripperies. All you have to do is bring somebody to share your "I do" moment. The wedding package might cost you $1,000 or so over the price of your cabin.

In Alaska this year, Carnival, Celebrity, NCL, Royal Caribbean, and Holland America Line allow you to hold your marriage ceremony in a specially decorated lounge on board while in port, officiated by a local clergyman or justice of the peace. Princess goes those lines one better. The *Diamond, Sapphire,* and *Coral Princesses* are equipped with wedding chapels in which the captain himself can conduct the ceremony. It's all perfectly legal, and the masters of those ships formalize half a dozen or so nuptials a week in various destination areas.

If you want guests to attend your special onboard moment while in port, the ship line must be notified well in advance, and your guests will be required to produce valid ID and to go through the same kind of screening process that passengers go through. Princess makes it easy for friends and family on shore to share the event by filming the entire process and then posting it on a special webcam found on its website (www.princess.com). Click on "Ships" and then "Bridge Cams." And, no, it's not really live. The images are there for all to see long after the rites are concluded.

No matter where you wed, you have to have a valid U.S. marriage license (or a Canadian license, if you want to bid farewell to the single life in one of the British Columbia ports). The cruise line's wedding planner will help you set that up. Just remember to plan in advance—these things take time.

cruises because it's closer to Anchorage. Those lines that do not have a strong investment in Alaska land components still tend to stick with the Vancouver (or Seattle) originating round-trip.

For your convenience, we've listed the **cruisetours and add-ons** you can book with your cruise, and we've provided brochure prices for these as well—where possible! Cruise lines do not all make all of their rate decisions (or even their fleet deployment decisions) at the same time. Some get the word out very early—and pretty much stick to it. Others take their time about deciding. Hence, at press time, some of the numbers were not readily available.

## PRICES

We've listed the prices for cabins and suites. We stress that all of the prices listed reflect the line's **brochure rates,** so depending on how early you book and on any special deals the lines are offering, you are likely to get a rate substantially below what we've listed. (Discounts can run as high as 60% or thereabouts.) Rates are for a 7-night cruise, per person, and are based on double occupancy. If the ship does not sail 7-night itineraries, we've noted that and offer rates for whatever itineraries it does sail. (*Crystal Harmony,* for instance, does 12-day cruises from San Francisco.) Our rates based on the basic types of accommodations:

- Inside cabin (one without windows)
- Outside cabin (one with windows)
- Suite

Remember that cruise ships generally have several different categories of cabins within each of these three basic divisions, all priced differently, which is why on some ships you'll see a rather broad range in each category.

Please keep something else in mind. As they say in the business, "Buy as much cruise as you can afford." If you go in with the attitude that you refuse to buy anything but the least expensive inside cabin, you may be doing yourself a disservice. The idea that "Oh, I'm not going to spend any time in my cabin anyway so what does it matter if it's inside or outside, big or small?" isn't really valid. You *will* spend time in your cabin, and sometimes having no exposure to the outside world can be awfully claustrophobic. You may find that for a few hundred dollars more you can upgrade to an outside room. Or, if you're planning to invest in an outside cabin, you may find that you could reserve a room with a balcony if you dug just a little deeper into the purse. This is not to say you have to go deeply into debt to buy the best, just that you should investigate the possibility of buying something a little better.

## 2 Carnival Cruise Lines

Carnival Place, 3655 NW 87th Ave., Miami, FL 33178-2428. ✆ **800/CARNIVAL.** Fax 305/471-4740. www. carnival.com.

Almost the definition of mass market, 31-year-old Carnival is the Big Kahuna of the industry, boasting a modern fleet of big ships that are the boldest, most innovative, and most successful on the seas. Why? Like the line's now-famous ad campaign says, the experience of being on the ships is "fun"—as in fun, fun, *fun!* As Kathie Lee Gifford used to sing, "In the morning, in the evening" you'll find fun on Carnival ships, with plenty of parties and party-going fellow passengers. But don't feel that because you're on a Carnival ship you *must* boogie all the time. There are more than enough quiet spots for you to "get away from it all," especially on the line's more recent ships. Notice that Carnival doesn't characterize itself as the ultimate in luxury. It leaves the hyperbole to others. It doesn't claim to offer the last word in cuisine (although what it does serve is pretty darned good—especially in the supper club now featured on all of its new builds). It doesn't promise round-the-clock pampering of guests. Nowhere in its brochures will you find mention of priceless works of art on the walls. All the company says is "Sail with us and you'll have fun." And, thanks to its superb entertainment package, friendly staff, and creative cruise directors who are forever thinking up new ways to spice up the experience (some of them, admittedly, a little corny), that's exactly what the company delivers.

**THE EXPERIENCE**    The decor on Carnival's ships is eclectic and definitely glitzy, offering an ambience that's akin to a theme park. Translating the line's warm-weather experience to Alaska has meant combining the "24-hour orgy of good times" philosophy with opportunities to experience the natural wonders of the state, so you may find yourself bellying up to the rail with a multicolored party drink to gawk at a glacier. Drinking and R-rated comedians are part of the scene, as are "hairy-chest contests" and the like. This, of course, is either a plus or a minus, depending on your taste.

## Pros

- **Entertainment.** Carnival's entertainment is among the industry's best, with each ship boasting dozens of dancers, a 10-piece orchestra, comedians, jugglers, and numerous live bands, as well as a big casino.
- **Children's program.** Carnival attracts a slew of families, and its children's program does an expert job of keeping them occupied, with some Alaska-specific activities thrown into the mix of other amusements. The line offers a special series of shore excursions designed for teens.

## Cons

- **Service.** The international crew doesn't provide terribly refined service, but that's not the point here, is it?
- **Loud public announcements.** All the Carnival ships are well run and maintained, but there are minor annoyances like lines and frequent loud public announcements—features that are characteristic of mass-market cruise lines.

**THE FLEET**    The 2,124-passenger megaship *Carnival Spirit* is returning to Alaska in 2005. It offers almost innumerable activities, great pool and hot-tub spaces (some covered for use in chillier weather), a big oceanview gym and spa, and more dining options than your doctor would say is advisable.

**PASSENGER PROFILE**    Overall, Carnival has some of the youngest demographics in the industry: Most passengers are under 50. You'll find couples, singles, and a good share of **families.** In fact, the line carries some 350,000 kids a year. This is the same crowd that can be found in Las Vegas and Atlantic City and at Florida's megaresorts. Even though passengers on the Alaska sailings may be older than those on Caribbean sailings, they tend to be young at heart. This is not your average sedentary, bird-watching crowd. Passengers want to see whales and icebergs, but they will also dance the Macarena on cue. If you are the type who wants to sit on deck, binoculars around your neck, waiting for a humpback whale to breach or a bald eagle to circle overhead, you may be happier aboard one of the more sedate lines—Holland America, for example. *Singles take note:* Carnival officials estimate that their ships attract more of you than any other line.

## Carnival Fleet Itineraries

| Ship | Itineraries |
| --- | --- |
| Carnival Spirit | **7-night northbound Gulf of Alaska:** From Vancouver to Whittier, visiting Ketchikan, Juneau, Skagway, and Sitka, and cruising Prince William Sound (to view College Fjord). **7-night southbound Gulf of Alaska:** From Whittier to Vancouver, visiting Sitka, Juneau, Skagway, and Ketchikan, and cruising Prince William Sound (to view College Fjord). **7-night Glacier Bay:** Sails round-trip from Vancouver (offered only in May and Sept), visiting Juneau, Skagway, Ketchikan, the Inside Passage, and Glacier Bay. |

**DINING**   Food is bountiful, and the cuisine is traditional American: Red meat is popular on these ships. Recent improvements have led to some surprisingly good preparations in the dining room, including fine renditions of old favorites, such as beef Wellington and duck a l'orange. In addition, they do delicious preparations of more "nouveau" dishes such as broiled Chilean sea bass with truffle butter, and smoked turkey tenderloin with asparagus tips. Broiled lobster is featured 1 night on each cruise. Special menus are offered in Alaska featuring salmon and other local ingredients. Health-conscious, pasta, and vegetarian options are offered nightly. Meals are served at assigned tables, with two seatings per meal. The casual lunch buffets include Chinese, deli, and pizza stations; and the breakfast buffet, in the same location—La Playa Grill, on Lido Deck—offers everything from made-to-order egg dishes to cold cereals and pastries. Many passengers prefer to eat these meals in La Playa rather than in the main dining room. The *Spirit* also adds the special treat of a truly superb reservations-only supper club, where for a fee of $25 per person, you can dine on a great steak and the famous Joe's Stone Crab, dancing between courses to music provided by a singer and keyboardist.

**ACTIVITIES**   "Nonstop" is the key word here. If Atlantic City and Las Vegas appeal to you, Carnival will, too. What you'll get is fun—lots of it, professionally and insistently delivered and spangled with glitter. Cocktails inevitably begin to flow before lunch. Singles and newlyweds parties are frequent. You can learn to country line dance or ballroom dance, take cooking lessons, learn to play bridge, watch first-run movies, practice your golf swing by smashing balls into a net, and join in a knobby-knee contest—a typical East-End-of-London type of frolic, in which men roll up their pants legs and show off their knees to the howls of their womenfolk. The one who earns the loudest roars of approval from the audience usually wins a bottle of champagne or some such. It's not particularly dignified and you won't find it on, say, Crystal, but, in the right setting, it's fun enough. Plus, there are always the onboard staple activities of eating, drinking, and shopping, and the Alaska-specific naturalist lectures that are delivered daily. Once in port, Carnival lives up to its "more is more" ethos by offering more than **100 shore excursions in Alaska.** These are divided into categories of easy, moderate, and adventure. Internet cafes offer Internet access for 75¢ a minute, with a 10-minute minimum.

**CHILDREN'S PROGRAM**   The line offers Camp Carnival, an expertly run program for children and teens with a plethora of kid-pleasing activities designed to keep the younger generation occupied so that parents can enjoy some downtime. In Alaska, these activities include everything from Native American arts-and-crafts sessions to lectures conducted by wildlife experts, and there are special shore excursions for teens. On the *Spirit,* parents of little kids can even request beepers so that they can keep in touch.

**ENTERTAINMENT**   Carnival consistently offers the most lavish entertainment extravaganzas afloat, spending millions on stage sets, choreography, and acoustical equipment that leave many other floating theaters in their wake. Each Carnival megaship carries flamboyantly costumed dancers and singers (on the *Spirit,* there's a cast of about 20) and a 10-piece orchestra, plus comedians, jugglers, acrobats, rock-'n'-roll bands, country-western bands, classical string trios, pianists, and big bands.

**SERVICE**   As we said above, it ain't exactly what you'd call "refined," but it is professional. All in all, a Carnival ship is a well-oiled machine, and you'll certainly get what you need—but not much more. When you board the ship, for instance, you're welcomed by polite staff at the gangway, given a diagram of the ship's layout, and then pointed in the right direction to find your cabin on your own, carry-on luggage in tow. It is possible on the *Spirit* to have your gratuities (about $10 per passenger per day) automatically charged to your shipboard account.

There is a **laundry service** on board (for washing and pressing only) that charges by the piece, as well as a handful of **self-service laundry rooms** with irons and coin-operated washing machines and dryers. Dry cleaning is not available.

**CRUISETOUR & ADD-ON PROGRAMS**   Two-, 3-, and 4-night land packages are available in the Denali corridor in conjunction with the services of one of Carnival's affiliate companies, Holland America Line. These range in price from $590 to $1,165 per two people, in addition to the cruise price. Pre- and post-cruise nights are available in a number of hotels in Seattle and Vancouver, starting at $120 a night, double.

## Carnival Spirit

Carnival Spirit *(photo: Gero Mylius, Indav Ltd.)*

### Specifications

| Size (in tons) | 88,000 | Officers | Italian |
|---|---|---|---|
| Number of Cabins | 1,062 | Crew | 920 (Int'l) |
| Number of Outside Cabins | 849 | Passenger/Crew Ratio | 2.3 to 1 |
| Cabins with Verandas | 682 | Year Built | 2001 |
| Number of Passengers | 2,124 | Last Major Refurbishment | n/a |

**THE SHIP IN GENERAL**   The *Spirit* is big and impressive, although some may find the interior a bit over the top. Rooms reflect a purposeful mismatch of styles, including Art Nouveau, Art Deco, Empire, Gothic, and Egyptian, with the decor featuring expensive materials, such as burled wood, marble, leather, copper, and even gold gild. In other words, legendary Carnival designer Joe Farcus showed little restraint. Love it or not, you'll certainly be wowed.

**CABINS**    Some 80% of the cabins on this ship boast ocean views, and of those, 80% boast private balconies, a big plus in a market like Alaska where views are the main draw. Cabins are larger than those you'll find on other lines in the same price category, and they are mostly furnished with twin beds that can be converted to king-size. (A few have upper and lower berths that cannot be converted.) All cabins come with a TV, wall safe, and telephone; oceanview cabins also come with bathrobes and coral-colored leather couches with nifty storage drawers underneath. There are connecting cabins available for families or groups traveling together. Suites are offered at several different levels, and each boasts separate sleeping, sitting, and dressing areas, plus double sinks, a bathtub, and a large balcony. Sixteen cabins are wheelchair accessible.

## Cabins & Rates

| Cabins | Brochure Rates | Bathtub | Fridge | Hair Dryer | Sitting Area | TV |
|---|---|---|---|---|---|---|
| *Inside Passage* | | | | | | |
| Inside | $1,579–$1,679 | no | yes | yes | no | yes |
| Outside | $1,929–$2,129 | no | yes | yes | yes | yes |
| Suites | $2,929 | yes | yes | yes | yes | yes |
| *Gulf of Alaska* | | | | | | |
| Inside | $1,919–$2,019 | no | yes | yes | no | yes |
| Outside | $2,269–$2,469 | no | yes | yes | yes | yes |
| Suites | $3,269 | yes | yes | yes | yes | yes |

**PUBLIC AREAS**    The ship's soaring atrium spans 11 decks and is topped with a red stained-glass dome that is part of the Nouveau Supper Club, a reservations-only steakhouse-type restaurant with fine dining and live entertainment (as we mentioned, a fee of $25 per person is charged). There are dozens of bars and lounges, including a piano bar, a sports bar, and a jazz club. A lobby bar offers live music and a chance to take in the vast dimensions of the ship. A particularly fun room is the two-level Jackson Pollock–inspired disco, with paint-splattered walls. That disco, we've found, is one of the busiest rooms on the *Spirit*. Many cruise lines tout their discos as "lively," "jumping," "rockin'," and so on. Often they are anything but. Especially in Alaska, where the passenger age demographic generally tends to edge up, the disco is a much-underused facility. Not so on the *Spirit*. When Carnival says it rocks 'til dawn, it does. That, of course is a reflection of the younger group that maybe cut its cruising teeth on Carnival in the Caribbean and now includes Alaska on its calendar, retaining its loyalty to the line. There is a two-level main dining room done up in Napoleonic splendor, and a bevy of other food service offerings (including a 24-hr. pizzeria) to keep your gourmet side happy and full.

The ship represents a new class for Carnival and offers the best features of the line's earlier ships, including an expansive outdoor area with three swimming pools (there is a retractable dome over the main pool so that you can take a dip no matter what the weather), four whirlpools, and a water slide; a high-tech children's play center with computers and wall of video monitors; a multilevel oceanview fitness facility; numerous clubs and lounges; and a variety of eating and entertainment options. Among the interesting features is the line's first wedding chapel, as well as a mostly outdoor promenade (if you are doing a full tour around the ship, you have to take a few steps inside). The ship also has ultramodern engines and waste treatment and disposal systems to make it more environmentally friendly. And the *Spirit* offers more space per passenger than most ships in the Alaska market.

The hundreds of onboard activities for which Carnival is famous, including Vegas-style shows and casino action (the ship's Louis XIV casino is one of the largest at sea), keep passengers on the *Spirit* on the fast track to that famous and oft-mentioned fun. It's up to you to find time to stop and catch the scenery, which you can do both from the generous open-deck spaces and from some (but not a lot) of indoor spaces. For kids, there's a children's playroom, children's pool, and video arcade. The *Spirit's* library doubles as an Internet cafe, and the clicking of the computers may be annoying to those who want to read a book there. Shoppers will find plenty of enticements at the ship's shopping arcade, including Fendi and Tommy Hilfiger products.

**POOL, SPA & FITNESS FACILITIES**    The ship boasts three pools, including one with a retractable dome, as well as a children's splash pool. There is a freestanding water slide on the top deck. The gym offers an interesting tiered design and more than 50 exercise machines, as well as a spacious aerobics studio. There are windows, so you don't miss the scenery. The spa has a dozen treatment rooms and an indoor sunning area with a whirlpool. The ship also offers three additional whirlpools and a jogging/walking track (15 laps = 1 mile).

## 3 Celebrity Cruises

1050 Caribbean Way, Miami, FL 33132. © **800/437-3111** or 305/262-8322. Fax 800/437-5111. www.celebritycruises.com.

With a premium fleet that's among the youngest and best designed in the cruise industry, Celebrity Cruises offers a great product: a classy, tasteful, and luxurious cruise experience at a moderate price.

**THE EXPERIENCE**    Each of the Celebrity ships is spacious, glamorous, and comfortable, mixing sleekly modern and vaguely Art Deco styles and throwing in an astoundingly cutting-edge art collection. The line's genteel service is exceptional: Staff members are exceedingly polite and professional, and contribute greatly to the elegant atmosphere. Dining-wise, Celebrity shines, offering innovative cuisine that's a cut above the fare offered by all the other mainstream lines.

Celebrity gets the "best of" nod in a lot of categories: The AquaSpas on the line's megaships are the best at sea, the art collections fleetwide are the most compelling, the cigar bars are the plushest, and the onboard activities are among the most varied. Like all the big-ship lines, Celebrity offers lots for its passengers to do, but its focus on mellower pursuits and innovative programming sets it apart.

It's interesting to note that this year Celebrity (and its affiliate company, Royal Caribbean International) are using a brand-new port—Icy Strait Point. The port—little more than a cannery dock, to be honest—lies between Juneau and Glacier Bay and offers a prime vantage point for whale- and wildlife-watching and easier access to the Alaskan wilderness. A small Indian village about a mile away will be included on shore excursions. Why add the stop at all? Simply because a growing number of Alaska passengers have begun to outgrow the historic ports of call. A "been-there-done-that" attitude among past guests has made it essential that cruise lines find new ways to stimulate public interest in the destination. Hence, Icy Strait Point. It will never make passengers forget the bustling streets and stores of, say, Juneau or Ketchikan, but the lines are hoping that the combination of hitherto pretty much unseen (at least by cruise passengers) wilderness and exposure to a real Indian village experience will make it a memorable stop.

## Pros

- **Spectacular spas and gyms.** Beautiful to look at and well stocked, the spas and gyms on the *Infinity, Mercury,* and *Summit* (and Celebrity's other non-Alaska megaships) are among the best at sea today.
- **Fabulous food.** Celebrity's cuisine is tops among mainstream cruise lines.
- **Innovative everything.** Celebrity's entertainment, art, cigar bars, service, spas, and cuisine are some of the most innovative in the industry. Its ships were among the first in the industry to display major art collections on board, it had one of the earliest cigar bars, and its menus have long recognized the need for vegetarian, low-sodium, heart-conscious, and other dishes.

## Cons

- **Occasional crowding.** Pack a couple thousand people onto a ship (pretty much any ship), and you'll get crowds sometimes, such as at buffets and when debarking.

**THE FLEET**   Celebrity's current Alaska fleet comprises two of the line's newest ships, the *Infinity* (91,000 tons, 1,950 passengers) and the similarly dimensioned *Summit,* and the stunning and only slightly older *Mercury.* All three ships are designed with sharp attention to detail and a high degree of decorative panache, and offer just the right combination of elegance, artfulness, excitement, and fun.

**PASSENGER PROFILE**   The typical Celebrity guest is one who prefers to pursue his or her R & R at a relatively relaxed pace, with a minimum of aggressively promoted group activities. The overall atmosphere leans more toward sophistication and less to the kind of orgiastic Technicolor whoopee that you'll find aboard, say, a Carnival ship. Celebrity passengers are the type who prefer wine with dinner and maybe a tad more decorum than on some other ships, but by and large they can kick up their heels with the beer-and-skittles crowd just fine if the occasion warrants. Most give the impression of being prosperous but not obscenely rich, congenial but not obsessively proper, animated and fun but not the types to wear a lampshade for a hat. You'll find everyone from kids to retirees.

**DINING**   Celebrity's cuisine is extra special. Due to the influence of executive chef Michel Roux, one of Britain's top French chefs, the fare leans toward the French. This means that dishes are generally not low fat, although healthy alternatives are always available. Food is plentiful and served with style.

Alaska cruises offer an array of **Pacific Northwest regional specialties,** and vegetarian dishes are featured at both lunch and dinner. If three meals a day in both informal and formal settings are not enough for you, Celebrity offers one of the most extensive 24-hour room-service menus in the industry, plus late-night buffets and gourmet snacks offered by waiters who rove all the public areas with trays of goodies. Meals in the alternative dining rooms on the *Infinity* and *Summit,* offered on a reservations-only basis, show Roux at his finest and are worth the $25 charge of admission.

You can dine formally in the dining room or informally at buffets for breakfast and lunch; dinner is served at two seatings in the dining room.

## Celebrity Fleet Itineraries

| Ship | Itineraries |
| --- | --- |
| Infinity | **7-night Inside Passage:** Round-trip cruises from Vancouver visit Icy Strait Point, Ketchikan, Juneau, Sitka, and Hubbard Glacier. |
| Mercury | **7-night Inside Passage:** Round-trip cruises from Seattle visit Icy Strait Point, Ketchikan, Hubbard Glacier, Skagway, Juneau, and Prince Rupert, B.C. |
| Summit | **7-night north and southbound Gulf of Alaska:** Sails from Vancouver to Anchorage/Seward and reverse, visiting Ketchikan, Juneau, Skagway, Hubbard Glacier, Valdez, and Icy Point. |

**ACTIVITIES**    The line offers a variety of different activities, although many passengers prefer to go it on their own, enjoying the passing landscape and the company of friends. A typical day might offer bridge, darts, a culinary demonstration, a trapshooting competition, a fitness fashion show, an art auction, and a volleyball tournament. **Lectures** on the various ports of call, the Alaska environment, glaciers, and Alaska culture are given by resident experts, who also provide commentary from the bridge as the ships arrive in port and, at other times, are available for one-on-one discussions with passengers. Cybercafes offer e-mail access for 95¢ a minute.

**CHILDREN'S PROGRAM**    For children, Celebrity ships employ a group of counselors who direct and supervise a camp-style children's program with activities geared toward different age groups. There's an impressive kids' play area and a separate lounge area for teens. Private and group babysitting are both available.

**ENTERTAINMENT**    Although entertainment is not generally cited as a reason to sail with Celebrity, the line's **stage shows** are none too shabby. You won't find any big-name entertainers, but you also won't find any obvious has-beens either—there's just a whole lot of singin' and dancin'. If you tire of the glitter, you can always find a cozy lounge or piano bar to curl up in, and if you tire of that, the disco and casino stay open late.

**SERVICE**    In the cabins, service is efficient and so discreet and unobtrusive you might never see your steward except at the beginning and end of your cruise. In the dining rooms, service is polite, professional, and cheerful. Five-star service can be had at the onboard beauty parlor or barbershop, and massages can be scheduled at any hour of the day. **Laundry, dry-cleaning,** and **valet services** are fast and precise.

**CRUISETOUR & ADD-ON PROGRAMS**    Celebrity offers a couple of dozen cruisetours in conjunction with its three Alaska ships this year, ranging in length from 9 to 13 nights and priced from $1,700 per person double to $3,190 per person double, depending on the season and the staterooms chosen. Sixteen of the tours include a ride in Royal Celebrity Tours' luxurious domed rail cars on the Denali Corridor and 2- or 3-night stays in the park area. These land portions complement the Gulf of Alaska cruises of the *Summit.* Other packages feature the Kenai Peninsula and the 650,000-acre Kenai Fjords National Park. Pre- and post-cruise hotel packages are also offered: from $249 per person per night, double occupancy, in Anchorage; from $149 per person per night, double occupancy, in Vancouver.

# Infinity • Summit

Infinity *(photo: Celebrity Cruises)*

## Specifications

| | | | |
|---|---|---|---|
| Size (in tons) | 91,000 | Officers | Greek |
| Number of Cabins | 975 | Crew | 997 (Int'l) |
| Number of Outside Cabins | 785 | Passenger/Crew Ratio | 1.96 to 1 |
| Cabins with Verandas | 582 | Year Built | 2001 |
| Number of Passengers | 1,950 | Last Major Refurbishment | n/a |

**THE SHIPS IN GENERAL**   When Celebrity's *Infinity* debuted in 2001, it was hailed as one of the most spectacular ships afloat; guests were equally struck by the debut of its sister ship *Summit* in 2002. We're talking the finest materials, first-class artwork, and expert design, including lots of glass through which to view the spectacular Alaska vistas.

**CABINS**   There's not a bad cabin on these ships. Even the smallest inside cabins are 170 square feet and boast a minibar, a sitting area with a sofa, and an entertainment unit with a TV. Premium oceanview cabins are a very generous 191 square feet, and large oceanview cabins with verandas are indeed large—271 square feet, with floor-to-ceiling sliding-glass doors leading outside. Suites come in several sizes and offer such accoutrements as whirlpool tubs, VCRs, and walk-in closets. The fanciest suites also have whirlpools on the veranda. The two apartment-size Penthouse Suites (1,432 sq. ft. each), designed to evoke Park Avenue apartments, offer all of the above plus separate living and dining rooms, a foyer, a grand piano, a butler's pantry, a bedroom, exercise equipment, outbound fax, and—sure to be a favorite accessory—motorized drapes. Twenty-six cabins are wheelchair accessible.

## Cabins & Rates

| Cabins | Brochure Rates | Bathtub | Fridge | Hair Dryer | Sitting Area | TV |
|---|---|---|---|---|---|---|
| *Summit* | | | | | | |
| Inside | $960–$1,060 | no | yes | yes | yes | yes |
| Outside | $1,235–$1,770 | no | yes | yes | yes | yes |
| Suites | $2,530–$6,350 | yes | yes | yes | yes | yes |
| *Infinity* | | | | | | |
| Inside | $1,000–$1,105 | no | yes | yes | no | yes |
| Outside | $1,200–$2,065 | no | yes | yes | yes | yes |
| Suites | $2,550–$6,550 | yes | yes | yes | yes | yes |

## Golf Simulators

Certain ships have golf simulator rooms on board. In these rooms, golf enthusiasts "drive" a ball (from an Astroturf-type mat) at a screen on which is displayed the holes of famous courses—St. Andrews, for instance, or Los Angeles' Riviera Country Club. The screen (theoretically) calculates how far your ball would have gone had you played that shot in real life. It then shows you where your ball landed and the picture changes to the shot that lies ahead of you. You go on like that until you're in the hole. It's far from being golf and the screen is far from accurate, but it helps golfers get over their withdrawal pains while they're on the ship.

**PUBLIC AREAS**   Highlights on the *Infinity* and *Summit* include the flower-filled botanical conservatories located on top of each ship. Pull up a rattan chair, sit under a ceiling fan, and enjoy a drink. You won't miss the Alaska views from this oasis thanks to two-story-high windows. The conservatories offer classes in flower arranging.

Both ships also boast dramatic two-tier dining rooms that feature live music by a pianist or a quartet. And they also offer gourmet dining experiences in intimate alternative restaurants: the SS United States on the *Infinity* and Normandie Room on the *Summit* (a fee of $25 is charged to dine in these classy escapes, and reservations are required). Breakfast and lunch are offered in both formal and informal venues. Dinner is served in the main dining room, a two-story affair, in two seatings. After dinner, Michael's Club (on both ships), decorated like the parlor of a London men's club and devoted to the pleasures of fine cigars and cognac, comes into its own. Each ship also offers a coffee bar, and if you're looking to spend the evening socializing with friends, there are various other bars tucked into nooks and crannies throughout the ship.

Want more? How about a music library, shopping center, pizzeria, casino, champagne bar, martini bar, cinema, theater, sports bar (with live ESPN), beauty salon, medical center, library, cybercafe, children's center, teen room, and arcade?

**POOL, SPA & FITNESS FACILITIES**   Spa aficionados, listen up: The *Infinity* and *Summit* will not disappoint. The 25,000-square-foot AquaSpa complexes on both ships feature a range of esoteric hydrotherapy treatments; site-specific attractions such as the Persian Garden, a suite of beautiful New Age steam rooms and saunas; and a huge free-of-charge thalassotherapy whirlpool. In addition, there is the usual array of massage and beauty procedures, plus some unusual offerings, such as an Egyptian ginger-and-milk treatment. Next door to the spa, there's a very large, well-equipped cardio room and a large aerobics floor. On the top decks are facilities for basketball, volleyball, quoits (a game akin to horseshoes), and paddle tennis; a jogging track; a golf simulator; two pools; four whirlpools; and a multitiered sunning area. The swimming pool boasts a waterfall.

# Mercury

Mercury *(photo: Matt Hannafin)*

## Specifications

| | | | |
|---|---|---|---|
| Size (in tons) | 77,713 | Officers | Greek |
| Number of Cabins | 948 | Crew | 900 (Int'l) |
| Number of Outside Cabins | 639 | Passenger/Crew Ratio | 2 to 1 |
| Cabins with Verandas | 220 | Year Built | 1997 |
| Number of Passengers | 1,896 | Last Major Refurbishment | n/a |

**THE SHIP IN GENERAL**   It's difficult to say what's most striking about the *Mercury.* The elegant spa and its 15,000-gallon thalassotherapy pool? The twin three- and four-story atria with serpentine staircases that seem to float without supports, and domed ceilings of painted glass? The distinguished Michael's Club cigar lounge with its leather wingbacks, velvet couches, and hand-rolled stogies? The two-story, old-world dining room set back in the stern, with grand floor-to-ceiling windows, allowing diners to spot the glow of the wake under moonlight? An absolutely intriguing modern-art collection unmatched in the industry (except aboard Celebrity's other megaships)? Take your pick: Any one points to a winner.

**CABINS**   Overall, there are no really bad cabins on this ship. Inside cabins are about par for the industry standard, but outside cabins are larger than usual, and suites, which come in five different categories, are particularly spacious. Some, such as the Penthouse Suites, offer more living space than you find in many private homes, and the Sky Suites offer verandas that, at 179 square feet, are among the biggest aboard any ship.

Cabins are accented with wood trim and outfitted with built-in vanities. Closets and drawer space are roomy, and all standard cabins have twin beds that, when pushed together, convert into one full-size bed. Bathrooms are sizable and stylish. Celebrity is fond of high-tech gizmos, and you can actually order food, gamble, or check your bill from the comfort of your cabin via your interactive TV.

Butler service is offered to suite passengers. Eight cabins are wheelchair accessible.

## Cabins & Rates

| Cabins | Brochure Rates | Bathtub | Fridge | Hair Dryer | Sitting Area | TV |
|---|---|---|---|---|---|---|
| Inside | $850–$890 | no | yes | yes | no | yes |
| Outside | $1,100–$1,500 | no | yes | yes | yes | yes |
| Suites | $1,650–$5,350 | yes | yes | yes | yes | yes |

**PUBLIC AREAS**   The interior of this ship is the product of a collaboration between a dozen internationally acclaimed design firms, working together to create a stylistically diverse yet harmonious whole that provides just the right amount of drama without resorting to glitz. The result is impressive. Our favorite is the champagne bar with champagne bubbles etched into the wall.

Throughout the ship, works from a multimillion-dollar, cutting-edge art collection sometimes greet you at unexpected moments. Read the tags and you'll be impressed to find names such as Sol LeWitt, who designed a mural specifically for the vessel.

Meals are a standout feature on all Celebrity ships. Breakfast on the *Mercury* is offered either in the dining room or at a vast buffet on the Lido Deck that manages to accommodate everyone's preferred waking hour. As on all Celebrity ships, lunch is also offered in both formal and informal venues. Dinner is served in the main dining room, a two-story affair, in two seatings. For posh relaxation after dinner, there's Michael's Club, a cigar and cognac bar similar to those on the other two Alaska ships in the fleet. Definitely a male hangout! There is a coffee bar for those craving caffeine, and various other bars pepper the ship and are great venues to spend time with friends.

There's a two-deck theater with an unobstructed view from every seat if you want to take in a stage show, and there's a cinema if you're in the mood for film. If you're looking for more active pleasures, there's always the disco and casino. For kids, there's a children's playroom, a children's pool, a teen center, and a video arcade.

**POOL, SPA & FITNESS FACILITIES**    The *Mercury*'s spa is not your average spa: It's an incredible AquaSpa that provides a world of sensual pleasure. It features a Moorish theme, with ornate tile work and latticed wood. There is a large hydrotherapy pool, plus steam rooms and saunas. The spa also features sometimes-pricey Steiner of London health and beauty services, including hairdressing, pedicures, manicures, massages, and various herbal treatments. We highly recommend the Rasul mud treatment for two. It's both relaxing and giggle-inducing. The attached fitness area offers exceptionally large cardiovascular floors and a full complement of exercise machines. An 18-member fitness staff is on hand in the spa and gym area to assist you. Prearranged spa packages that you book before your cruise are available and are a wise idea, as some services (including Rasul) sell out fast.

The Resort Deck features a pair of good-size swimming areas rimmed with teak benches for sunning and relaxation. Even when the ship is full, these areas don't seem particularly crowded. A retractable dome covers one of the swimming pools during inclement weather. A basketball court, jogging/walking track, fitness center, golf simulator, and volleyball court fill out the offerings.

## 4 Crystal Cruises

2049 Century Park E., Suite 1400, Los Angeles, CA 90067. ℭ 800/446-6620 or 310/785-9300. Fax 310/785-3891. www.crystalcruises.com.

Crystal's brand of luxury cruising appeals to a discerning clientele. Everything is first class, with fine attention paid to detail and to making guests feel comfortable.

**THE EXPERIENCE**    The luxurious *Crystal Harmony* (1990) is the line's representative in Alaska for the 6th consecutive year. The *Harmony* and its sister ships, *Crystal Symphony* and *Crystal Serenity,* operate on a formula of offering all the amenities of much bigger ships in a more luxurious and intimate atmosphere, with only 940 passengers.

Japanese-owned and Los Angeles–based, Crystal had the Great Land's luxury market to itself for a while. Radisson Seven Seas is now also on the scene, with a product that offers a slightly more casual definition of luxury. (In 2004, there was yet a third ship in the luxury field, Silversea's *Silver Shadow*. In keeping with Silversea's policy of offering past guests as much variety as possible and trying to avoid repetition, that vessel is not returning to the 49th state this year.) Like Radisson Seven Seas, Crystal offers the chance to dress up and act like a millionaire, even if you're not one.

## Pros

- **The best of everything.** Superb cuisine, elegant service, handsome public areas, sparkling entertainment, excellent guest quarters—this ship has it all. It's a six-star ship in a five-star field.
- **Great itinerary.** Another of the *Harmony*'s selling points is its itinerary: Sailing out of San Francisco, it calls at both Victoria and Vancouver, B.C., as well as the traditional best of Alaska. For those who love sea days, the San Francisco–originating itinerary is ideal; there's at least 1 port-free day at the beginning of the cruise and one at the end.

## Cons

- **Fairly rigid dining schedule.** For many upscale travelers, the *Harmony*'s major failing is that, like all biggish ships, it has two seatings at dinner, locking passengers into 6:30 or 8:30pm appointments in the main dining room. (There are, however, two very fine alternatives available for a suggested gratuity of $6 per person.)
- **Lack of closet space.** One more quibble is that some of the cabins on the *Harmony*'s lower decks are not as generously equipped with closet space as they could be.

**THE FLEET**     Plush, streamlined, extravagantly comfortable, and not as overwhelmingly large as the megaships used by less glamorous lines, the 940-passenger *Crystal Harmony* offers a broad choice of onboard diversions and distractions, more than you'd expect on a luxury vessel. In an industry first, the line brought feng shui to the high seas, renovating space on some of its vessels in accordance with this ancient and now very hip practice of balance and harmony.

**PASSENGER PROFILE**     Generally, the passengers aboard Crystal's ships are people of some discernment—say, successful businesspeople who can afford to pay for the best. Item: On one Panama Canal cruise aboard the *Harmony* a few years ago, we heard of a 70-something couple, occupying one of the better suites, who visited the future-bookings desk in the lobby and signed up for about $200,000 worth of the next round-the-world cruise, scheduled for a few months later. If memory serves, they were unable to take the entire 99-day world cruise because of a family commitment, so they "settled"—and paid on the spot—for two-thirds of it! These people may not have been typical, but they weren't all that out of the ordinary, either.

At one time, that couple might have been closer to the average age of passengers on an Alaska Crystal cruise, but they no longer are. Probably thanks to Crystal's excellent shore-excursion program, its Caesars Palace–operated casino, and its entertainment package, the *Harmony* is attracting a younger breed of cruiser, many under 50. The average age is, in fact, dropping fast. Those new 40- and 50-something millionaire types have to vacation somewhere. Perhaps the post-WorldCom, post-Enron stock market plunge, having left fewer of those types, explains why Crystal does a little more discounting now than it used to! Whatever their age, Crystal guests tend to be people who like to dress up rather than down. Casual nights don't mean the same thing to Crystal guests as they do to passengers on some other lines.

## Crystal Fleet Itineraries

| Ship | Itineraries |
|------|-------------|
| Crystal Harmony | **12-night Inside Passage:** Round-trip from San Francisco, visiting Victoria, B.C., Sitka, Skagway, Juneau, Ketchikan, Glacier Bay, and Hubbard Glacier. |

**DINING**   Cuisine aboard the *Harmony* is superbly prepared and professionally served. Dinner, which is served in the main dining room, offers a nightly choice of at least four entrees, health-conscious vegetarian dishes, and a pasta dish. The Lido Cafe, an indoor/outdoor area, puts on a lavish breakfast and lunch buffet daily, and the poolside Trident Grill serves up hot dogs, hamburgers, pizza, and sandwiches from lunchtime through the afternoon. There is also the new casual option, on select nights, of dining at an open-air grill (weather permitting, of course). An alternative Italian restaurant (Prego) and Asian restaurant (Kyoto) are open on a reservations-only basis. The Italian restaurant includes the option of a five-course "Valentino" dinner, thanks to a special agreement between the cruise line and the famed Los Angeles restaurant of that name.

There's also an ice-cream and frozen-yogurt bar and 24-hour room service. The wine cellar features some 25,000 bottles.

**ACTIVITIES**   *Crystal Harmony* carries a battery of **Alaska naturalists,** environmentalists, and National Park Service rangers to educate and entertain passengers in the wilderness areas of the 49th state. Once again in 2005, it will repeat its **food-and-wine series,** carrying one of the great chefs of San Francisco on selected sailings—a different chef on each sailing (the participants were not finalized as this book went to press). Each chef will offer food preparation demonstrations, lecture on the art of cookery, and, on 1 evening of each cruise, prepare a gala dinner for passengers. If that's the kind of experience you're after, ask for the dates of the food-and-wine cruises when you make your reservation.

As far as non-food-related activities, a PGA-approved golf pro accompanies practically every *Harmony* cruise, conducting clinics along the way. The *Harmony* also has a flourishing computer room on board, with training for the uninitiated, and Internet access for a fee not yet established by the cruise line. There are few things as gratifying as seeing the smile on the face of a hitherto computer-illiterate grandma after she's sent her first e-mail to her grandkids in Cincinnati.

**CHILDREN'S PROGRAM**   Crystal focuses its attention on adults, so it's generally not a line for kids. That said, the *Harmony*'s small but bright children's playroom does see some action in Alaska, when as many as 20 to 40 kids may be on board any given cruise. Counselors are on hand to supervise activities for several hours in the morning and in the afternoon, and babysitting can be arranged privately through the concierge.

**ENTERTAINMENT**   Although it's probably not going to be the high point of your cruise, Crystal's onboard entertainment is good and plentiful. Shows in the lounge feature everything from classical concertos by accomplished pianists to comedy to a troupe of lip-synching dancers and a pair of lead singers doing a Vegas-style performance. After dinner each night, a second large, attractive lounge is the venue for ballroom-style dancing to a live band. Gentlemen hosts are available to dance with single ladies. There's also a small, separate (and usually empty) disco featuring karaoke a couple of nights per cruise. A pianist plays popular show tunes and pop hits before and after dinner in the dark, paneled, romantic Avenue Saloon. A movie theater shows first-run movies several times a day, and cabin TVs feature a wonderfully varied and full movie menu as well.

Gamblers will feel at home in the roomy casino, which is supervised directly by Caesar's Palace Casinos at Sea, offering the bonus (unusual on ships) of free drinks.

**SERVICE**   Service on the ship is nothing short of superb. Crystal has a corporate philosophy that states that its staff will exhibit "The Crystal Attitude." Catchy promotional slogan, huh? The thing is, it actually works. You can usually tell when service people are faking it: the plastic smiles, the look that's meant to say "I care" while the actions clearly demonstrate "I don't give a hoot." That doesn't happen on Crystal. From the officers to the dining-room staff, cabin stewards, reception-desk employees, and guys who swab the deck and paint the rails, these people are genuinely glad to welcome passengers and to accommodate them in every way possible. It's not obsequiousness. It's not overpowering. It's just, well, the right attitude!

In addition to **laundry** and **dry-cleaning services, self-service laundry rooms** are available.

**CRUISETOUR & ADD-ON PROGRAMS**   Crystal is offering no cruise-tours or add-on programs in Alaska this year.

## Crystal Harmony

Crystal Harmony
*(photo: Crystal Cruises)*

### Specifications

| Size (in tons) | 51,044 | Officers | Int'l |
| --- | --- | --- | --- |
| Number of Cabins | 470 | Crew | 545 (Int'l) |
| Number of Outside Cabins | 461 | Passenger/Crew Ratio | 1.7 to 1 |
| Cabins with Verandas | 260 | Year Built | 1990 |
| Number of Passengers | 940 | Last Major Refurbishment | 2000 |

**THE SHIP IN GENERAL**   A handsome ship by any standard, *Crystal Harmony* was designed by an international team from Scotland, England, Denmark, and Italy, led by one of the bright lights of the ship-architecture world, Sweden's Robert Tillberg. A multimillion-dollar refurbishment in 2000 made a good thing even better. The ship's dining room was gutted and rebuilt virtually from scratch; it is now a roomier space with softer decor and improved acoustics. The atrium reception area was also overhauled to considerable effect, and the top suites were totally done over.

The tones throughout the ship are pastel, and the material used on banister rails, bar and tabletops, walls, and so on is classy—all teak, marble, stainless steel, and the like. There's not a bit of cheap plastic or vinyl to be found anywhere. Stairwells and public rooms are dotted with quality artwork, and the entertainment activities tend to be more decorous than on most other ships. Don't look for amateur night in the show lounge, for instance, or any raucous audience participation games.

The ship has one of the highest passenger-to-space ratios (a measurement of the amount of cubic space throughout the ship—both public and private—divided by the number of passengers) of any cruise ship. In industry parlance, that ratio is 54.3, a number that may not mean much to the layperson—until he or she cruises on the ship. Then the spaciousness becomes obvious.

**CABINS**    The cabins are large, well appointed, and tastefully decorated in warm agreeable colors, with quality fittings. Almost half have private verandas. The one small criticism is that space to hang clothes is a little tight in some of the lower cabin categories.

The very smallest of the *Harmony's* cabins is almost 200 square feet, while the upper-end guest quarters are huge, with the Crystal Penthouse measuring 982 square feet. There are four of these Crystal Penthouses on the *Harmony,* each with a large sitting room, a wet bar, a big Jacuzzi with a view of the ocean (ah, bliss!), a dining area, a massive bedroom, two bathrooms, and walk-in closets.

The *Harmony's* 26 Penthouse Suites are a little less than 500 square feet each, and the 32 "regular" penthouses are 370 square feet. All of these, like the Crystal Penthouses, come with butler service and verandas. Be careful with the terminology when booking a cabin on the *Harmony:* Crystal Penthouse, Penthouse Suite, and penthouse sound awfully similar, but they're different categories. Four cabins are wheelchair accessible, two on the Penthouse Deck and two on the Promenade Deck. There are, incidentally, 418 cabins that don't carry "penthouse" designations and have the amenities listed in the "Cabins & Rates" chart below.

## Cabins & Rates

| Cabins | Brochure Rates* | Bathtub | Fridge | Hair Dryer | Sitting Area | TV |
|---|---|---|---|---|---|---|
| Inside | $3,120 | yes | yes | yes | yes | yes |
| Outside | $3,390–$6,385 | yes | yes | yes | yes | yes |
| Suites | $9,510–$19,365 | yes | yes | yes | yes | yes |

*__Note:__ *Crystal designates some cruises as "Value Collection" sailings and offers them at lower rates, sometimes at savings as much as two for the price of one. Check with your travel agent.*

**PUBLIC AREAS**    Let's hear it for *Crystal Harmony's* public areas. Like the rest of the ship, they're pure class. It's our opinion that Palm Court is the prettiest public space afloat. Bright and airy, with enticing and comfortable wicker furniture and natural greenery all around, it's the kind of room that reeks of that good old-fashioned "understated elegance." There's also the large, well-designed casino, and the intimate amidships bistro and piano bar. The two-story lobby, the Crystal Atrium, with its tinkling waterfall and classy hand-cut glass sculptures, is a refreshing change from the garishness of some of the lobbies on the new ships. The elegance carries over to the rest of the ship. Sip a glass of wine in the Crystal Cove, which is in the lobby alongside the atrium, or in the snug Avenue Saloon, located one deck up (Jerry's favorite ship bar, by the way), and you'll see what we mean.

The *Harmony's* two **alternative restaurants,** Prego (Italian, mostly northern) and Kyoto (Asian/Japanese), introduce variety to the dining experience. Meals at the alternative restaurants are included in the fare (except for the "suggested gratuity" of $6 a head), and dining is by reservation only.

The dramatic Vista Lounge, with wall-to-ceiling windows, is perfect for glacier and wildlife viewing. And there's a playroom to occupy the kids.

**POOL, SPA & FITNESS FACILITIES**   The *Harmony* offers a lot of outdoor activities and spacious areas in which to perform them. There are two outdoor swimming pools separated by a bar, ice-cream stand, and sandwich grill, as well as two hot tubs. One of the pools is refreshingly oversized, stretching almost 40 feet across one of the Sun Decks; the other can be covered with a retractable glass roof and has a swim-up bar. The gym and separate aerobics area are positioned for a view over the sea, and the adjacent spa and beauty salon are sizable. Crystal is dedicated to the proposition that no two people need the same kind of health and fitness training, and therefore offers an excellent personalized program. The *Harmony*'s instructors are trained to recognize which passenger might need to work, say, on the weight machines. Others may benefit most from an aerobics workout, or from a spell on the cardio machines or exercise bikes. Once they've identified the need, the instructors create the program. Pilates, yoga, stress-reduction exercises, and more are popular features of the ship's Crystal Spa and Fitness Center. There's also a pair of golf-driving nets, a putting green, a large paddle-tennis court, and Ping-Pong tables. For runners and walkers, just under four laps equals 1 mile on the broad, uninterrupted, teak Promenade Deck.

## 5 Holland America Line

300 Elliott Ave. W., Seattle, WA 98119. ℰ 800/426-0327 or 206/281-3535. Fax 206/286-7110. www.holland america.com.

More than any other line in Alaska, Holland America has managed to hang on to some of its seafaring history and tradition, offering a moderately priced, classic, casual yet refined ocean liner–like cruise experience.

**THE EXPERIENCE**   In Alaska terms, everybody else is an upstart when it comes to the cruise and cruisetour business. The line calls itself Alaska's most experienced travel operator, and the key to its status as such was HAL's 1971 acquisition of the tour company Westours, founded in 1947 by Charles B. "Chuck" West, often called "Mr. Alaska" and widely recognized as the absolute pioneer of tourism to and within the state. (West later founded the small-ship line known as Cruise West.)

Over the years, Holland America Line has picked up a lot of "stuff"—Holland America Tours (formed by the merger of Westours and Gray Line of Alaska), Gray Line of Seattle, Westmark Hotels, the *Yukon Queen II* river-/day boat that operates between Eagle and Dawson City on the Yukon River, the MV *Ptarmigan* day boat that visits Portage Glacier outside Anchorage, rail cars (eight of them less than 2 years old), motorcoaches, and a lot more. HAL's control of so many of the components of tour packages once gave the cruise company a position of preeminence in the Alaska market, though that's been challenged in the past decade by Princess, which now has a heavy presence in the accommodations and ground-transportation business as well. There are many similarities between the two lines besides their land-tour holdings. Both lines have large fleets of primarily late-model ships, both strive for (and achieve) consistency in the cruise product, and both are pursuing and acquiring younger passengers and families. It is interesting to note that HAL's philosophy is to stick with ships in the 1,200- to 1,800-passenger range, eschewing the 2,200- and 2,600-passenger megaships being built by some other lines, including Princess. The one notable exception to the middle-sized ship that HAL prefers is the *Prinsendam,* its smallest and most intimate vessel, carrying just 794 passengers and weighing 38,000 tons. The *Prinsendam* will not be in Alaska this year.

Cruising with HAL is less hectic than cruising on most other ships. The line strives for a quieter, sometimes almost sedate, presentation, although it has brightened up its entertainment package and its menus in recent years. Overall, the ships tend to be more evocative of the days of grand liners, with lots of dark wood and displays of nautical artifacts.

Late in 2003, the company embarked on a $225-million Signature of Excellence product and service enhancements program aimed at bringing all of the ships in the fleet up to the standards of the new *Westerdam,* which debuted in 2004, and the *Oosterdam,* which entered service in 2003. One problem that always faces cruise lines is ensuring that their new builds—which are invariably fitted with all of the latest "bells and whistles" of the day—don't overshadow their existing, older fleet mates. HAL's $225-million investment is one way to minimize the disparity between the old and the new.

In the 2 years or so since the initiative began, HAL has spent much of the $225 million on such items as new amenities in all staterooms—massage showerheads; lighted, magnifying makeup mirrors; hair dryers; extra fluffy towels; terry-cloth robes; upgraded mattresses; and Egyptian-cotton bed linens. Guests in all rooms are now welcomed with a complimentary fruit basket. Suites will have plush duvets on every bed, VCR/DVD players, and access to a well-stocked library of tapes and discs, and a fully stocked minibar.

The Pinnacle Grill, a popular alternative restaurant on eight of the ships in the fleet, has been added to all of the others. Table service and a wider range of hot meals will be added for evening dining in the Lido, formerly a buffet-style bistro on most of the HAL ships.

In addition, the company now allows passengers to board as early as 11:30am—a couple of hours earlier than the norm. And it makes the sometimes tedious and lengthy process of disembarking less onerous by letting passengers stay longer in their staterooms until they are called to leave.

There's more. Kid's centers, shore excursions, onboard educational programs—the HAL program, nearly completed, has upgraded them all.

## Pros

- **The expertise that comes with experience.** The company's ships are young, but Holland America's experience is apparent. You want to know what experience is? The company was formed way back in 1873 as the Netherlands-America Steamship Company. It figures that you'd get to know a little about operating oceangoing vessels in 131 years!
- **Warm Interiors.** Holland America ships, especially the more recent builds, tend to be understated, inviting, and easy on the eye.

## Cons

- **Sleepy nightlife.** If you're big on late-night dancing and barhopping, you may find yourself partying mostly with the entertainment staff, although the company is making an effort to offer more for night owls on its newer ships. You'll find more piano lounges, a bigger casino, and the like on the line's new ships.
- **Homogenous passenger profile.** To a certain degree, passengers tend to be a pretty homogenous group of low-key, 55+, North American couples who aren't overly adventurous. However, this profile is changing as younger passengers and families come aboard.

**THE FLEET**   The company's 1,266-passenger Statendam-class ships—the *Statendam* (1993), *Maasdam* (1993), *Ryndam* (1994), and *Veendam* (1996)—are virtual carbon copies of the same attractive, well-crafted design, with a dash of glitz here and there. The 1,440-passenger *Volendam* officially debuted in November 1999 and the 1,440-passenger *Zaandam* debuted in May 2000. Brighter and bolder than the earlier ships, the *Volendam* and *Zaandam* share many features of the Statendam-class ships, though the *Volendam* and *Zaandam* are slightly larger in size (63,000 tons, as opposed to 59,652) and carry more passengers (1,440, against the Statendam class's 1,266). The 1,380-passenger *Amsterdam* is 61,000 tons and is one of two flagships in the fleet. (The other is the *Amsterdam*'s sister ship, the *Rotterdam*.) The *Oosterdam* (85,000 tons and carrying 1,848 passengers) is the second of what HAL calls its Vista-class ships (the other being the *Zuiderdam,* which entered service in the winter of 2002 and is not scheduled to be in Alaska). The *Westerdam,* also a Vista-class ship, joined the fleet last year and another similarly dimensioned vessel, to be called the *Noordam,* is scheduled to check in early in 2006.

The company has never shown any inclination to plunge into the 100,000-plus-ton megaship market. Keeping the size down allows HAL to maintain its high service standards and a degree of intimacy while enabling the line's ships to offer all of the amenities of its larger brethren.

**PASSENGER PROFILE**   Holland America's passenger profile used to reflect a much older crowd. Now the average age is dropping, partly thanks to an increased emphasis on the line's Club HAL program for children and partly due to some updating of the onboard entertainment offerings. HAL's passenger records in Alaska show a high volume of middle-aged-and-up vacationers (the same demographic as aboard many of its competitors' ships), but on any given cruise, records are also likely to list a few dozen passengers between the ages of, say, 5 and 16. This trend gathered its initial momentum a few years ago in Europe, a destination that, parents seem to think, has more kid appeal. It's spilled over into Alaska recently, mainly thanks to the cruise line's added emphasis on generational travel and family reunion travel, a growing segment of the market.

The more mature among Holland America's passengers are likely to be repeat HAL passengers, often retirees. They are usually not Fortune-500 rich—they are looking for solid value for their money—and they get it from this line.

**DINING**   Years ago, HAL's meals were as traditional as its architecture and its itineraries. In the last few years, though, it's become a lot more adventurous in all three areas. The variety of dishes on the menu is as good as on any other premium line, and the quality of the food is generally high throughout the fleet. Don't look for lots of pastas; do look for excellent soups. Vegetarian options are available at every meal, and the line has excellent veggie burgers at the on-deck grill.

The kids' menu usually includes spaghetti, pizza, hamburgers, fries, and hot dogs. In addition, a few variations on what's being offered to the adults at the table are often served.

Buffets are offered at the Lido Restaurant as an alternative to breakfast and lunch in the main dining room. HAL also recently expanded its dinner options to include a casual dinner on the Lido Deck in addition to its formal dining-room dinner service (the buffet is offered on all nights except the final night of the cruise). There are also intimate, reservations-required alternative Italian restaurants on the *Amsterdam, Volendam, Oosterdam,* and *Zaandam.*

**ACTIVITIES**    Young swingers need not apply. Holland America's ships are heavy on more mature, less frenetic activities and light on boogie-till-the-cows-come-home party-hearty pursuits. You'll find good bridge programs and music to dance to or listen to in the bars and lounges, plus health spas and all of the other standard activities found on most large ships—bingo, golf-putting contests (on the carpet in the lobby), dance lessons, art auctions, and the like. All ships offer Internet access for 75¢ a minute, with a 5-minute minimum.

In 2005 the line will continue its **Artists in Residence Program,** arranged through the Alaska Native Heritage Center in Anchorage, with Alaska Native artists accompanying all 7-night cruises and demonstrating traditional art forms such as ivory and soapstone carving, basket weaving, and mask making. The line will also be continuing its Huna Interpretive Program, with a member of the Huna tribe joining National Park Service employees in providing commentary as the ship visits Glacier Bay. The Huna tribe has called Glacier Bay home for centuries.

**CHILDREN'S PROGRAM**    Club HAL is more than just one of those half-hearted give-'em-a-video-arcade-and-hot-dogs-at-dinner efforts. This children's program offers expert supervisors, a fitness center, and dedicated kids' common rooms (adults keep out!) on the *Amsterdam, Zaandam, Volendam, Oosterdam,* and *Ryndam.* On the other ships, some of the meeting rooms and lounges—the Half Moon Lounge on the *Veendam,* for instance—are set aside for the younger set during the day and revert to their general-population purposes at night.

Kids' activities are arranged in three divisions, by age—5 to 8, 9 to 12, and teens. The youngest group might have, say, singalongs, while the older kids will try their hand at karaoke. The middle group will compete in golf putting and the teens in fake Monte Carlo nights. (Don't worry, Mom, there's no real gambling involved!) The line also has a portfolio of **kids-only shore excursions** (floatplane rides, treasure hunts, hikes, and the like), on which parents can send their teens and preteens before setting off for their own adventure.

**ENTERTAINMENT**    The line has improved its nightly show-lounge entertainment, which was once, frankly, not so hot. Again, the change to some extent reflects the younger passengers who are starting to book with HAL. Each week includes a crew talent show in which the Indonesian and Filipino staff members perform their countries' songs and dances. Even if that sounds a bit amateurish and corny, try it—many of the staff members are fabulous!

**SERVICE**    The line employs primarily Filipino and Indonesian staff members, and from the welcome by a white-gloved steward who guides you to your cabin to the final gala dinner and everything in between, they are gracious and friendly without being cloying.

Jerry once sailed on the old *Rotterdam V* alongside one of those passengers who must make service people cringe. Three times in 6 nights in the dining room he sent a dish back with a complaint—"Needs more paprika" was one of his more exotic gripes. Nobody else at the table had any problem with the food—just this obnoxious character. He never once wanted a meal as is. Whatever the menu said, it was always, "I'd like this on the side," or, "That instead of such and such," or, "Don't put any of those in it." In short, the guy was an absolute pain. But the waiters never once reacted negatively to this aggravating little man. No matter what, the staff (the table captain and the maitre d' as well as the waiters) treated him exactly as they did the others at the table—with courtesy and warmth. He always got an apology when he sent his food back, no matter how spurious his

## HAL Fleet Itineraries

| Ship | Itineraries |
|------|-------------|
| Amsterdam/ Oosterdam | **7-night Inside Passage:** Round-trip from Seattle, visiting Juneau, Hubbard Glacier, Sitka, Ketchikan, and Victoria, B.C. |
| Volendam/ Zaandam | **7-night Inside Passage:** Round-trip from Vancouver, visiting Juneau, Skagway, Ketchikan, and Glacier Bay. |
| Statendam/ Ryndam/ Veendam | **7-night Gulf of Alaska:** North- and southbound between Vancouver and Anchorage/Seward, visiting Juneau, Ketchikan, Sitka, and either Tracy Arm, Glacier Bay, or Hubbard Glacier. |

complaint. The manner in which the dining-room staffers dealt with this diffi-cult customer (even though they must have been seething inside) told Jerry a great deal about their commitment to service.

On another occasion, Jerry somehow managed to get his baggage on board a Holland America ship in Vancouver in preparation for sailing—while his keys were lying on the bedside table at home 1,000 miles away. (You may well feel that you haven't heard many dumber moves than that!) Whatever, the cabin steward refused to let him break the locks and ruin the rather expensive (and brand-new) luggage. Instead, he called an engineer and together they toiled patiently with a variety of tools—and a huge ring of keys—until, about half an hour after boarding, they managed to free the offending locks. Luggage saved—and score one for the HAL service spirit!

Onboard services on every ship in the fleet include **laundry** and **dry clean-ing.** Each ship also maintains several **self-service laundry rooms** with irons.

**CRUISETOUR & ADD-ON PROGRAMS**    As might be expected of a com-pany that owns its own tour company (Royal Caribbean and Princess also own tour companies in the Alaska market), HAL offers a wide variety of land arrangements in combination with its cruises. Prices vary depending on the cabin category and hotel category you choose. The offerings are extensive. Cruisetours are available in lengths ranging from 11 to 18 days (cruise and land sections included) in Denali, Kenai, the Yukon, and the Canadian Rockies. Overnight hotel stays are also avail-able in Fairbanks, Vancouver, Seattle, and Anchorage—again, with a wide price range. This year the cruisetour brochure includes some new features. For instance, one tour features Tombstone Territorial Park, 90 minutes' drive from Dawson City in the heart of Canada's Yukon Territory. In 2004, the company introduced exclu-sive tours to the Yukon Territory's Kluane National Park, designated by UNESCO as a World Heritage Site, and will repeat the program this year. The opening up of these two vast, hitherto untouched wilderness areas reflects HAL's preeminent posi-tion in the Yukon tourism market. Whereas other lines (in particular Princess and Celebrity/Royal Caribbean) have tended to concentrate their investment focus in the Denali Corridor, HAL has built instead in the Canadian interior. Its entry into Kluane and Tombstone allows it to offer, in conjunction with Parks Canada, fixed-wing flightseeing over Kathleen Lake, a Tatshenshini River white-water rafting out-ing, a hike though the King's Throne region (all in Kluane), and a motorcoach tour from Dawson City to Tombstone for wildlife viewing and hiking. Also new: a tour that allows an overnight stay in Seward and direct service by motorcoach to Denali. Historically, Denali tours have gone first to Anchorage from Seward for an overnight stay. It's a long drive from the Resurrection Bay port to the park, but the scenery en route is certain to make you forget the passing of the hours.

# Amsterdam

Amsterdam
*(photo: Holland America Line)*

## Specifications

| | | | |
|---|---|---|---|
| Size (in tons) | 61,000 | Officers | Dutch |
| Number of Cabins | 690 | Crew | 647 (Indonesian/ Filipino) |
| Number of Outside Cabins | 557 | Passenger/Crew Ratio | 2.13 to 1 |
| Cabins with Verandas | 172 | Year Built | 2000 |
| Number of Passengers | 1,380 | Last Major Refurbishment | n/a |

**THE SHIP IN GENERAL**    The *Amsterdam* is one of a line of attractive, mid-size ships in the Holland America fleet. It appeals to a broad range of cruise-goers thanks to its classic style and tradition combined with innovation. The ship's splendid focal point, for instance, is a giant clock tower in the atrium lobby, a da Vinci–like masterpiece with carillon bells. The ship's revolutionary propulsion system enables it to cruise a little faster than most ships, which allows it to arrive in some ports earlier and leave a little later. It features an all-suite deck with butler service and a private lounge for guests in the suites. The *Amsterdam* offers open expanses and dramatic staircases leading to the lobby level and between decks. Broad, teak decks and subdued hues give the ship a feel of elegance.

The ship is, in fact, the third in the Holland America fleet to bear the *Amsterdam* name. It shares flagship status with its sister ship, the *Rotterdam VI*.

**CABINS**    Don't look for a lot of frills and fripperies on the *Amsterdam*. Its accommodations are warm, comfortable, low-key—and totally functional. Its inside rooms go as big as 182 square feet—not huge, but more than adequate by today's standards. Outside rooms range up to a very comfortable 197 square feet, while mini- and full suites are between 284 and 1,226 square feet. Cabin decor is subdued, with lots of pastels and white wood trim, splashed with tasteful additions of rich, deep maroons and dark oak. There's nothing garish here.

The smallest inside cabins have showers only, while the rest of the cabins have tub/shower combinations. The suites feature whirlpool tubs—the one in the penthouse is an oversize affair, quite big enough for two. Suite guests also get VCRs (you can borrow tapes from the ship's video library). The full suites include a dressing room, living room, minibar, and refrigerator. Passengers on the all-suite Navigation Deck enjoy concierge service and exclusive use of a small lounge, the Neptune Room, on that level.

Twenty-one cabins on four decks are wheelchair accessible.

## Cabins & Rates

| Cabins | Brochure Rates | Bathtub | Fridge | Hair Dryer | Sitting Area | TV |
|---|---|---|---|---|---|---|
| Inside | $1,461–$1,764 | no | no | yes | some | yes |
| Outside | $1,857–$2,946 | yes | no | yes | yes | yes |
| Suites | $3,300–$6,075 | yes | yes | yes | yes | yes |

**PUBLIC AREAS**    The first thing to catch passengers' eyes is the centerpiece of the atrium: an enormous, elaborate astronomical timepiece. The celestial clock has a carillon that chimes tunes at certain hours of the day, and a constantly changing map of the heavens as they appear from Amsterdam (the city from which the ship takes its name).

Strategically located around the ship are depictions of big ol' Alaskan grizzly bears. British artist Susanna Holt, a world-renowned sculptor, spent weeks in the 49th state studying these creatures and preparing to create the bronzes that now decorate some of the public areas of the *Amsterdam.*

The **La Fontaine Room,** the ship's main dining room, is a two-level facility where the friendly Indonesian waitstaff serves food on Rosenthal china. The room's ambience of elegance and richness is heightened by an impressive stained-glass ceiling. An alternative dining room, **The Odyssey,** is located amidships on the Promenade Deck. Reservations for this classy eatery are a must and there is an additional charge of $10 to eat there.

The double-decker **Queen's Lounge,** the main showroom, is an excellent spot to view some of Holland America's improved (and still improving) evening entertainment.

For after-hours (or, for that matter, daytime) relaxing and imbibing, we particularly like the elegant **Explorer's Lounge** or the less formal **Crow's Nest.** Other public rooms include a casino, a library (intellectually named the Erasmus Library), additional lounges, and a coffee bar.

**POOL, FITNESS & SPA FACILITIES**    The ship has two pools (including one that can be covered in inclement weather), a jogging track, a well-equipped gymnasium, and two paddle-tennis courts. The oceanview spa offers saunas, a loofah scrub room, massage specialists, steam rooms, and beauty and hair salons. It's not the most imaginative spa in the world, but it does cover all the bases.

## Statendam • Ryndam • Veendam

Veendam
*(photo: Holland America Line)*

### Specifications

| Size (in tons) | 55,451 | Officers | Dutch |
|---|---|---|---|
| Number of Cabins | 633 | Crew | 588 (Int'l) |
| Number of Outside Cabins | 502 | Passenger/Crew Ratio | 2.2 to 1 |
| Cabins with Verandas | 150 | Year Built | 1993/1994/1996 |
| Number of Passengers | 1,266 | Last Major Refurbishment | n/a |

**THE SHIPS IN GENERAL**    These three nearly identical vessels were built within a 3-year span and fall somewhere between midsize and megaships. They demonstrate an extremely good use of space that pays attention to passenger traffic flows. The interiors feature leather, glass, cabinets, textiles, and furniture from around the world. Touches of marble, teakwood, polished brass, and around $2-million worth of artwork on each vessel evoke the era of the classic ocean liners. The decor often illustrates the Netherlands's seafaring traditions and the role of Holland America in opening commerce and trade between Holland and the rest of the world.

**CABINS**    All the cabins have a sitting area that can be closed off from the sleeping area with curtains, plus lots of closet and drawer space. The outside doubles have either picture windows or verandas. The least expensive inside cabins run almost 190 square feet (quite large by industry standards) and have many of the amenities of their higher-deck counterparts—sofas, chairs, desk-cum-dressers, stools, hair dryers, safes, and coffee tables. All cabins have TVs and telephones and some have bathtubs (including some whirlpool tubs), VCRs, and minibars. Penthouses (one only on each ship) are huge—almost 1,200 square feet.

Six cabins on each ship are wheelchair accessible.

## Cabins & Rates

| Cabin | Brochure Rates | Bathtub | Fridge | Hair Dryer | Sitting Area | TV |
|-------|----------------|---------|--------|------------|--------------|-----|
| Inside | $1,052–$1,302 | no | no | yes | some | yes |
| Outside | $1,880–$2,773 | yes | no | yes | yes | yes |
| Suites | $2,902–$5,730 | yes | yes | yes | yes | yes |

**PUBLIC AREAS**    The striking dining rooms and the two-tiered showrooms are among these ships' best features; the latter are comfortable and have great views of the stage area from all seats. It helps, of course, that Holland America has made huge strides in upgrading its entertainment package.

The lobby area on each ship is not just the place to board the ship, but a place to hang out in as well. The *Statendam's* lobby houses a magnificent three-story fountain, the *Ryndam* has a smaller version of the same fountain, and the *Veendam* has a huge glass sculpture called *Jacob's Ladder.*

Other public rooms include a coffee bar, a card room, a casino, a children's playroom, a cinema, conference facilities, and a library. We especially like the **Crow's Nest** forward bar and lounge up on the sports deck, an inviting place to while away an hour or three.

**POOL, SPA & FITNESS FACILITIES**    All three ships have a sprawling expanse of teak-covered aft deck surrounding a swimming pool. One deck above that is a second swimming pool plus a wading pool, spacious deck area, bar, and two hot tubs that can be sheltered from inclement weather with a sliding-glass roof. Both areas are well planned and wide open. There's a practice tennis court and, on the *Statendam,* an unobstructed track on the Lower Promenade Deck for walking or jogging. The ships' roomy, windowed gyms have a couple dozen exercise machines, a large separate aerobics area, steam rooms, and saunas. The spas lack pizzazz but offer the typical menu of treatments.

# Volendam • Zaandam

Volendam
*(photo: Holland America Line)*

## Specifications

| | | | |
|---|---|---|---|
| Size (in tons) | 63,000 | Officers | Dutch/Int'l |
| Number of Cabins | 720 | Crew | 647 (Indonesian/Filipino) |
| Number of Outside Cabins | 581 | Passenger/Crew Ratio | 2.2 to 1 |
| Cabins with Verandas | 197 | Year Built | 2000 |
| Number of Passengers | 1,440 | Last Major Refurbishment | n/a |

**THE SHIPS IN GENERAL** Holland America pulled out all the stops on these two ships: The centerpiece of the striking triple-decked oval atrium on the *Volendam,* for instance, is a glass sculpture by Luciano Vistosi, one of Italy's leading practitioners of the art, and that's just part of the ship's $2-million art collection, which reflects a flower theme. On the *Zaandam,* the focal point of the atrium is a 22-foot-tall pipe organ that is representative of the ship's music theme, which is filled out by a collection of guitars signed by rock musicians including the Rolling Stones, Iggy Pop, David Bowie, and Queen (an attempt to attract a younger, baby-boomer clientele?). Apart from the artwork and overall decorating themes, there aren't many differences between these two magnificent vessels; they really are virtually indistinguishable from one another. The *Zaandam* may look just the teeniest bit brighter than the *Volendam,* but hardly enough to make a real difference.

**CABINS** The 197 suites and deluxe staterooms on each ship have private verandas, and the smallest of the remaining 523 cabins is a comfortable 190 square feet. All cabins come complete with sofa seating areas, hair dryers, telephones, and TVs. The suites and deluxe rooms also have VCRs, whirlpool baths, and minibars. Both ships have more balcony cabins than other HAL vessels.

Twenty-three of the cabins are equipped to accommodate wheelchairs.

## Cabins & Rates

| Cabins | Brochure Rates | Bathtub | Fridge | Hair Dryer | Sitting Area | TV |
|---|---|---|---|---|---|---|
| *Volendam* | | | | | | |
| Inside | $1,104–$1,746 | no | no | yes | yes | yes |
| Outside | $1,875–$2,946 | yes | no | yes | yes | yes |
| Suites | $3,300–$6,057 | yes | yes | yes | yes | yes |
| *Zaandam* | | | | | | |
| Inside | $1,461–$1,961 | no | no | yes | yes | yes |
| Outside | $2,175–$3,532 | yes | some | yes | yes | yes |
| Suites | $3,745–$7,103 | yes | yes | yes | yes | yes |

**PUBLIC AREAS**   Each ship has five entertainment lounges, including the main two-tiered showroom. The Crow's Nest, a combination nightclub and observation lounge, is a good place to watch the passing Alaska scenery during the day.

Both ships have an alternative restaurant serving Italian cuisine, available on a reservations-only basis. The *Volendam's* alternative restaurant is designed as an artsy bistro and features drawings and etchings on the walls. The *Zaandam's* alternative eatery features a collection of 17th-century still-life paintings that the ship's interior designers happened upon and decided to display. Each ship also has a casino, a children's playroom, a cinema, a library, an arcade, and an Internet center where you can surf for 75¢ a minute, with a 5-minute minimum.

**POOL, SPA & FITNESS FACILITIES**   On both ships, the gym is downright palatial, with dozens of state-of-the-art machines surrounded by floor-to-ceiling windows. There is an adjacent aerobics room. The spa and hair salon are not quite as striking. Three pools are on the Lido Deck, with a main pool and a wading pool under a retractable glass roof that also encloses the cafelike Dolphin Bar. A smaller and quieter aft pool is located on the other side of the Lido buffet restaurant. On the Sports Deck is a pair of paddle-tennis courts as well as a shuffleboard court. Joggers can use the uninterrupted Lower Promenade Deck for a good workout.

## Oosterdam

Oosterdam
*(photo: Holland America Line)*

### Specifications

| Size (in tons) | 85,000 | Officers | Dutch/Int'l |
|---|---|---|---|
| Number of Cabins | 924 | Crew | 825 (Indonesian/Filipino) |
| Number of Outside Cabins | 786 | Passenger/Crew Ratio | 2.2 to 1 |
| Cabins with Verandas | 621 | Year Built | 2003 |
| Number of Passengers | 1,848 | Last Major Refurbishment | n/a |

**THE SHIP IN GENERAL**   This will be the *Oosterdam's* second summer in the 49th state. Its thoughtful layout prevents bottlenecks at key points—outside the dining room, for instance, and at the buffet and pool area. Art worth about $2 million, according to HAL, is well displayed throughout the vessel, and the decor reflects Holland's (and Holland America's) contribution to the development of cruising and, indeed, of ships as a trade and transportation medium. The nautical pieces on display are plentiful, but never overwhelming.

**CABINS**   Nearly 85% of the *Oosterdam's* cabins have ocean views, and 67% of the ship's cabins have verandas. The smallest of the inside cabins is just 136 square feet—tiny enough to induce claustrophobia in some people. But the standard outside rooms start at 185 square feet, a considerable improvement.

Suites range up to 951 square feet, putting them (along with those of the *Zuiderdam*) among the biggest in the HAL fleet. All rooms have Internet/e-mail dataports. All of the rooms—even the smallest—have ample drawer and closet space, are tastefully decorated in quiet colors, and have quality bathroom fittings. All have VCRs and minibars.

Twenty-eight of the cabins, in several categories, are wheelchair accessible.

## Cabins & Rates

| Cabin | Brochure Rates | Bathtub | Fridge | Hair Dryer | Sitting Area | TV |
|---|---|---|---|---|---|---|
| Inside | $1,602–$1,887 | no | no | no | no | yes |
| Outside | $2,123–$2,695 | no | yes | yes | yes | yes |
| Suites | $3,445–$7,387 | yes | yes | yes | yes | yes |

**PUBLIC AREAS**   The *Oosterdam*'s 10 decks include a disco, a two-level main dining room; a library; a 24-hour cafe; an alternative, reservations-requested restaurant; and seven lounges/bars, including HAL's signature Crow's Nest observation lounge/nightclub. Plus, the *Oosterdam* has not one but two showrooms—a spectacular three-level main showroom and a smaller "cabaret-style" venue for smaller-scale performances.

The Club HAL children's facilities are extensive and have both indoor and outdoor components. The ship has two interior Promenade decks, affording walkers protection against the elements—these decks can prove very useful in Alaska!

Wheelchair users are well catered to on this vessel. Besides the 28 cabins specially designed for them, the ship has a wheelchair elevator dedicated for use in boarding the tenders in port, two tenders equipped with special wheelchair-accessible platforms, and accessible areas at virtually all public desks, bars, and lounges.

The ship has a well-equipped casino, offering passengers the chance to try their hands at stud poker, slots, craps, and roulette. And dozens of original art works, whose combined value ranks in the millions, dot the public areas.

**POOL, SPA & FITNESS FACILITIES**   The main pool on the Lido Deck has a retractable dome—a feature that has proven popular on other ships in Alaskan waters and will on this one as well. A couple of hot tubs and a smaller pool complement the main pool. A huge spa, complete with the usual array of treatments and services (reserve in advance), occupies part of the *Oosterdam*'s topmost deck.

## 6 Norwegian Cruise Line

7665 Corporate Center Dr., Miami, FL 33126. ℂ **800/327-7030** or 305/436-4000. Fax 305/436-4120. www.ncl.com.

The very mass-market Norwegian Cruise Line offers an informal and upbeat atmosphere on medium- to megasize ships. This year the *Norwegian Sun* relocates to Vancouver (from Seattle), and the *Norwegian Dream, Star,* and *Spirit* take over in rotation out of Seattle. The line offers 7- and 10-night itineraries.

**THE EXPERIENCE**   NCL excels in the activities department—if the line added any more to the list, passengers would be completely exhausted. Recreational and fitness programs are among the best in the industry, and include programs where attendance at fitness events earns you points that you can cash in for prizes. The line's children's program and entertainment offerings are also top-notch.

The company, which was bought by Star Cruises of Malaysia in 2000, has gradually changed its program to what it calls "freestyle" cruising, which makes life a whole lot easier for passengers. The line was, in fact, one of the pioneers of the concept. One of the main components of freestyle cruising is freedom in when and where passengers dine. Guests can eat in their choice of a variety of restaurants pretty much any time between 5:30pm and midnight (you must be seated by 10pm), with no prearranged table assignment or dining time. Other perks of freestyle cruising are that tips are automatically charged to room accounts, dress codes are more relaxed (resort casual) at all times, and at the end of the voyage, passengers can remain in their cabins until their time comes to disembark, rather than huddling in lounges or squatting on luggage in stairwells until their lucky color comes up. Freestyle cruising has since been copied, to whatever extent possible, by other lines operating in the U.S., although it's been standard for Star Cruises in Asia for years.

## Pros

- **Sports orientation.** Sports fans will be happy to find that major weekend sports games are broadcast into passengers' cabins and at the sports bars.
- **Smoke-free zones.** Norwegian promotes a smoke-free environment for those who want it. At least half the cabins on its ships are nonsmoking cabins, and on any ship with more than one dining room, one will be nonsmoking. There are even blackjack tables in the casinos that are reserved for nonsmokers.
- **Flexible dining.** NCL's dining policy lets you sit where and with whom you want, dress as you want, and dine when you want (dinner is served between 5:30pm and midnight).

## Cons

- **Inflated self-opinion.** One thing to watch out for is that the line tends to promote itself as more luxurious than it really is.
- **Unmemorable food.** The food is plentiful and okay, but it's not the line's strongest point. An exception is the cuisine served in some of the alternative dining rooms.

**THE FLEET**    The 1,936-passenger *Norwegian Sun* joined the fleet in September, 2001, and the 2,240-passenger *Norwegian Star* just 3 months later. The *Norwegian Spirit,* formerly the *SuperStar Leo,* was built for Star Cruises in 1999 and was renamed and transferred to the NCL fleet last year. The oldest of the NCL ships in Alaska this year, the *Norwegian Dream,* entered service in 1992. All three ships have lots of windows for great viewing. Though these ships are relatively large and have a lot of public areas, some of the cabins are on the small side and some have insufficient closet space.

**PASSENGER PROFILE**    In Alaska, the demographic tends more toward fairly affluent retirees than on the line's warmer-climate sailings, but you'll also find an increasing number of families as well, including grandparents bringing along the grandkids. Generally, passengers are not seeking high-voltage activities or round-the-clock action. The disco is seldom the most-used room on an NCL ship. There is a good mix of first-timers and veteran cruisers (many of whom have cruised with this line before).

**DINING**    None of the NCL vessels would win a prize for cuisine, but the cruise line handles the business of dining in an innovative way. And you can dress pretty much however you like, too—even jeans and T-shirts are acceptable.

## NCL Fleet Itineraries

| Ship | Itineraries |
| --- | --- |
| Norwegian Spirit | **7-night Inside Passage:** Round-trip from Seattle, visiting Ketchikan, Juneau, Skagway, and Prince Rupert, B.C., and cruising Sawyer Glacier. |
| Norwegian Sun | **7-night Inside Passage:** Round-trip from Vancouver, visiting Ketchikan, Juneau, Skagway, and Wrangell, and cruising Sawyer Glacier. |
| Norwegian Star | **7-night Inside Passage:** Round-trip from Seattle, visiting Ketchikan, Juneau, Skagway, and Victoria, B.C., and cruising Glacier Bay. |
| Norwegian Dream | **10-night Inside Passage:** Round-trip from Seattle, visiting Sitka, Whittier, Juneau, Ketchikan, and Prince Rupert, B.C., and sailing College Fjord. |

There is 1 optional formal night for those who want to dress up. On this night, some of the dining outlets are formal and others remain casual. As on all ships, breakfast and lunch are available either in the dining room, on an open-seating basis, or in the buffet up top, where passengers can help themselves, dress pretty much as they please (many of them have come straight from the pool), and enjoy a more relaxed meal.

In addition to the main dining rooms, the ships all have a variety of other food options. The *Spirit,* for instance, has 8 places to eat; the *Star,* 11; and the *Sun,* 9. Included in the mix, depending on the ship, are sushi, sashimi, and teppanyaki rooms; Italian eateries; and an a la carte Californian/Hawaiian/Asian outlet for which reservations are strongly recommended. A midnight chocolate buffet, offered once during each cruise, has become an NCL standard on all its ships.

**ACTIVITIES**    In Alaska the line offers a lecturer on the history and culture of the state, wine-tasting demonstrations, art auctions, trapshooting, cooking classes, craft and dance classes, an incentive fitness program, daily quizzes, board games, lotto, and bingo, among other activities. Passengers also tend to spend time at sports activities, which include basketball. The ships all have Internet cafes that cost 75¢ a minute.

**CHILDREN'S PROGRAM**    NCL ships tend to be very family-friendly: There's at least one full-time youth-activity coordinator, a kids' activity room, video games, an ice-cream stand, and guaranteed babysitting, plus a Polar Bear Pajama Party and sessions with park rangers. The line is constantly upgrading its kids' program to include escorted shore excursions for youngsters (an NCL youth counselor goes along). This year, for example, there is an Alaskan bush plane ride in Ketchikan and a White Pass train-and-bicycle tour in Skagway, among other choices.

**ENTERTAINMENT**    Entertainment is generally strong, with Vegas-style productions that are surprisingly lavish and artistically ambitious. On some nights, the showrooms also feature comedians and juggling acts. The three ships boast the NCL fleet's big splashy casinos, and all three ships have intimate lounges that present pianists and cabaret acts. Music for dancing—usually by a smallish band and invariably the kind of dancing that mature passengers can engage in (that is, not a lot of rock 'n' roll)—is popular aboard, and takes place before or after shows. Each ship also has a late-night disco for those who *do* like to dance to a more frenetic beat.

**SERVICE**   In the past, service has been inconsistent, ranging from just okay to great, but the line is working at focusing on personalized service. Generally, room service and bar service fleetwide is speedy and efficient, and the waitstaff is attentive and accommodating. With the introduction of the line's flexible dining program, additional crewmembers, mostly waiters and kitchen staff, have been added to each ship. To eliminate tipping confusion, the line automatically adds a charge of $10 per passenger per day to shipboard accounts (you are free to adjust the amount up or down as you see fit based on the service you received). (There was no tipping confusion on a recent cruise Jerry made on the *Norwegian Star.* In fact, for perhaps the first time ever, a crewmember on a mainstream ship absolutely rejected an effort to reward him with a small gratuity for an extra service rendered. Jerry inquired of a waiter in the luncheon buffet area whether it was likely that he would need to make a reservation for the alternative restaurant that night. The question was not, strictly speaking, within the purview of this young man. But he made it his business to go and call the restaurant in question and what's more, he came back and asked what time we'd like to eat—and then returned to the telephone and made the reservation. Service like that deserves recognition but he firmly refused to accept a gratuity, noting that he had done "nothing at all.") **Full-service laundry** and **dry cleaning** are available.

**CRUISETOUR & ADD-ON PROGRAMS**   With three ships calling Seattle home, the line expects considerable demand for its 3-night pre- or post-cruise packages to Victoria, B.C., complete with city tours and sightseeing (Butchart Gardens and Graigdarroch Castle, for example), starting at $499 per person, based on double occupancy; and its 2-night Seattle/Mount Rainier tour, available from $359 per person, based on double occupancy. These cruisetours are available only in conjunction with the sailings of the Seattle-based ships. One- and 2-night hotel packages are available in Vancouver for passengers on the *Sun* starting at $119 per night, per person, based on double occupancy, depending on the accommodations chosen.

## Norwegian Dream

Norwegian Dream *(photo: NCL)*

### Specifications

| Size (in tons) | 50,764 | Officers | Norwegian |
|---|---|---|---|
| Number of Cabins | 874 | Crew | 700 (Int'l) |
| Number of Outside Cabins | 716 | Passenger/Crew Ratio | 2.5 to 1 |
| Cabins with Verandas | 48 | Year Built | 1992 |
| Number of Passengers | 1,748 | Last Major Refurbishment | 1998 |

**THE SHIP IN GENERAL**   The *Norwegian Dream* is one of the line's oldest vessels. Built as the *Dreamward* (before all of the ships were named Norwegian something), it built up a following for itself for 6 years. Then it was midsectioned (that is, the ship was cut in half and a middle section of 130 ft. inserted) in Bremerhaven, Germany, adding another 150 or so cabins to its inventory. At that time, the ship was given its current name. The refurbishment that was done in Germany gave NCL essentially a new ship. Anybody who has built up an affinity for the ship and wants to see Alaska from its decks had better do so this year; in October, after its season in the 49th state, it is being deployed in Houston year-round for Western Caribbean/Mexico/Central America cruises.

**CABINS**   The smallest of the rooms is about 140 square feet, about average for this kind of ship. That's not big but it's not too cramped, either. The bigger accommodations go up to nearly 400 square feet. One complaint often voiced is the age-old bugbear—not enough closet and drawer space. But the rooms are tastefully furnished—no glitz, no glare.

## Cabins & Rates

| Cabins | Brochure Rates* | Bathtub | Fridge | Hair Dryer | Sitting Area | TV |
|--------|-----------------|---------|--------|------------|--------------|-----|
| Inside | $1,601–$1,732 | no | yes | yes | yes | yes |
| Outside | $1,882–$2,892 | yes | yes | yes | yes | yes |
| Suites | $3,512–$4,372 | yes | yes | yes | yes | yes |

*\* For 11-day sailing*

**PUBLIC AREAS**   The extensive refurbishment that accompanied the midsectioning in 1998 left the *Dream* with a more contemporary look and feel than might be expected of a ship that was launched in 1992. The public areas are bright and airy and more spacious than you would expect. What the process could not accomplish, however, was to give the ship as many dining facilities as some of its fleet mates; it has only five. Its main dining room, The Four Seasons, seats 482. The Terraces holds 334 and The Sun Terrace, the buffet breakfast and lunchroom, seats 258. These three operate on NCL's pioneering freestyle dining system—go when you like, with whom you like. The reservations-only facility, The Bistro, is the smallest of all, with room for just 72, and is open only for lunch and dinner. A fifth restaurant (of sorts) is the outdoor Café/Pizzeria on Sun Deck, serving breakfast and lunch snacks, pizza, hot dogs, and the like.

In addition to all of these the *Dream* has numerous lounges and bars, including NCL's signature Sports Bar, with its wall of multiple television sets (with ESPN feed when in range) showing major sporting events of the day and which serves light buffet snacks and beverages. Champs, on Sports Deck, is the outdoor bar, with 12 stools for those seeking liquid sustenance after taking their exercise. The Observatory Lounge is an ideal place to view the passing scenery; its floor-to-ceiling windows open the world to loungers. Among the other lounges are the Rendezvous Bar, an intimate cocktail bar; Dazzles Night Club, where you can listen or dance to a small combo; and the Wet Bar, a 15-seat facility near the pool, the hangout of those taking a break from their swimming labors.

Two other attractive facilities are the ship's Casino Royale (seven blackjack tables, one for roulette, another for dice games, and two more for Caribbean Stud Poker—plus 158 slot machines) and the main showroom, the Stardust Lounge, a 710-seat facility with a huge stage for some pretty ambitious Broadway-style revues.

There is a Kids' Korner with trained supervisors tending to youngsters from 3 to 17 years, and a youth center video arcade, with video games, a jukebox, and a 45-inch TV set on which are shown movies appropriate to specific age groups.

There is an Internet cafe, which really isn't a cafe at all, but in which, sans coffee and pastries, passengers can keep in electronic touch with the outside world for 75¢ a minute.

**POOL, SPA & FITNESS FACILITIES**  The *Dream* has two pools—a large one on Sun Deck, with lots of lounging and sunning space around, and a somewhat smaller one on International Deck. There are two Jacuzzis on Sports Deck, up top. The full-service spa and beauty center is operated by Mandara, a big name in seagoing spas.

The Fitness Center, on Sports Deck, features a large aerobics room and a variety of state-of-the-art exercise equipment, including a number of Lifecycles and Lifesteps.

## Norwegian Spirit

Norwegian Spirit *(photo: NCL)*

## Specifications

| | | | |
|---|---|---|---|
| Size (in tons) | 77,000 | Officers | Norwegian |
| Number of Cabins | 983 | Crew | 965 (Int'l) |
| Number of Outside Cabins | 618 | Passenger/Crew Ratio | 2 to 1 |
| Cabins with Verandas | 590 | Year Built | 1999 |
| Number of Passengers | 1,966 | Last Major Refurbishment | n/a |

**THE SHIP IN GENERAL**  In its previous incarnation, as the *SuperStar Leo* with Star Cruises, this ship was hugely successful in the Asian market. It was Star Cruises' first new build and its largest ship by far. Now, as the *Norwegian Spirit,* it is carving out a niche for itself in the U.S. It assumed its new identity last summer. Although there may be nearly 2,000 people on board, the ship seldom seems to be overly crowded. And the variety of dining options takes a lot of the sting out of meal times.

**CABINS**  The cabins are not huge, by prevailing industry standards but, at about 140 square feet, even the smallest are adequate. However, some of them lack closet and drawer space. In addition some of the color schemes in those low-end rooms are a trifle loud—like bright green carpeting and the same bright green (with pink stripes) on the bed coverlets. Rich reds and deep blues tend to prevail in the outside staterooms and the 18 suites. The spacious suites have whirlpool baths with separate shower and, of course, verandas.

## Cabins & Rates

| Cabins | Brochure Rates | Bathtub | Fridge | Hair Dryer | Sitting Area | TV |
|---|---|---|---|---|---|---|
| Inside | $944–$1,114 | no | no | yes | no | yes |
| Outside | $1,204–$1,764 | yes | no | yes | some | yes |
| Suites | $2,524–$3,714 | yes | yes | yes | yes | yes |

**PUBLIC AREAS**  The ship's Moulin Rouge Showroom, a multilevel affair, is a pretty spectacular room for the company's Broadway and Las Vegas–style extravaganzas. The facility seats 1,000 at a time and the sightlines are generally good.

Maharajah's Casino offers the usual cruise ship array of table games and slots in a comfortable, airy setting. The ship has a couple of locations for those wishing to trip the light fantastic. You just have to decide how strenuous you want your tripping to be! The Celebrity Disco is a high-energy site with loud music and laser lights into the wee, small hours. For a somewhat less frenzied dance floor, try the Galaxy of the Stars on the top of the ship, a lively, but to many tastes, more comfortable spot in which to whisk your partner around the floor.

The *Norwegian Spirit's* dining facilities offer a vast choice of styles and cuisines. The opulent Windows Restaurant, so called because of its two-story window offering panoramic views of the ocean and passing scenery, and Maxim's, an elegant steak house, are the dressier of the alternatives. For less formal dining there are Shogun Asian, The Garden Room, La Trattoria, Raffles Buffet, and the 24-hour-a-day Blue Lagoon. You might also like to look in on Champagne Charlie's bar or the Bier Garten, which need no explanation.

An Internet cafe allows passengers to link up with home (or Wall St.) for 75¢ a minute.

**POOL, SPA & FITNESS FACILITIES**   The Tivoli Pool has plenty of lounging space around it, as well as four hot tubs. Nearby the ship's Roman Spa and Fitness Center offers an Aquaswim jet current exercise pool—an increasingly popular exercise tool—as well as a full gymnasium with an ample complement of weight machines, treadmills, exercise bikes, and the like. There is also a jogging track up top.

## Norwegian Star

Norwegian Star *(photo: NCL)*

### Specifications

| Size (in tons) | 91,000 | Officers | Norwegian |
|---|---|---|---|
| Number of Cabins | 1,120 | Crew | 1,100 (Int'l) |
| Number of Outside Cabins | 784 | Passenger/Crew Ratio | 2 to 1 |
| Cabins with Verandas | 515 | Year Built | 2001 |
| Number of Passengers | 2,240 | Last Major Refurbishment | n/a |

**THE SHIP IN GENERAL**   The *Norwegian Star* came to Alaska last year straight from the other noncontiguous state, Hawaii. In Hawaii, it operated an imaginative interisland itinerary with a trip to and from Fanning Island, a day's sail west of Hawaii, thrown in.

The *Star* differs from many other ships—including its fleet mates in Alaska this year—in that it has a blunt rear end, a style that is becoming more common in new builds, but which is still a little unusual when the ship is viewed in profile. But that doesn't detract in any way from the quality of the interior. The decor is modern, but not jarringly so, with muted, but not washed-out colors.

There are lots of pastel shades of green and blue, some gold (on drapes and bed-top covers, for instance) and a lot of blond wood. The overall effect is a pleasing meld of functionality and esthetics.

**CABINS**    Almost 800 of the *Star*'s accommodations are outside, and more than two-thirds of those have verandas. The inside cabins are small, ranging from 130 to 150 square feet. Suites have floor-to-ceiling windows, refrigerators, and private balconies. All cabins are equipped with TVs, telephones, small dressing tables, soundproof doors, individual climate control, and sitting areas that are actually big enough to stretch out in. Closet and drawer space is quite limited, so pack lightly.

Twenty cabins are suitable for wheelchair access.

## Cabins & Rates

| Cabins | Brochure Rates | Bathtub | Fridge | Hair Dryer | Sitting Area | TV |
|---|---|---|---|---|---|---|
| Inside | $1,004–$1,114 | no | no | yes | no | yes |
| Outside | $1,264–$1,634 | no | no | yes | some | yes |
| Suites | $1,844–$3,734 | yes | yes | yes | yes | yes |

**PUBLIC AREAS**    The *Star* has no fewer than 11 rooms in which passengers can eat, depending on the time of day—and not counting room service. The two main dining rooms (Versailles and Aqua), which offer traditional (that is to say, six- or seven-course meals) and a range of lighter fare, are joined by a variety of alternatives. Le Bistro, a French/Mediterranean restaurant, requires a $10 cover charge. Then there is Blue Lagoon, a casual eatery offering fish and chips, hamburgers, wok dishes, and the like; Ginza, serving Japanese cuisine; and the SoHo Room, which specializes in Pacific Rim/Hawaiian/Californian fusion dishes. In addition, the *Star* has Endless Summer, a Hawaiian-themed restaurant; the Market Café, an indoor/outdoor food station; Las Ramblas Tapas Bar & Restaurant, serving Spanish-influenced dishes; and the Italian-themed La Trattoria. As if that weren't enough, The Grill, a 24-hour buffet-style eatery, dispenses hamburgers, hot dogs, soups, salads, and pizza. When NCL says freestyle cruising, it means *freestyle* cruising!

A card room, casino, cigar bar, conference facilities, disco, library, karaoke bar, wine-tasting cellar, English pub, ice-cream counter, and three-level show lounge round out the public room offerings. For kids, there's a children's playroom (Planet Kids) and a video arcade.

**POOL, SPA & FITNESS FACILITIES**    The *Star* is well equipped for the sports-minded and active vacationer. In addition to the fitness center, there are three heated pools (one with a swim-up pool bar, and a children's pool and adults' pool that adjoin one another), a jogging/walking track (3.5 laps = 1 mile), and a wide array of sports facilities, including Ping-Pong tables and two golf driving ranges.

The Fitness Center, on Deck 12, and the Barong Spa and Beauty Salon, on Deck 11, are well stocked with Jacuzzis, hydro baths, and saunas. The spa has facilities for couples to take their treatments together.

# Norwegian Sun

Norwegian Sun *(photo: NCL)*

## Specifications

| | | | |
|---|---|---|---|
| Size (in tons) | 78,000 | Officers | Norwegian |
| Number of Cabins | 968 | Crew | 968 (Int'l) |
| Number of Outside Cabins | 650 | Passenger/Crew Ratio | 2 to 1 |
| Cabins with Verandas | 432 | Year Built | 2001 |
| Number of Passengers | 1,936 | Last Major Refurbishment | n/a |

**THE SHIP IN GENERAL**　　The *Norwegian Sun* was a groundbreaker for NCL when it debuted late in 2001 because it was the first ship specifically built by the company with the freestyle cruising concept in mind. The *Sun* was designed and constructed with all of the features that its owners envisioned as vital to the idea of dining flexibility—most specifically, nine different restaurants. It's possible on this ship (as it is on the *Star*) to eat in a different place every night of the week and not enter either of the two main dining rooms.

It's a peaceful ship, with plenty of room to get away from it all, if that's what you have in mind. The *Sun*'s eight-story midships atrium is not as ornate as those on some other ships (*Crystal Harmony* has a gentle waterfall and etched glass windows, for instance, and the *Amsterdam* has a grandiloquent giant timepiece). But it is nevertheless a striking area, giving a great feeling of airiness. Bright and airy is not a bad way to sum up the *Sun,* including its sleeping accommodations.

**CABINS**　　More than two-thirds of the ship's guest rooms have ocean views, a total of about 650 cabins in all. Of these, 432 have balconies. The smallest cabins are 172 square feet and, and having noted earlier passenger comments, NCL has built in additional closet and drawer space. Thirty minisuites each measure 267 square feet. All rooms have TV, radio, telephone, refrigerators, and safes, as well as individually controlled air-conditioning units. The ship has 20 wheelchair-accessible cabins.

## Cabins & Rates

| Cabins | Brochure Rates | Bathtub | Fridge | Hair Dryer | Sitting Area | TV |
|---|---|---|---|---|---|---|
| Inside | $959–$1,174 | no | yes | yes | yes | yes |
| Outside | $1,204–$1,564 | yes | yes | yes | yes | yes |
| Suites | $1,934–$3,964 | yes | yes | yes | yes | yes |

**PUBLIC AREAS**　　Besides Le Bistro, a standard on NCL's Alaska ships, the *Sun* offers Il Adagio, a rather formal Italian dining room; Ginza, for Japanese food; East Meets West, presenting a fusion of California, Asian, and Hawaiian cuisine, with a live lobster tank in the middle of the room as a focal point; a Spanish tapas bar called Las Ramblas; the Garden Buffet/Great Outdoor Café, serving lunch and dinner; a healthy-living restaurant called Pacific Heights; and two main dining rooms. Those with a sweet tooth should look for Sprinkles Ice Cream Parlor, near the pools. There is also a 24-hour room-service menu.

Located midships, the glass-domed, eight-story atrium of the *Sun* is a striking feature, built to offer at least the illusion of space. Bright and airy, it is the place to find the purser's desk, the shore-excursions office, and so on. Four glass elevators whisk passengers to the higher decks. A grand spiral staircase, also midships, links the Atlantic Deck with the International Deck, two flights up. Internet facilities (24 terminals) are available at 75¢ a minute. The two-story show lounge doubles as a disco that jumps into the wee small hours. The *Sun* has a large casino and eight bar/lounges, one of which is open to cigar smokers.

**POOL, SPA & FITNESS FACILITIES**    The ship has two pools and four hot tubs on Pool Deck 11, and a children's splash pool one deck up, on the Sports Deck, forward. The Sports Deck features a golf driving net, a basketball/volleyball court, a batting cage, shuffleboard courts, and sunbathing areas.

As might be expected of a ship built so recently, the *Sun*'s spa is rather more extensive than those on the ships that were built before it. Mandara, one of the premier spa operators in the world, manages this spa, as well as the spas on all NCL ships. Simultaneous spa treatments for couples, in-cabin spa service, hydrotherapy baths incorporating milk and honey or mineral salts, exotic Asian treatments, de-stress treatments, and all of Mandara's signature "Best of East and West" techniques are available here.

## 7 Princess Cruises

24305 Town Center Dr., Santa Clarita, CA 91355. ℂ **800/LOVE-BOAT** or 661/753-4999. Fax 310/277-6175. www.princess.com.

Consistency is Princess's strength. With new, large premium ships joining its fleet like so many cars off a Detroit assembly line (all seven of its ships in Alaska this year were built since 1991—four of them in the last 3 years—two of them in less than a year!), the company's major challenge now has been to maintain the service standards that passengers have come to expect, an effort in which it has generally succeeded.

**THE EXPERIENCE**    If you were to put Carnival, Royal Caribbean, Celebrity, and Holland America in a big bowl and mix them all together, you'd come up with Princess Cruises' megas. The *Coral, Island, Diamond,* and *Sapphire Princesses*—its latest creations—are less glitzy and frenzied than the ships of, say, Carnival and Royal Caribbean; not quite as cutting-edge as Celebrity's *Infinity* and *Summit;* and more exciting, youthful, and entertaining than Holland America's near-megas. The Princess fleet appeals to a wider cross section of cruisers by offering loads of choices and activities, plus touches of big-ship glamour, along with plenty of the private balconies, quiet nooks, and calm spaces that characterize smaller, more intimate-size vessels. Aboard Princess, you get a lot of bang for your buck, attractively packaged and well executed. The *Dawn* and the *Sun Princesses* are older vessels—the *Sun* is all of 10 years old and the *Dawn* is 2 years younger. The *Regal* is the oldest in the Alaska fleet, having been built in 1991. As a result, these three vessels lack some of the pizzazz of their newer fleet mates; they don't have as many dining options, for instance. All three are, nevertheless, worthy representatives of the Southern California–based line, and each has its own loyal following.

Although its ships serve every corner of the globe, nowhere is the Princess presence more obvious than in Alaska. Through its affiliate, Princess Tours, the company owns wilderness lodges, motorcoaches, and rail cars in the 49th state, making it one of the major players in the Alaska cruise market, alongside Holland America. In 2002 Princess unveiled its fifth wilderness lodge—near Wrangell–St. Elias National Park.

This year, Princess will again use the rather nondescript Whittier as the northern terminus for its Gulf cruises, instead of the more commonly used Seward. Whittier's primary advantage over Seward seems to be that it's about 60 miles closer to Anchorage. What's more, Princess passengers bound for rail tours of Denali National Park will be able to board their trains right on the pier, instead of taking a bus to Anchorage and then embarking on their rail carriages. It is the latest effort by the line to gain a competitive edge over its Alaska rivals. The battle for the minds and wallets of the public is being fought as much on land as at sea these days. With so many ship lines striving to attract new passengers or persuade old ones to come back, every little bit helps. Princess adds a lodge. Holland America signs a contract with the Yukon Territory government to offer Kluane and Tombstone. Royal Celebrity builds new domed rail cars; Princess and Holland America follow suit. The beat goes on—to the benefit of the traveling public. Princess Cruises is now a member of the same group that owns Holland America and Carnival, both of them highly visible in the Alaska cruise market. That gives the parent Carnival Corp. control of no fewer than 15 ships in Alaska in 2005.

## Pros

- **Good service.** The warm-hearted Italian, British, and Filipino service crew do a great job. On a Princess cruise a few years ago, one barman with a glorious Cockney accent (which we noted he could mute or emphasize at will) was a huge hit with our group, dispensing one-liners, simple magic tricks, and drinks with equal facility. We've met others on Princess ships with the same gift for making passengers feel welcome without being overly familiar.
- **Private verandas.** Virtually all of the line's Alaska ships have scads and scads of verandas, some of them in as many as 75% of the cabins.

## Cons

- **Average food.** The ships' cuisine is perfectly fine if you're not a gourmet, but if you are, you'll find it's pretty banquet hall–esque and not as good as, say, Crystal's or Celebrity's.

**THE FLEET**    Princess's diverse fleet in Alaska essentially comprises seven megaships, six launched since 1995 and one built in 1991. The fleet includes the *Diamond* and *Sapphire,* which were completed just last year; the *Coral* and *Island,* of 2002/2003 vintage; the *Sun* (1995); and the *Dawn* (1997). The *Regal,* operating this summer out of San Francisco, is the old-timer in the fleet. The ships generally are pretty but not stunning, bright but not gaudy, spacious but not overwhelmingly so, and decorated in a comfortable, restrained style that's a combination of classic and modern. They're a great choice when you want a step up from Carnival, Royal Caribbean, and NCL but aren't interested in the slightly more chic ambience of Celebrity.

**PASSENGER PROFILE**    Typical Princess passengers are likely to be between about 50 to 65, and are often experienced cruisers who know what they want and are prepared to pay for it. (Although they don't have to pay as much as they would on, say, Crystal.) The line's recent additional emphasis on its youth and children's facilities has begun to attract a bigger share of the **family market,** resulting in the passenger list becoming more active overall.

**DINING**    In general, Princess offers meals that are good, if hardly gourmet. But you've got to give them points for at least trying to be flexible: A few years ago, Princess implemented a new fleetwide dining option known as Personal Choice. Basically, this plan allows passengers to sign up for the traditional first or second seating for dinner, or for a come-as-you-please restaurant-style dining option. The latter allows you to eat dinner any time between 5:30pm and midnight (you must be seated by 10pm) each night. If they choose the restaurant-style option, passengers may request a cozy table for two or bring half a dozen shipmates with them, depending on their mood that evening. A $6.50-a-day gratuity will be automatically added to your bill for the restaurant service. If you want to raise or lower that amount, you should do so when you make your cruise reservation (it will be harder to do it once you're on board). It's also possible to eat all your meals in the 24-hour Lido Deck cafe on all Princess ships in Alaska. If you don't go to the main dining room, though, you may miss one of Princess's best features: its pastas, prepared tableside several times during each cruise by your dining-room captain. The newest ships also offer a variety of alternative-dining restaurants—Italian, Mexican, New Orleans, and the like— and it's our experience that meals at these restaurants are well worth the price of admission, ranging from $8 to $15 per person on most of the ships. This year, on the new *Sapphire* and *Diamond,* Princess is implementing yet another dining-flexibility program (see ship reviews on p. 106).

**ACTIVITIES**    Princess passengers can expect enough onboard activity to keep them going from morning to night if they've a mind to, and enough hideaways to allow them to do absolutely nothing if that's their thing. The line doesn't go out of its way to make passengers feel that they're spoilsports if they don't participate in the amateur-night tomfoolery, or putt for dough, or learn to fold napkins. These activities are usually there, along with the inevitable bingo, shuffleboard, and the rest, but they're low-key. Internet access is offered on all the ships for $30 an hour with a 15-minute ($7.50) minimum. The line's ScholarShip@Sea program, which allows passengers to learn all there is to know about subjects as diverse as photography, computers, cooking, and even pottery, has been hugely popular since its inception 18 months ago.

Specifically in Alaska, the line has naturalists and park rangers on board to offer commentary.

**CHILDREN'S PROGRAM**    Supervised activities are offered year-round for ages 2 to 17, and are divided into two groups: "Princess Pelicans" for ages 2 to 12, and teens, ages 13 to 17. Princess is seeking to broaden its appeal and distance itself from its old image as a staid, adults-only line, and all of the ships are now well equipped for children and clearly intended to cater to families. Each ship has a spacious children's playroom and a sizable area of fenced-in outside deck for kids only, with a shallow pool and tricycles. Teen centers have computers, video games, and a sound system. Wisely, these areas are placed as far away as possible from the adult passengers.

**ENTERTAINMENT**    From glittering, well-conceived, and well-executed Vegas-style shows to New York cabaret-singer performances to a rocking disco, this line offers a terrific blend of musical delights, and you'll always find a cozy spot where

## Princess Fleet Itineraries

| Ship | Itineraries |
|---|---|
| Dawn/Sun/ Island/Coral Princess | **7-night Gulf of Alaska:** North- and southbound between Vancouver and Whittier/Anchorage, visiting Ketchikan, Juneau, and Skagway, and cruising Glacier Bay and College Fjord. |
| Sapphire/ Diamond Princess | **7-night Inside Passage:** Round-trip from Seattle, visiting Juneau, Skagway, Tracy Arm, Ketchikan, and Victoria. |
| Regal Princess | **10-night Inside Passage:** Round-trip from San Francisco, visiting Victoria, Juneau, Skagway (or Haines), and Ketchikan (or Sitka). |

some soft piano or jazz music is being performed. You'll also find entertainment like hypnotists, puppeteers, and comedians, plus karaoke for you audience-participation types. In the afternoons there are always a couple of sessions of that ubiquitous cruise favorite, the "Newlywed and Not-So-Newlywed Game." Each of the ships also has a wine bar selling caviar by the ounce and vintage wine, champagne, and iced vodka by the glass. The Princess casinos are sprawling and exciting places, too, and are bound to keep gamblers entranced (hypnotized?) with their lights and action. Good-quality piano-bar music and strolling musicians, along with dance music in the lounge, are part of the pre- and post-dinner entertainment.

For years, Princess has had a connection to Hollywood—this is the Love Boat line, after all. It's the only line we know of where you can watch yesterday's and today's television shows on your in-room TV. Also shown are A&E, Biography, E! Entertainment TV, Nickelodeon, Discovery Channel, BBC, and National Geographic productions, as well as recently released movies, some of them shown on a giant screen on Pool Deck when the weather permits.

**SERVICE**   Throughout the fleet, the service in all areas—dining room, lounge, cabin maintenance, and so on—tends to be of consistently high quality. An area in which Princess particularly shines is the efficiency of its shore-excursion staffs. Getting 2,000 people off a ship and onto motorcoaches, trains, and helicopters—all staples of any Alaska cruise program—isn't as easy as this crew makes it look. And a real benefit of the Princess shore-excursions program is that passengers are sent the options about 60 days before the sailing and can book their choices on an advanced-reservations basis before the trip (tickets are issued on board), either by mail or on the Internet at **www.princesscruises.com**. The program improves your chances of getting your first choice of tours before they sell out.

All of the Princess vessels in Alaska offer **laundry** and **dry-cleaning services** and have their own **self-service laundromats.**

**CRUISETOUR & ADD-ON PROGRAMS**   Princess offers an array of land packages this year that can be used in more than 50 different cruisetour itineraries in Alaska in conjunction with its Gulf of Alaska and Inside Passage voyages (not to mention another dozen or so options in the Canadian Rockies). Virtually every part of the state is covered—from the Kenai Peninsula to the Interior to the Far North. The land portions come in 4- to 7-night segments, all combinable with a 7-night cruise.

# Coral Princess •
# Island Princess

Coral Princess *(photo: Matt Hannafin)*

## Specifications

| Size (in tons) | 88,000 | Officers | British/Italian |
|---|---|---|---|
| Number of Cabins | 987 | Crew | 900 (Int'l) |
| Number of Outside Cabins | 879 | Passenger/Crew Ratio | 2.2 to 1 |
| Cabins with Verandas | 727 | Year Built | 2002/2003 |
| Number of Passengers | 1,974 | Last Major Refurbishment | n/a |

**THE SHIPS IN GENERAL**   The two ships are essentially twins, offering the same amenities and services, with nothing but relatively minor cosmetic differences between them. Roominess is the key here. Weighing 11,000 tons more than the *Dawn* and *Sun,* each nevertheless carries only about 24 additional passengers.

The ships reflect the marine design inventiveness that is becoming more obvious with the arrival of every new ship. Each has a 9-hole putting green, a world-class art collection, a spacious kids' and teen center, a wedding chapel, cigar lounge, a martini bar (the last two features have become almost standard on new ships), and much more. Decor is tasteful and rich, with a lot of teak decking, stainless steel and marble fittings, and prominent use of light shades of gray, blue, and brown in the soft furnishings.

**CABINS**   The two ships have a remarkable number of outside rooms (almost 90%) and a huge number of private balconies—727, or more than 7 out of 10 of the outside units. The smallest accommodations on either of the ships are about 160 square feet and the largest, the 16 top suites, stretch to 754 square feet, including the veranda. In between, the *Coral* and *Island* offer rooms with square footage ranging from 217 to 302. Don't assume when making a reservation that a minisuite will necessarily come with a veranda; each of the ships has eight minisuites without that amenity, so ask. Twenty of the cabins (16 outside, 4 inside) are configured for wheelchair use. They are very spacious—between 217 square feet and 374 square feet.

## Cabins & Rates

| Cabins | Brochure Rates | Bathtub | Fridge | Hair Dryer | Sitting Area | TV |
|---|---|---|---|---|---|---|
| Inside | $1,479–$1,569 | no | yes | yes | no | yes |
| Outside | $1,589–$1,919 | no | yes | yes | no | yes |
| Suites | $1,939–$3,249 | yes | yes | yes | yes | yes |

**PUBLIC AREAS**   In keeping with the trend on so many ships these days, the *Coral* and *Island* each offer a comfy cigar bar and a martini lounge—the Churchill Lounge and the Rat Pack Bar, respectively.

The ships have two main dining rooms and four alternatives. There's Sabatini's Trattoria, a fast favorite on most recent vintage Princess ships; a New Orleans restaurant called The Bayou Café; the poolside hamburger grill; and the poolside pizza bar. In combination, they allow passengers to eat pretty much when they want, and to be as formal or as relaxed as they wish.

One of the most appealing rooms is the nautical-themed Wheelhouse Bar, a warm, inviting place to spend time after-hours. Also inviting is the Explorers Lounge, though it's likely to be a little more hectic, and also functions as the disco after dinner.

The huge casino on each ship is a London-themed room, with frescos and knickknacks reflective of the ships' British heritage. An AOL Internet cafe, a wedding chapel, children's and teens' centers, a golf putting green, and a golf simulator are located on the top deck.

**POOL, SPA & FITNESS FACILITIES**   There are three pools and five whirlpool tubs. The fitness center is a large, well-stocked, airy room with absolutely the last word in equipment. The Lotus Spa offers one of the widest arrays of massage and beauty treatments afloat, including oxygenating facials, an "aromaflex" package that combines the ancient healing therapies of massage and reflexology, and a treatment that involves the placing of heated, oiled volcanic stones on key energy points of the body to release muscular tension and promote relaxation. (It should perhaps be noted here that Jerry's wife believes this to be the best spa treatment she's ever had!)

## Sun Princess • Dawn Princess

Sun Princess *(photo: Princess Cruises)*

### Specifications

| Size (in tons) | 77,000 | Officers | Italian |
|---|---|---|---|
| Number of Cabins | 975 | Crew | 900 (Int'l) |
| Number of Outside Cabins | 603 | Passenger/Crew Ratio | 2.2 to 1 |
| Cabins with Verandas | 410 | Year Built | 1995/1997 |
| Number of Passengers | 1,950 | Last Major Refurbishment | n/a |

**THE SHIPS IN GENERAL**   As in the case of the *Coral* and *Island Princesses,* these two ships are indistinguishable from one another but for cosmetics. Despite their size and passenger complement, you'll probably never feel crowded: There always seems to be lots of space on deck, in the buffet dining areas, and in the lounges.

**CABINS**   More than 400 of each ship's 975 cabins and suites have private balconies, including many in the midprice range, such as those on Baja Deck. All cabins, including the 408 inside units, come equipped with minibars, TVs, and twin beds that are easily converted to queens. Closet space is adequate, although it's a little cramped in the lower-end cabins.

The smallest cabins are a spacious 175 square feet, and the six suites aft measure up at 754 square feet, offering a large living room, separate bedroom/dining area, stall shower and bathtub with whirlpool, two TVs, refrigerator, and safe. The 32 minisuites are somewhat less lavish, though they're still highly desirable accommodations.

The ships have 19 wheelchair-accessible cabins located on several decks and in several different categories.

## Cabins & Rates

| Cabins | Brochure Rates | Bathtub | Fridge | Hair Dryer | Sitting Area | TV |
|--------|----------------|---------|--------|------------|--------------|-----|
| Inside | $1,309–$1,429 | no | yes | yes | no | yes |
| Outside | $1,499–$1,939 | no | yes | yes | no | yes |
| Suites | $2,399–$3,039 | yes | yes | yes | yes | yes |

**PUBLIC AREAS**   These ships shine when it comes to communal areas. They have a decidedly unglitzy decor that relies on lavish amounts of wood, glass, and marble. Collections of original paintings and lithographs worth $2.5 million are featured. The one-story showrooms offer unobstructed viewing from every seat, and several seats in the back are reserved for passengers with mobility problems. The smaller Vista Lounge also offers shows with good sightlines and comfortable cabaret-style seating. The twin dining rooms on each ship are broken up by dividers topped with frosted glass. The elegant, nautical-motif Wheelhouse Bar is done in warm, dark-wood tones and features live entertainment; it's the perfect spot for pre- or post-dinner drinks. There's a dark and sensuous disco; a bright, spacious, enticing casino; a card room; a cinema; a show lounge; and lots of little lounges that are perfect for an intimate rendezvous, such as the Entre Nous and the Atrium Lounge (which is so popular with passengers that it's where the captain holds his opening cocktail party). Another striking feature on these ships is the library, with leather easy chairs equipped with built-in headphone sound systems. They absolutely cry out, "Sit here!"

If you're hungry, options besides the usual main dining rooms and the buffet include an all-night sit-down restaurant (you can get a full dinner until 4am) and Lago's Pizzeria, a sit-down restaurant open afternoons and nights. Sorry, no takeout or delivery. Pizza is also available by the slice in the Horizon Court between 4 and 7pm daily.

The ships have extensive children's playrooms with ball drop, castles, computer games, puppet theaters, and more.

**POOL, SPA & FITNESS FACILITIES**   There are a total of four pools (one of which is the kids' wading pool), and hot tubs scattered around the Riviera Deck. The ships boast some of the best-designed, most appealing health clubs of any of Princess's vessels, though the gyms are on the small side for ships of these proportions. The spa offers all of the requisite massages and spa treatments. A teakwood deck encircles the ship for joggers, walkers, and shuffleboard players, and a computerized golf center called Princess Links simulates the trickiest aspects of some of the world's most legendary golf courses.

Fitness classes are available throughout the day in a very roomy aerobics room, where stretching and meditation classes are also offered.

## Sapphire Princess •
## Diamond Princess

Diamond Princess
(photo: Princess Cruises)

### Specifications

| Size (in tons) | 116,000 | Officers | British/Italian |
|---|---|---|---|
| Number of Cabins | 1,337 | Crew | 1,100 (Int'l) |
| Number of Outside Cabins | 960 | Passenger/Crew Ratio | 2.4 to 1 |
| Cabins with Verandas | 746 | Year Built | 2004 |
| Number of Passengers | 2,670 | Last Major Refurbishment | n/a |

**THE SHIPS IN GENERAL**    For all practical purposes, these two giants are also virtual twins, offering only the inevitable cosmetic (no structural) differences. Built in Nagasaki, Japan, they are by far the youngest ships in the fleet, each about a year old.

**CABINS**    Almost 60% of these ships' accommodations come with private balconies (78% of all the outside rooms)—a lot, though not as high a percentage as on some other ships in the market, including some of their own fleetmates. But it should be borne in mind that these are very much mass-market vessels. That requires that there be ample space for people who want less pricey inside and standard outside (nonbalcony) cabins. The rooms range from 168 square feet in the low-end inside units to between 535 and 1,329 square feet (including the veranda) in the suite category.

Twenty-seven cabins (16 outside, 11 inside) are wheelchair accessible.

### Cabins & Rates

| Cabins | Brochure Rates | Bathtub | Fridge | Hair Dryer | Sitting Area | TV |
|---|---|---|---|---|---|---|
| Inside | $1,689–$2,049 | no | yes | yes | no | yes |
| Outside | $2,199–$2,688 | no | yes | yes | yes | yes |
| Suites | $2,799–$4,849 | yes | yes | yes | yes | yes |

**PUBLIC AREAS**    As in the case of other ships in the fleet, these two vessels cater to a range of tastes. There is, for example, the high-tech Club Fusion, a lounge with flashing lights and modernistic furnishings. At the other end of the spectrum, for those with a more traditional bent, there is the Wheelhouse Bar, a classic nautical-themed room with dark wood and a warm feeling.

You wanna dance? Take your pick. For those whose taste runs to the more frenzied, there's Skywalkers, a lounge/disco in the sky with a balcony where you can cool off, and the Explorers Lounge, another disco lower on the ship. For those who prefer more sedate venues, numerous lounges and bars throughout the ships offer more traditional, less hectic dance opportunities. There's also a cozy, well-stocked library, a large casino, an Internet cafe, children's and teens' centers, a wedding chapel, and an art gallery. Up top there's a Sports Deck with a jogging track, basketball/paddle tennis courts, a golf putting course, and a golf simulator.

The *Sapphire* and *Diamond* each offer multiple dining venues. And what a variety of choices guests have! The main dining room, aft, is a handsome, somewhat traditional large room with two seatings for dinner. And that's where the tradition ends! There are four other themed rooms on Decks 5 and 6. One is a steakhouse, another is an Italian eatery, another is an Asian restaurant, and the fourth serves Southwestern cuisine. Meals in these restaurants are available at no extra charge. Plus, in each of the alternative restaurants, passengers may eat from the themed menu or have the same food that is being served that night in the main dining room. And, in the main dining room, the menu will include at least one item from each of the four alternative restaurants each night. Phew! If that's not enough variety for you, you can go to Sabatini's, an upscale Italian restaurant (cover charge $20). Princess aims to offer guests as much flexibility as possible. And that's a lot of flexibility!

During strategic times of the day, hamburgers, hot dogs, and sandwiches are available at the Trident Grill, located poolside, and Häagen-Dazs ice cream is served at Sundae's, also on the Pool Deck. And, of course, 24-hour room service is also available. There is, alas, no pizza parlor, as there is on the other Princess ships in Alaska. It was eliminated on these two vessels to make way for Sabatini's, which was not included in the original plans but which has proven so popular on the other ships that the company decided to install it on these ships as well.

**POOL, SPA & FITNESS FACILITIES**   There are three major outdoor pool areas and a generously supplied spa and fitness center on each ship, each offering the expected (and demanded) full range of treatments, facials, herbal wraps, and massage. Trainers are present to conduct stretching, meditation, and aerobics classes.

## Regal Princess

Regal Princess
*(photo: Princess Cruises)*

### Specifications

| Size (in tons) | 70,000 | Officers | British/Italian |
|---|---|---|---|
| Number of Cabins | 795 | Crew | 696 (Int'l) |
| Number of Outside Cabins | 614 | Passenger/Crew Ratio | 2.3 to 1 |
| Cabins with Verandas | 184 | Year Built | 1991 |
| Number of Passengers | 1,590 | Last Major Refurbishment | 1999 |

**THE SHIP IN GENERAL**   The *Regal* is a warm and inviting ship—inside. Its profile leaves a little to be desired. It was designed by architect Renzo Piano, who has some very, er, different, ideas about how his creations should look. In this case, he gave the ship a modernistic, graceful, dolphinlike dome at the front and then, looking, as he said, for a blend of the old and the new, stuck a straight-up-and-down smokestack—a decidedly outdated style—behind it. He got the old and the new in the design all right, but the blend isn't so hot. Nevertheless, once you're on board and don't have to look at the ship from the side, the *Regal* still delivers the goods, even in its 15th year—positively ancient by Princess standards!

**CABINS**   The cabins are among the better features of this ship. They're spacious (standard dimensions are about 190 sq. ft.), well furnished, and decorated in tasteful, easy-on-the-eyes colors. All rooms have safes, generous drawer space, and terry-cloth robes. Most have minibars. Closet space is ample. The bathrooms in standard and lower-end accommodations have shower stalls, while suites have both showers and tubs. Suites, minisuites, and some outside cabins have verandas.

Four cabins are wheelchair accessible.

## Cabins & Rates

| Cabins | Brochure Rates | Bathtub | Fridge | Hair Dryer | Sitting Area | TV |
|--------|---------------|---------|--------|-----------|--------------|-----|
| Inside | $2,139–$2,479 | no | yes | yes | no | yes |
| Outside | $2,699–$3,189 | no | yes | yes | no | yes |
| Suites | $3,369–$4,459 | yes | yes | yes | yes | yes |

**PUBLIC AREAS**   The dome up front was meant to be the observation lounge but it proved to be far too big for that purpose—so big, in fact, that Princess moved the casino and a bar in there as well. The best areas to view the passing Alaska scenery, if you don't care for the dome, are outside on Promenade Deck or aft on Lido Deck.

The three-story Plaza Atrium is an oval-shaped area including the reception desk, a patisserie, and retail stores. The dominant feature is the fountain sculpture on the lowest level. Other public areas include four bars (including a wine bar), a card room, disco, library, and show lounge.

The *Regal*'s interior is warm and inviting, and the ship boasts a multimillion-dollar art collection that is easier on the eye than the eclectic displays seen on some ships. One of the few disappointments is its exterior space; there isn't enough of it for the number of passengers. That means crowding for prime sunbathing space, especially around the pools. Another (admittedly purely personal) gripe: The ship has no wraparound Promenade Deck. That means that those in search of walking exercise must walk one way until they hit the blank wall, then turn and walk around the deck in the other direction. But the comfortable chairs and pleasant surroundings inside make the ship a worthy representative for Princess.

**POOL, SPA & FITNESS CENTER**   The gymnasium and aerobics rooms are situated on a low deck, much lower than they are on most other ships. But they are well equipped and well maintained under the watchful eye of expert trainers. The *Regal* also has two large pools, four whirlpools, and the obligatory Sports Deck topside, with a golf driving net and half basketball court. The *Regal*'s spa, which is smaller than those on the ship's newer fleetmates, offers an array of massage rooms as well as steam rooms and saunas.

## 8 Radisson Seven Seas Cruises

600 Corporate Dr., Suite 410, Fort Lauderdale, FL 33334. ℭ **800/285-1835.** www.rssc.com.

Radisson carries passengers in style and extreme comfort. Its brand of luxury is casually elegant and subtle, and its cuisine is among the best in the industry. The line operates five upscale small to midsize ships and one expedition ship, geared toward taking affluent and worldly travelers to such locations as Europe, South America, Antarctica, Tahiti, and Alaska. This year marks the line's fifth full season in Alaska, and the return for the third year of the all-suite and all-balcony

## Radisson Fleet Itineraries

| Ship | Itineraries |
| --- | --- |
| Seven Seas Mariner | **7-night Gulf cruises** between Vancouver and Seward and reverse, visiting Prince Rupert, B.C., Tracy Arm, Juneau, Skagway, Sitka, and Hubbard Glacier. |

*Seven Seas Mariner.* The line has announced plans to eliminate the Radisson from its title, but as of this writing, it had not done so.

**THE EXPERIENCE**    The Radisson Seven Seas experience offers the best in food, service, and accommodations in an environment that's a little more casual than Crystal's more determined luxury, as evidenced by the country-club casual attire that passengers wear throughout the cruise.

### Pros

- **Overall excellence.** The line has a no-tipping policy, excellent food, open seating for meals, generally fine service, great accommodations, and creative shore excursions.
- **Great room service.** Room service is about the best we've found on a ship, with the food served promptly, fresh, and course by course (rather than all at once).

### Cons

- **Sedate nightlife.** Most passengers, exhausted after a full day in port, or perhaps wanting to watch a movie on their in-suite VCR, head back to their cabins after the show (or around 11pm), leaving only a few night owls in the disco and other lounges.

**THE FLEET**    For 2005, Seven Seas has returned to Alaska the very upscale *Seven Seas Mariner.* It's one of the largest ships in the fleet (the other being its sister, the *Seven Seas Voyager,* which debuted in Apr 2003), and it offers an elegant yet comfortable modern design and a graceful yet casual onboard atmosphere.

**PASSENGER PROFILE**    Radisson tends to attract passengers in their 50s, with a household income of more than $100,000 who don't like to flaunt their wealth. The typical passenger is well educated, well traveled, and inquisitive.

**DINING**    Radisson's cuisine is among the best on the high seas, and would gain high marks even if it were on land. Service by professional waiters adds to the experience, as do little touches such as fine china and fresh flowers on the tables. Complimentary wines are served at dinner. Complimentary, that is, unless you want a very expensive bottle of champagne, say, or Opus One. But because the line serves excellent wines, there's very little reason to want to trade up. The main dining room has open seating, so you can eat when and with whom you wish. You can also dine at the lavish buffets offered for breakfast and lunch in the Veranda Room or in the other alternative dining restaurants, Signatures and Latitudes—the latter being the only reservations-only dining room on board. (Unlike on some other ships, no fee is charged for this room.) There is also a casual outdoor grill.

**ACTIVITIES**    The line assumes that, for the most part, passengers want to entertain themselves on board, but that doesn't mean there isn't a full roster of activities including lectures by local experts and well-known authors, plus instruction in the fine arts of pom-pom making, juggling, and such. There are card and board games, blackjack and Ping-Pong tournaments, bingo, and big-screen movies with popcorn. Bridge instructors are on board on select sailings, and the ships offer facilities to send and receive e-mail. Le Cordon Bleu–trained chefs offer cooking classes and gentlemen hosts are on hand each evening to dance with single ladies.

**CHILDREN'S PROGRAM**   The line is adult-oriented, but a children's program, Club Mariner, is offered on Alaska cruises, and you may find a dozen or so youngsters on any given sailing. Activities, held in borrowed spaces such as the nightclub or card room (there is no dedicated children's facility), include games, tournaments, Alaska-oriented crafts projects, storytelling, and opportunities to use Sony PlayStations. There are also a limited number of special kids' shore excursions.

**ENTERTAINMENT**   Entertainment includes small-scale production shows, cabaret acts, and headliners including comedians and magicians, and sometimes members of philharmonic orchestras and other musical groups. The library stocks books and movies that guests can play on their in-cabin VCRs.

**SERVICE**   The dining-room waiters generally have experience at fine hotels as well as on ships, and they provide service so good that you don't really notice it. Ditto for the excellent room stewards. The *Mariner* offers full-service and self-service **laundry** and **dry cleaning.**

**CRUISETOUR & ADD-ON PROGRAMS**   Land packages along the Denali Corridor between Anchorage and Fairbanks, to the Arctic Circle, and in the Canadian Rockies are among the cruisetour options available in conjunction with the Gulf schedule of the *Mariner.* As an example of the prices, a 2-night sky-trekking tour of the Interior with a private pilot/guide starts at $2,495 per person double, while a 5-night Fairbanks/Arctic Circle package starts at $2,005 per person double. A 3-night package at British Columbia's venerable Chateau Whistler is priced at $1,600 per person double.

Pre- or post-cruise hotel nights are available in Anchorage (from $235 per person double) and in Vancouver (from $160 per person double).

## Seven Seas Mariner

Seven Seas Mariner
*(photo: Radisson)*

## Specifications

| Size (in tons) | 50,000 | Officers | Italian |
|---|---|---|---|
| Number of Cabins | 350 | Crew | 445 (Int'l) |
| Number of Outside Cabins | 350 | Passenger/Crew Ratio | 1.6 to 1 |
| Cabins with Verandas | 350 | Year Built | 2001 |
| Number of Passengers | 700 | Last Major Refurbishment | n/a |

**CABINS**   The cabins are all oceanview suites, and all have private verandas. The Standard Suite is a large 301 square feet, and the largest two suites are a whopping 1,580 square feet and boast two bedrooms and two balconies. Some of the suites interconnect if you want to book two for a family or just to have additional space. All the suites offer separate living-room areas, and top levels of suites have dining areas as well. All the cabins come with queen-size beds that convert to twins, walk-in closets, marble-appointed bathrooms with full-size tubs and separate showers, TVs and VCRs, refrigerators stocked with complimentary bottled water and soft drinks, complimentary in-suite bar setups, safes, phones, and 24-hour room service. You can even order full meals from the dining room menu served in-suite. Fifteen of the cabins are wheelchair accessible.

## Cabins & Rates

| Cabins | Brochure Rates | Bathtub | Fridge | Hair Dryer | Sitting Area | TV |
|--------|---------------|---------|--------|------------|--------------|-----|
| Suites | $4,599–$18,899 | yes | yes | yes | yes | yes |

**PUBLIC AREAS**    The *Mariner* features an eclectic modern design that's elegant yet comfortable. Italian-designed and built, its officers are Italian and its crew is international. An impressive atrium starts on Deck 4 and reaches to Deck 12. The Constellation Theater is two-tiered and designed to resemble a 1930s nightclub. There are two additional lounges and a Connoisseur Club, a cushy venue for pre-dinner drinks and after-dinner fine brandy and cigars. The casino offers blackjack, roulette, Caribbean stud poker, and slots. Shoppers can indulge in two small boutiques offering clothes, jewelry, and your usual array of cruise-line logo items. The library offers books and videos, as well as a few computer terminals. Additional computer terminals fill the adjacent classroom. You can send and receive e-mail for about $1 per message.

Meals are served in the pretty, windowed Compass Rose main dining room on an open-seating basis. Buffets are also offered at breakfast and lunch at the indoor/outdoor La Veranda. At night, part of La Veranda is closed off and serves Mediterranean cuisine in a casual, intimate dining space.

**POOL, SPA & FITNESS FACILITIES**    The ship's Carita of Paris spa offers treatments using a variety of herbal and water-based therapies, as well as a variety of beauty services. The seawater pool is flanked by three heated whirlpools and surrounded by lots of open deck space. Recreational facilities include a fitness center, golf-driving cages, paddle tennis, a jogging track, Ping-Pong, and shuffleboard.

## 9 Royal Caribbean International

1050 Caribbean Way, Miami, FL 33132. ℰ **800/327-6700** or 305/379-4731. www.rccl.com.

A bold, brash industry-innovating company, which ranks up there in size with Carnival and Princess, Royal Caribbean introduced the concept of the megaship with its *Sovereign of the Seas* in 1988. The mass-market style of cruising that Royal Caribbean sells aboard its megaships is reasonably priced and offers nearly every diversion imaginable.

**THE EXPERIENCE**    The ships are more informal than formal and are well run, with a veritable army of friendly service employees paying close attention to day-to-day details. Dress is generally casual but neat during the day and informal most evenings, with 1 formal night per 7-night cruise.

The contemporary decor on Royal Caribbean vessels doesn't bang you on the head with glitz like, say, Carnival. It's more subdued, classy, and witty, with lots of use of glass, greenery, and art. All the Royal Caribbean vessels feature the line's trademark Viking Crown Lounge, an observation area located in a circular glass structure on the upper deck (in some cases encircling the smokestack), which looks like a Martian spacecraft atop the vessels. Another popular trademark feature are the ships' nautically themed Schooner bars.

## Pros

- **Great spas and recreation facilities.** Royal Caribbean's Alaska ships for 2005 all have elaborate health club and spa facilities, a covered swimming pool, and large, open sun-deck areas.
- **Great observation areas.** The Viking Crown Lounge and other glassed-in areas make excellent observation rooms for gazing at the Alaska sights.
- **Quality entertainment.** Royal Caribbean spends big bucks on entertainment, which includes high-tech show productions. Headliners are often featured.

## Cons

- **Crowds.** In common with some other big ships, you almost need a map to get around, and you'll likely experience the inevitable lines for buffets, debarkation, and boarding of buses during shore excursions.

**THE FLEET**   Royal Caribbean owns the largest ships in the world, the four 142,000-ton Voyager-class vessels. Although those four 3,000-plus passenger ships—which introduced such cruise ship design features as ice-skating rinks, rock-climbing walls, and cabins overlooking interior atrium areas—are not in the Alaska market, Royal Caribbean does have in the market for a third year its very up-to-date 2,500-passenger *Radiance of the Seas,* which in 2001 introduced a new category of ship for the line, and offers many innovations, including a billiards room with self-leveling pool tables. The big news for RCL last year was the arrival in Alaska of the *Radiance*'s new sister ship, the similarly dimensioned *Serenade of the Seas.* Apparently, that was a sound marketing move; the ship is returning this year. Also returning to Alaska in 2005 is the 2,452-passenger *Vision of the Seas.*

**PASSENGER PROFILE**   The crowd on Royal Caribbean ships, like the decor, tends to be a notch down on the whoopee scale from what you'll find on Carnival. Passengers represent an age mix from 30 to 60, and a good number of families are attracted by the line's well-established and fine-tuned kids' programs.

In Alaska, Royal Caribbean is focusing more on international sales than the entrenched market leaders, Princess and Holland America, which has resulted in sailings populated by a good many overseas passengers, including many from Asia and Europe.

**DINING**   Food on Royal Caribbean has been upgraded and improved recently, and occasionally a dish will knock your socks off. Dining rooms feature two seatings with assigned tables at breakfast, lunch, and dinner. Every menu contains selections designed for low-fat, low-cholesterol, and low-salt dining, as well as vegetarian and children's dishes. On the *Radiance* and *Serenade,* you also have the option of dining on a reservations-only basis at Chops, a classy steakhouse; or Portofino, an upscale Italian eatery. A fee of $20 a head is charged at these venues, but in our experience, the food soars above what's offered in the dining room. Casual dining, with table service, is offered in Cascades at all three meals as an alternative for those who don't want to sit in the dining room (no extra charge). Casual buffet-style breakfasts and lunches are available in the Windjammer Café, on Deck 10. In addition to the midnight buffet, sandwiches are served throughout the night in the public lounges. A basic menu is available

## Royal Caribbean Fleet Itineraries

| Ship | Itineraries |
| --- | --- |
| Serenade of the Seas | **7-night Inside Passage:** Round-trip from Vancouver, visiting Hubbard Glacier, Skagway, Juneau, Ketchikan, and Misty Fjords. |
| Vision of the Seas | **7-night Hubbard Glacier (Inside Passage):** North- and southbound between Vancouver and Seward, visiting Ketchikan, Juneau, Skagway, Hubbard Glacier, and Sitka. (Southbound cruises also cruise Misty Fjords.) |
| Radiance of the Seas | **7-night Inside Passage:** Round-trip from Vancouver, visiting Juneau, Skagway, Hubbard Glacier, and Ketchikan. |

from room service 24 hours a day, and during normal dinner hours, a cabin steward can bring you anything being served in the dining room that night. Royal Caribbean bans smoking in the dining rooms on all its vessels.

**ACTIVITIES**    On the activity front, Royal Caribbean offers plenty of the standard cruise-line fare (craft classes, horse racing, bingo, shuffleboard, deck games, line-dancing lessons, wine-and-cheese tastings, cooking demonstrations, and art auctions), but if you want to take it easy and watch the world go by or scan for wildlife, no one will bother you or cajole you into joining an activity. Port lectures are offered on topics such as Alaska wildlife, history, and culture. The ships also offer an extensive **fitness program** called ShipShape.

You can e-mail home from Internet cafe areas for 50¢ a minute.

**CHILDREN'S PROGRAM**    Children's activities are some of the most extensive afloat, and include a teen disco, children's play areas, and the Adventure Ocean program, which offers a full schedule of scavenger hunts, arts-and-crafts sessions, and science presentations—so many activities, in fact, that kids get their own daily activities program delivered to their cabin.

**ENTERTAINMENT**    Practically no one does entertainment as well as Royal Caribbean, which incorporates sprawling, high-tech cabaret stages into each of its ship's showrooms, some with a wall of video monitors to augment live performances. Entertainment begins before dinner and continues late, late into the night. There are musical acts, comedy acts, sock hops, toga parties, talent shows, and that great cruise favorite, karaoke. The Vegas-style shows are filled with all the razzle-dazzle passengers have come to expect, and these large-cast revues are among the best you'll find on any ship. Royal Caribbean uses 10-piece bands in its main showroom. Show bands and other lounge acts keep the music playing all over the ship. All of the entertainment options are first-rate.

**SERVICE**    Overall, service in the restaurants and cabins is friendly, accommodating, and efficient. You're likely to be greeted with a smile by someone polishing the brass in a stairwell. That said, big, bustling ships like Royal Caribbean's are no strangers to crowds and lines, and harried servers may not be able to get to you exactly when you'd like them to. Considering the vast armies of personnel required to maintain a line as large as Royal Caribbean, it's a miracle that staffers appear as motivated and enthusiastic as they do.

**Laundry** and **dry-cleaning** services are available on all the ships, but none have self-service laundromats.

**CRUISETOUR & ADD-ON PROGRAMS**    Royal Caribbean offers 10- and 12-night cruisetours combining a 7-night cruise with a 3- to 5-night land package in the Denali Corridor (between Anchorage and Fairbanks) in conjunction with the Gulf of Alaska itinerary of the *Vision of the Seas.* In addition, it features similar-length programs in the Canadian Rockies in combination with the Vancouver-based Inside Passage itineraries of the *Serenade* and the *Radiance.* Prices for the packages vary greatly according to cabin category, length of land itinerary, departure date, and other factors. A 12-night Denali package, for example, starts at $3,317 per person, double, while a 12-night Canadian Rockies package starts at $3,775 per person, double. In addition, RCL offers pre- and post-cruise hotel stays in Anchorage (from $239 per person, double) and Vancouver (from $89 per person, double).

## Vision of the Seas

Vision of the Seas *(photo: RCCL)*

## Specifications

| Size (in tons) | 78,491 | Officers | Norwegian/Int'l |
|---|---|---|---|
| Number of Cabins | 1,000 | Crew | 834 (Int'l) |
| Number of Outside Cabins | 593 | Passenger/Crew Ratio | 2.4 to 1 |
| Cabins with Verandas | 229 | Year Built | 1998 |
| Number of Passengers | 2,000 | Last Major Refurbishment | 2000 |

**THE SHIP IN GENERAL**   The *Legend of the Seas,* not in Alaska, was the first ship in Royal Caribbean's Vision class; the *Vision of the Seas* is another in that class, as are the *Grandeur, Rhapsody, Enchantment,* and *Splendour of the Seas.* The *Vision* is a true floating city, offering elegant trappings from multimillion-dollar art collections to a wide range of onboard facilities. Plenty of nice touches— sumptuous, big-windowed health clubs/spas with lots of health and beauty treatments, and loads of fine shopping, dining, and entertainment options— give the *Vision* the feel of a top-flight shore resort.

**CABINS**   Cabins are not large—inside cabins measure 138 square feet and outsides 153 square feet (compared to Carnival's 190 sq. ft. for standard cabins)—but do have small sitting areas. All cabins have TVs, telephones, and twin beds that convert to queen-size. They have ample storage space and well-lit, moderately sized bathrooms. TVs feature movies, news, and information channels, and excursion and debarkation talks are rebroadcast in-room just in case you missed something. Nearly a quarter of the cabins have private verandas, and about a third of the cabins are designed to accommodate third and fourth passengers. For big digs, check out the Royal Suite on the *Vision*—it measures a mammoth 1,150 square feet and even has a grand piano. Fourteen cabins on the ship are wheelchair accessible.

## Cabins & Rates

| Cabins | Brochure Rates | Bathtub | Fridge | Hair Dryer | Sitting Area | TV |
|---|---|---|---|---|---|---|
| Inside | $761–$881 | no | no | no | yes | yes |
| Outside | $961–$1,141 | no | some | no | yes | yes |
| Suites | $1,611–$5,211 | yes | yes | no | yes | yes |

**PUBLIC AREAS**    The *Vision* soars 10 stories above the waterline and features a seven-story, glass-walled atrium with glass elevators (a la Hyatt Regency) and a winding brass-trimmed staircase. At the top of the staircase, the Viking Crown Lounge affords a 360-degree view of the passing scenery. You'll also appreciate the view through the glass walls of the bi-level dining room. Actually, other than in the windowless casino and show lounge, there are great views to be found virtually everywhere on this ship—perfect for scoping glaciers.

A playroom, teen center, and video arcade provide plenty to keep kids happily occupied while parents relax, gamble, attend one of the many activities (there are dozens to select from each week, including informative nature lectures), take in a show in the theater, or dance the night away in the disco or one of numerous lounges and bars, which include a champagne/caviar bar and piano bar. Other rooms include a card room, library, several shops, and a conference room.

Meals are served both in the windowed, two-story dining room and in the casual open-seating Windjammer Café (an indoor/outdoor facility open for breakfast and lunch), so there's freedom as to when you dine and, since the menus in each venue are different, choices as to what you'll eat. Pizza is served in the Solarium.

**POOL, SPA & FITNESS FACILITIES**    The spa on the ship is one of the most attractive around—truly a soothing respite from the hubbub of ship life. It offers a wide selection of treatments, as well as the standard steam rooms and saunas. Adjacent to the spa, the spacious solarium has a pool, lounge chairs, floor-to-ceiling windows, and a retractable glass ceiling. This is a peaceful place to repose before or after a spa treatment, or any time at all. Surprisingly, the gym is small for the ship's size—and in comparison to those on Carnival's, Holland America's, and Celebrity's megaliners—but it's well equipped.

The main pool area has four whirlpools and there are two more in the Solarium. Glass windbreaks out on deck shelter an observatory (complete with stargazing equipment). The *Vision* also offers a cushioned jogging track and a half basketball court.

## Radiance of the Seas •
## Serenade of the Seas

Radiance of the Seas *(photo: RCCL)*

### Specifications

| Size (in tons) | 90,090 | Officers | Norwegian/Int'l |
|---|---|---|---|
| Number of Cabins | 1,250 | Crew | 859 (Int'l) |
| Number of Outside Cabins | 813 | Passenger/Crew Ratio | 2.3 to 1 |
| Cabins with Verandas | 577 | Year Built | 2001 |
| Number of Passengers | 2,550 | Last Major Refurbishment | n/a |

**THE SHIPS IN GENERAL**    These are Royal Caribbean's first ships of the 21st century, as well as being the first vessels in a new class, and they continue the line's tradition of being an innovator in the industry, with such features as a billiards room with custom-made, self-leveling tables (in case there are big waves), and a revolving bar in the disco.

The ships are designed to remind guests that they are at sea. With that goal in mind, they literally feature walls of glass through which to view the passing Alaska scenery. You won't even miss the views when you are in the 12-story lobby elevators because they, too, are made of glass and face the ocean. Even the Internet cafe has an ocean view!

These ships are slightly more upscale than the line's other vessels—Royal Caribbean seems to have borrowed a page from sister company Celebrity. They feature wood, marble, and lots of nice fabrics and artwork, adding up to a pretty, low-key decor that lets the views provide most of the visual drama.

**CABINS** Cabins on these vessels are larger than on the *Vision*—the smallest is 170 square feet—and more come with verandas than on the earlier vessels. All cabins are equipped with an interactive TV (which allows guests to check their bills, contact the purser's office, and, on some ships, make shore excursion reservations), a telephone, a computer jack, a vanity table, a refrigerator/minibar, and a hair dryer. Suites also come with a veranda, a sitting area with a sofa bed, a dry bar, a stereo and VCR, and a bathtub and double sinks. The Royal Suite on each ship has a separate bedroom (with a king-size bed) and living room, a whirlpool bathtub, and a baby grand piano. Family cabins and suites can accommodate five. Fourteen cabins are wheelchair accessible.

## Cabins & Rates

| Cabins | Brochure Rates | Bathtub | Fridge | Hair Dryer | Sitting Area | TV |
|--------|----------------|---------|--------|------------|--------------|-----|
| *Serenade of the Seas* | | | | | | |
| Inside | $899–$1,029 | no | yes | no | no | yes |
| Outside | $1,049–$1,419 | no | yes | yes | yes | yes |
| Suites | $1,699–$5,699 | yes | yes | yes | yes | yes |
| *Radiance of the Seas* | | | | | | |
| Inside | $799–$889 | no | yes | no | no | yes |
| Outside | $1,049–$1,374 | no | yes | yes | yes | yes |
| Suites | $1,649–$5,699 | yes | yes | yes | yes | yes |

**PUBLIC AREAS** These ships are full of little surprises. There's that billiards room we mentioned, and a card club where five tables are dedicated to poker. (The others are for bridge, chess, and so on.) You can, of course, also find more gaming options in the ships' massive French Art Nouveau–inspired Casino Royale. Bookworms will want to check out the combo bookstore and coffee shop (a first at sea).

The numerous cushy bars and lounges include a champagne bar and piano bar. If you tire of the ocean views, you can gaze into the atrium, eight decks below, from a portholelike window in the floor of the Crown and Anchor Lounge. The ships' Viking Crown Lounge holds the disco and its revolving bar, as well as an intimate cabaret area. The three-level theater on each ship recalls the glacial landscapes of not only Alaska but the North Pole as well. The elegant two-level main dining room features a grand staircase but is a rather noisy space. On both ships, casual buffet breakfasts and lunches are offered in the Windjammer Café, and casual dinners, with waiter service, are offered in the Windjammer Café and the Seaview Café. The ships also boast two alternative, reservations-only restaurants: Chops Grill, featuring steaks and chops, and Portofino, featuring Italian cuisine. Pizza is served in the Solarium. Other public rooms include a show lounge, conference center, library, shopping mall, and business center. For kids, there's a children's center equipped with computer and crafts stations. Teens get their own hangout space. There's also a video arcade.

**POOL, SPA & FITNESS FACILITIES**    For the active sort, there's a rock-climbing wall and a 9-hole golf course on the *Radiance* (the latter designed as a baroque garden, of all things). On both vessels, there is a nice spa (including a sauna and steam rooms), an oceanview fitness center with dozens of machines (including 18 Stairmaster treadmills), a jogging track, a sports court (including basketball), golf simulators (for those who like to play virtual golf), and three swimming pools—one outside, one enclosed (the indoor pool features an African theme complete with 17-ft.-high stone elephants and cascading water-falls), and the third a teen/kiddie pool with slide. Whirlpools can be found in the Solarium and near the outdoor pool.

# 6

# The Cruise Lines, Part 2: The Small Ships

**W**hereas big ships allow you to see Alaska while immersed in a vibrant, resort-like atmosphere, small ships allow you to see it from the waterline. There's no distraction from anything un-Alaskan—no glitzy interiors, no big shows or loud music, no casinos, no spas, and no crowds. The largest of these ships (the new stern-wheeler, *Empress of the North*—more on that later) carries only 235 passengers. On the small ships you're immersed in the 49th state from the minute you wake up to the minute you fall asleep, and for the most part, you're left alone to form your own opinions.

These vessels allow you to visit more isolated parts of the coast. Thanks to their smaller size and shallow draft (the amount of hull below the waterline), they can go places larger ships can't, and they have the flexibility to change their itineraries as opportunities arise—say, to go where whales have been sighted. Depending on the itinerary, ports of call might include popular stops such as Sitka or Ketchikan, lesser-visited areas such as Elfin Cove or Warm Springs Harbor, or a Tlingit Native village such as Kake. Plus, all itineraries include **glacier viewing and whale-watching.** Most of the itineraries also have time built in for passengers to explore the wilder parts of Alaska, ferrying passengers ashore for **hikes in wilderness areas** and, in some cases, carrying **sea kayaks and Zodiacs** for passenger use. Rather than glitzy entertainment, you'll likely get **informal and informative lectures** and, sometimes, video presentations on Alaskan wildlife, history, and Native culture. In most cases, at least some shore excursions are included in your cruise fare. (An exception is Clipper, which charges extra.) Meals are served in open seatings, so you can sit where and with whom you like, and time spent huddled on the outside decks scanning for whales fosters great camaraderie among passengers. It must be noted, though, that the size of the ships precludes any kind of spacious dining rooms. Generally, they're quite small—some people would even say cramped.

Cabins on these ships don't generally offer TVs or telephones, and they tend to be tiny and sometimes spartan. (See the individual reviews below for exceptions.) Most do not have e-mail access of any kind (though the *Clipper Odyssey* does). There are no stabilizers on most of these smaller ships, so the ride can be bumpy in rough seas. Since the vessels tend to spend most of their time in the somewhat protected waters of the Inside Passage, this is not usually a major concern. But it can be a problem when the vessels ply open seas.

Of the small ships, only Cruise West's *Spirit of '98* and *Spirit of Oceanus*, Clipper's *Clipper Odyssey*, and American West Steamboat Company's *Empress of the North* are even moderately wheelchair friendly. Small ships may not be the best choice for families with children, unless those kids are avid nature buffs and are able to keep themselves entertained without a lot of outside stimuli.

> **Tips** **Whale & Other Wildlife Info**
>
> See the appendix of this book for information on spotting and identifying whales and wildlife.

## READING THE REVIEWS

See the explanation of itineraries, prices, and ship reviews at the beginning of chapter 5, which applies equally to this chapter. In this chapter, you'll also see the following terms used to describe the various small-ship experiences:

- **Soft adventure:** These ships don't provide grandeur, organized activities, or entertainment but instead give you a really close-up Alaska experience. These ships often avoid large ports.
- **Active adventure:** These ships function less like cruise ships than like base camps. Passengers use them only to sleep and eat, getting off the ship for hiking and kayaking excursions every day.
- **Port-to-port:** These ships are for people who want to visit the popular Alaska ports (and some lesser-known ones) but also want the flexible schedules and maneuverability of a small ship and a more homey experience than you would find aboard a glitzy big ship.

## TIPPING

Tipping on small ships is a little different than on big ships. Tips on the following vessels are pooled among the crew. Below is a rundown of suggested tips (you are free to move the numbers up or down as you see fit).

Suggested tips, per passenger, for a 1-week cruise:

- **American Safari Cruises:** 5% to 10% of the cost of the cruise.
- **America West Steamboat Company:** $84 to $98 ($12–$14 per day).
- **Clipper:** $70 for the week ($10 per day), plus tips to bartenders at your discretion.
- **Cruise West:** $70 ($10 per day).
- **Glacier Bay Cruiseline:** $84 to $105 ($12–$15 per day).
- **Lindblad Expeditions:** $56 to $70 ($8–$10 per day).

*Note:* Rates in these reviews are brochure rates. Some discounts may apply, including early booking and last-minute offers, although small-ship lines do not traditionally discount their fares as much as bigger ship lines.

## 1 American Safari Cruises

19101 36th Ave. W., Suite 201, Lynnwood, WA 98036. ℂ **888/862-8881.** Fax 425/776-8889. www. amsafari.com.

Directed toward the slightly jaded high-end traveler, American Safari Cruises sails luxury soft-adventure cruises aboard three full-fledged luxury yachts.

**THE EXPERIENCE**    American Safari Cruises promises an intimate, all-inclusive yacht cruise to some of the more out-of-the-way stretches of the Inside Passage. The price is considerable, as is the pampering. The company books only 12 to 22 people per cruise, guaranteeing unparalleled flexibility, intimacy, and privacy. Once passenger interests become apparent, the expedition leader shapes the cruise around them. Black-bear aficionados can chug off in a Zodiac boat for a better look, active adventurers can explore the shoreline in one of the yacht's four kayaks, and lazier travelers can relax aboard ship. A crew-to-passenger ratio of about one to two ensures that a cold drink, a clever meal, or a sharp eagle-spotting eye is always nearby on the line's comfortable 120-foot ships.

## Pros

- **Almost private experience.** With only one or two dozen fellow passengers, it's like having a yacht to yourself. (In fact, if you have the money and the inclination, you can literally have the yacht to yourself; whole charters are available for a couple of weeks for a mere $120,000.)
- **Built-in shore excursions.** All off-ship excursions, including a flightseeing trip, are included in the cruise fare, as are drinks.
- **Night anchorages.** A great boon to light sleepers is that the route taken allows time for the vessels to overnight at anchor, making for quieter sleeping than aboard most ships, which travel through the night.

## Cons

- **The price.** Shore excursions and drinks are included, but even when you remove these costs, the price is still high. And, at a recommended 5% to 10% of the tariff, gratuities can add mightily to the outlay. You pay for all the luxury you get.

**THE FLEET**   The 22-passenger *Safari Quest* (1992) and the newest vessel, the 12-passenger *Safari Escape* (1993), are the closest things you'll find to private yachts in the Alaska cruise business. They're sleek, they're stylish, and they're as far as you can get from the megaship experience without owning your own boat. The 12-passenger *Safari Spirit,* built in 1991, has left the fleet after spending much of last year in the repair yard after having been damaged in a disagreement with a submerged object in the Canadian Inside Passage.

**PASSENGER PROFILE**   Passengers—almost always couples—tend to be more than comfortably wealthy and range from about 45 to 65 years of age. Most hope to get close to nature without sacrificing luxury. (You know the old saying: "Some people will go to the ends of the air-conditioned earth in search of adventure.") They've paid handsomely for food, drink, and service, all of which American Safari delivers—and then some! Dress is always casual, with comfort being the prime goal.

**DINING**   A shipboard chef assails guests with multiple-course meals and clever snacks (wild-mushroom cups, rack of lamb, thyme-infused king salmon, amaretto cheesecake, fresh-baked bread), barters with nearby fishing boats for the catch of the day, and raids local markets for the freshest fruits and vegetables—say, strawberries the size of a cub's paw and potent strains of basil and cilantro. Between meals, snacks such as Gorgonzola and brie with pears, walnuts, and table crackers are set out. Guests may always serve themselves from the ludicrously well-stocked bar, which during our visit had two kinds of sherry and four brands of gin alone, all of them premium.

**ACTIVITIES**   When passengers aren't eating or drinking, an expedition leader is helping them into Zodiac boats or kayaks to investigate shoreline black bears or prancing river otters, or to navigate fjords packed with ice floes and lolling seals. Expeditions include trips to boardwalked cannery towns and Tlingit villages,

Travel Tip: He who finds the best hotel deal has more to spend on facials involving knobbly vegetables.

Hello, the Roaming Gnome here. I've been nabbed from the garden and taken round the world. The people who took me are so terribly clever. They find the best offerings on Travelocity. For very little cha-ching. And that means I get to be pampered and exfoliated till I'm pink as a bunny's doodah.

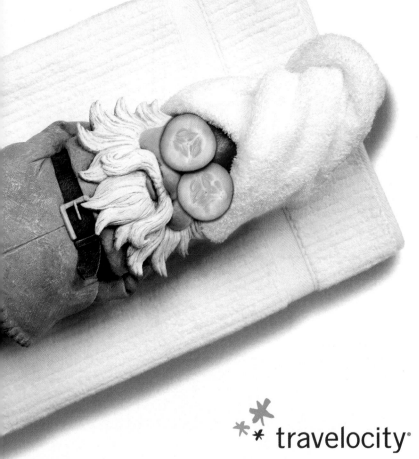

travelocity®

1-888-TRAVELOCITY / travelocity.com / America Online Keyword: Travel

## American Safari Cruises Fleet Itineraries

| Ship | Itineraries |
|---|---|
| Safari Escape | **8-night Inside Passage:** North- and southbound between Juneau and Prince Rupert, B.C., and Juneau and Sitka, visiting Foggy Cove, B.C., Ketchikan, Misty Fjords, Traitors Cove, Meyers Chuck, Wrangell Narrows, Canoe Cove, Petersburg, Frederick Sound, and Tracy Arm.* |
| Safari Quest | **7-night Inside Passage:** North- and southbound between Juneau and Sitka, visiting Tracy Arm, Admiralty Island, Frederick Sound, Thomas Bay, Petersburg (with LeConte Glacier flightseeing trip included), the Native village of Kake, Red Bluff Bay on Baranof Island, Warm Springs Bay, Chatham Channel, and Schultz Bay.* |

*\* In addition to the itineraries above, the ship offers 14-night repositioning cruises between Seattle and Juneau (from Seattle to Juneau in May and the reverse in Sept). Rates start at $4,395.*

where local people receive the yachts more personally and gracefully than they might a larger ship. Activities throughout the day are well spaced, with many opportunities to see wildlife.

From time to time, local bush pilots may swoop down for a landing beside the ships and take two or three passengers for a whirl over a glacier or a nearby fjord. Because these are private operations, they're not included in the cruise fare.

**CHILDREN'S PROGRAM** None—these aren't ships for kids, unless you charter the whole thing and bring your extended family. (The ships are small enough that that's a realistic option for some, but it will cost you!)

**ENTERTAINMENT** A big-screen TV in the main lounge forms a natural center for impromptu lectures during the day and movie watching at night. Guests may choose from a library of 100-odd videotapes (guests in the Owner's and Captain's staterooms have TV/VCRs in their cabins) or opt for a casual game of cards or Scrabble in the public rooms upstairs.

At the beginning or end of a trip, the crew and passengers gather for an all-you-can-eat salmon bake and local saloon crawl, and from time to time, the ship docks at a town with a measure of nightlife—at the least, you may get to shoot a game of pool and have a drink among the locals.

**SERVICE** Crew members cosset passengers cheerfully and discreetly, fussing over such details as the level of cilantro in lunchtime dishes or making elaborate cocktails from the fully stocked open bar. They've even been known to call ahead to upcoming anchorages to arrange for a passenger's favorite brand of beer to be brought aboard. Laundry service is not available on board except in "emergency situations." (The company recommends, by the way, a crew gratuity of 5%–10% at the end of each voyage; as we said, a hefty sum when you're paying, say, $4,500 for a cruise.)

**CRUISETOURS & ADD-ON PROGRAMS** There are no organized land tours for 2005. Instead the line will feature a "sampling" of 1- to 6-day exclusive shore adventures in Alaska and British Columbia. When clients book a cruise, they can inquire about what's available and the line will help tailor a land-tour program geared toward their specific interests. Also see the line's website for information on these opportunities.

# Safari Escape •
# Safari Quest

Safari Quest
*(photo: American Safari Cruises)*

## Specifications

| Size (in tons) | n/a* | Officers | American |
|---|---|---|---|
| Number of Cabins | 6/11 | Crew | 6/9 (American) |
| Number of Outside Cabins | 6/11 | Passenger/Crew Ratio | 2 to 1 (approx.) |
| Cabins with Verandas | 0 | Year Built | 1993/1992 |
| Number of Passengers | 12/22 | Last Major Refurbishment | 2001/2000 |

*\* These ships' sizes were measured using a different scale than the others in this book, so comparison is not possible.*

**THE SHIPS IN GENERAL**    More private yachts than cruise ships, American Safari Cruises' vessels are an oddity in the cruise community: One old tar we met called them "Tupperware ships," a pretty accurate description for their exceedingly sleek, contoured, Ferrari-looking exteriors. Inside, there are very few areas out of bounds, lending to the feel that you're vacationing on an impossibly rich friend's space-age yacht.

**CABINS**    Sleeping quarters are comfortable and clean, with large, firm beds; adequate light; and art (of varying quality) on the walls. Bathrooms are roomy, even in the standard cabins; cabins on the *Safari Escape* have showers only. The showers shoot a steady but not spectacular stream of reliably hot water. The Admiral's Cabins have a large picture window and a small sitting area. Down below, deluxe rooms are tidy, filled with a surprising amount of natural light, and fairly spacious. A few of the top staterooms have televisions with VCRs.

There are no special facilities for travelers with disabilities and no cabins designed specifically for single occupancy.

## Cabins & Rates

| Cabins | Brochure Rates | Bathtub | Fridge | Hair Dryer | Sitting Area | TV |
|---|---|---|---|---|---|---|
| *Safari Escape* | | | | | | |
| Outside | $3,895–$4,795 | no | no | yes | some | yes |
| *Safari Quest* | | | | | | |
| Outside | $3,990–$4,995 | no | no | yes | some | yes |

**PUBLIC AREAS**    Sitting rooms are intimate and luxurious, almost as if they had been transported intact from a spacious suburban home. Four or five prime vantages for spotting wildlife (one is a hot tub!) ensure as little or as much privacy as you desire. All public rooms have generous panoramic windows to gaze out of when you can't be on deck because of cold or inclement weather. All three meals are served at a wooden table in a casual room, usually when the ship is at anchor. Expect paper napkins at lunch and cloth serviettes at dinner. There are 24-hour coffee/tea facilities, a fully stocked open bar, and a small library/video library.

**POOL, SPA & FITNESS FACILITIES**    There's a stair-stepper on *Safari Quest,* and sea kayaks for passenger use: eight on *Safari Quest,* and two on *Safari Escape;* both ships have a hot tub on the top deck.

## 2 American West Steamboat Company

2101 4th Ave., Suite 1150, Seattle, WA 98121. © **800/434-1232** or 206/292-9606. Fax 206/340-0975. www.columbiarivercruise.com.

Although it clearly belongs in the small-ship category, the *Empress of the North* is quite a bit bigger than the others in its field. Carrying 235 passengers, it has almost twice the capacity of the second largest of the small ships. In a very real sense, this ship belongs in a whole new category—stern-wheelers. There had not been a paddle-wheel-driven ship in the Inside Passage for a century or more until the *Empress of the North* debuted there 3 years ago. The *Empress* operates with its companion ship, *Queen of the West*, on the Columbia/Snake rivers when not in Alaska. Positioning a ship of that design in the waters of the 49th state was a bold, and apparently successful, move, which is being continued in 2005. Its owner, by the way, is . . . a rail company! Oregon Rail Corp., of Portland, Oregon, owned by entrepreneur Henry Hillman Jr., is the parent company of America West Steamboat. This year the company has tweaked its itineraries. Instead of 11-night voyages between Juneau and Seattle, the *Empress* will concern itself primarily with 7-night round trip sailings out of Juneau. The new routing keeps the vessel in the waters of the Inside Passage rather than in the open seas of the Pacific out of Seattle. It has also dropped Sitka, on the western side of Baranof Island, from the itinerary, thereby again offering passengers greater protection from rough going. The ship will, however, make an 11-day Seattle–Juneau and Juneau–Seattle positioning cruise at the beginning and end of the season.

**THE EXPERIENCE**   Clearly, the appeal here is the nostalgia. Pure Americana—that's what the *Empress of the North* and *Queen of the West* represent. Steamboats—both side-wheelers and stern-wheelers (like these two)—were how most of the gold-rush pioneers made their way to Alaska to join the hunt for Yukon riches more than a century ago. Who can travel on such a vessel in Alaska and not think of the Stampede of '98, of the glory days of riverboats on the mighty Mississippi and other great American waterways, of calliopes, of Mark Twain, of banjo-strumming performers on the upper decks with excited townsfolk on the riverbank swaying to the music? We may not have been around when these colorful vessels held sway over America's rivers and waterways. But we've all read about them.

The experience is laid-back: no hassle, no heavy entertainment schedule, no formality. The boats move slowly—top speed is about 14 knots on the open seas. That leaves plenty of time for contemplation of the passing scenery. The unstuffy atmosphere makes it easy to meet and mingle with complete strangers who quickly become friends.

### Pros
- **Nostalgia.** The ship has a romantic, old-time atmosphere.
- **Lots of private verandas.** All outside cabins and more than 90% of cabins on the *Empress* have verandas.
- **Shore excursions included.** Most explorations ashore are covered in the price.

### Cons
- **Shallow draft.** Despite the presence of state-of-the-art stabilizers, ships with drafts as shallow as that of the *Empress* are liable to feel heavy seas more than some other ships. But that's not a huge problem in the protected waters of the Inside Passage.

## American West Steamboat Company Itinerary

| Ship | Itineraries |
|---|---|
| **Empress of the North** | **7-night Inside Passage:** Round-trip Juneau, visiting Skagway, Wrangell, Ketchikan, and cruising in Icy Strait, Misty Fjord, and Tracy Arm. |

\* *The itinerary on the pre-, and post-season 11-day cruises features Petersburg, Vancouver, and Victoria as well.*

**THE FLEET**    *Empress of the North,* built in 2003, is a fleet mate of the 163-passenger *Queen of the West* (1995), another stern-wheeler. (Hmmm . . . wonder if an empress outranks a queen?) The latter is in service on the Columbia and Snake rivers year-round.

**PASSENGER PROFILE**    Not necessarily filthy rich, but probably comfortably off. And they are experienced cruisers. Not many people would choose a stern-wheeler in open water for their first experience at sea. Many of them have already tried the *Empress of the North* or the *Queen of the West* on the Columbia/Snake rivers. They're not looking for wild adventure ashore or frenzied activity on board.

**DINING**    Casually elegant, with an emphasis on local produce. Don't look for five or six choices on the menu. With the number of passengers on these ships, it's difficult to get too extensive. But nobody ever left the table hungry.

**ACTIVITIES**    Not a lot of organized fun and games. *Empress* and *Queen* passengers don't require it and don't want it. A lecturer accompanies each cruise, offering insights into the passing scenery and cultures. But don't look for kayaks off the back of the vessel, or scuba diving, or anything of that nature.

**CHILDREN'S PROGRAM**    There isn't one.

**ENTERTAINMENT**    Live entertainment—music for dancing—begins in the early evening in the showrooms and continues after dinner in the Paddlewheel Lounge on both ships. Local performers will board in port to present Native song and dance shows.

**SERVICE**    All American, which isn't unusual in the small-ship category these days. The seeming lack of sophistication shown by some of the crew is refreshing. It's part of their appeal and you can't help but become friends with them in very short order.

**CRUISETOUR & ADD-ON PROGRAMS**    The company does not offer any cruisetour or add-on programs.

## Empress of the North

Empress of the North
*(photo: American West
Steamboat Company)*

### Specifications

| Size (in tons) | 3,388 | Officers | American |
|---|---|---|---|
| Number of Cabins | 112 | Crew | 84 (American) |
| Number of Outside Cabins | 112 | Passenger/Crew Ratio | 2.8 to 1 |
| Cabins with Verandas | 105 | Year Built | 2003 |
| Number of Passengers | 235 | Last Major Refurbishment | n/a |

**THE SHIP IN GENERAL**   This ship got—and continues to get—a lot of attention in Alaska because of its distinctive profile and the historical musings it evokes. It has four decks, two lounges, and two elevators. Although it is a stern-wheeler, it must be noted that the 360-foot ship does have other propulsion capability—for the technically minded it has two Z drives which rotate 360 degrees and which provide additional power in any direction.

**CABINS**   Cabins are large by small-ship standards. The least expensive is a roomy 200 square feet and the accommodations range up to two-bedroom suites measuring 525 square feet. All of the cabins have views of the ocean and 105 (out of 112) also have verandas. Two of the cabins are wheelchair accessible.

## Cabins & Rates

| Cabins | Brochure Rates* | Bathtub | Fridge | Hair Dryer | Sitting Area | TV |
|--------|-----------------|---------|--------|------------|--------------|-----|
| Outside | $2,999–$4,549 | no | yes | no | yes | yes |
| Suites | $5,139 | no | yes | no | yes | yes |

*\* Rates are for 8-day Alaska sailings.*

**PUBLIC AREAS**   Elegance and opulence are the bywords in the *Empress*'s public rooms. Plush maroon and dark green–hued carpeting, drapes, and upholstery; windows all over the place; two elevators; comfy lounge seating—it's all here. And we must say that one of the most interesting rooms afloat is the Paddlewheel Lounge aft, from which tipplers and dancers can be mesmerized by the thrum, thrum of the paddle wheel seen through the floor-to-ceiling window.

**POOL, SPA & FITNESS FACILITIES**   There are none of any consequence.

## 3 Clipper Cruise Line

11969 Westline Industrial Dr., St. Louis, MO 63146. ℂ **800/325-0010** or 314/655-6700. Fax 314/655-6670. www.clippercruise.com.

Not your typical cruise vessels, these down-to-earth, comfortable small ships focus on offbeat ports of call, learning, and mingling with your fellow passengers. It's the ideal small-ship cruise for people who've tried Holland America or Princess and now want a more intimate cruise experience.

**THE EXPERIENCE**   Clipper caters to mature, seasoned, easygoing, relatively affluent, and well-traveled older passengers seeking a casual vacation experience. Being small ships, the ambience is intimate and conducive to making new friends. You won't find any glitter, glitz, or Las Vegas–style gambling here.

The line is particularly strong in providing information on the nature, history, and culture of the ports visited, and each ship carries one or more naturalists on every sailing. These experts also accompany some shore excursions. A cruise director helps organize the days, answers questions, and assists passengers.

Unfortunately, like many of the American-crewed small ships, cruise rates are not cheap.

### Pros

- **Great learning opportunities.** Naturalists and educators sail with the ships, offering informal lectures on board and accompanying guests on shore excursions.
- **Informal atmosphere.** No need to dress up here—everything's casual.

- **Young, enthusiastic American crew.** Although they may not be the most experienced, they're sweet, engaging, and hardworking, and add a homey feel to the trip.

## Cons
- **No stabilizers.** If you hit some choppy waters and you're prone to seasickness, good luck.
- **Noisy engines on *Yorktown Clipper.*** If you can help it, don't book a cabin on the lowest deck (Main Deck), where noise from the engines can get quite loud.

**THE FLEET**   The 138-passenger *Yorktown Clipper* (1988) is a spacious, comfortable small ship that's an ideal choice for someone who's sailed with a big-ship line and wants to try a small-ship experience. In 1999 the line acquired the more luxurious 120-passenger ***Clipper Odyssey,*** which was built in 1989 and previously sailed as the *Oceanic Odyssey* from Spice Islands Cruises of Bali, Indonesia.

**PASSENGER PROFILE**   The majority of Clipper passengers are well-traveled, 50+ couples who are attracted by the casual intimacy of small ships and by the opportunities Clipper offers for learning something about the places its ships visit. Most passengers are well educated though not academic, casual though not sloppily so, and adventurous in the sense that they're up for a little hiking but are happy to be able to get back to their comfortable cabins or have a drink in the lounge afterwards. As a company spokesperson notes, "We provide a soft adventure for travelers who may shy away from roughing it, and we think of ourselves not as a cruise line, but as a travel company that just happens to have ships."

Clipper attracts a remarkably high number of repeat passengers: From 40% to 45% on any given cruise have sailed with the line before, and many have also sailed with other small-ship lines such as Lindblad Expeditions and American Caribbean Cruise Line (ACCL). On one Clipper cruise Fran took in the Caribbean, repeaters were thanked verbally at the captain's cocktail party, and the list went on for several minutes. Many, many passengers were on board for their second Clipper cruise, and many more were taking their third or fourth, but the winner that day was a husband and wife who were on their eighth. That must say something about customer satisfaction!

**DINING**   The fare is all-American, prepared by graduates of the Culinary Institute of America, and incorporates local ingredients whenever possible. Although relatively simple in ingredients and presentation, the cuisine easily equals all but the best that is served aboard mainstream megaships.

Breakfast is served in both the lounge and dining room, with cereals, fruit, toast, and pastries at the former and a full breakfast menu in the latter. Similarly, you can create your own sandwich in the lounge from an assortment of cold cuts, or get a full lunch in the dining room. Set lunches offer a hot luncheon platter (perhaps crab cakes, baby back ribs, or pasta primavera); a lighter, cold entree (Cobb salad, chicken Caesar salad, seafood salad, and more); and one or another kind of omelet, and there's always the option of a platter of fresh fruit and cottage cheese.

Dinner is served in a single open seating in the dining room, at tables set up for four to six, and offers four courses with five main entree options: seafood (perhaps herb-marinated halibut, stuffed lobster tail, or Chilean sea bass), a meat entree (such as roast duck, veal Marsala, or prime rib), a vegetarian entree (maybe marinated grilled portobello mushrooms, vegetarian lasagna, or 10-vegetable couscous), a pasta entree, and a "starch and vegetables" entree (steamed vegetables over saffron rice).

## Clipper Fleet Itineraries

| Ship | Itineraries |
| --- | --- |
| Clipper Odyssey | **14-night Gulf of Alaska/Bering Sea:** Sails between Anchorage and Petropavlovsk visiting Nome, Gambell, Boxer Bay, St. Matthew Island, St. Paul Island, Chagaluk Island, Kiska, Kommandor Island, Utashud Island, and Vestnik Bay. |
| Yorktown Clipper | **7-night Inside Passage:** Round-trip from Juneau, visiting Skagway, Haines, Elfin Cove, Idaho Inlet, Glacier Bay, Sitka, and Tracy Arm. |

Clipper can accommodate dietary preferences or restrictions if you give the staff notice before your trip.

Although the onboard dress code is casual at all times, most passengers tend to get a bit more gussied up at dinner, and men may even wear jackets at the captain's welcome-aboard and farewell parties (though you can get away with a nice shirt and slacks if you don't want to pack the fancies).

In the lounge you can get coffee, tea, iced tea, orange and cranberry juice, and lemonade 24 hours a day. Some kind of crunchy snack food (Goldfish crackers, cashew nuts, rice crackers, and so on) is also on the bar during the day. The famous (and really delicious) "Clipper Chipper" cookies are set out here as well in the late afternoon, and hors d'oeuvres are served here before dinner. These may include mushroom caps stuffed with escargot or perhaps smoked salmon with petite pieces of toast.

As aboard almost all small ships, there is no room service unless you're too ill to attend meals.

**ACTIVITIES** By design, these ships don't offer much in the way of typical cruise ship pastimes. Instead, they offer activities designed to focus your attention on the area you're visiting, giving you the opportunity to return home from your vacation not only relaxed but enriched. Throughout the cruise, onboard naturalists offer a series of informal lectures. Organized shore excursions are offered at each port (not included in the price), including flightseeing, sport fishing, and city tours with commentary by local residents. E-mail access is offered on the *Clipper Odyssey* only: You can send and receive e-mail from a shipboard account (but you can't check your e-mail back home) for about $1 a page.

**CHILDREN'S PROGRAM** None.

**ENTERTAINMENT** As is true of the vast majority of small-ship companies, Clipper offers no casino, no dancing girls, no comedy and/or magic acts—nothing, in fact, that is usually standard-issue on one of the megas (except for the occasional second-run movie shown in the lounge). That said, the line does bring aboard local musicians and/or dancers, when possible, to perform in the evenings.

The *Yorktown Clipper* has an observation lounge where you'll find a bar, a piano, and a small library well stocked with books on Alaska history, culture, nature, and geography (as well as a smattering of bestsellers). The *Clipper Odyssey* also has an observation lounge with a piano and a second lounge, as well as a very small gym and separate library.

**SERVICE** Service staffers aboard Clipper's ships are basically collegiate or post-collegiate Americans having an adventure before getting on with whatever it is they're getting on with. In other words, these aren't the same folks you'll find serving at the Four Seasons. They're amateurs—fresh-faced, willing to work, and happy to help, but don't expect them to bow when you cross the threshold. Not that you'd want them to—which is, we think, the point. As Clipper's demographic base is generally couples over 50, we suspect the line has a nefarious plot to staff its ships with young men and women of approximately the same age as passengers' children and grandchildren, who (unlike those real offspring) *actually do what you tell them to.* What a refreshing change!

There is neither room service, nor are there any laundry facilities or services. In a nod to water conservation and a more detergent-free environment, bathroom towels are changed on an as-needed basis only: If you want fresh towels, leave the old ones on the bathroom floor; if you don't, leave them hanging.

**CRUISETOURS & ADD-ON PROGRAMS** A 4-night Fairbanks/Denali/Anchorage package by motorcoach and train is offered for $1,695 per person in addition to cruise fare. Pre- and post-cruise hotel options in Seattle start at $115 per person.

## Clipper Odyssey

Clipper Odyssey
*(photo: Clipper Cruise Line)*

### Specifications

| Size (in tons) | 5,200 | Officers | International |
|---|---|---|---|
| Number of Cabins | 64 | Crew | 72 (American/Int'l) |
| Number of Outside Cabins | 64 | Passenger/Crew Ratio | 1.8 to 1 |
| Cabins with Verandas | 9 | Year Built | 1989 |
| Number of Passengers | 128 | Last Major Refurbishment | 1999 |

**THE SHIP IN GENERAL** Acquired by Clipper in 1999, the *Clipper Odyssey* has been sailing in the Far East for most of the time since then. It's Clipper's sleekest and most luxurious vessel, and sails a very limited number of beyond-the-norm, even exotic, Alaska itineraries (see above).

**CABINS** Cabins are all outside, with twin lower beds that can be converted to a single queen-size bed. All have a small sitting area, and the two top levels have small private verandas—almost unheard of on a small ship, and completely unheard of on the other small ships sailing in Alaska.

This vessel is one of only four small ships in Alaska that has an elevator, making it a better bet than most for people with mobility problems. (The other three with elevators are Cruise West's *Spirit of Oceanus* and *Spirit of '98,* and American West's *Empress of the North.*) All public rooms and one cabin are wheelchair accessible.

### Cabins & Rates

| Cabins | Brochure Rates* | Bathtub | Fridge | Hair Dryer | Sitting Area | TV |
|---|---|---|---|---|---|---|
| Outside | $5,630–$7,190 | yes | yes | yes | yes | yes |
| Suites | $8,270 | yes | yes | yes | yes | yes |

*\* Rates for 14-night Alaska cruise.*

**PUBLIC AREAS**   The *Odyssey* boasts more extensive public rooms than your average small ship, with the usual lounge/bar and dining room augmented by a second lounge, a library, and a beauty salon.

**POOL, SPA & FITNESS FACILITIES**   If these amenities are important to you, the *Odyssey* is just about the only small ship in Alaska that offers them. It's got a heated outdoor pool, a small gym, a Jacuzzi, and a dedicated jogging track.

## Yorktown Clipper

Yorktown Clipper
*(photo: Clipper Cruise Line)*

### Specifications

| | | | |
|---|---|---|---|
| Size (in tons) | 2,354 | Officers | American |
| Number of Cabins | 69 | Crew | 40 (American/Int'l) |
| Number of Outside Cabins | 69 | Passenger/Crew Ratio | 3.5 to 1 |
| Cabins with Verandas | 0 | Year Built | 1988 |
| Number of Passengers | 138 | Last Major Refurbishment | n/a |

**THE SHIP IN GENERAL**   The impression we kept coming back to when sitting in the spacious lounge of this ship, or in our cozy cabin, was that someone had taken one of the Holland America or Princess ships and shrunk it to a fraction of its normal size. Though not boasting the multitude of public rooms of those large ships, the four-deck *Yorktown Clipper* offers similar clean styling and easy-to-live-with colors, fabrics, and textures, while also offering a small ship's ability to take passengers into shallow-water ports and other out-of-the-way locations away from the megaship crowds.

The ship has no elevator, nor does it have any cabins designed for passengers with disabilities.

**CABINS**   Although smallish (average cabin size is 123–140 sq. ft.), cabins are very pleasantly styled, with blond-wood writing desks, chairs, and bed frames; "not really there"-style paintings (better than a bare wall, we guess); and a goodly amount of closet space, plus additional storage under the beds. There are no phones or TVs, but each cabin does have music channels. There are no cabin safes as such, but two drawers in the closet can be locked.

Cabins come in six different categories, differentiated mostly by their location rather than their size. Each has two lower-level beds, permanently fixed in either an L-shaped corner configuration or as two units set parallel to one another (taller passengers—over 6 ft., 2 in.—would be better off with the L-shaped arrangement, as the others are abutted by wall and headboard and are not much longer than 6 ft., 4 in.). No cabins have beds that can be pushed together to form a king- or queen-size, so these ships are off the list for honeymooners or congenitally randy couples. Some cabins contain upper berths that unfold from the wall to accommodate a third person.

All cabins have picture windows except for a few Category 1 cabins on the Main Deck, which have portholes. All cabins on the Promenade Deck and a handful at the stern on the Lounge Deck open onto the outdoors (rather than onto an interior corridor). While we normally prefer this layout because it makes us feel closer to nature, here it doesn't seem to matter because the doors open out—meaning you can't really leave the door open to breezes without blocking the deck. It's worth noting that passengers in the Promenade Deck cabins should be careful when opening their doors from the inside, lest you end up braining one of your poor fellow passengers walking around the promenade.

Cabin bathrooms are compact, though not nearly so tiny as aboard many of Cruise West's and all of Glacier Bay's ships. Toilets are wedged between the shower and sink area and may prove tight for heavier people. Bathrooms have showers but no tubs.

There are no special facilities on board for travelers with disabilities and no cabins designed specifically for single occupancy.

## Cabins & Rates

| Cabins | Brochure Rates* | Bathtub | Fridge | Hair Dryer | Sitting Area | TV |
|---|---|---|---|---|---|---|
| Outside | $2,450–$3,730 | no | no | no | no | no |

*Rates for 7-night sailings.*

**PUBLIC AREAS**   As on board most small ships, there are only two public areas: the dining room and the Observation Lounge. The pleasant lounge has big windows, a bar, a small but informative library, a piano (that gets little use), and enough space to comfortably seat everyone on board for lectures and meetings. It's the main hub of onboard activity. The dining room is spacious and comfortable. Other than that, there are no cozy hideaways on board other than your cabin. There is, however, plenty of outdoor deck space for wildlife- and glacier-watching.

**POOL, SPA & FITNESS FACILITIES**   For exercise, you can jog or walk around the deck (18 laps = 1 mile). Other than this, there are no exercise facilities.

## 4 Cruise West

2401 4th Ave., Suite 700, Seattle, WA 98121. ℂ **800/426-7702** or 206/441-8687. Fax 206/441-4757. www.cruisewest.com.

Like all small ships, Cruise West's ships can navigate in tight areas such as Misty Fjords and Desolation Sound, visit tiny ports such as Petersburg and Haines, and scoot up close to shore for wildlife-watching. But these are not adventure cruises. Like Clipper Cruise Line's itineraries, these trips are for people who want to visit Alaska's coastal communities and see its wilderness areas up close and in a relaxed, comfortable, small-scale environment without big-ship distractions. They're not for people who want to spend their days hiking and kayaking—unless they really want to, that is.

**THE EXPERIENCE**   The operative words here are casual, relaxed, and friendly. At sea, the lack of organized activities on the line's port-to-port itineraries leaves you free to scan for wildlife, peruse the natural sights, or read a book. In port—whether one of the large, popular ports or a less visited one—the line arranges some novel, intimate shore excursions, such as a visit with local artists at their homes outside Haines or an educational walking tour led by a Native guide in Ketchikan.

## Like a Road Trip, but by Boat

In addition to the cruises profiled here, Cruise West offers what it calls its **"Daylight Yacht Tours"** series of 5-day packages aboard the 70-passenger motor yacht *Sheltered Seas*. The craft, which has no sleeping accommodations, cruises Alaska's waterways by day and deposits you at a hotel each night. Additional travel by rail or motorcoach allows visits to Fairbanks and Denali National Park, and the timing of your arrival in ports—generally in the early evening—means you'll be hitting the town after the crowds from larger cruise ships have left. If you can't decide between cruising Alaska and seeing it by land, this is an option worth exploring. **Rates:** 4-night trips from $2,299. Prices include all shore accommodations, port charges, luggage handling, and meals aboard ship.

## Pros

- **The staff.** The line's friendly, enthusiastic staffs are a big plus, making guests feel right at home.
- **Great shore excursions.** Cruise West's list includes some real gems.
- **Comfort.** A couple of the line's ships—the *Spirit of Endeavour,* a sleek, yachtlike vessel, and *Spirit of '98,* a re-creation of a late-19th-century coastal steamer—offer snazzier surroundings than most of their small-ship competitors. And the line's newest vessel, *Spirit of Oceanus,* which entered the fleet in April 2001, is its nicest ship yet.
- **Itineraries.** Because the line has six ships in Alaska service, it's able to offer more of the varied itineraries that aficionados have come to expect from small ships.

## Cons

- **Wacky bathrooms on some ships.** Some of the line's ships have the kind of awkward, head-style bathrooms that are common to many small vessels.

**THE FLEET**    The 96-passenger *Spirit of '98* (1984) is the most distinctive small ship in Alaska, having been built as a replica of a 19th-century coastal steamer. It was even featured as such in the Kevin Costner film *Wyatt Earp.* The 102-passenger *Spirit of Endeavour* (1983) formerly sailed as the *Newport Clipper* of Clipper Cruise Line and has a similar design and the same kind of low-key, comfortable feel as that line's current *Yorktown Clipper.* The 78-passenger *Spirit of Alaska* (1980) and *Spirit of Columbia* (1979) and the 84-passenger *Spirit of Discovery* (1976) are all extremely similar ships, with less fancy decors than the *Endeavour* and *'98.* On the other hand, the line's newest ship, the 114-passenger *Spirit of Oceanus* (1984), the former *Renaissance V* of Renaissance Cruises, is the line's most luxurious ship.

**PASSENGER PROFILE**    Passengers with Cruise West tend to be older (typically around 60–75), financially stable and well educated, and consider themselves adventuresome. When we sailed the first time, there were a good number of current or retired physicians and teachers aboard, a smattering of farmers and ranchers, a pair of behavioral psychologists, several computer specialists and

## Cruise West Fleet Itineraries

| Ship | Itineraries |
| --- | --- |
| Spirit of '98 | **7-night:** One-way between Juneau and Ketchikan or reverse, visiting Desolation Sound, Misty Fjords, Frederick Sound, Tracy Arm, and Glacier Bay. |
| Spirit of Alaska | **8-night Inside Passage:*** Round-trip from Juneau, visiting Kake and Sitka and cruising Glacier Bay, and around Admiralty, Chichagof, and Baranof islands. |
| Spirit of Discovery | **8-night Inside Passage:*** Same as *Spirit of Alaska.* |
| Spirit of Endeavour | **7-night Inside Passage:*** Same as *Spirit of '98.* |
| Spirit of Columbia | **7-night Wilderness Waterways:*** Round-trip from Juneau, visiting Tracy Arm, Endicott Arm, Sitka, Glacier Bay, and Icy Strait. |
| Spirit of Oceanus | **15-night Bering Sea:*** Cruise between Anchorage and Nome, visiting Homer, Kodiak, Katmai National Park, Dutch Harbor, the Pribilof Islands, and Provideniya and Yanrakynnot (Russia). |

*\* Includes one pre- or post-cruise hotel overnight.*

other high-tech types, and a few 30-ish and 40-ish adults traveling with their single parents. On another cruise, the passenger list included a group of 30-odd Yale alumni, including one delightful, 80-something lady from New Haven (widow of a Yale professor) who didn't miss a thing—hiking, kayaking, the lot. Passengers such as these want to visit Alaska's ports and see its natural wonders in a relaxed, dress-down atmosphere—and on this count, Cruise West delivers.

**DINING**   Breakfast, lunch, and dinner are served at set times at one unassigned seating. An early riser's buffet is set out in the lounge before the set breakfast time, but if you're a late riser you'll miss breakfast entirely, as no room service is available. A late-afternoon snack is provided every day to tide passengers over until dinner, and the chef will occasionally whip up a batch of cookies. At all meals the fare is primarily home-style American—not overly fancy, but tasty and varied. Chefs make a point of stocking up on fresh salmon and crabs while in port. The galley can accommodate special diets (vegetarian, kosher, low salt, low fat), but make special arrangements for this when you book your cruise. Service can sometimes be slow, as each waitperson must cover several tables, though when we overslept coming into Skagway and thought we'd only have time for toast and coffee, our waiter assured us he could have scrambled eggs and hash browns out in 30 seconds—and, amazingly, he did.

**ACTIVITIES**   As with other small ships, Cruise West vessels don't offer much in the way of diversions. What onboard activities there are might include post-dinner discussions of the port or region to be visited the next day, afternoon talks by expert guests while at sea, and perhaps a tour of the engine room or galley. (On one *Spirit of Endeavour* cruise, Jerry was somewhat nonplussed to find that one of the lecturers was a forester whose presentation would be on the area's trees. Ho hum, thought Jerry. Guess what? The speaker turned out to be highly entertaining and informative. Just goes to show you—never dismiss any speaker without a fair hearing!) Onboard fitness options are limited to the exercise bike and/or Stairmaster that each ship carries. One shore excursion in each port is included in the cruise fare, and there are additional options for an extra charge.

A cheerful and knowledgeable **cruise coordinator** accompanies each trip to answer passengers' questions about Alaska's flora, fauna, geology, and history; and

Forest Service rangers, local fishers, and Native Alaskans sometimes come aboard to teach about the culture and industry of the state. Binoculars are provided for onboard use. If you have your heart set on a port activity that the line doesn't offer—say, salmon fishing in Sitka—the cruise coordinator will do his or her best to set something up for you.

**CHILDREN'S PROGRAM**    None.

**ENTERTAINMENT**    Videos are available on some ships for in-cabin use, and organized entertainment, such as it is, is sometimes provided by the crew or by your fellow passengers, often in a humbly (and perhaps appropriately) titled "No-Talent Night" or in a game of Truth or Dare.

**SERVICE**    The line strives for a family feeling, and toward this end, employs a young, energetic crew (mostly college students) who radiate enthusiasm and perform all shipboard tasks, waiting tables at breakfast, making beds and cleaning cabins, polishing the handrails, and unloading baggage at journey's end. They may not be consummate pros, but passengers tend to find them adorable. Just be sure you don't come aboard expecting luxury and white-glove service. Crew members once told us of being sent into crisis mode when the occupants of the ship's most deluxe suite went into spasms because they couldn't order room service. If you see yourself in that scenario, cruise elsewhere.

**CRUISETOURS & ADD-ON PROGRAMS**    Cruise West offers land extensions in Denali, Prince William Sound, and the Interior Region, around Fairbanks in combination with its cruises; packages vary greatly in price depending on the cruise length and cabin category chosen. Its brochure also lists overnight hotel opportunities in Seattle (from $145 per person, double), Anchorage (from $160 per person, double), Vancouver (from $140 per person, double), and Juneau and Ketchikan (both from $120 per person, double).

## Spirit of '98

Spirit of '98 *(photo: Cruise West)*

### Specifications

| Size (in tons) | 96 | Officers | American |
|---|---|---|---|
| Number of Cabins | 49 | Crew | 23 (American) |
| Number of Outside Cabins | 49 | Passenger/Crew Ratio | 4.2 to 1 |
| Cabins with Verandas | 0 | Year Built | 1984 |
| Number of Passengers | 96 | Last Major Refurbishment | 1995 |

**THE SHIP IN GENERAL**    The *Spirit of '98* is a time machine. Built in 1984 as a replica of a 19th-century steamship and extensively refurbished in 1995, it carries its Victorian flavor so well that fully two-thirds of the people we've met on board think the ship was a private yacht at the turn of the century.

If you use a wheelchair or otherwise have mobility problems, note that the '98 is one of only four small ships in Alaska that has an elevator. (Cruise West's *Spirit of Oceanus,* Clipper's *Clipper Odyssey,* and American West's *Empress of the North* are the others.)

If you want to get a look at this ship, rent Kevin Costner's *Wyatt Earp* at your local video store—one of the final scenes was filmed on board. Also, Sue Henry's 1997 mystery novel *Death Takes Passage* is set entirely aboard the '98 and provides detailed descriptions of the ship.

**CABINS**    Cabins are comfortable and of decent size, and continue the Victorian motif. Each features TV/VCR combos and either twin, convertible twin, or double beds with firm, comfortable mattresses. Deluxe cabins have a refrigerator, a seating area, and a trundle bed to accommodate a third passenger. One Owner's Suite provides a spacious living room with a meeting area, a large bathroom with whirlpool tub, a king-size bed, a stocked bar with refrigerator, a TV/VCR, a stereo, and enough windows to take in all of Alaska at one sitting. Bathrooms are larger than aboard most other small ships, though they lack any hint of Victorian frills.

Cabin 309, located on the upper deck right next to the elevator, is fully wheelchair accessible. Two cabins (321 and 322, in the stern) are singles.

## Cabins & Rates

| Cabins | Brochure Rates | Bathtub | Fridge | Hair Dryer | Sitting Area | TV |
|---|---|---|---|---|---|---|
| Outside | $3,799–$4,549 | no | some | no | some | yes |
| Suites | $5,049 | yes | yes | no | yes | yes |

**PUBLIC AREAS**    The Grand Salon Lounge has the ship's main bar, a suitably plinky-sounding 19th-century-ish player piano, a 24-hour tea/coffee station, and a small video library. The Klondike Dining Room is beautifully decorated and large enough to seat all guests in booths and around center tables. The booths seem to suffer less ambient noise than the round tables in the middle, so try to snag one of those if you can. Both rooms carry the 19th-century theme with pressed-tin ceilings (aluminum actually, but why be picky?), balloon-back chairs, ruffled draperies, and plenty of polished woodwork and brass throughout. A small bar called Soapy's Parlour sits just aft of the dining room. There's a bartender at Soapy's at mealtime, but it otherwise gets little use—meaning it's a good spot to sneak off and read.

Out in the air, passengers congregate in the large bow area, on the open top deck, or at the railing in front of the bridge, which is open to visitors except when the ship is passing through rough water.

**POOL, SPA & FITNESS FACILITIES**    The ship has none.

## Spirit of Endeavour

Spirit of Endeavour
*(photo: Matt Hannafin)*

## Specifications

| Size (in tons) | 99 | Officers | American |
|---|---|---|---|
| Number of Cabins | 51 | Crew | 25 (American) |
| Number of Outside Cabins | 51 | Passenger/Crew Ratio | 4 to 1 |
| Cabins with Verandas | 0 | Year Built | 1983 |
| Number of Passengers | 102 | Last Major Refurbishment | 1996 |

**THE SHIP IN GENERAL**    Formerly the *Newport Clipper* of Clipper Cruise Line, the *Endeavour* closely resembles that line's *Yorktown Clipper* in style and layout. Along with the Clipper ships, Cruise West's new *Spirit of Oceanus,* and Glacier Bay's *Executive Explorer,* it offers a higher level of comfort than most other small ships in the Alaska market.

**CABINS**    Well appointed, with a writing desk and two large windows in all but the lowest price category (which has portholes), all cabins have firm, comfortable twin beds (convertible to queen-size only in Deluxe cabins); TV/VCRs; adequate closet space; and decent-size bathrooms. Deluxe cabins feature a refrigerator, and several in the top two categories have a Pullman berth to accommodate a third passenger. Six pairs of cabins have the option of being adjoined.

There are no special facilities aboard for travelers with disabilities and no cabins designed specifically for single occupancy.

## Cabins & Rates

| Cabins | Brochure Rates | Bathtub | Fridge | Hair Dryer | Sitting Area | TV |
|---|---|---|---|---|---|---|
| Outside | $3,799–$5,049 | no | some | no | no | yes |

**PUBLIC AREAS**    As with almost all small ships, the *Endeavour* has two indoor public areas: the dining room—the largest room on the ship, lined with wide picture windows and round dinner tables—and the plush piano lounge/bar, decorated with considerable style. Up top, a large Sun Deck and Stern Deck (both of beautiful teakwood) and a bow viewing area just below the bridge allow plenty of space for wildlife and nature observation. There's a 24-hour tea/coffee station and a video library in the lounge.

**POOL, SPA & FITNESS FACILITIES**    There's a single exercise machine.

## Spirit of Oceanus

Spirit of Oceanus *(photo: Cruise West)*

## Specifications

| | | | |
|---|---|---|---|
| Size (in tons) | 126 | Officers | International |
| Number of Cabins | 57 | Crew | 59 (Int'l) |
| Number of Outside Cabins | 57 | Passenger/Crew Ratio | 2 to 1 |
| Cabins with Verandas | 12 | Year Built | 1984 |
| Number of Passengers | 114 | Last Major Refurbishment | 2001 |

**THE SHIP IN GENERAL**    Cruise West took ownership of the former *Renaissance V* in June 2002. The addition of the oceangoing vessel has allowed Cruise West to pursue itineraries outside its traditional coastal cruising waters, such as Southeast Asia and the South Pacific.

## Cabins & Rates

| Cabins | Brochure Rates | Bathtubs | Fridge | Hair Dryer | Sitting Area | TV |
|---|---|---|---|---|---|---|
| Suites | $13,299–$19,995* | no | no | no | yes | yes |

*\* For 15-night itinerary. Rate includes pre- or post-cruise hotel stay and select shore excursions.*

**CABINS**   Launched in 1990, the renamed *Spirit of Oceanus* has 57 outside suites ranging in size from 215 to 353 square feet, each containing a walk-in closet or wardrobe, a marble-topped vanity, a lounge area separated from the bedroom by a curtain, an in-room safe, a minibar, and satellite telephone access. Twelve cabins have private teak balconies. None of the cabins are wheelchair accessible.

**PUBLIC AREAS**   Public rooms include two lounges, a library, a beauty salon, laundry, an outdoor dining terrace, a piano bar, and a small swimming pool. The vessel is one of the few small ships in Alaska with an elevator, making it a better choice for passengers with mobility problems.

**POOL, SPA & FITNESS FACILITIES**   Small swimming pool and one exercise machine.

## Spirit of Alaska • Spirit of Columbia • Spirit of Discovery

Spirit of Alaska *(photo: Cruise West)*

## Specifications

| Size (in tons) | 97/97/94 | Officers | American |
|---|---|---|---|
| Number of Cabins | 39/39/43 | Crew | 21/21/21 (American) |
| Number of Outside Cabins | 27/27/43 | Passenger/Crew Ratio | 3.7 to 1 (average) |
| Cabins with Verandas | 0 | Year Built | 1980/1979/1976 |
| Number of Passengers | 78/78/84 | Last Major Refurbishment | 1995/1995/1992 |

**THE SHIPS IN GENERAL**   Though of slightly different sizes and passenger capacities, the *Spirit of Alaska, Columbia,* and *Discovery* are easily lumped together because they are similarly designed ships, all offering the friendly Cruise West experience, though in somewhat less fancy surroundings than the *Spirit of Endeavour, Oceanus,* and *'98* (reviewed above). Though they're older ships, all have been extensively refurbished.

Interestingly, the *Columbia* is like Glacier Bay Cruiseline ships *Wilderness Adventurer* and *Wilderness Discoverer,* both formerly of the American Canadian Caribbean Line, which seems to be supplying half the small-ship lines around with its patented shallow-draft expedition vessels. All of these ships share a problem common to all ACCL-built vessels: They're not good choices for very tall people, as ceilings throughout are set at about 6 feet, 4 inches; many beds are also too short for those 6 feet, 2 inches or taller. On a positive note, though, the *Alaska* and *Columbia* have ACCL's patented bow ramp, which in combination with their shallow draft allows the ships to basically beach themselves, disembarking passengers right onto shore in wild areas without ports.

**CABINS**   Cabins aboard all three ships are very snug (smaller than those on the *Spirit of '98* and *Endeavour*) but comfortable, with light, airy decor and lower twin or double beds. Aboard the *Discovery,* one category has upper and lower bunks, and deluxe cabins have queen-size beds. Storage space is ample, and outside cabins feature picture windows. Bathrooms aboard the *Discovery* and *Columbia* are slightly better than those aboard the *Alaska,* which has tight, head-style arrangements.

There are no special facilities aboard for travelers with disabilities. There are two single-occupancy cabins on *Discovery*, and three (small) suites on *Spirit of Columbia*.

## Cabins & Rates

| Cabins | Brochure Rates | Bathtub | Fridge | Hair Dryer | Sitting Area | TV |
|---|---|---|---|---|---|---|
| *Spirit of Alaska* | | | | | | |
| Inside | $2,999 | no | no | no | no | no |
| Outside | $3,149–$5,049 | no | some | no | some | some |
| *Spirit of Columbia* | | | | | | |
| Inside | $3,099 | no | no | no | some | some |
| Outside | $3,249–$5,149 | no | some | no | some | some |
| *Spirit of Discovery* | | | | | | |
| Inside | $3,699 | no | no | no | no | no |
| Outside | $3,899–$5,149 | no | no | no | some | no |

**PUBLIC AREAS**  All three ships have a dining room and lounge with similar amenities as *Endeavour* and *'98* (see reviews earlier in this section), such as a bar, a 24-hour tea/coffee station, and a video library, though the rooms have a less fancy feel than you'll find on those other ships. Lounges are a little too small to accommodate all passengers when the ships are full.

**POOL, SPA & FITNESS FACILITIES**  There's a single exercise machine on each ship.

## 5 Glacier Bay Cruiseline

107 Denny Way, Suite 303, Seattle, WA 98119. ℂ 800/451-5952 or 206/623-2417. Fax 206/623-7809. www.glacierbaycruiseline.com.

Glacier Bay Cruiseline offers adventure cruises, mostly of the soft variety, and port-to-port sailings, with the balance weighted toward the soft-adventure side. The adventure sailings are for a particular type of traveler, one interested in exploring Alaska's wilds rather than its towns. In 2004, the company was sold to an investor group that included Bob Brennan, a former Princess Cruises and Holland America executive. At press time, its plans for 2005 were still somewhat fluid, especially in the area of cruisetours.

**THE EXPERIENCE**  On this line's average soft-adventure cruise, the focus is not on cities and towns where souvenir shopping is a key activity; instead, the emphasis is on kayaking, hiking in remote regions, exploring glaciers, and cruising the waterways looking for whales and other wildlife. On board the Sport Utility Vessels—the line's term, not ours—the atmosphere is casual and friendly, with the staff providing just enough attention while leaving you the space to enjoy your vacation however you want.

### Pros

- **Kayaking!** The line's adventure ships carry a fleet of stable two-person sea kayaks, which are launched from dry platforms at the ships' sterns. A week-long sailing typically includes three kayak treks.
- **Informality.** It's casual all the way, and you and the crew will bond in no time.
- **Focus on environment and Native culture.** No casinos and showgirls here; instead, you'll learn something about Alaska with this line.
- **Built-in shore excursions.** All off-ship excursions on the adventure cruises are included in the cruise price.

## Glacier Bay Fleet Itineraries

| Ship | Itineraries |
| --- | --- |
| Wilderness Adventurer | **7-night Inside Passage:** Juneau to Ketchikan (or reverse) including kayaking, shore walks, and wildlife-/glacier-watching in Glacier Bay, Warm Springs Bay, Petersburg, Wrangell Narrows, and Misty Fjords. |
| Wilderness Discoverer | **7-night Inside Passage:** Juneau and Sitka (or reverse) including visits to Frederick Sound, Tracy Arm, Skagway, Haines, Icy Strait, and Glacier Bay. |
| Wilderness Explorer | **5-night Glacier Bay:** Round-trip from Glacier Bay. Itinerary includes 4 full days of intensive kayaking, shore walks, and wildlife-/glacier-watching in Icy Strait and Glacier Bay.* |

*Includes 1 hotel night in Glacier Bay.*

## Cons

- **Spartan accommodations.** Most accommodations are very basic. In general, cabins are tiny, and most bathrooms are minuscule head-style units. (The toilet and sink are in the shower stall.)

**THE FLEET**    Glacier Bay Cruiseline has three vessels. The 36-passenger *Wilderness Explorer* (1969) is the most basic, but it also sails the most adventurous itineraries, basically diving right into wilderness for 6 days and not emerging again until the 7th. The 74-passenger *Wilderness Adventurer* (1984) and 86-passenger *Wilderness Discoverer* (1992) are very similar ships and a notch up in comfort and spaciousness (especially the suites on the *Discoverer*), though still very basic. The *Adventurer* sails 7-night itineraries that pretty much avoid civilization, as well as some that visit a few out-of-the-way ports, while the *Discoverer* mixes kayaking and hiking days with visits to various ports.

**PASSENGER PROFILE**    Passengers tend to be on the youngish side, with as many couples in their 40s and 50s as in their 60s and 70s, and a scattering of 30-somethings filling out the list. Whatever their age, passengers tend to be active and interested in nature and wildlife, especially on the adventure itineraries. They're definitely not looking to spend their trip shopping in the ports of call, and they don't want to get dressed up for dinner. They're individuals, happy to get away from TV, highway traffic, and the day-to-day grind; happy with the unstructured and casual ambience aboard ship; and happy with the flexible itinerary, which allows the captain complete freedom to sail wherever the passengers will get the best Alaska experience that day, taking into account factors such as weather and wildlife sightings.

**DINING**    Meals are pretty standard middle-American fare (plus the expected delicious newly caught Alaska salmon) and are served in single open seatings. One dinner per cruise is designated the captain's dinner, and here the cuisine is ratcheted up a notch, perhaps to lobster and free champagne.

Each ship has a single bar (near which pre-dinner snacks of the chicken-wing and nacho variety are served). Other than that, coffee, tea, the occasional bowl of chips, and the fresh cookies baked at midafternoon are the only snacks available between scheduled mealtimes.

Special diets (vegetarian, kosher, low fat, low salt) can be accommodated with some advance warning.

**ACTIVITIES**   Activities aboard the adventure vessels are the integral elements of the trip: kayaking, hiking, and wildlife-watching (for which the line makes binoculars available, though you should bring your own if you have them since there may not be enough to go around). Naturalists sail with every cruise to point out features and lead off-ship expeditions. One naturalist we encountered was a Native Aleut who had taken it upon herself to learn a number of Tlingit legends, which she told to the passengers in a traditional manner. It was a big, big highlight of the trip. Guest lecturers on select sailings mingle with guests and speak on such topics of local interest as glaciers, marine life, and whale training.

**CHILDREN'S PROGRAM**   None.

**ENTERTAINMENT**   Entertainment facilities are minimal, consisting of board games; a piano (aboard the *Wilderness Explorer* only); and a TV/VCR in the lounge of each ship, on which passengers can view tapes on wildlife, Alaska history, and Native culture, and a few feature films.

**SERVICE**   One of the line's greatest strengths is the extreme informality of the passenger/crew dynamic—the two groups tend to become so friendly so fast that after a couple of days, you'll find off-duty deckhands watching nature videos with passengers in the lounge and naturalists sitting with passengers on the top deck at night, watching the stars. Most crew members are from Alaska and the Pacific Northwest, and a number are Native Alaskans. As with most small-ship lines, members of the staff do double- and triple-duty, cleaning the cabins, serving meals, and loading and unloading your luggage.

**CRUISETOURS & ADD-ON PROGRAMS**   At press time, the company had no cruisetours scheduled. Hotel nights in Juneau and Sitka are available starting at $100 per night.

## Wilderness Adventurer • Wilderness Discoverer

Wilderness Discoverer
*(photo: Glacier Bay)*

### Specifications

| Size (in tons) | 89/95 | Officers | American |
| --- | --- | --- | --- |
| Number of Cabins | 35/43 | Crew | 22 (American) |
| Number of Outside Cabins | 34/37 | Passenger/Crew Ratio | 3.4/3.9 to 1 |
| Cabins with Verandas | 0 | Year Built | 1984/1992 |
| Number of Passengers | 74/86 | Last Major Refurbishment | 2000/2001 |

**THE SHIPS IN GENERAL**   Both of these vessels were purchased from American Canadian Caribbean Line, for whom they sailed as the *Caribbean Prince* and *Mayan Prince,* respectively. Because of this heritage, these ships have all the innovative features for which ACCL founder Luther Blount's ships are known. They are low-slung, maneuverable, and quiet; have an incredibly shallow draft; and are outfitted with Blount's patented bow ramp, which allows them to nose right up onto dockless shorelines so passengers can easily disembark and explore. In addition, Glacier Bay has outfitted both vessels with a fleet of stable sea kayaks and a dry-launch platform in the stern that allows passengers to take off right from the ship. Some other small-ship operators offer kayaking in Alaska, but in every other instance, you must first take a boat to shore, where you then launch your kayak.

The downside to all this innovation? Former owner Blount has never been known for making fancy ships. These are spartan vessels for people who want adventure, not cushy comfort.

**CABINS** *Basic* is the word to remember here. Most of the cabins on these ships are just big enough for two to maneuver in simultaneously, decor is on the drab side, and closet space is minimal (though there's more space under the beds). Twin beds (convertible to queen- or king-size) are simply thin (though comfortable) mattresses over wooden platforms. All AA- and A-class cabins (plus Deluxe cabins and suites on the *Discoverer*) have picture windows, while cabins on the lower deck are smaller than the rest and have no closet, nightstand, or windows. Some AA cabins can accommodate a third person, albeit tightly.

Bathrooms are referred to as "marine heads," and what they are is one-piece, one-space units where the toilet faces the sink, from which projects the shower head on a hose. Your whole bathroom is, in effect, the shower stall. Luxury it ain't.

There are no special facilities aboard for travelers with disabilities, and none designated for single travelers.

## Cabins & Rates

| Cabins | Brochure Rates | Bathtub | Fridge | Hair Dryer | Sitting Area | TV |
|---|---|---|---|---|---|---|
| *Wilderness Adventurer* | | | | | | |
| Inside | $2,520* | no | no | no | no | no |
| Outside | $2,735–$3,390* | no | no | no | no | no |
| *Wilderness Discoverer* | | | | | | |
| Inside | $2,740 | no | no | no | no | no |
| Outside | $2,900–$3,770 | no | no | no | no | no |

*Rates include a shore excursion in each port.*

**PUBLIC AREAS** The public rooms on both ships—the forward lounge and adjacent dining room—are similarly bare-boned but are lined with windows, so even at mealtimes you can keep watch for natural wonders. The lounges have TV/VCR setups and a selection of tapes, plus a small library, board games, and a 24-hour tea/coffee station.

On both ships, prime outdoor viewing areas are in the bow and stern of the main deck and on the top deck (a portion of which is covered with a plastic tarp for viewing in rainy weather). These three spots are where passengers spend most of their time on board, making any deficiencies in the interior decor pretty much a moot point.

**POOL, SPA & FITNESS FACILITIES** The sea-kayak excursions that are integral to these ships' itineraries will provide all the exercise you'll need, but you can also walk all the way around each ship on the Sun Deck.

## Wilderness Explorer

Wilderness Explorer
*(photo: Glacier Bay)*

### Specifications

| | | | |
|---|---|---|---|
| Size (in tons) | 98 | Officers | American |
| Number of Cabins | 18 | Crew | 13 (American) |
| Number of Outside Cabins | 18 | Passenger/Crew Ratio | 2.8 to 1 |
| Cabins with Verandas | 0 | Year Built | 1969 |
| Number of Passengers | 36 | Last Major Refurbishment | n/a |

**THE SHIP IN GENERAL**   The *Wilderness Explorer,* which the line refers to as its "cruising base camp," offers the most active cruise experience available in Alaska. Cruises are structured so passengers are out exploring most of each day and only use the vessel to eat, sleep, and get from place to place. It's the line's most basic ship, having been built in 1969 by American Canadian Caribbean Line's Luther Blount—one of his first ships and still going strong.

**CABINS**   Tiny, tiny, tiny. All cabins feature upper and lower bunks, the same kind of head-style bathrooms as aboard the *Wilderness Adventurer* and *Discoverer,* and minimal storage space. Tiny windows in A-class cabins let in light but aren't much good for seeing the sights. AA-class cabins are one deck up and have more space and actual windows, while one Deluxe cabin is located right behind the wheelhouse and has more space and windows at both port and starboard.

There are no special facilities aboard for travelers with disabilities, and none are designated for single travelers.

### Cabins & Rates

| Cabins | Brochure Rates | Bathtub | Fridge | Hair Dryer | Sitting Area | TV |
|---|---|---|---|---|---|---|
| Outside | $1,780–$2,290 | no | no | no | no | no |

**PUBLIC AREAS**   As on all the line's other vessels, there's a lounge with a bar, a 24-hour tea/coffee station, a library, and a TV/VCR, plus a dining room and an observation deck, part of which is covered for inclement weather.

**POOL, SPA & FITNESS FACILITIES**   These cruises are based around active adventures like sea kayaking and hiking. That's all the exercise you'll need.

## 6 Lindblad Expeditions

720 5th Ave., New York, NY 10019. ℂ **800/397-3348** or 212/765-7740. Fax 212/265-3770. www. expeditions.com.

In 1984, Sven-Olof Lindblad, son of adventure-travel pioneer Lars-Eric Lindblad, followed in his father's footsteps by forming Lindblad Expeditions, which specializes in providing environmentally sensitive soft-adventure/educational cruises to remote places in the world, with visits to a few large ports.

## Lindblad Expeditions Fleet Itineraries

| Ship | Itineraries |
| --- | --- |
| Sea Bird/Sea Lion | **11-night Alaska, British Columbia, San Juan Islands:** North- and southbound between Juneau and Seattle, visiting Point Adolphus, Glacier Bay, Sitka, Frederick Sound, Misty Fjords, Alert Bay and Johnstone Strait, B.C., and the San Juan Islands, Washington. **7-night Coastal Wilderness:** North- and southbound between Juneau and Sitka, visiting Tracy Arm, Petersburg, Frederick Sound, Chatham Strait, Glacier Bay, Point Adolphus, and Chichagof Island. |

**THE EXPERIENCE**    Lindblad cruises are explorative and informal, designed to appeal to the intellectually curious traveler seeking a vacation that's educational as well as relaxing. Your time is spent learning about the outdoors (from high-caliber expedition leaders trained in botany, anthropology, biology, and geology) and observing the world around you either from the ship or on shore excursions, which are included in the cruise package. Lindblad Expeditions' crew and staff emphasize respect for the local ecosystem, and flexibility and spontaneity are keys to the experience, as the route may be altered at any time to follow a pod of whales or school of dolphins. Depending on weather and sea conditions, there are usually two or three excursions every day.

### Pros
- **Great expedition feeling.** Lindblad's programs offer innovative, flexible itineraries; outstanding lecturers/guides; and a friendly, accommodating staff.
- **Built-in shore excursions.** Rather than rely on outside concessionaires for their shore excursions (which is the case with most other lines, big and small), Lindblad Expeditions runs its shore excursions as an integral part of its cruises and includes all excursion costs in the cruise fare.

### Cons
- **Cost.** Cruise fares tend to be a little higher than the line's small-ship competition.

**THE FLEET**    The 70-passenger *Sea Lion* and *Sea Bird* (built in 1981 and 1982, respectively) are nearly identical in every respect and are, in fact, very similar to many of the other small ships in the Alaska market, including Glacier Bay Cruiseline's *Wilderness Adventurer* and *Wilderness Discoverer,* and Cruise West's *Spirit of Columbia, Spirit of Discovery,* and *Spirit of Alaska.* As a matter of fact, the *Spirit of Alaska* and the two special expedition ships all sailed at one time for the now-defunct Exploration Cruise Lines. All are basic vessels built to get you to beautiful spots, and feature a minimum of public rooms and conveniences: one dining room, one bar/lounge, and lots of deck space for wildlife and glacier viewing.

**PASSENGER PROFILE**    Lindblad Expeditions tends to attract well-traveled and well-educated, professional, 55+ couples who have "been there, done that" and are looking for something completely different in a cruise experience. The passenger mix may also include some singles and a smattering of younger couples. Although not necessarily frequent cruisers, many passengers are likely to have been on other Lindblad Expeditions programs, tend to share a common interest in wildlife (whale- and bird-watching), and are also intellectually curious about the culture and history of the region they're visiting.

**DINING**    Hearty buffet breakfasts and lunches and sit-down dinners feature a good choice of both hot and cold dishes with plenty of fresh fruits and vegetables. Many of the fresh ingredients are obtained from ports along the way, and meals may reflect regional tastes. Although far from haute cuisine, dinners are well prepared and presented and are served at single open seatings that allow passengers to get to know each other by moving around to different tables. Lecturers and other staff members dine with passengers.

**ACTIVITIES**    During the day, most activity takes place off the ship, aboard Zodiac boats and/or on land excursions. While on board, passengers entertain themselves with the usual small-ship activities: wildlife-watching, staring off into the wilderness, reading, and engaging in conversation.

**CHILDREN'S PROGRAM**    There are no organized programs, as there are few children aboard.

**ENTERTAINMENT**    Lectures and slide presentations are scheduled throughout the cruise, and documentaries or movies may be screened in the evening in the main lounge. Books on Alaskan topics are available in each ship's small library.

**SERVICE**    Dining-room staff and room stewards are affable and efficient and seem to enjoy their work. As with other small ships, there's no room service unless you're ill and unable to make it to the dining room.

**CRUISETOURS & ADD-ON PROGRAMS**    Lindblad offers a 6-night land extension to Anchorage, Denali, and Fairbanks priced from $3,290 per person, based on double occupancy.

## Sea Lion • Sea Bird

Sea Bird *(photo: Lindblad Expeditions)*

### Specifications

| Size (in tons) | 100 | Officers | American |
|---|---|---|---|
| Number of Cabins | 37 | Crew | 22 |
| Number of Outside Cabins | 37 | Passenger/Crew Ratio | 3.2 to 1 |
| Cabins with Verandas | 0 | Year Built | 1981/1982 |
| Number of Passengers | 70 | Last Major Refurbishment | n/a |

**THE SHIPS IN GENERAL**    The shallow-draft *Sea Lion* and *Sea Bird* are identical twins, right down to their decor schemes and furniture. Not fancy at all, they have just two public rooms and utilitarian cabins.

**CABINS**    Postage-stamp cabins are tight and functional rather than fancy. No cabins are large enough to accommodate more than two, and each features twin or double beds, a closet (there are also drawers under the bed for extra storage), and a sink and mirror in the main room. Behind a folding door lies a Lilliputian bathroom with a head-style shower (toilet opposite the shower nozzle). All cabins are located outside and have picture windows that open to fresh breezes (except the lowest-price cabins, which have a small "portlight" that allows light in but provides no view). The vessels have no handicapped-accessible cabins.

## Cabins & Rates

| Cabins | Rates | Bathtub | Fridge | Hair Dryer | Sitting Area | TV |
|---|---|---|---|---|---|---|
| Outside | $3,980-$5,850* | no | no | no | no | no |
| Outside | $3,840-$4,990** | no | no | no | no | no |

*Rates for 11-night cruise.
** Rates for 7-night cruise.

**PUBLIC AREAS** Public space is limited to the open Sun Deck and bow areas, the dining room, and an observation lounge that serves as the nerve center for activities. In the lounge, you'll find a bar; a library of atlases and books on Alaska's culture, geology, history, plants, and wildlife; a gift shop tucked into a closet; and audiovisual aids for the many naturalists' presentations.

**POOL, SPA & FITNESS FACILITIES** As is the case with the majority of small ships, there is no gym aboard either ship, nor are there any other onboard exercise facilities. However, Lindblad's style of soft-adventure travel means you'll be taking frequent walks/hikes in wilderness areas, usually accessed via Zodiac landing craft.

## 7 And Now for Something Completely Different: Cruising Using the Alaska Marine Highway System

3132 Channel Dr., Juneau, AK 99801. (℃ **800/642-0066.** Fax 907/277-4829. www.dot.state.ak.us/amhs. (**Note:** There is a proposal to move the company's headquarters from Juneau to Ketchikan, possibly as early as 2005.)

In Alaska, which has fewer paved roads than virtually any other state, getting around can be a problem. There are local airlines, of course, and small private planes—lots and lots of small private planes, some with wheels, some with skis, some with floats for landing on water. But given the weather conditions in many areas for large parts of the year, airplanes are not always the most reliable way of getting from Point A to Point B in Alaska.

That's why the Alaska Marine Highway System (aka the Alaska Ferry, or AMHS) is so important. Even the state capital, Juneau, cannot be reached by road and relies heavily on the ferryboats of the AMHS, which bring in visitors, vehicles, supplies, and even, when air travel is impeded by inclement weather, the legislators who run the state.

Although the ferry system was originally created with the aim of providing Alaska's far-flung, often-inaccessible smaller communities with essential transportation links with the rest of the state and with the Lower 48, the boats have developed a following in the tourism business as well. Each year, thousands of visitors eschew luxury cruise ships in favor of the more basic services of the 10 vessels of the AMHS. The service is of particular value to independent travelers, enabling visitors to come and go as they please among Alaska's outposts.

**THE EXPERIENCE** It must be stressed that ferry-riding vacations are different than cruise vacations, to say the least. Don't even think about one if you're looking for a lot of creature comforts—fancy accommodations, gourmet food, spa treatments, Broadway-style shows, and the rest. You won't find any of the above on the sturdy vessels of the AMHS. In fact, not all ferry passengers get sleeping berths!

It's in the lounges or on deck that riders may encounter the only entertainment on board, all created by passengers on a strictly impromptu basis. It might be a backpacker strumming a guitar and singing folk songs. It might be a bearded, burly local reciting the poetry of Robert Service ("A bunch of the boys were whooping it up in the Malamute Saloon . . . "). Or it could be a father keeping his children occupied by performing magic tricks. Occasionally, spirited discussion groups will form in which all are welcome to participate. The subject might be the environment, politics (Alaskan or federal), the northern lights, the effect of tourism on wildlife, or any of a thousand other topics.

## Pros

- **Unique way to travel.** The ferry system offers the chance for adventuresome travel that is not too taxing.
- **Lots of flexibility.** Passengers can combine the varied journeys that the ferry system has scheduled to customize their vacation package.

## Cons

- **No doctor on board.** None of the vessels carries a doctor, so this may not be a good way to travel if you have health concerns.
- **Space books up quickly.** The only way you will be able to find a space on most of the ferries is by booking promptly. Don't call in May and expect to get what you want in June. It ain't gonna happen! If you're serious about experiencing Alaska by ferry, book now. Call the company at ℂ **800/ 642-0066** or book electronically through the website at **www.dot.state. ak.us/amhs**.
- **Spartan cabins.** Sleeping accommodations are basic, to say the least—no fridges, no telephones, no VCRs, and so on.

**THE FLEET**   All of the AMHS boats are designated M/V, as in motor vessel. Below is a thumbnail sketch of each one.

- The newest, and AMHS's fastest, is the *Fairweather,* which operates between Juneau and Sitka, and between Juneau and Haines and Juneau and Skagway through the Lynn Canal. It is a 235-foot, 250-passenger (and 35-car) catamaran that cuts travel times in half. Interestingly, and somewhat surprisingly, while it links Juneau with Skagway and Haines, it does not link those two latter, neighboring communities. The vessel has no sleeping quarters; it is designed purely to provide fast access to and from the capital. Its value to locals is immense; they can now be in the grocery and clothing stores of Juneau, or in the offices of the Legislature, twice as fast as they once were. Its value to tourists is that it enables them to spend less time in transit. A sister high-speed vessel, the *Chenega,* is due to debut in summer 2005.
- Another vessel that joined the fleet in 2004, just after the *Fairweather,* is the *Lituya,* which just happens to be the smallest and slowest of the ferry company's boats. Carrying just 149 passengers and 18 vehicles, the *Lituya* was built to operate between Ketchikan and the Indian village of Metlakatla. Although built with a specific local market in mind, it also allows tourists to visit an Indian community 17 miles from Ketchikan.

- The *Kennicott* (which began service in 1998) was built in Gulfport, Mississippi. It is 382 feet long (about one-third as long as the biggest of today's cruise ships), has a service speed of just under 17 knots, and carries 748 passengers. Five of its cabins are wheelchair accessible. The *Kennicott* has a dining room for sit-down fine dining and a cafeteria.
- The *Taku* was built in 1981 in Seattle. It is 352 feet long and carries 450 passengers at 16.5 knots. Two of its cabins are wheelchair accessible. The *Taku* has a cocktail lounge and cafeteria.
- The Wisconsin-built *Aurora,* which is used only for runs of a few hours, has room for 250 riders. Although it offers no sleeping berths, it has a cafeteria.
- The *Columbia* is the largest (though it doesn't have the biggest capacity) of the AMHS vessels. The ferry, built in Seattle in 1974, is 418 feet long and holds 625 passengers and 134 vehicles. Of its 104 sleeping rooms, 3 are suitable for wheelchair users. The vessel has a cafeteria, dining room for fine dining, and cocktail lounge.
- The 250-passenger (34 vehicle) *Le Conte,* built in Wisconsin in 1973, is a no-sleeper short-run ferry that offers food service.
- The *Matanuska* entered service in 1968 after leaving the builder's yard in Seattle. In 1972, the boat was lengthened and renovated in Portland, bringing it to its current capacity of 500, with room for 88 vehicles. It has 107 cabins, 1 of which can accommodate a wheelchair user. The vessel has a cafeteria and a cocktail lounge.
- Another Wisconsin product, the *Tustumena,* began in Alaska waters in 1964 and was extensively renovated in San Francisco 5 years later. Its sleeping rooms number 26, with 1 adapted to wheelchair use. It carries 210 passengers. The *Tustumena* has a cafeteria and a cocktail lounge.
- The 500-passenger *Malaspina,* another Seattle build, has 88 vehicle spaces and 73 cabins. One is suitable for a wheelchair user. The *Malaspina* has a cafeteria and a cocktail lounge.

**PASSENGER PROFILE**    The travelers who use the ferries are looking for a laid-back, totally casual Alaska experience. Jeans and climbing boots (sometimes not removed for days), anoraks and backpacks . . . these are the basic accessories of ferry travelers in the 49th state. Ferry passengers who are on vacation (the AMHS is also heavily used as basic transportation by Alaska locals) are mostly young and don't often bring their families. They are definitely *not* looking for luxury.

**PORTS OF CALL**    Those seeking a change from the more popular and frequently congested larger Inside Passage and Gulf ports find that the ferries are an ideal way to get around the less-visited Alaska, where paved roads are in short supply and reliable air connections—especially when the weather turns ugly—are nonexistent. A trip on one of the ferries can deposit you in, say, Pelican, on Chichagof Island, where you can enjoy fishing and scenery and join in the banter of the local fisherfolk in Rosie's Bar, the center of activity in town. A trip on another ferry will transport you to Tenakee Springs, a popular spa as far back as the gold-rush days, where you can "take the waters" and take advantage of saltwater fishing opportunities. The ferry will get you to Port Lions, which is located on the northeast coast of Kodiak Island at the eastern end of the Aleutian Chain; to other areas of the Aleutians—False Pass and King Cove for instance; to Chenega Bay, in Prince William Sound; to the Indian settlements at Kake, on Kupreanof Island; and to Metlakatla, on Annette Island, among many other destinations. These are not, and never will be, ports with mass appeal. No luxury liner will ever disgorge 2,600 cruise passengers in any of them. But those people who seek a taste of down-home spirit, Alaska-style, find these ports to be attractive destinations. In short, the Alaska Marine Highway System can get you to places that cruise ships just don't go. Of course, the ferry system can also get you to big-ship cruise ports such as Ketchikan, Juneau, Whittier, and the rest, but much of the system's appeal, to many visitors, is its ability to transport travelers to lesser-known outposts.

**DINING**    Only 2 of the 10 AHMS ferries, the aforementioned *Kennicott* and *Columbia,* have full-service, sit-down dining rooms. The others have cafeteria-style facilities that serve hot meals and beverages. There are also vending machines on all of the boats, which dispense a variety of snacks and drinks. Food prices—ranging from $1 for a vending machine snack to $7.50 for a hot meal in the dining room—are not included in the fares.

**ACTIVITIES**    No organized activities, but lots of scenic viewing.

**CHILDREN'S PROGRAM**    None.

**ITINERARIES**    The ferries operate in two distinct areas—year-round in the Southeast or Inside Passage (from Bellingham to Skagway/Haines), and in the summer months across to the Aleutians (in Alaska's Southwestern region) by way of Prince William Sound and the Kenai Peninsula. The reason for the seasonality of the Aleutians service is the weather: The seas become too rough, the fog too thick, and the cold too intense for the ferries to operate safely or profitably in the winter. See the website (www.dot.state.ak.us/amhs) for details on the many routes that the AMHS offers and the ports that it services.

**SERVICE**    Service is not one of the things that the Alaska Marine Highway System is noted for. The small American staff on each vessel works enthusiastically but without a great deal of distinction.

**CRUISETOUR & ADD-ON PROGRAMS**    The company does not offer any cruisetour or add-on programs.

**CABINS**    The great majority of the cabins are small and spartan, coming in two- and four-bunk configurations, and either inside (without windows) or outside (with windows), but for a premium you can reserve a more comfortable sitting-room unit on some vessels. Most cabins have tiny private bathrooms with showers. Try to get an outside cabin so that you can watch the world go by. Cabins can be stuffy, and the windowless units can be claustrophobic as well.

Those who do not book their ferry passage in time to snag a cabin must spend their time curled up in chairs in the lounges if it's cold, or out on deck in a tent when the days lengthen and the sun stays high until late into the night. The patio-furniture lounge chairs on the covered outdoor solarium, on the top deck, are the best public sleeping spot on board, in part because the noise of the ship covers other sounds. If you're tenting, the best place is behind the solarium, where it's not too windy. On the *Columbia,* that space is small, so grab it early. Bring duct tape to secure your tent to the deck in case you can't find a sheltered spot, as the wind over the deck of a ship in motion blows like an endless gale. The recliner lounges are comfortable too, but can be stuffy. Bring a pillow. If the ship looks crowded, grab your spot fast to get a choice location. Showers are available, although there may be lines. Lock the valuables and luggage you don't need in the coin-operated lockers.

**RATES**   A word about fares: First you pay the cost of basic transportation. The journey between, say, Bellingham, Wash., the southernmost port in the system, and Ketchikan, Alaska (a trip that takes 37 hr.), costs $192 one-way. From Haines to Skagway, just an hour-long journey, the fare is $25 one-way.

Once you've booked your passage, you choose and pay for the cabin that you will sleep in. That's extra. For the Bellingham/Ketchikan leg, a two-berth outside cabin, with facilities, goes for $206. There are three- and four-berth cabins on some of the vessels, and some of the cabins are inside, some are outside, some have private facilities, and some don't.

After you've reserved and paid for your passage on the boat and your cabin, you then have to pay still more for your automobile or recreational vehicle, if you're taking one along. Here, again, the prices vary widely by size of vehicle. There are also fees for kayaks, inflatables, and bicycles. (Only in Alaska!)

The price for the 2-hour trip between, say, Haines and Juneau on the new *Fairweather,* is $35 one-way without a vehicle, $101 one-way with a vehicle.

**PUBLIC AREAS**   All of the ferries have warm if somewhat sparse interiors, with room for all when the weather is foul. They have solariums with high windows for viewing the passing scenery, which, you should bear in mind, doesn't change because you're on a ferry and not a megaship.

**POOL, SPA & FITNESS FACILITIES**   There are none available.

# 7

# The Ports of Embarkation

Most Alaska cruises operate either round-trip from Vancouver or Seattle, or one-way northbound or south-bound between Vancouver or Seattle and Seward/Anchorage. This year Princess will be joined by Carnival Cruises in using Whittier, an unprepossessing little place that has the advantage of being 60 miles closer to Anchorage, as the northern turn-around port for their combined five Gulf of Alaska ships. Seattle and San Francisco are other popular ports of embarkation: This year, Crystal and Princess will each operate one ship in Alaska rotation out of San Francisco; and Norwegian, Princess, Cruise West, Holland America, and American West Steamboat Company have cruises from Seattle. Most of the small adventure-type vessels sail from popular Alaska ports of call such as Juneau,

Ketchikan, and Sitka. In this chapter, we'll cover the most common of these home ports: Anchorage, Seward, Vancouver, Seattle, Juneau, and Whittier.

You may want to consider traveling to your city of embarkation at least a day or two before your cruise departure date. This will give you time to check out local attractions, alleviate any fears you might have about your plane being delayed (worrying that you'll miss the boat is not fun), and, if you're traveling between coasts, give you time to overcome jet lag.

In addition to the port-city information provided here, you may want to refer to *Frommer's Alaska*, *Frommer's Vancouver & Victoria*, *Frommer's Seattle*, or *Frommer's San Francisco* guides for more details, particularly if you're planning to spend a few days in the port.

## 1 Anchorage

Anchorage, which started as a tent camp for workers building the Alaska Railroad in 1914, stands between the Chugach Mountains and the waters of upper Cook Inlet. It was a remote, sleepy railroad town until World War II, when a couple of military bases were located here and livened things up a bit. Even with that, though, Anchorage did not start becoming a city in earnest until the late 1950s, when oil was discovered on the Kenai Peninsula, to the south.

Fortunes came fast and development was haphazard, but the city seems at this point to have settled into its success. It now boasts good restaurants, good museums, and a nice little zoo. In addition, it features an excellent cultural attraction—the Alaska Native Heritage Center, a 26-acre re-creation of the villages of Alaska's five Native groups. As always, wilderness lies so close that moose regularly annoy gardeners in the town, and even bears occasionally show up in the streets.

Anchorage's downtown area, situated near Ship Creek, is about 8 by 20 blocks wide, but the rest of the city spreads some 5 miles east and 15 miles south. Most visitors, whether heading off on a cruise ship or not, spend a day or two in town

# Anchorage

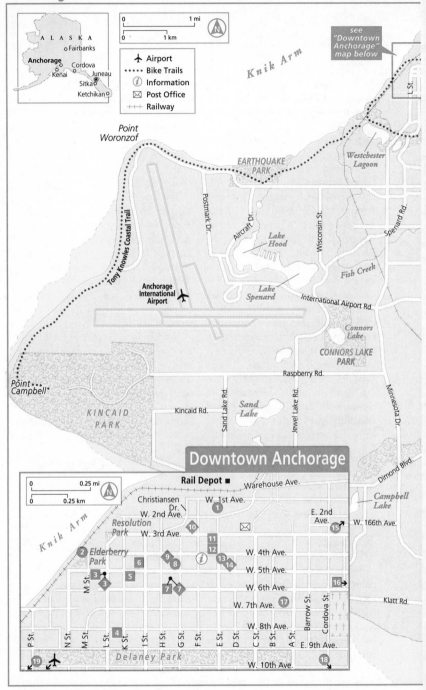

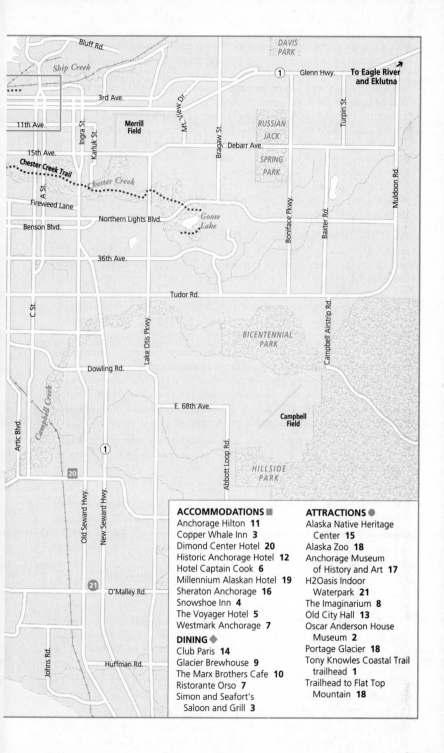

ACCOMMODATIONS ■
Anchorage Hilton **11**
Copper Whale Inn **3**
Dimond Center Hotel **20**
Historic Anchorage Hotel **12**
Hotel Captain Cook **6**
Millennium Alaskan Hotel **19**
Sheraton Anchorage **16**
Snowshoe Inn **4**
The Voyager Hotel **5**
Westmark Anchorage **7**

DINING ◆
Club Paris **14**
Glacier Brewhouse **9**
The Marx Brothers Cafe **10**
Ristorante Orso **7**
Simon and Seafort's
  Saloon and Grill **3**

ATTRACTIONS ●
Alaska Native Heritage
  Center **15**
Alaska Zoo **18**
Anchorage Museum
  of History and Art **17**
H2Oasis Indoor
  Waterpark **21**
The Imaginarium **8**
Old City Hall **13**
Oscar Anderson House
  Museum **2**
Portage Glacier **18**
Tony Knowles Coastal Trail
  trailhead **1**
Trailhead to Flat Top
  Mountain **18**

before going somewhere more remote. The city center is pleasant, but we recommend you try to see more than just the streets of tourist-oriented shops. Check out the **coastal trail** and the **museums,** and if you have time, plan a day trip about 50 miles south along **Turnagain Arm** to explore the receding **Portage Glacier** and visit the mountains.

And don't forget the **Alaska Native Heritage Center** we mentioned. It's well worth a visit, even at $21 a head, providing an introduction to the state's Native groups through storytelling, dance, music, a crafts workshop, a museum, and an outdoor area in which five traditional homes have been constructed. Most lines' shore-excursion books include it this year.

The H2Oasis Indoor Waterpark, Anchorage's newest—and perhaps most unusual—attraction, opened in 2002. The facility has been a draw with both the locals and cruise ship passengers.

## GETTING TO ANCHORAGE & THE PORT

Cruise ships dock in Seward or Whittier on the east coast of the Kenai Peninsula, so as to avoid the extra day that cruising all the way around the peninsula to Anchorage adds to Gulf of Alaska itineraries. It's quicker to transport passengers between the towns in motorcoaches or by train than it is to sail all the way around the peninsula. Most visitors will use Anchorage as a hub because, thanks to the international airport, it's where Alaska links with the rest of the world. You can spend a day or two in Anchorage before heading off on a cruise.

**BY PLANE**   If you're arriving or leaving by plane before or after your cruise, you'll land at the **Ted Stevens Anchorage International Airport** (how come they always name airports after politicians?). The facility is located within the city limits, a 15-minute drive from downtown. Taxis run about $19 for the trip downtown, and the **Borealis Shuttle** (© 907/276-3600) and **Mom's Shuttle** (© 907/344-6667) each charge $12 per couple.

**BY CAR**   By car, there is only one road into Anchorage from the rest of the world: the Glenn Highway. The other road out of town, the Seward Highway, leads to the Kenai Peninsula.

## EXPLORING ANCHORAGE

**INFORMATION**   The **Anchorage Convention and Visitor Bureau** (© 907/276-4118) maintains five information centers. The main one is the **Log Cabin Visitor Information Center** at 4th Avenue and F Street (© 907/274-3531). It's open daily from 7:30am to 7pm June through August, and from 8am to 6pm in May and September.

**GETTING AROUND**   Most car-rental companies operate at the airport. A midsize car costs about $55 a day, with unlimited mileage. (There aren't many of those $9.99-a-day specials that you see advertised in some other states!) Advanced bookings are recommended. Anchorage's bus system is an effective way of moving to and from the top attractions and activities. The buses operate between 6am and 10pm daily, and passage costs $1.25 for adults and 75¢ for those between the ages of 5 and 18. In the 20-block downtown area, which consists of 5th and 6th avenues between Denali and K streets, the bus operates as a free people mover.

### ATTRACTIONS WITHIN WALKING DISTANCE

With its old-fashioned grid of streets, Anchorage's downtown area is pleasant, if a bit touristy. The 1936 **Old City Hall,** at 4th Avenue and E Street, offers an interesting display on city history in its lobby, including dioramas of the early streetscape. For a better sense of what Alaska's all about, though, you'll want to check out the heritage museums or take a ride outside the city to the Chugach Mountains. You can also take a walk on the **Tony Knowles Coastal Trail,** which comes through downtown and runs along the water for about 11 miles, from the western end of 2nd Avenue to Kincaid Park. You can hop onto the trail at several points, including Elderberry Park, at the western end of 5th Avenue.

**Anchorage Museum of History and Art**    In the Alaska Gallery, you can enjoy an informative walk through the history and anthropology of the state, and in the art galleries you can see what's happening in Alaska art today. The cafe serves excellent lunches, and Native dancers perform in the auditorium daily at 12:15, 1:15, and 2:15pm.

121 W. 7th Ave. ℂ **907/343-4326.** www.anchoragemuseum.org. Admission $6.50 adults, $6 seniors 65 and older, free for children 17 and under (a $2 donation is suggested). May 15–Sept 15 Fri–Wed 9am–6pm, Thurs 9am–9pm; Sept 16–May 14 Tues–Sat 10am–6pm, Sun 1–5pm.

**The Imaginarium**    This science museum is geared toward kids, with concise explanations and lots of fun learning experiences. There's a strong Alaska theme to many of the displays. The saltwater touch tank, one of the stars of the museum, is like an indoor tide pool.

737 W. 5th Ave., Suite G. ℂ **907/276-3179.** www.imaginarium.org. Admission $5 ages 13–64, $4.50 ages 2–12 and 65 and older. Mon–Sat 10am–6pm; Sun noon–5pm.

**The Oscar Anderson House Museum**    This house museum shows how an early Swedish butcher lived. It's a quaint dwelling surrounded by a lovely little garden, and the house tour provides a good explanation of the city's short history. Furnishings include a working 1909 player piano.

420 M St., in Elderberry Park. ℂ **907/274-2336.** www.anchoragehistoric.org. Admission $3 adults, $1 children 5–12. Summer Mon–Fri noon–5pm. Closed in winter.

## ATTRACTIONS OUTSIDE THE DOWNTOWN AREA

**The Alaska Native Heritage Center**    Years in the planning, this 26-acre center introduces visitors to the lives and cultures of the state's five major Alaska Native groupings: the Southeast (Inside Passage) region's Tlingits, Eyaks, Haida, and Tsimshians; the Athabascans of the Interior; the Inupiat and St. Lawrence Island Yupik Natives of the far north; the Aleuts and Alutiiqs of the Aleutian Islands; and the Yup'ik and Cup'ik tribes of the extreme west. A central "Welcome House" holds a small museum, a theater, a workshop where Native craftspeople demonstrate techniques, and a rotunda where storytelling, dance, and music performances are presented throughout the day. Outside, spaced along a walking trail around a small lake, five traditional dwellings represent the five regional Native groupings, each hosted by a member of that group.

From the Glenn Hwy. take the North Muldoon exit. ℂ **800/315-6608** or 907/330-8000. www.alaskanative. net. Admission $21 adults, $19 seniors and military, $16 children 7–16. Alaska residents $9 adults, $6 children. Summer daily 9am–6pm.

**The Alaska Zoo**    Don't expect a big city zoo. Instead, come to experience a little Eden complete with Alaskan bears, seals, otters, musk oxen, mountain goats, moose, caribou, and waterfowl. There are also decidedly non-Alaskan elephants, tigers, and the like here.

4731 O'Malley Rd. ℂ **907/346-3242.** www.alaskazoo.org. Admission $9 adults, $8 seniors, $5 children 12–17, $4 children 3–12, free under 3. May–Aug daily 9am–6pm, till 9pm Tues and Sat in June and July, summer

## The Iditarod

Few things fire up Alaska's residents like the Iditarod Trail Sled Dog Race, a 1,000-mile run from Anchorage to Nome that takes place in mid-March. Winners cover the distance in 9 or 10 days, which includes mandatory stopovers of up to 24 hours to rest the dogs. The race is big news—TV anchors speculate on the mushers' strategies at the top of the evening news, and school children plot the progress of their favorite teams on maps. When the event hits Nome, the town over-flows with visitors kept busy by the many local events and activities that coincide with the race. Even if the first team crosses the finish line at 3am in –30°F (–34°C) degree weather, a huge crowd turns out to congratulate the winner.

This is Alaska's Super Bowl, its World Series. The victors are feted and admired throughout the state as much as any sports star ever is in the Lower 48. They're not compensated quite as well, mind you. First prize in the grueling event varies but usually runs about $65,000—with sometimes a truck thrown in for good measure! The cruise lines long ago recognized the significance of the Iditarod, whose start has been featured several times on ABC's *Wide World of Sports.* Princess, for instance, has a contract with Libby Riddles, the first woman to win the race. She comes aboard in port in Juneau to talk about her mushing experience and her win in the 1985 event, to show slides, and to sign copies of her autobiography. The *Riverboat Discovery,* a popular day cruise on the Chena River in Fairbanks—an outing included in the cruisetour itinerary of every line with programs in the Denali Corri-dor—stops for a while on each of its sailings at the summer training facility of Susan Butcher. An Alaska legend, Butcher won the Iditarod four times—in 1986, 1987, and 1988 and again in 1990. Butcher shows off some of her animals and demonstrates her riding skills around the camp on a wheel-equipped sled. (Yes, men have also won the Iditarod; Riddles and Butcher are the only two women to have done so in its 31-year history!) The Iditarod Trail Sled Dog Race headquarters are located in Wasilla, near Anchorage, and are also a part of the shore excursion schedule of virtually all Gulf of Alaska cruise operators.

Cruise aficionados may never be in the state to see the race itself, since it takes place off season—very much off season. But they are likely to see and hear plenty about it during their summer ship vacations.

educational programs Tues at 7pm, live music Friday at 7pm; off season open daily at 10am, closing time varies so call ahead. Drive out the New Seward Hwy. to O'Malley Rd., then turn left and go 2 miles; it's 20 min. from downtown, without traffic.

**Flat Top Mountain**    Rising right behind Anchorage, this mountain is a great and easy climb, and perfect for an afternoon hike. The parking area at Glen Alps, above the tree line, is a good starting point.

In the Chugach Mountains. From the New Seward Hwy., drive east on O'Malley Rd., turn right on Hillside Dr. and left on Upper Huffman Rd., then right on the narrow, twisting Toilsome Hill Dr.

**The H2Oasis Indoor Waterpark** This aquatic attraction features a lazy river perfect for idling away an hour, a wave pool that generates rollers that can reach up to 4 feet, a water coaster more than 40 feet high and 500 feet long, a 150-foot-long enclosed slide, and a children's lagoon with a pirate ship and water cannons.

The Castle on O'Malley, 1520 O'Malley Rd. (about 5 miles from downtown). ✆ **907/522-4420**. Day pass $20 adults, $15 children 3–21. Daily 10am–10pm. Take the New Seward Hwy. from downtown past O'Malley Rd. Park is between O'Malley and Huffman roads.

**Portage Glacier** In 1985 the National Forest Service spent $8 million building a visitor center at Portage. Imagine its chagrin when the glacier then started receding, moving away from the center so fast that at this point you can't even see one from the other. You must now board a tour boat to get close to the glacier face. Portage is not the best glacier Alaska has to offer—it's relatively small—but if you haven't had enough of them after your cruise (or want a preview before your cruise), it's well worth a stop. The visitor center itself is still worth a visit; it's a sort of glacier museum and an excellent place to learn about the glaciers you'll be seeing (or saw) on your cruise. Many bus tours are offered (your cruise line may offer one, too), including a 7-hour **Holland America Tours** (✆ **907/277-5581**) trip from Anchorage, which includes the boat ride to the glacier and a stop at the town of Girdwood. The cost is $59, and the trip is offered twice daily in the summer.

About 50 miles south of the city on the Seward Hwy. (toward Seward). Visitor Center Memorial Day to Labor Day daily 9am–6pm; Labor Day to Memorial Day Sat–Sun 10am–5pm.

## THE BEST SHORE EXCURSIONS
See the "Anchorage City Tour," on p. 160.

## ORGANIZED TOURS
**Anchorage Historic Properties** This 1-hour tour covers 2 miles, and the volunteer guides are both fun and knowledgeable. Meet at the lobby of Old City Hall, next door to the Log Cabin Visitor Information Center (p. 152).

645 W. 3rd Ave. ✆ **907/274-3600**. Guided walking tour of historic downtown Anchorage June–Aug weekdays at 1pm, for a reasonable $5 per person, $1 for kids. You can also buy a combination ticket with the Oscar Anderson House Museum (p. 153).

## WHERE TO STAY
Rooms can be hard to come by in Anchorage in the summer, so be sure to arrange lodging as far in advance of your trip as possible, whether through your cruise line or on your own. In addition to the listings below, you can try the luxurious **Anchorage Hilton,** 500 W. 3rd Ave. (✆ 800/245-2527 or 907/272-7411; www. hilton.com); the **Hotel Captain Cook,** 4th and K Street (✆ 800/843-1950 or 907/276-6000; www.captaincook.com); the **Westmark Anchorage,** 720 W. 5th Ave. (✆ 800/544-0970 or 907/276-7676; www.westmarkhotels.com); the **Sheraton Anchorage,** 401 E. 6th Ave. (✆ 800/325-3535 or 907/276-8700; www. sheraton.com); the small and charming **Historic Anchorage Hotel,** right next door to the Hilton on E Street (✆ 800/544-0988 or 907/272-4553; www. historicanchoragehotel.com); the **Dimond Center Hotel,** 700 E. Dimond Blvd. (✆ 866/775-5002 or 907/770-5000; www.dimondcenterhotel.com); or the **Millennium Alaskan Hotel,** 480 Spenard Rd. (✆ 800/544-0535 or 907/245-2300; www.millenniumhotels.com). Room rates in Anchorage average between $210

and $340 per night, so expect all of these properties to charge rack rates in that range. Hotels will accept all major credit cards. The hotels mentioned above are among the city's more upscale. The following are some lower-priced alternatives:

**Copper Whale Inn**   There's a wonderfully casual feeling to this place. A pair of clapboard houses overlooks the water and Elderberry Park right on the coastal trail downtown, with charming rooms of every shape and size. The rooms in the newer building, lower on the hill, are preferable, with cherrywood furniture and high ceilings. All rooms are hooked up for TVs, phones, and voice mail, but you have to ask for the actual instrument to be connected. A few bikes are available for loan, and a full breakfast is included in the price.

440 L St., Anchorage, AK 99501. ℂ 907/258-7999. Fax 888/WHALE-IN or 907/258-6213. www.copper whale.com. 15 units, 9 with bathroom. $125 double with shared bathroom; $165–$245 double with private bathroom. Additional person in room $10 extra. AE, DC, DISC, MC, V.

**Snowshoe Inn**   This cheerful, family-run hotel on a quiet downtown street has comfortable, sunlit, and attractively decorated rooms with bright fabrics, all perfectly clean. The six rooms with shared bathrooms are in pairs, and the bathrooms are close and secure. There's no better bargain downtown. Freezer and storage space and a coin-op laundry are available. No smoking.

826 K St., Anchorage, AK 99501. ℂ 907/258-SNOW (907/258-7669). Fax 907/258-SHOE (907/258-7463). 17 units, 13 with bathroom. $89 double without bathroom; $99–$149 double with bathroom. Rates include continental breakfast. Additional person in room $10 extra. AE, DISC, MC, V.

**The Voyager Hotel**   The Voyager is just about right. The size is small, the location central, the rooms large and light (all with kitchens), and the housekeeping exceptional. The desks have modem ports and extra electrical outlets, and the hospitality is warm yet highly professional. There's nothing ostentatious or outwardly remarkable about the hotel, yet the most experienced travelers rave about it the loudest. No smoking.

501 K St., Anchorage, AK 99501. ℂ 800/247-9070 or 907/277-9501. Fax 907/274-0333. www.voyagerhotel. com. 38 units. $140–$169 single or double. Additional person in room $10 extra. AE, DC, DISC, MC, V.

## WHERE TO DINE

**Club Paris** STEAK/SEAFOOD   Walking from a bright spring afternoon under a neon Eiffel Tower into midnight darkness, past a smoke-enshrouded bar, and sitting down at a secretive booth for two, we felt as if we should be plotting a shady 1950s oil deal. And we would probably not have been the first. Smoky Club Paris may be too authentic for some, but it's the essence of the old Anchorage boomtown years, when the streets were dusty and an oilman needed a class joint in which to do business. Beef, of course, is what to order, and it'll be done right. Full liquor license.

417 W. 5th Ave. ℂ 907/277-6332. www.clubparisrestaurant.com. Reservations recommended. Lunch $5.75–$12; dinner $14–$44. AE, DC, DISC, MC, V. Mon–Sat 11:30am–2:30pm and 5–11pm; Sun 5–10pm.

**Glacier Brewhouse** GRILL/SEAFOOD   A tasty, eclectic, and ever-changing menu is served in a large dining room with lodge decor, where the pleasant scent of the wood-fired grill hangs in the air. This place brews five hearty beers behind a glass wall. It's noisy and active, with lots of agreeable if trendy touches, such as the bread—made from spent brewery grain—that's set out on the tables with olive oil. An advantage for travelers is the wide price range—a feta cheese, spinach, and artichoke pizza is under $10.

737 W. 5th Ave. ℂ **907/274-BREW**. www.glacierbrewhouse.com. Reservations recommended for dinner. Lunch $8–$15; dinner $9–$34. AE, DISC, DC, MC, V. Summer 11am–11pm; winter Mon 11am–9:30pm, Tues–Thurs 11am–10pm, Fri–Sat 11am–11pm, Sun 4–9:30pm.

**The Marx Brothers Cafe** ECLECTIC/REGIONAL    A restaurant that began as a hobby among three friends nearly 20 years ago is still a labor of love and has become a standard of excellence in the state. The cuisine is varied and creative, ranging from Asian to Italian, but everyone orders the Caesar salad made at the table. The decor and style are studied casual elegance. Beer and wine license.

627 W. 3rd Ave. ℂ **907/278-2133**. www.marxcafe.com. Reservations required. Main courses $18–$36. AE, DC, MC, V. Summer Tues–Sat 5:30–10pm; winter Wed–Sat 5:30–10pm.

**Ristorante Orso** ITALIAN    Despite its Italian orientation (excellent pastas, great sauces), this restaurant also offers superb wood-grilled steaks and locally caught seafood in an elegant, comfortable setting.

737 W. 5th Ave. ℂ **907/222-3232**. www.orsoalaska.com. Reservations recommended. Lunch $8–$18; dinner $12–$30. AE, DC, DISC, MC, V. Summer Mon–Fri 11:30am–2:30pm, daily 5–11pm; winter Sun–Mon 5–9:30pm, Tues–Thurs 5–10pm, Fri–Sat 5–11pm.

**Simon and Seafort's Saloon and Grill** STEAK/SEAFOOD    This is one of the city's great dinner houses, with turn-of-the-century decor, a cheerful atmosphere, warm service, and fabulous sunset views of Cook Inlet. Prime rib and seafood are the specialties. Light meals are served in the bar.

420 L St. ℂ **907/274-3502**. Reservations recommended (reserve a couple of days in advance in summer). Lunch $7–$15; dinner $16–$40. AE, MC, V. Mon–Fri 11:15am–3:30pm; daily 5–10pm.

## 2 Seward

Since Seward—new competition from Whittier notwithstanding—is the northern embarkation and disembarkation port for most Gulf of Alaska cruise operators, passengers can almost be forgiven if they sometimes think the correct name of this Resurrection Bay community is "Seward-the-port-for-Anchorage." Although the majority of 7-day Gulf cruises are advertised as "Vancouver to Anchorage" (or the reverse), the ships don't actually sail to Anchorage proper. Instead, they dock in Seward and guests are carried by motorcoach (or, more recently, by rail) to or from Anchorage. Why? Because Seward and Whittier lie on the south side of the Kenai Peninsula, and Anchorage on the north. Sailing around the peninsula would add another day to the cruise.

This means that most people pass through Seward on their way to or from their ship but never really see much of the town. And that's a pity. Seward is an attractive little town rimmed by mountains and ocean, with streets lined with old wood-frame houses and new fishermen's residences. It's also home to the spectacular **Alaska SeaLife Center** (a marine research, rehabilitation, and public education center where visitors can watch scientists uncovering the secrets of nearby **Prince William Sound**). Seward is an ideal spot from which to make wildlife-watching day trips by boat into the sound or to begin one of a variety of road and rail trips through the **Kenai Peninsula,** one of Alaska's most beautiful expanses.

Seward was hit hard on Good Friday 1964 when a massive earthquake rattled Anchorage, the peninsula, and everything in between. The villagers (there were only about 2,500 of them) watched the water in the harbor drain away after the shaking stopped and realized immediately what was about to happen: a tidal wave. Because they were smart enough to read the signs and run for high ground, loss of life was miraculously slight when the towering 100-foot wall of water struck. The town itself, however, was heavily damaged, so many of the buildings that visitors see today are of a more recent vintage than might be expected.

## GETTING TO SEWARD & THE PORT

Most cruise passengers will arrive at Seward either by ship (at the end of their cruise) or by bus from the nearest major airport, **Anchorage International Airport.** The bus trip takes about 3 hours, taking passengers through the beautiful Chugach National Forest. If you haven't made transportation arrangements through your cruise line, **Seward Bus Line** (© **907/224-3608**) offers one trip a day (9am check-in) from Anchorage for $40 one-way. **Holland America Tours' Alaskan Express** (© **800/544-2206**) does the same for $44.

**BY PLANE**   Commuter air service is provided by **Era Aviation** (© **800/866-8394**) and **F. S. Air** (© **907/248-9595**) from Anchorage for about $69 one-way.

**BY CAR**   For those arriving by car, Seward and the Kenai Peninsula are served by a single major road, the Seward Highway.

**BY TRAIN**   The **Alaska Railroad** (© **800/544-0552** or 907/265-2494; www.akrr.com) offers extraordinarily scenic train service between Anchorage and Seward for $55 one-way ($90 round-trip).

## EXPLORING SEWARD

**INFORMATION**   The **Seward Chamber of Commerce** (© **907/224-8051;** www.sewardak.org) operates an information booth right on the cruise ship dock; it's open from 8am to noon and 3 to 7pm daily. If you're going to have time to look beyond the boundaries of the village, drop in at the **Kenai Fjords National Park Visitor Center,** near the waterfront on 4th Avenue (© **907/224-3175** or 907/224-2132), to pick up some literature, learn about what's new in the area, and peruse a list of hiking trails in Seward's environs. They're open May through Labor Day daily from 9am to 6pm, off season Monday through Friday from 9am to 5pm.

**GETTING AROUND**   The downtown area is within walking distance of the cruise ship dock, and you can easily cover downtown Seward on foot, although a little help is handy to get back and forth from the boat harbor. If it's not raining, a bike may be the best way. **Seward Mountain Bike Shop** (© **907/224-2448**), in a rail car near the depot at the harbor, rents high-performance mountain bikes as well as models that are good for just getting around town, plus other equipment. A cruiser is $18 for a half-day, $32 for a full day. For motorized transport, the **Chamber of Commerce Trolley** runs every half-hour from 10am to 7pm daily in summer; it goes south along 3rd Avenue and north on Ballaine Street, stopping at the railroad depot, the cruise ship dock, the Alaska SeaLife Center, and the harbor visitor center. The fare is $2 per trip, or $5 for an all-day pass.

There's a little bus, known as the Seward Trolley, that will carry you between the downtown area and the waterfront. It costs $3 for a day pass—use the service as often as you like. But it's not much more than a mile and it's a pleasant walk if the weather cooperates.

**ACCOMMODATIONS** ■
The Breeze Inn **3**
Hotel Seward **6**
The New Seward Hotel **6**
The Seward Windsong
    Lodge **2**
The Van Gilder Hotel **5**

**DINING** ◆
The Harbor Dinner Club **7**
Ray's Waterfront **2**

**ATTRACTIONS** ●
Alaska SeaLife Center **8**
The Seward Museum **4**

✈ Airport
🚢 Cruise Ship
    Dock
ⓘ Information
⊠ Post Office

## ATTRACTIONS WITHIN WALKING DISTANCE

**The Alaska SeaLife Center**    Opened in 1998, this center allows scientists to study, in their natural habitat, the Steller's sea lions, porpoises, sea otters, harbor seals, fish, and other forms of marine life that abound in the area, as well as the umpteen species of local seabirds—colorful rock puffins, cormorants, and more. The important thing, of course, is that you can study them, too—through windows that show you the undersea world. The center itself is something of a phoenix, rising from the metaphorical ashes of the 1989 *Exxon Valdez* disaster that so drastically affected the area's marine ecology and the creatures that inhabit the sound. Much of the $60 million needed to create the center came from an oil-spill reparation fund established by Exxon Corporation. It would be nice to record that the center has been an unqualified financial success, but it hasn't. The planners way overestimated the potential visitation, and the facility, strapped for cash, has been forced to request state government grants to cover the shortfall. The failure of this great facility to turn a profit is a pity—and probably caused by the fact that visitors tend to land in Seward and almost immediately board trains and coaches for Anchorage, leaving very little time for touring and sightseeing. Nevertheless, the SeaLife Center will continue operations and should be on everybody's must-see list.

301 Railway Ave. ✆ **800/224-2525** or 907/224-6300. www.alaskasealife.org. $14 adults, $11 children 7–12, free for children 6 and under. May–Aug daily 8am–8pm; Sept–Apr daily 9am–6pm.

**The Seward Museum**    This is a charming grandma's attic of a place, with clippings, memorabilia, and curiosities recalling town history, painter Rockwell Kent, and the ways of the past. An interesting exhibit revolves around the Russian ships built here in the 18th century.

Corner of 3rd and Jefferson sts. ℂ 907/224-3902. www.akohwy.com/s/semuseum.htm. $3 adults, 50¢ children 5–18, free for children under 5. Summer daily 9am–5pm.

## THE BEST SHORE EXCURSIONS

**Anchorage City Tour** (3–9 hr.; $39–$98): A restroom-equipped motorcoach takes you on a 3-hour drive from Seward through the Chugach National Forest and along Turnagain Arm between Seward and Anchorage. Once you hit Anchorage, the bus makes a circuit through the downtown area, pointing out sights of interest, good shops, and popular restaurants. You'll then be free for a few hours to shop, eat, or visit the Museum of History and Art. The tour is either an all-day round-trip affair from Seward or a half-day trip that ends in Anchorage (either downtown at Egan Center or at the Anchorage Airport).

**Exit Glacier** (3 hr.; $54): This excursion includes a quick orientation trip through Seward before heading out the Resurrection River Valley to Exit Glacier. After a short hike along nature trails, you'll come to the glacier face. *Note:* Chunks fall off the glacier regularly, so keep your distance—park rangers are on hand to see that you do.

**Mount McKinley Flightseeing** (3 hr.; $330): This tour is often canceled because of weather conditions, but if the skies are clear, you'll board a private plane at the Seward Airport and swoop over the dramatic valleys of the Kenai Peninsula to watch for wildlife, before heading over Anchorage and up the Susitna Valley and Kahiltna River to towering Mount McKinley, the highest peak in North America. On the return flight you'll pass over Prince William Sound for a different perspective.

**Portage Glacier** (2–8 hr.; $35–$96): This tour is typically done en route to Anchorage via motorcoach, but it's also available as a daylong round-trip excursion from Seward, hence the higher of the two prices. The MV *Ptarmigan,* an enclosed cruiser with an open top deck, sails up Portage Lake for an hour-long sojourn that sometimes brings you within 300 yards of the glacier.

**Resurrection Bay Wildlife Cruise** (4–5 hr.; $95–$115): A 90-foot touring vessel will take you for a 50-mile narrated tour into Resurrection Bay and the Kenai Fjords area. The highlight of this excursion is wildlife-watching—the region is teeming with birds and sea mammals, so chances are good that you'll see eagles, puffins, kittiwakes, cormorants, harbor seals, otters, sea lions, porpoises, and maybe even humpbacks.

## ORGANIZED TOURS

Downtown Seward can be explored with the help of a **walking-tour map,** available from the Chamber of Commerce visitor centers at the docks (p. 158) and at establishments throughout town. **Alaska Railroad** day tours are available for $50 per person on weekends by calling ℂ **800/544-0552** (better to do it in advance of arrival). The ride is as far as Portage and back, one of the state railway's most scenic segments. **Kenai Fjords Tours** (ℂ **800/478-8068** or 907/224-8068) has a wide variety of land excursions and day cruises in Resurrection Bay and the Kenai Fjords National Park. A 6-hour cruise is priced at $115 for adults and $58 for children, while a 9½-hour, 150-mile cruise, including deli-style lunch, is priced at $139 for adults and $69 for children under 12. **Coastal**

**Kayaking and Custom Adventures Worldwide** (© 800/288-2134 or 907/258-3866) offers kayaking day trips in Resurrection Bay for $95, as well as longer trips into Kenai Fjords National Park. **IditaRide dog-sled tours,** Old Exit Glacier Road, 3¾ miles out the Seward Highway (© **800/478-3139** or 907/224-8607), offers dog-sled demonstrations and rides on a wheeled dog sled.

In addition to these tours, fishing charters are available from various operators in the harbor.

## WHERE TO STAY

**The Breeze Inn**  Located right at the boat harbor, this large, three-story motel-style building offers good standard accommodations with the most convenient location for a fishing or Kenai Fjords boat trip. Twenty new rooms, at the upper end of the price range, are especially nice. A restaurant and lounge are across the parking lot.

1306 Seward Hwy. (P.O. Box 2147), Seward, AK 99664-2147. © **907/224-5237.** Fax 907/224-7024. www.breezeinn.com. 86 units. $109 single; $130–$188 double. Additional person in room $10 extra. AE, DC, DISC, MC, V.

**Hotel Seward**  The rooms here are large, fresh, and attractively decorated. Many rooms have big bay windows, and all have VCRs, refrigerators, and coffeemakers. The rooms with a view at the front go for a premium. Avoid the south-facing rooms, which look out onto the back of another hotel. This place was formerly the Best Western Hotel Seward.

217 5th Ave., Seward, AK 99664. © **907/224-2378.** Fax 907/224-3112. 38 units. $179–$224 double. Additional person in room $10 extra. AE, MC, V.

**The New Seward Hotel**  This place shares a lobby, an address, and a common ownership with the Hotel Seward, but the rooms are smaller and less expensive.

217 5th Ave., Seward, AK 99664. © **907/224-8001.** Fax 907/224-3112. 28 units. $69 double without private bathroom; $96 double with private bathroom. AE, DISC, MC, V.

**The Seward Windsong Lodge**  This hotel is the only one near Kenai Fjords National Park with a national park atmosphere. The location is out of town, among spruce trees in the broad, unspoiled valley of the Resurrection River. The collection of buildings goes on and on, with rooms set in separate lodges with entry from exterior porches. All accommodations have a crisp feel and feature two queen beds, rustic-style furniture, and good amenities.

Mailing address: 2525 C St., Suite 405, Anchorage, AK 99503. © **888/959-9590** or 907/224-7116. www.sewardwindsong.com. 12 units. $189 double. Extra person over age 11 $15. AE, MC, V. Exit Glacier/Herman Leirer Rd. Continue for ½ mile.

**The Van Gilder Hotel**  This charming if creaky old place was founded in 1916 and is listed on the National Register of Historic Places. Some rooms have a lot of charm, but authenticity means they tend to be small and unique, so choose carefully.

308 Adams St. (P.O. Box 609), Seward, AK 99664. © **800/204-6835** or 907/224-3079. Fax 907/224-3689. www.vangilderhotel.com. 24 units. High season $105 double with shared bathroom, $135–$155 double with private bathroom, $185 suite; low season $55–$75 double with shared bathroom, $65–$110 double with private bathroom, $115–$145 suite. Extra person $10. AE, DC, DISC, MC, V.

## WHERE TO DINE

**The Harbor Dinner Club** STEAK/SEAFOOD  This old-fashioned family restaurant has been the same reliable place as long as anyone can remember.

With white tablecloths and a menu that ranges from fine seafood to a basic but delicious hamburger, you don't have to spend a lot of money to eat in a quiet, well-appointed dining room. Full liquor license.

220 5th Ave. ℭ 907/224-3012. Main courses $9.50–$19; lunch $7–$15. AE, DC, DISC, MC, V. Daily 11am–2:30pm and 5–11pm.

**Ray's Waterfront** STEAK/SEAFOOD   The lively, noisy dining room here has big windows that look out across the small-boat harbor. This is where the locals will send you, and for good reason: The food is just right, and the atmosphere is fun. The specialty is salmon served on a cedar plank. To eat well and less expensively, order the delicious fish chowder and a small Caesar salad. Don't count on speedy seating or service. Full liquor license.

At the small-boat harbor. ℭ 907/224-5606. Lunch $6–$15; dinner $16–$25. AE, DISC, MC, V. 18% gratuity added for parties of 6 or more. Mid-Mar to Sept daily 11am–11pm. Closed Oct to mid-Mar.

## 3 Vancouver

Located in the extreme southwestern corner of British Columbia, Vancouver has the good fortune to be surrounded by both mountains and ocean. The city has been expanding and growing rapidly, thanks to an influx of foreign money (especially from Hong Kong), and has undergone a major construction boom. But the development has not diminished the quality of life in Vancouver, which has a rich cultural heritage that includes Northwest Coast Native tribes and a flourishing Asian community. The city also has a thriving arts scene, including numerous summertime festivals focusing on various forms of entertainment such as folk music, jazz, and comedy. Residents and visitors alike relish the proximity of opportunities to sailboard, rock climb, mountain bike, wilderness hike, kayak, and ski on a world-class mountain. You can do it all in the same day if you have the energy. For day-trippers, the city offers easily accessible attractions including the historic **Gastown district,** with its shops and cafes, and a thriving **Chinatown.** And with the worth of the U.S. dollar strong against the Canadian currency (the exchange rate at press time was US$1 = C$1.27), a visit to the stores on Robson Street and **Granville Island** is practically a must.

You'll likely visit Vancouver at the beginning or end of your Alaska cruise, as it's the major southern transit point. Crystal—with its longer itinerary from San Francisco—also offers it as a port of call. We recommend that you try to come in at least a day before your cruise (or if you'll be here at the end of your cruise, plan to stay an extra day) so that you have time to explore.

*Note:* Rates below are calculated in U.S. dollars and could change based on the exchange rate at the time of your trip.

## GETTING TO VANCOUVER & THE PORT

Most cruise ships dock at **Canada Place** (ℭ 604/666-7200) at the end of Burrard Street. A landmark in the city, the pier terminal is noted for its five-sail structure, which reaches into the harbor. It's located at the edge of the downtown district and is just a quick stroll from the **Gastown** area (see below), with its cafes, art and souvenir shops, and Robson Street, where trendy fashions can be found. Right near the pier are hotels, restaurants, and shops, as well as the **Tourism Vancouver Infocentre.** Ships also sometimes dock at the **Ballantyne** cruise terminal, a 5-minute cab ride away from Canada Place.

**BY PLANE**   Vancouver International Airport is located 13km (8 miles) south of downtown Vancouver. The average taxi fare from the airport to downtown is

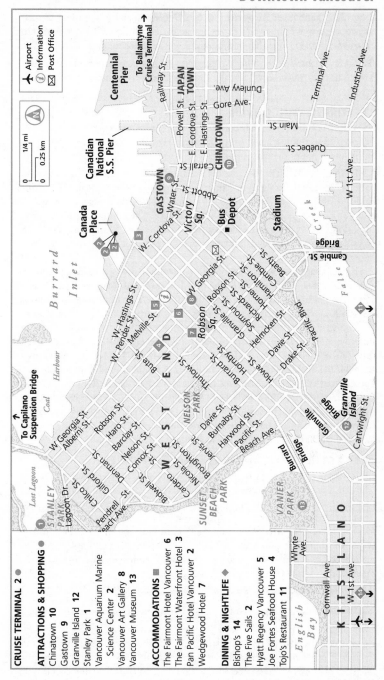

# Downtown Vancouver

**CRUISE TERMINAL 2** ●

**ATTRACTIONS & SHOPPING** ●
Chinatown **10**
Gastown **9**
Granville Island **12**
Stanley Park **1**
Vancouver Aquarium Marine
Science Center **2**
Vancouver Art Gallery **8**
Vancouver Museum **13**

**ACCOMMODATIONS** ■
The Fairmont Hotel Vancouver **6**
The Fairmont Waterfront Hotel **3**
Pan Pacific Hotel Vancouver **2**
Wedgewood Hotel **7**

**DINING & NIGHTLIFE** ◆
Bishop's **14**
The Five Sails **2**
Hyatt Regency Vancouver **5**
Joe Fortes Seafood House **4**
Tojo's Restaurant **11**

✈ Airport
ⓘ Information
⊠ Post Office

0    1/4 mi
0    0.25 km

about $20. **Vancouver Airporter** (℅ **604/946-8866**) buses offer service one-way to the city for about $7.75 per person for adults (less for kids). **AirLimo** (℅ **604/273-1331**) offers flat-rate limousine service at $28 for up to six passengers.

**BY CAR**    Don't look for a freeway to carry you from the airport to downtown. There isn't one. All you can do is take Granville Street in and hope that the traffic's light.

## EXPLORING VANCOUVER

**INFORMATION**    The **Vancouver Tourist InfoCentre,** 200 Burrard St. (℅ **604/683-2000**), is open May to Labor Day daily from 8am to 6pm, daily 8:30am to 5:30pm the rest of the year.

**GETTING AROUND**    Because of its shape, it is often necessary to get around parts of Vancouver by using one of several bridges—Burrard Bridge, Granville Bridge, Cambie Street Bridge, and, of course, Lions Gate Bridge, under which cruise ships pass going from and to Canada Place. These sometimes make driving a slow process. (If you've ever crossed, say, the George Washington Bridge in New York or San Francisco's Bay or Golden Gate bridges during rush hour, you know what we mean!)

Car-rental agencies with local branches include Avis, Budget, Hertz Canada, and Thrifty. You can easily walk the downtown area of Vancouver, but if you want transportation, you've got a few options. The **Translink system** (℅ **604/ 521-0400**) includes electric buses, ferries, and the magnetic-rail SkyTrain. Service on the main routes runs from 5am to 2am, and schedules are available at many hotels and online (www.translink.bc.ca). Taxis are available through **Black Top** (℅ **604/731-1111**), **Yellow Cab** (℅ **604/681-1111**), and **MacLure's** (℅ **604/731-9211**), and can either be called or found around the major hotels. You can rent a bicycle from **Spokes and Stanley Park Bicycle Rentals,** 1798 W. Georgia St. (℅ **604/688-5141**) from $2.75 per hour, $7.50 for a half-day, and $11 for a full day. Helmets are required by law and, along with locks, are included in the rate. The city has several great bicycle runs, including Stanley Park and the Seawall Promenade, and Pacific Spirit Park.

### ATTRACTIONS WITHIN WALKING DISTANCE

**Chinatown**    Vancouver's Chinatown is one of the largest in North America (though it doesn't hold a candle to those in New York and San Francisco), and like Gastown, it's also a historic district. Chinese architecture and the **Dr. Sun Yat-sen Garden** (578 Carrall St., ℅ **604/689-7133;** admission $4 adults, $2.50 kids) are among the attractions, along with great food and shops selling Chinese wares. In addition to photogenic Chinese gates, bright-red buildings, and open-air markets, you'll find the amazing 6-foot-wide **Sam Kee Building,** at 8 W. Pender St.

In the area bordered by E. Pender and Keefer sts., from Carrall St. to Gore Ave.

**Gastown**    Gastown is named for "Gassy" Jack Deighton, who in 1867 built a saloon in Maple Tree Square (at the intersection of Water, Alexander, and Carrall sts.) to serve the area's loggers and trappers. The Gastown of today offers cobble-stone streets, historic buildings, gaslights, a steam-powered clock (near the corner of Water and Cambie sts.), street musicians, and a touch of bohemia. It's so close to the ship pier that it's a must-see. There are boutiques, antiques and art shops, and lots of tourist-geared shops, along with restaurants, clubs, and cafes.

Located in the area bordered by Water and Alexander sts., from Richard St. east to Columbia St.

(*Tips* **Safety**

In Vancouver, it's advisable not to wander too far off the beaten path. Only a block or two from Gastown, you can encounter parks that drug-users frequent, plus other places that you wouldn't want to wander into.

**Granville Island**   Granville Island is nirvana for shoppers, with a vibrant daily market and streets lined with fine-art studios. Downtown, **Robson Street** is chockablock with boutiques, souvenir shops, coffeehouses, and bistros. The massive **Pacific Centre Mall** fills the city blocks between Robson, Dunsmuir, Howe, and Granville streets. It's within easy walking distance of the pier.

Across False Creek. (It's a hearty walk from downtown, so depending on where you're staying, you may want to take a cab.)

**Stanley Park**   Just a few miles from the heart of downtown Vancouver, Stanley Park's 405 hectares (1,000 acres) contain rose gardens, totem poles, a yacht club, a kids' water park, miles of wooded hiking trails, great vantage points for views of Lions Gate Bridge, and the outstanding **Vancouver Aquarium Marine Science Center** (② 604/659-3400; $12 adults, $9.75 youths, $6 kids 4–12).

Downtown Vancouver, northwest of the cruise ship terminal.

**Vancouver Art Gallery**   Located within easy walking distance of the pier, the gallery is housed in a building constructed in 1906 as the provincial courthouse. It contains an impressive collection that includes works by British Columbia artist Emily Carr and the Canadian Group of Seven. Also on display are international and other regional paintings, sculptures, graphics, photography, and video ranging from classic to contemporary. The Annex Gallery features rotating educational exhibits geared toward younger audiences.

750 Hornby St. ② 604/662-4719. $9.25 adults, $6.60 seniors (half-price Tues), $5.90 students, free for children under 12. Mon–Wed and Fri–Sun 10am–5:30pm; Thurs 10am–9pm.

**Vancouver Museum**   This museum offers a history of the city, from the Coast Salish Indian settlement to the arrival of early pioneers to European settlement to 20th-century expansion. The exhibit allows visitors to walk through the steerage deck of a 19th-century immigrant ship, peek into a Hudson's Bay Company trading post, and sit in an 1880s Canadian-Pacific passenger car. Re-creations of Victorian and Edwardian rooms show how early Vancouverites decorated their homes.

1100 Chestnut St. ② 604/736-4431. $7.50 adults, $4.75 youths. Fri–Wed 10am–9pm, Thurs 10am–5pm throughout the summer.

## ATTRACTIONS OUTSIDE THE DOWNTOWN AREA

**Capilano Suspension Bridge**   Sure it's touristy, but it's still a kick to cross this narrow, historic, 137m (450-ft.) walking bridge, located 70m (230 ft.) above the Capilano River in North Vancouver (about a 10-min. drive, or about a $13 cab ride from downtown). From this vantage point, even the towering evergreens below look tiny (this attraction is not for those with a fear of heights). The adjacent park offers hiking trails, history and forestry exhibits, a carving center, and Native American dance performances (in the summer months only), as well as restaurants and a gift shop.

3735 Capilano Rd., North Vancouver. ② 604/985-7474. Admission $13 adults, $9.25 seniors and students, $2 children 6–12, free for children 5 and under. May–Sept daily 8:30am–dusk; Oct–Apr daily 9am–5pm.

## ORGANIZED TOURS

**Stanley Park Horse-Drawn Tours** (© **604/681-5115**) has offered tours of the 405-hectare (1,000-acre) Stanley Park by horse-drawn trolley for more than a century. The narrated, 1-hour tours depart from the Coal Harbour parking lot beside the Stanley Park information booth on Park Drive. Tickets are $15 for adults, $12 for students, and $7 for kids 3 to 12. **The Vancouver Trolley Company** (© **888/451-5581** or 604/801-5515) has old-fashioned (engine-powered) trolleys offering narrated tours on a circuit that includes Gastown, Chinatown, Granville Island, Stanley Park, and other areas of interest. You can get off and on as you like. Stop no. 1 is in Gastown. Tickets are $17 for adults and $8 for kids.

## THE BEST SHORE EXCURSIONS

**Capilano Canyon Nature Tour** (4 hr.; $55 adults, $29 kids 12 and under): Walk alongside the canyon and through a rainforest with 500-year-old trees, as guides describe the ecosystem and wildlife habitats. Then cross the Lions Gate Bridge, with its spectacular views of the skyline, and eat a picnic lunch before returning to the airport or your downtown hotel.

**City Tour** (2½–3 hr.; $35): This bus tour covers major sights like Gastown, Chinatown, Stanley Park, and high-end residential areas. You'll also visit Queen Elizabeth Park, located at the city's highest southern vantage point, and the Bloedell Conservatory, located in the park's environs and offering a commanding 360-degree city view plus an enclosed tropical rainforest complete with free-flying birds.

*Note:* This tour is usually offered after the cruise and is available only to passengers with late-afternoon or evening flights. At the end of the tour, you are dropped off at the airport for your flight home.

**Vancouver by Night** (2 hr.; $35): Enjoy the visual splendors of the city—Gastown, Granville Park, Chinatown, Canada Place, and the rest—on an after-dark motorcoach ride.

## WHERE TO STAY

Virtually all of Vancouver's downtown hotels are within walking distance of shops, restaurants, and attractions, but for safety reasons you might want to avoid places around Hastings and Main after dark. Granville Street downtown is an area that has been "cleaned up" and is now home to some lower-end, boutique-type hotels. The area has clubs and an active nightlife that attracts a younger set—but also lots of panhandlers.

**The Fairmont Hotel Vancouver**   After extensive renovations, the grande dame of Vancouver's hotels has been restored beyond its former glory. Designed on a generous scale, with a copper roof, marble interiors, and massive proportions, the hotel conveys unparalleled luxury and spaciousness in its lobby and public areas. High tea is a proud tradition here. Guest rooms have marble bathrooms and mahogany furnishings and offer city, harbor, and mountain views.

900 W. Georgia St., Vancouver, BC V6C 2W6. © **800/441-1414** (Fairmont Hotels & Resorts) or 604/684-3131. Fax 604/662-1929. www.fairmont.com. 544 units. $215–$310 double; from $390 suite. AE, DC, DISC, MC, V. Parking $19.

**The Fairmont Waterfront Hotel**   Made up of 23 stories of blue reflective glass, this ultramodern hotel takes advantage of its harborside location, offering spectacular waterfront and mountain views from 70% of the rooms. The rooms include amenities such as two-line phones. A concourse links the hotel to the rest of Waterfront Centre, Canada Place, and the Alaska cruise ship terminal.

900 Canada Place Way, Vancouver, BC V6C 3L5. ℂ **800/828-7447** (Fairmont Hotels and Resorts) in the U.S., or 604/691-1991. Fax 604/691-1999. www.fairmont.com. 518 units. $190–$250 double; from $290 suite. AE, DC, MC, V. Parking $14.

**Hyatt Regency Vancouver**   The Hyatt is a modern white tower built over the Royal Centre Mall, which contains 60 specialty shops. The very large guest rooms are tastefully decorated with understated yet comfortable furnishings. Corner rooms on the north and west sides have balconies with lovely views.

655 Burrard St., Vancouver, BC V6C 2R7. ℂ **800/233-1234** or 604/689-3707. Fax 604/643-5812. www.hyatt.com. 644 units. From $190 double; $442 suite. AE, DC, DISC, MC, V. Parking $13.

**Pan Pacific Hotel Vancouver**   Vancouver's most distinctive landmark is Canada Place Pier, with five gleaming white Teflon sails that recall a giant sailing vessel. The pier houses the Vancouver Trade and Convention Centre as well as the Alaska cruise ship terminal. It also offers a splendid **IMAX theater** (ℂ **604/682-4629**) where, for about $7, cruise passengers can while away an hour or so viewing the wonders of Alaska and other places, such as Mount Everest and the Galapagos Islands. Atop the terminal is the spectacular 23-story Pan Pacific Hotel Vancouver. This and the Fairmont Waterfront Hotel are the closest accommodations to the cruise ship dock. All of the guest rooms are modern, spacious, and comfortably furnished. All come with such amenities as coffeemakers, irons, and ironing boards. Try to book a harborside room so you can enjoy the view.

300–999 Canada Place, Vancouver, BC V6C 3B5. ℂ **800/937-1515** or 604/662-8111. Fax 604/685-8690. www.panpac.com. 506 units. $316–$381 double; $419–$452 suite. AE, DC, MC, V. Valet parking $14.

**Wedgewood Hotel**   This small boutique property near the Robson Street shops features individually furnished rooms filled with nice amenities. Penthouse suites also offer fireplaces, wet bars, Jacuzzis, and scenic garden terraces. Public rooms boast antiques and fresh flowers, and the hotel has one of the best watering holes in town, Bacchus, an upscale piano bar where you can sink into a plush chair or couch, enjoy an excellent martini, and take in the local scene. The Bacchus restaurant has also won awards for its fine cuisine.

845 Hornby St., Vancouver, BC V6Z 1V1. ℂ **800/663-0666** or 604/689-7777. Fax 604/608-5348. www.wedgewoodhotel.com. 89 units. $296–$370 double; $444–$666 suite. AE, DC, MC, V. Parking $11.

## WHERE TO DINE

**Bishop's** PACIFIC NORTHWEST   The atmosphere is all candlelight, white linen, and soft jazz; the service is impeccable; and the food is even better. Owner John Bishop greets you personally, escorts you to your table, and introduces you to an extensive catalog of fine wines and a menu he describes as "contemporary home cooking"—which means dishes such as roast duck breast with sun-dried Okanagan Valley fruits and candied ginger glacé, steamed smoked black cod with new potatoes and horseradish sabayon, and marinated sirloin of lamb. If you have only 1 evening to dine out in Vancouver, spend it here.

2183 W. 4th Ave. ℂ **604/738-2025**. Reservations required. Main courses $21–$26. AE, DC, MC, V. Mon–Sat 5:30–11pm; Sun 5:30–10pm.

**The Five Sails** PACIFIC NORTHWEST/SEAFOOD   The Five Sails' view of Coal Harbour, Stanley Park, and the Coast Mountains is utter magic, a vision of the rugged nirvana that is Vancouver. Even more enchanting, the Five Sails' food is a match for the view. Those dining in twosomes and feeling flush should not pass up on the Voyage of Discovery, a spectacular fresh seafood platter featuring tuna crab roll, freshly shucked oysters with red-wine mignonette, smoked wild sockeye, scallop seviche, and other delicacies too numerous to list. Other inventive appetizers include an albacore tuna hot pot, and Dungeness crab ravioli. Main courses feature pan-seared halibut, oven-roasted lobster, crispy sea bass, and a slow-roasted B.C. sockeye. Ingredients are excellent here, and preparation is inventive without being too clever. The nonpiscivorous are catered to with a trio of duck, beef, and lamb dishes, and though they are excellent, well-prepared dishes, this is not really where the menu's heart lies.

999 Canada Place Way, in the Pan Pacific Hotel. (C) **604/891-2892.** Reservations recommended. Main courses $15–$23; tasting menu $34–$42. AE, DC, MC, V. Daily 6–10pm.

**Joe Fortes Seafood and Chop House** SEAFOOD This two-story, dark-wood restaurant with an immensely popular bar is always filled with Vancouver's young-and-successful crowd. The decor and atmosphere are reminiscent of an oyster bar, and the spacious covered and heated roof garden (where cigar smokers gather) is pure Vancouver. Pan-roasted oysters are a menu staple. A daily selection of up to a dozen types of oysters is offered raw or cooked in a variety of ways, along with fresh fish, Dungeness crab, and live lobsters (at market prices). The wine list has earned well-deserved awards 8 years and running.

777 Thurlow St. (C) **604/669-1940.** Reservations recommended. Most main courses $13–$27. AE, DC, DISC, MC, V. Daily 11am–4pm lunch menu (brunch Sat–Sun); 4–10:30pm dinner.

**Tojo's Restaurant** JAPANESE Located above an A&W burger joint, this restaurant has an unimpressive decor but nice city views if you can snag a window seat. And Hidekazu Tojo's sushi is Vancouver's best, attracting Japanese businessmen, Hollywood celebrities, and anyone else who's willing to pay for the finest. Tell Tojo how much you want to spend, and he'll prepare an incredible meal to fit your budget.

777 W. Broadway. (C) **604/872-8050.** Reservations required for sushi bar. Main dishes $17–$74. AE, DC, MC, V. Mon–Sat 5–10pm.

## 4 Seattle

Americans have more opportunities than ever now to begin and end their cruise on U.S. soil—in Seattle. Since the events of September 11, 2001, caused cruise lines to redeploy their ships to destination areas and home ports that were perceived as less threatening (that is, to move them out of Europe), Alaska has become more and more popular as a cruise destination. And its popularity has not waned, even now, several years removed from the World Trade Center tragedy, because Americans remain skittish about long-distance air travel to the European and Mediterranean cruise markets. In the interest of variety and also because the port of Vancouver is bursting at the seams with cruise ships (so many cruise passengers needed air transportation into the Canadian city that the airlines were unable to accommodate them all), Seattle has become an attractive port for large oceangoing passenger liners. In 2000, only one major ship was based in Seattle for the Alaska cruise season. In 2005, six large vessels will be based in the city. And they will be joined by Cruise West's small (80–140 passengers) ships and the vessels of other smaller lines that have operated a few cruises out of Seattle every summer for years.

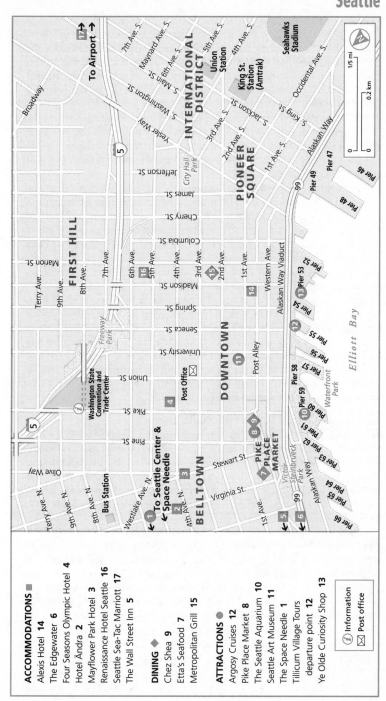

# Seattle

**ACCOMMODATIONS** ■
Alexis Hotel **14**
The Edgewater **6**
Four Seasons Olympic Hotel **4**
Hotel Ändra **2**
Mayflower Park Hotel **3**
Renaissance Hotel Seattle **16**
Seattle Sea-Tac Marriott **17**
The Wall Street Inn **5**

**DINING** ◆
Chez Shea **9**
Etta's Seafood **7**
Metropolitan Grill **15**

**ATTRACTIONS** ●
Argosy Cruises **12**
Pike Place Market **8**
The Seattle Aquarium **10**
Seattle Art Museum **11**
The Space Needle **1**
Tillicum Village Tours
departure point **12**
Ye Olde Curiosity Shop **13**

ⓘ Information
✉ Post office

As cruise ports go, Seattle need bow the knee to no other. It is every bit as scenically appealing as, say, Vancouver. Its skyline is dominated by the 607-foot-high revolving Space Needle, built in 1962 for the World's Fair and linked to the heart of downtown by a monorail. Seattle has shopping, fine restaurants, attractions galore, good air service, culture, a wide range of accommodations, internal transportation—everything you need, in fact, to enjoy a day or two before or after your cruise.

Seattle is very much a water-oriented city, set between Puget Sound and Lake Washington, with Lake Union in the center. Practically everywhere you look, the views are of sailboats, cargo ships, ferries, windsurfers, and anglers. One of our favorite pastimes on nice days in Seattle is to take one of the local ferries— to anywhere. Just for the fun of it!

The **Seattle Waterfront,** along Alaskan Way from Yesler Way North to Bay Street and Myrtle Edwards Park, is the city's single most popular attraction, and much like San Francisco's Fisherman's Wharf area, that's both good and bad. Yes, it's very touristy, with tacky gift shops, saltwater taffy, T-shirts galore, and lots of overpriced restaurants, but it's also home to the Seattle Aquarium, the Pike Place Market and its many vendors, and Ye Olde Curiosity Shop (king of the tacky gift stores). Your ship will dock right along this strip. There are companies located here that offer sailboat and sea-kayak tours.

At Pier 54, you'll find companies offering sea-kayak tours, sport-fishing trips, jet-boat tours, and bicycle rentals. At Pier 55, boats leave for 1½-hour harbor cruises, as well as the **Tillicum Village** excursions to Blake Island (see "Attractions Outside the Downtown Area," below). At Pier 57 you'll find the **Bay Pavilion,** which has a vintage carousel and a video arcade to keep the kids busy. At Pier 59 you'll find the **Seattle Aquarium** and a waterfront park. Meanwhile Pier 69 is the dock for the ferries that ply the waters between Seattle and Victoria. Sunset and jazz cruises also leave from this pier.

## GETTING TO SEATTLE & THE PORT

**BY PLANE    Seattle-Tacoma International Airport (© 800/544-1965** or 206/ 431-4444), also known as **Sea-Tac,** is located about 14 miles south of Seattle. It's connected to the city by Interstate 5. Generally, allow 30 minutes for the trip between the airport and downtown. Since the Bell Street passenger ship pier is so superbly located, a few minutes' walk from the heart of downtown, airport taxis will drop you at the terminal for about the same price as they would charge to go to any of the major Seattle hotels.

A **taxi** between the airport and downtown will cost you around $30. **Gray Line Airport Express (© 800/426-7532** or 206/626-6088) provides service between all the airport terminals and seven downtown hotels, with the first hotel pickup at 4:50am and continuing every half-hour through the day until the last pickup at 11:20pm. The fares are $9.50 one-way, $15 round-trip; children ages 2 to 12 pay $6 one-way and $10 round-trip. **Shuttle Express (© 425/981-7000)** also gets you between Sea-Tac and downtown. The company's check-in desk is on the third floor of the parking garage at the airport, and a one-way fare for up to three people is $21 to most downtown areas.

**BY CAR**    The major freeway running through Seattle is Interstate 5. Follow it south from downtown to Sea-Tac. Interstate 5 runs north to the Canadian border, which leads, ultimately, to the road to Vancouver. Alaskan Way, a busy street, runs along the waterfront and past the cruise ship terminal. It's only a very short car or cab ride from any city hotel to the cruise terminal, which is not more than 10 minutes from even the most distant of the hotels listed here.

## EXPLORING SEATTLE

**INFORMATION**    The **Seattle-King County Convention and Visitors Bureau** operates a visitor information center in the Washington State Convention and Trade Center, 800 Convention Place, Galleria Level, at the corner of 8th Avenue and Pike Street (© **206/461-5840**). It's open 8:30am to 5pm Monday through Friday, 10am to 4pm Saturday and Sunday late May through August, and varying shorter hours during the remainder of the year.

**GETTING AROUND**    Nearly every major car-rental company has an outlet at Sea-Tac, and many also have offices in downtown hotels. Prices will depend on the season and even on the day of the week (rentals on Fri, for example, when cruise passengers are likely to arrive in large numbers, will probably cost more than they will on, say, Wed). **Seattle Metro** (© **800/542-7876** or 206/553-3000) offers free bus transportation within the downtown area between the hours of 6am and 7pm, and charges a couple of dollars for rides outside the downtown area. The company also operates a waterfront service using old-fashioned streetcars, some of it in the ride-free area, some of it outside. Visitors to the Space Needle can use the **monorail** from downtown, 1¼ miles away, for $1.25 one-way.

## ATTRACTIONS WITHIN WALKING DISTANCE

**Pike Place Market**    City officials have worked overtime to ensure that the Pike Place Market, begun in 1907 and one of Seattle's most enduring institutions, remains true to its roots. A big push was made a few years ago to add more tourist-friendly T-shirt and souvenir shops, but the market fought to keep the emphasis on food and flowers. The market remains the single best place in the city to find fresh produce and seasonal specialties like Rainier cherries, Washington asparagus, fresh king salmon, and Northwest hazelnuts. The food grazing is unsurpassed: Don't leave without trying a Dungeness crab cocktail, a fresh-baked piroshki or cinnamon roll, and, of course, coffee from any number of vendors, including the original Starbucks. Explore below the main floor to find wonderful specialty shops, including one of the best stores devoted to magic and old magic posters in the country, a fragrant store dedicated to spices, and an exotic bird store where the parrots squawk in your face. A 90-minute Market Heritage Tour is offered Wednesday through Sunday at 11am and 2pm, beginning at the Market Heritage Foundation Visitor Center on Western Avenue. At night the vendors clear out, but the several excellent restaurants, bars, and theater in the market keep on hopping.

Between Pike and Pine sts., at 1st Ave. © 206/682-7453. Mon–Sat 9am–6pm; Sun 11am–5pm.

**The Seattle Aquarium**    The Seattle Aquarium presents well-designed exhibits dealing with the watery worlds of the Puget Sound region. One of the aquarium's most popular exhibits is an interactive tide pool and discovery lab that re-creates Washington's wave-swept intertidal zone. From the underwater viewing dome, you get a fish's-eye view of life beneath the waves. Each September you can watch salmon return up a fish ladder to spawn.

1483 Alaskan Way, Pier 59, Waterfront Park. © 206/386-4320. Admission $12 adults, $8.75 seniors, $7.50 ages 6–15, $5 ages 3–5. Extra charges and package rates for the ImaxDome films. Daily 9:30am–7pm.

**Seattle Art Museum**   You can't miss this place, with its stark cement facade and giant Jonathon Borofsky *Hammering Man* sculpture outside. Inside, the Seattle Art Museum is a repository for everything from African masks, old masters, and Andy Warhol to one of the nation's premier collections of Northwest Coast Indian art.

100 University St., 2 blocks from Pike Place Market. © **206/654-3100.** Admission $7 adults, $5 seniors and students, free for children 12 and under, free to all 1st Thurs of the month. Tues–Sun 10am–5pm (to 9pm Thurs).

**The Space Needle**   From a distance, this structure resembles a flying saucer on top of a tripod. When it was built for the World's Fair, it was meant to suggest future architectural trends; today, the soaring structure is the quintessential symbol of Seattle. At 518 feet above ground level, the views from the observation deck are stunning. High-powered telescopes let you zoom in on distant sights, and there's a lounge and two very expensive restaurants inside.

203 6th Ave. N., Seattle Center. © **206/443-2111.** Admission $13 adults, $11 seniors, $6 children 6–13. Daily 9am–11pm.

**Ye Olde Curiosity Shop**   A cross between a souvenir store and Ripley's Believe It or Not! It's weird! It's tacky! It's always packed! See Siamese-twin calves, a natural mummy, the Lord's Prayer on a grain of rice, a narwhal tusk, shrunken heads, a 67-pound snail, fleas in dresses, and walrus and whale oosiks (the bone of the male reproductive organ). The collection of oddities was started in 1899 by Joe Standley, who had developed a more-than-passing interest in strange curios.

1001 Alaskan Way, on Pier 54. © **206/682-5844.** Free admission. Mon–Fri 9:30am–6pm; Sat–Sun 9am–6pm.

## ATTRACTIONS OUTSIDE THE DOWNTOWN AREA

**Tillicum Village/Tillicum Village Tours**   Located at Blake Island State Marine Park across Puget Sound from Seattle, and only accessible by tour boat or private boat, **Tillicum Village** was built in conjunction with the 1962 Seattle World's Fair. The "village" is actually a large restaurant and performance hall fashioned after a traditional Northwest Coast Indian longhouse. With totem poles standing vigil out front, the forest encircling the longhouse, and the waters of Puget Sound stretching out into the distance, it's a beautiful spot. **Tillicum Village Tours** operates tours that include the scenic boat ride to and from the island, a lunch or dinner of alder-smoked salmon, and a performance by traditional masked dancers—members of 11 Northwest tribes. After the meal and the dance performance, you can strike out on forest trails to explore the island.

Pier 56. © **206/443-1244.** 4-hr. tour $70 adults, $59 seniors, $25 children 5–12.

## THE BEST SHORE EXCURSIONS

**Experience Music Project** (4 hr.; $24): Visit a museum dedicated to the development and social significance of popular music. Many of the exhibits include interactive features and state-of-the-art technology, and there is a gallery containing a large collection of the memorabilia of local boy Jimi Hendrix. Country, jazz, rock, punk, hip-hop . . . whatever your taste, you're likely to know more about it when you leave this place than you did when you went in.

**Mount Rainier 1-Day Tour** (10 hr.; $72): Take a coach ride to Mount Rainier National Park, home of the 14,410-foot peak that is visible on a clear day from much of the city, and heavily contributes to Seattle's scenic beauty. Located 90 miles southeast of Seattle, Mount Rainier and its surrounding 235,000 acres were designated a national park in 1899. If you're visiting it independently, be aware that there is a charge of $10 per vehicle for entry.

**Ride the Ducks of Seattle** (2 hr; $24 adults, $13 children 12 and under): See the wonders of the Emerald City by land and sea in a restored World War II amphibious landing craft, while a Coast Guard–certified captain offers (mostly) light-hearted commentary on the passing scene. You'll see the historic waterfront area, Pioneer Square, and Safeco Field ballpark, and then splash into Lake Union for a short cruise. This is a great family excursion.

## ORGANIZED TOURS

**Argosy Cruises**   This firm offers a variety of short cruises around the Seattle area, including a **Seattle harbor cruise,** a cruise through the **Hiram Chittenden Locks to Lake Union,** and cruises around **Lake Washington** (which, among other things, take you past the fabled Xanadu built by Bill Gates on the shore of Lake Washington).

Pier 55. ℂ 206/623-4252. Tickets $25 adults, $12 children 5–12, free for children under 5.

## WHERE TO STAY

**Alexis Hotel**   Unbelievable as it sounds, this elegant boutique hotel, located in an enviable location halfway between Pike Place Market and Pioneer Square, and only 2 blocks from the waterfront, was once a parking garage. Now listed in the National Register of Historic Places, the 90-year-old building is a sparkling gem, with a pleasant mix of old and new and a friendly staff. Classic styling prevails in the guest rooms, each of which is a little different (the nicest by far are the fireplace suites, so ask for one when you book).

1007 1st Ave. (at Madison St.), Seattle, WA 98104. ℂ **800/426-7033** or 206/624-4844. Fax 206/621-9009. www.alexishotel.com. 109 units. $230–$255 double; $245–$625 suite. AE, DC, MC, V. Valet parking $20.

**The Edgewater**   Built on a pier, Seattle's only waterfront hotel is incongruously designed to resemble a deluxe mountain lodge. Somehow, it works. A vaulted open-beamed ceiling, a deer-antler chandelier, a river-stone fireplace, and a wall of glass that looks out on busy Elliott Bay and gorgeous sunsets all combine to make the lobby a great place to hang out. Rooms feature rustic lodgepole pine furniture. Because the least expensive rooms here overlook the parking lot (and city), you really should opt for a water-view or partial-water-view room. It makes all the difference.

Pier 67, 2411 Alaskan Way, Seattle, WA 98121. ℂ **800/624-0670** or 206/728-7000. Fax 206/441-4119. www.edgewaterhotel.com. 236 units. $137–$250 double; $275–$750 suite. AE, DC, DISC, MC, V. Valet parking $18.

**Four Seasons Olympic Hotel**   This is one of the biggest, and absolutely one of the most elegant, hotels in Seattle. Reminiscent of an Italian Renaissance palace, complete with crystal and gilt chandeliers, marble facings, and dark oak walls and pillars, the hotel offers a health club, shopping area (upscale, of course), concierge, complimentary overnight shoeshine, and much more. Not cheap, to be sure, but worth the money.

411 University St., Seattle, WA 98101. ℂ **800/332-3442** or 206/621-1700. Fax 206/682-9633. www.fshr.com. 450 units. $315–$375 double; $355–$1,850 suite. AE, DC, DISC, MC, V. Valet parking $22; self-parking $21.

**Hotel Ändra**   Part Art Deco, part Buzz Lightyear—that describes this new boutique hotel located in the trendy Belltown enclave, an easy walking distance from Pike Place Market, the Seattle Art Museum, and downtown shopping.

Originally built in 1926, the classic brick-and-terra-cotta building was thoroughly reinvented in 2004 with design elements that meld the Northwest (the extensive use of woods and stones) with high-tech toys such as flat-screen TVs, wireless Internet connections, and blue-glass bedside lamps. All rooms score high for creature comforts too, especially with the Frette towels and plump goose-down pillows and comforters. One of Seattle's hottest new restaurants beckons downstairs: Lola, from top chef Tom Douglas, with a menu that ranges from local seafood to Greek cuisine.

2000 4th Ave., Seattle, WA 98121. ⓒ **877/448-8600** or 206/448-8600. Fax 206/441-7140. www.hotelandra. com. 119 units. $149–$189 double; $189–$750 suite. AE, DC, DISC, MC, V. Valet parking $20.

**Mayflower Park Hotel**   If shopping and sipping martinis are among your favorite recreational activities, there's no question of where to stay in Seattle. The Mayflower Park Hotel, built in 1927 and completely renovated a few years back, is connected to the upscale shops of Westlake Center and is flanked by Nordstrom and Bon Marché department stores. In Oliver's Lounge the hotel also serves up the best martinis in Seattle. (It's won the annual martini contest sponsored by a local newspaper umpteen times!) Most rooms are furnished with an eclectic blend of contemporary Italian and traditional European furnishings. If you crave space, ask for one of the large corner rooms or a suite. The smallest rooms here are very cramped.

405 Olive Way, Seattle, WA 98101. ⓒ **800/426-5100**, 206/382-6990, or 206/623-8700. Fax 206/382-6997. www.mayflowerpark.com. 192 units. $170–$195 double; $225–$365 suite. AE, DC, DISC, MC, V. Valet parking $15.

**Renaissance Hotel Seattle**   Despite its large size and its location a stone's throw from the freeway, this hotel manages to stay quieter and less hectic than most convention hotels, and with its rooftop restaurant and swimming pool with a view, it's a good choice for leisure travelers. All rooms are larger than average and many have views of either Puget Sound or the Cascade Range. For the best views, ask for a room on the west side of the hotel.

515 Madison St., Seattle, WA 98104. ⓒ **800/468-3571** or 206/583-0300. Fax 206/622-8635. www. renaissancehotels.com. 631 units. $140–$210 double; $250–$2,000 suite. AE, DC, DISC, MC, V. Valet parking $18; self-parking $15.

**Seattle Sea-Tac Marriott**   If you want to stay near the airport, this is a fantastic bet—a resortlike hotel with a huge central atrium that has a swimming pool, dense tropical greenery, a bar, two whirlpool tubs, and a scattering of totem poles. Rooms are sizable and comfortable, some with a view (on a clear day) of Mount Rainier.

3201 S. 176th St., Seattle, WA 98188. ⓒ **800/228-9290** or 206/241-2000. Fax 206/248-0789. www.marriott hotels.com/seawa. 464 units. $158 double ($178 double with breakfast for 2); $225–$550 suite. AE, DC, DISC, MC, V. Free parking.

**The Wall Street Inn**   Comfortable and conveniently located near the main activities in Seattle, the Wall Street Inn was once a boarding house run by the local sailor's union. The rooms, of course, have been spiffed up since those days, but some still have the kitchenettes favored by the old salts decades ago. The hotel is surrounded by a vast array of restaurants in a range of price categories. Plus, downstairs is El Gaucho, one of Seattle's best steakhouses.

2507 1st Ave., Seattle, WA 98121. ⓒ **800/578-7878** or 206/448-0125. Fax 206/448-2406. www.wallstreet inn.com. 17 units. $85–$145 double. Rates include continental breakfast. AE, DC, DISC, MC, V.

## WHERE TO DINE

Chez Shea PACIFIC NORTHWEST   Quiet, dark, and intimate, Chez Shea is one of the finest restaurants in Seattle. Its dozen candlelit tables with views across Puget Sound to the Olympic Mountains are the perfect setting for a romantic dinner. The menu changes with the season, and ingredients come primarily from Pike Place Market, conveniently located below the restaurant. There are usually five entree choices, along the lines of rabbit braised in wine with balsamic vinegar, sweet peppers, leeks, and rosemary; or halibut sautéed with blood-orange coulis, gaeta olives, red onion, coriander, white wine, and garlic. While there are equally fine restaurants in the city, none has quite the quintessential Seattle atmosphere as Chez Shea.

Corner Market Building, Suite 34, 94 Pike St., Pike Place Market. © 206/467-9990. Reservations highly recommended. Main dishes $22–$26; fixed-price 4-course dinner $44. AE, MC, V. Tues–Sun 5:30–10:30pm.

Etta's Seafood SEAFOOD   Etta's offers the best seafood in town. Located in the Pike Place Market area, this place serves chef/owner Tom Douglas's signature crab cakes (crunchy on the outside, creamy on the inside) and more. Consider the seared ahi tuna if it's on the menu. This almost-sushi has a wonderful texture. If you're not a lover of seafood, don't be afraid: Even though seafood makes up most of the menu, there are other fine options, too.

2020 Western Ave. © 206/443-6000. Reservations recommended. Main dishes $9.50–$23. AE, DC, DISC, MC, V. Mon–Thurs 11:30am–10pm; Fri 11:30am–11pm; Sat 9am–11pm; Sun 9am–10pm.

Metropolitan Grill STEAK   The Metropolitan is dedicated to carnivores. When you walk in, you'll see various cuts of meat, from filet mignon to triple-cut lamb chops, displayed on ice. Green-velvet booths and floral-design carpets create a sophisticated atmosphere, and mirrored walls and a high ceiling trimmed with elegant plasterwork make the dining room feel larger than it actually is. Perfectly cooked steaks are the primary attraction, and a baked potato and a pile of thick-cut onion rings complete the perfect steak dinner.

818 2nd Ave. © 206/624-3287. Reservations recommended. Main dishes lunch $8–$20, dinner $17–$35. AE, DC, DISC, MC, V. Mon–Fri 11am–3:30pm and 5–11pm; Sat 4–11pm; Sun 4:30–10pm.

## 5 Juneau

Since Juneau is also a major port of call, we refer you to the Juneau section in chapter 8, "Ports & Wilderness Areas along the Inside Passage," for a map and information on attractions and tours.

## GETTING TO JUNEAU & THE PORT

BY PLANE   Juneau is served by **Alaska Airlines** (© **800/426-0333** or 907/789-9791) with daily nonstop flights from Seattle and Anchorage. Because weather can wreak havoc with landing conditions, it's especially advisable if you're flying to Juneau to plan on getting there a day or two before your cruise embarkation date.

The vessels of the Alaska Marine Highway (www.dot.state.ak.us/amhs; commonly known as the Alaska Ferry) link Juneau with Alaska, British Columbia, and U.S. gateways as far south as Bellingham, Washington, but unless you have 2 or 3 days to spare, you probably won't use that service to get to your ship. And since you can't drive to Juneau (there are no road links to the outside world) or get there by train, that leaves you with airplanes, period.

A cab from the airport to downtown will cost about $20. The **Capital Transit city bus** (© **907/789-6901**) comes to the airport at 11 minutes past the hour on weekdays from 7:11am to 5:11pm and costs $1.50; your luggage has to fit under your seat or at your feet. Ask the driver for the stop closest to your hotel; you may need a short cab ride from there.

The passenger pier is right in town and an easy walk. But, with baggage, it might be necessary to take a taxi, which shouldn't cost more than, say, $5.

Major car-rental companies have offices at the airport.

## INFORMATION

The **Visitor Information Center** is in Centennial Hall at 101 Egan Dr., near the State Museum (© **888/581-2201** or 907/586-2201; fax 907/586-6304; www.traveljuneau.com). It's open May through September daily from 8:30am to 5pm, October through April Monday through Friday from 9am to 4:30pm. The visitor center at the cruise ship dock is open during the summer when the ships come in.

## WHERE TO STAY

**Goldbelt Hotel Juneau**   This is a recently renovated hotel with large, nicely appointed rooms favored by business travelers. The rooms on the front (which are more expensive) overlook the Gastineau Channel. The atmosphere is quiet and almost hermetic. There's a Mediterranean-themed restaurant off the lobby.

51 W. Egan Dr., Juneau, AK 99801. © **888/478-6909** or 907/586-6900. Fax 907/463-3567. www.goldbelt tours.com. 105 units. $169–$179 double. Additional person in room $15 extra. AE, DC, DISC, MC, V.

**Inn at the Waterfront**   This charming little inn across from the cruise ship dock feels like a small European hotel, with its narrow stairs, oddly shaped rooms, and understated elegance. The proprietors make the most of the building's gold-rush history as a semi-legal brothel, but the place does better than relying on the typical Victorian kitsch. The Summit, one of Juneau's most sophisticated restaurants, is downstairs.

455 S. Franklin St., Juneau, AK 99801. © **907/586-2050**. Fax 907/586-2999. 21 units, 12 with private bathroom. $78 double; $110 suite. Additional person in room $9 extra. AE, DC, DISC, MC, V.

**Prospector Hotel**   The Prospector is a comfortable hotel right on the waterfront, with large, standard rooms in attractive pastel colors. More than two dozen rooms have kitchenettes, and some of the more expensive ones are like nice furnished apartments. Those facing the channel have good views. The lower level, called the first floor, is half basement and somewhat dark.

375 Whittier St., Juneau, AK 99801-1781. © **800/331-2711** or 907/586-3737. Fax 907/586-1204. 58 units. $135–$155 double. AE, DC, DISC, MC, V.

**Westmark Baranof Hotel**   In winter the venerable old Baranof acts like an annex of the state capitol for conferring legislators and lobbyists; in the summer it's like a branch of the package-tour companies. The nine-story concrete building, built in 1939, has the feel of a grand hotel, although some rooms are on the small side. The upper-floor rooms are modern and have great views of the water. There are many room configurations, so make sure you get what you want. Kitchenettes are available.

127 N. Franklin St., Juneau, AK 99801. © **800/544-0970** or 907/586-2660. Fax 907/586-8315. www. westmarkhotels.com. 193 units. $149–$169 double. AE, DC, DISC, MC, V.

## WHERE TO DINE

**DiSopra/The Fiddlehead Restaurant and Bakery** SEAFOOD/ITALIAN
Upstairs, DiSopra serves finely crafted northern Italian cuisine in a dining room
with big windows, a mural, and solicitous service. The menu changes quarterly,
and Juneau friends have complained of inconsistency, but the food is still the
most sophisticated in town. Meanwhile, downstairs, the Fiddlehead has knotty
pine paneling and ferny stained glass. It serves from a long menu of flavorful
food, with a great variety of ethnic delicacies made into sandwiches. More
expensive dinner entrees of seafood, beef, or pasta, similar to those upstairs, are
also served in the Fiddlehead.

429 W. Willoughby Ave. *C* 907/586-3150. www.thefiddlehead.com. Reservations recommended for DiSopra.
Lunch $8–$12; dinner $9–$25. 15% gratuity added for parties of 6 or more. AE, DISC, MC, V. Summer DiSopra
daily 5–10pm, Fiddlehead daily 7am–10pm; winter DiSopra Tues–Sat 5:30–9pm, Fiddlehead daily 7am–9pm.

**Red Dog Saloon** SALOON FOOD   This is not by any means an elegant
eatery—it's more of an experience. The Red Dog is a Juneau landmark, and its
restaurant serves good, wholesome food in a frontier atmosphere. Just don't go
looking for speedy or particularly distinguished service. Enjoy the honky-tonk
piano and banjo and the emcee's constant stream of one-liners while you're waiting for your grub. It's noisy. It's crowded. And it's *fun!*

728 S. Franklin St. *C* 907/463-3777. Main courses $7.50–$11. AE, MC, V. Summer daily 11am–11pm.

## 6 Whittier

Whittier lies on the edge of a long fjord in the northwest corner of Prince
William Sound. For several years, it had only minor relevance to major-ship
cruise passengers. A dreary community of just 300 permanent residents (two-
thirds of whom live in one apartment building, by the way), it was used primarily by the small-ship lines as a gateway for daylong and half-daylong wildlife
sightseeing voyages in the picturesque sound. All that changed when Princess
announced that it would use Whittier, rather than Seward, as the northernmost
point of its Gulf of Alaska schedule in 2004. This year, of course, Carnival
Cruises, Princess' affiliate company in the Carnival Corp. family, is using the
port as well. Whittier has the distinct advantage of being closer to Anchorage,
where virtually all cruisers begin or end their Gulf vacations. Princess was a regular at Whittier until 1993 when it withdrew to Seward, primarily to protest the
$1-a-passenger head tax levied by the Whittier City Council. Three factors
encouraged the Santa Clarita, California, line to restore Whittier to its schedule.
First, the city built a new floating dock and 20,000-square-foot passenger terminal, suitable for major-ship use. Second, it repealed the onerous tax and gave
some assurance that it will not be reimplemented. And third, the nearly 3-mile-
long Alton Anderson Tunnel, on the outskirts of town, was recently refurbished
to accommodate both train and motorcoach traffic, making it vastly easier to
transfer thousands of passengers to and from Anchorage. In theory, access by
road vehicles to the tunnel puts Alaska's largest city and major airport not much
more than an hour away from Whittier—less than half the time it takes to drive
to or from Seward. In theory! The tunnel has its drawbacks. It has only one lane,
shared by train and road traffic. When a train is scheduled through, in either
direction, road vehicles are held until the train is well clear of the tunnel. Timing is crucial. Unless the ship can be cleared and passengers boarded on transportation on a strict timetable, a wait is almost assured.

---

**Tips**  **Be Prepared**

An ATM is located at the liquor store near the boat harbor, but Whittier lacks a bank and other services, so bring what money you need.

---

Besides the sightseeing in the sound, there's little other reason to go to Whittier, unless you're on a quest to find America's oddest towns. Most of the townspeople live in a single 14-story concrete building with dark, narrow hallways. The grocery store is on the first floor and the medical clinic is on the third. The rest of the people live in one other building. **The Begich Towers,** as the dominant structure is called, was built during the 1940s, when Whittier's strategic location on the Alaska Railroad and at the head of a deep Prince William Sound fjord made it a key port in the defense of Alaska. Today, with its barren gravel ground and ramshackle warehouses and boat sheds, the town maintains a stark military-industrial character. The pass above the town is a funnel for frequent whipping winds, it always seems to rain, and the glaciers above the town keep it cool even in summer. The official boosters look on the bright side: Having everyone live in two buildings saves on snow removal in a place that gets an average of 20 feet per winter. The kids don't even have to go outside to get to school—a tunnel leads from the tower to the classroom.

No matter how odd or dreary Whittier may seem, it has assumed huge importance to Princess and Carnival—and vice versa. The two companies' five Gulf ships will make a combined 50-odd stops there during the season, potentially exposing more than 120,000 embarking and disembarking visitors to the city. How long, and how much money, any of those thousands will spend on goods and services is an open question. But the cruise lines' docking fees alone will be worth big bucks to Whittier.

## GETTING TO WHITTIER & THE PORT

You can get to Whittier from Anchorage on the Alaska Railroad (© **800/ 544-0552** or 907/265-2494). The new dock is near the mouth of Whittier Creek. Nothing in Whittier is more than a 5-minute walk away. Don't look for taxi ranks or free shuttles: You won't need them.

## EXPLORING WHITTIER

**INFORMATION**    Probably because it doesn't have much to promote, Whittier has no tourist board per se, and there is no visitor center, but you can contact the city offices at © **907/472-2327,** ext. 101 (admin@ci.whittier.ak.us). The people at the harbormaster's office are also helpful and maintain public toilets and showers; it's the only two-story building at the harbor (© **907/472-2327,** ext. 110 or 115).

## ATTRACTIONS WITHIN WALKING DISTANCE

Everything's within walking distance; there just isn't much to see. Visit the yacht harbor and the town's apartment building—that's about it.

## ATTRACTIONS OUTSIDE THE DOWNTOWN AREA

You can take the train straight to Anchorage, a fun, scenic ride, for $45 one-way, $55 round-trip (half-price ages 2–11) on the **Alaska Railroad** (© **800/544-0552** or 907/265-2494). *But be warned:* A round-trip journey is a long, full

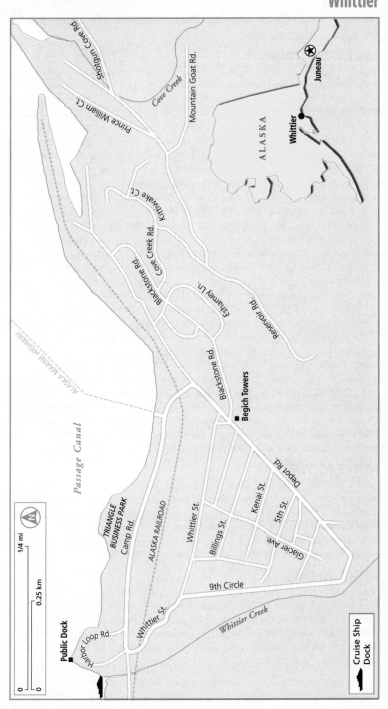

day—up to 10 hours, based on the timing of the railroad's services in each direction and depending on traffic.

## ORGANIZED TOURS

Several companies compete for your business for day-trip tours to the sound's western glaciers. Besides having incredible scenery, the water is calm, making seasickness unlikely—for the queasy, this is a much better choice than Kenai Fjords National Park. Each operator times departures to coordinate with the daily Alaska Railroad train from Anchorage, described above, which means they have up to 6 hours for the trip. Some try to see as much as possible, while others take it slower to savor the scenery and wildlife sightings. **Phillips' Cruises and Tours** (© **800/544-0529** or 907/276-8023) offers a 26-glacier cruise of the sound on a fast three-deck catamaran, counting the glaciers as they go. The boat ride is 4½ hours and costs $129, $69 for children under 12. There is a snack bar on board. **Major Marine Tours** (© **800/764-7300** or 907/274-7300) operates a smaller, 149-passenger vessel at a slower pace than Phillips'—they hit a mere 10 glaciers, but spend more time waiting for them to calve. The route goes up Blackstone Bay. The boat is comfortable, with reserved table seating. They also put more emphasis on their food, which costs extra; the all-you-can-eat salmon and prime rib buffet is $12 for adults, $6 for children. Time on the water is 5 hours. Price: $99 adults, $49 children under 12 (food not included). **Sound Eco Adventures** (© **888/471-2312** or 907/472-2312) is operated by a retired wildlife biologist who spent years researching the waterfowl and ecology of Prince William Sound. They carry up to six passengers at a time on wildlife, whale, and glacier tours and do kayak drop-offs from a 30-foot aluminum boat, which is suitable for wheelchairs. Prices range from $149 per person to $199 per person, depending on the duration and itinerary chosen. Lunch and a snack are included. **Honey Charters** (© **888/477-2493** or 907/472-2493) is a family-run small-boat business licensed to carry 6 to 10 passengers. For larger groups, their *Qayaq Chief* can carry 18 kayakers or 22 visitors on a sightseeing cruise. Bring lunch and snacks with you, as no food is available on board. For a 3-hour cruise, the price is $89 per person; for 6 hours, it's $139 per person; and for 11 hours, $189 per person.

## WHERE TO STAY

**June's Whittier Bed and Breakfast Condo Suites**    Nine of these condo units are in the top two floors of the Begich Towers, the concrete building that dominates Whittier, allowing guests to live as Whittier people do, with great views and hummingbirds feeding at the windows. All have full kitchens.

P.O. Box 715, Whittier, AK 99693. © 888/472-2396 or 907/472-2396. Fax 907/472-2503. www.breadnbutter charters.com. 10 units. $98–$225 double. Extra person over age 5 $15. AE, MC, V.

## WHERE TO DINE

Most meals served in Whittier are for people grabbing a sandwich while waiting for a boat or otherwise passing through. Several such restaurants are in the triangle at the east end of the harbor, including a good Chinese place, the Korean-owned **China Sea** (© **907/472-2222**). Lunch there is $8 or $9, dinner $12 to $19, and in the summer they serve specials such as kung pao halibut. Hours are 11am to 10pm daily.

# 8

# Ports & Wilderness Areas along the Inside Passage

The Inside Passage runs through the area of Alaska known as **Southeast.** It's that narrow strip of the state—islands, mainland coastal communities, and mountains—that stretches from the Canadian border in the south to the start of the Gulf in the north, just above Glacier Bay National Park. It's also known, by the way, as The Panhandle. Since the typical cruise itinerary begins or ends in Vancouver, British Columbia, or, increasingly this year, in Seattle (both of which we've covered in chapter 7, "The Ports of Embarkation"), we've arranged the ports chapters geographically, moving northward.

For ports and wilderness areas in the Gulf of Alaska, see chapter 9.

## 1 Victoria, British Columbia

We know it's in Canada, not Alaska, but cruises that start in Seattle or San Francisco typically include Victoria (on Vancouver Island) as a port of call on the way up to Alaska. This lovely city, the capital of British Columbia, offers Victorian architecture and a very proper British atmosphere—some say it's more British than Britain itself—with main attractions that include high tea and a visit to **Butchart Gardens** with its incredible botanical displays.

A former British outpost, Victoria has a history filled with maritime lore. Whalers and trade ships once docked in the city's harbors, transporting the island's rich bounty of coal, lumber, and furs throughout the world. More recently (as historical events go), John Wayne summered here, and the Nixons honeymooned here.

Take a tour around the island and you'll see gorgeous homes and gardens and views that include the snowcapped mountains of Washington State. Then head downtown for shopping bargains.

**COMING ASHORE**   Cruise ships dock at the Ogden Point terminal on Juan De Fuca Strait. It's not much more than a mile into town, so if you don't mind a stretch of the legs, walk west along Dallas Street from the dock and north on, say, Oswego Street or Menzies Street and you'll find yourself in the heart of the action. Every cruise ship, of course, operates a shuttle service to the Inner Harbour, where flowers, milling crowds, and street performers liven the scene under the watchful eye of the venerable **Empress Hotel,** famed setting for English-style high tea.

**INFORMATION**   You can pick up a map of the city at the **Visitors Information Center** (© 250/382-2127), located on the waterfront at 812 Wharf St. It's open daily from 9am to 8pm in May and June, 9am to 9pm in July and August, and 9am to 5pm the rest of the year.

# Southeast Alaska

CRUISE TERMINAL 5

Butchart Gardens **1**
Craigdarroch Castle **4**
Fairmont Empress Hotel **2**
Miniature World **2**
Royal British Columbia Museum
  and National Geographic
  IMAX Theatre **3**

## SHORE EXCURSIONS

(Note that shore excursion prices quoted here are representative of what's available but may differ slightly from cruise line to cruise line.)

**City Tour & Butchart Gardens** (3½–4 hr.; $54 adults, $29 children under 12): After an abbreviated tour of the sights in Victoria, the bus makes the 21km (13-mile) trip out on the Saanich Peninsula to world-renowned Butchart Gardens along Brentwood Bay, where you'll have 2 hours or so to explore the 53-hectare (130-acre) grounds. Expanded trips include high tea at the gardens (4 hr.; $79 adults, $47 children).

**City Tour with High Tea at the Empress** (4 hr.; $75 adults, $55 children): This guided excursion aboard a double-decker bus takes you by the major sights of the Inner Harbour, downtown, and residential areas, followed by a stop for afternoon high tea at the Empress Hotel.

## TOURING THROUGH LOCAL OPERATORS

Several local operators greet passengers right at the pier, offering rides into the city and longer tours using various modes of transportation. **Heritage Tours and Daimler Limousine Service** (✆ 250/474-4332) does tours using stretch limos, Rolls-Royces, and Daimlers. Fares range from about $45 an hour per vehicle for a small stretch limo, to $60 an hour per vehicle for a plush six-passenger stretch limousine. **Classic Car Tours** (✆ 250/883-8747) is a new company with a similar concept, offering tours in classic convertibles (perfect on a sunny day), with commentary that we found colorful and delightful. Fares are $50 an hour per car; the cars seat up to four guests. The bicycle rickshaws operated by **Kabuki Kabs** (© **250/385-4243**) and competing firms offer an unusual way to get into the city for about $40 an hour (for two people). The company actually charges by the minute as well—about 70¢ per person—so you can pay less depending on the length of your ride. For those seeking a more traditional bus tour, **Gray Line of Victoria** (© **250/388-5248**) offers tours of Victoria and Butchart Gardens, leaving from near the Empress Hotel. The 1½-hour Grand City Tour costs $15 for adults and $6 for children; the 3-hour tour including the gardens is $30 for adults, $13 for kids.

## ON YOUR OWN: WITHIN WALKING DISTANCE

**The Fairmont Empress Hotel**   Located right by the Inner Harbour, this ivy-covered 1908 landmark has a commanding view of the harbor and an opulent lobby. This is the place to go for your British-style high tea. Call ahead for reservations and ask about the dress code. (No shorts, no tank tops.) Tea with pastries, scones, sandwiches, and all the trimmings runs about $34 a person. Around the back of the hotel, you'll find the **Miniature World** museum (© **250/385-9731**), with quirky displays that include big dollhouses, the world's smallest working sawmill, and a model of London in 1670.

721 Government St. © 250/384-8111. Admission $8 adults, $7 youths 12–18, $5 children 5–11.

**Royal British Columbia Museum and National Geographic IMAX Theatre**   Outside the entrance to this modern, three-story concrete-and-glass museum is a glass-enclosed display of towering totem poles and other large sculptural works by Northwest Native artists. Inside, exhibits showcase the natural history of the province, illustrate Victoria's recent past, and demonstrate how archaeologists study ancient cultures, using artifacts from numerous local tribes. There's also an IMAX theater showing features on nonlocal places like the Amazon. (The shows change every few months.) Behind the museum is **Thunderbird Park,** with Native totem poles and a ceremonial house. **Helmecken House,** 10 Elliot St., next to the park, is one of the oldest houses in British Columbia. It was the home of a pioneer doctor, and there are lots of torturous-looking medical tools to shudder over.

675 Belleville St. © 888/447-7977 or 250/356-7226. Museum admission $17 adults, $12 youths 6–18, family admission $48, free for children age 5 and under. IMAX admission $9.75 adults, $7.50 youths, $5 for children 5 and under.

## ON YOUR OWN: BEYOND WALKING DISTANCE

**Butchart Gardens**   A ride by cab, public bus, or other transportation (see "Touring Through Local Operators," above) and several free hours will be required for a visit to this world-famous attraction. Well worth visiting, the gardens lie 21km (13 miles) north of downtown Victoria on a 53-hectare (130-acre) estate and feature English-, Italian-, and Japanese-style plantings, as well as water gardens and rose beds. There are also restaurants and a gift shop on-site. (*Note:* You can catch a public bus from downtown Victoria for less than $2 each way, or Gray Line offers a shuttle from near the Empress Hotel for $3 each way. A cab will cost you about $25 each way.)

800 Benevenuto Ave., in Brentwood Bay. © 250/652-5256. Admission $16 adults, $7.50 youths 13–17, $1.60 kids 5–12, free for kids 4 and under.

**Craigdarroch Castle**    You have to take a cab to see Craigdarroch Castle, the elaborate home of millionaire Scottish coal-mining magnate Robert Dunsmuir, who built the place in the 1880s. The four-story, 39-room Highland-style castle is topped with stone turrets and furnished in opulent Victoria splendor.

1050 Joan Crescent. ⓒ **250/592-5323.** Admission $7 adults, $2.40 children.

## 2 Canada's Inside Passage

Canada's Inside Passage is simply the part of an Inside Passage cruise that lies in British Columbia, south of the Alaskan border and running to Vancouver. On big ships, the first day out of Vancouver (or the last day going south) is usually a day at sea. Passengers get the chance to enjoy the coastal beauty of the British Columbia mainland to the east and Vancouver Island to the west, including some truly magnificent scenery in Princess Louisa Inlet and Desolation Sound.

In most cases, that's all the ships do, though: Go past the scenery. In their haste to get to Ketchikan, the first stop in Alaska, they invariably sail right past much of the Canadian Inside Passage.

One of the Canadian Inside Passage's loveliest stretches is **Seymour Narrows,** 5 or 6 hours north of Vancouver, just after the mouth of the Campbell River. It's so narrow that it can only be passed through at certain hours of the day, when the tide is right. Again, cruise visitors are often denied its full beauty because ships tend to reach it late in the day or in the wee small hours. On the long days of summer, it is often possible to enjoy Seymour Narrows if you're prepared to stay up late.

The U.S./Canadian border lies just off the tip of the Misty Fjords National Monument, 43 sailing miles from Ketchikan (and 403 miles from Glacier Bay, for those who are keeping count).

### Shopping for Native Art

If you're interested in Native Alaskan art, you need to be aware that there is a large market in fakes. There have been noted cases of shopkeepers' assistants being spotted removing "Made in Taiwan" stickers from supposedly Native art objects with razor blades.

Before you buy a piece of Native art, ask the art dealer for a biography of the artist and ask whether the artist actually carved the piece (rather than just lending his or her name for knockoffs). Most dealers will tell you where a work really comes from, but you have to ask.

Price should also be a tip-off to fakes, as real Native art is pricey. An elaborate mask, for instance, should be priced at $3,000, not $300. Be particularly wary of soapstone carvings, as most are not made in Alaska.

There are two marks used for Alaska products: a Made-in-Alaska **polar bear sticker,** which means the item was at least mostly made in the state, and a **silver hand sticker,** which indicates authentic Native art. An absence of the label, however, does not mean the item is not authentic; it may just mean the artist doesn't like labels. So just ask if you're curious about a piece of artwork that doesn't have a sticker.

## 3 Prince Rupert, British Columbia

Until recently this sleepy Canadian port just a few miles from the Alaska border has registered a very small blip on the cruise industry's radar screen. Now, though, with the number and size of ships in the Alaska trade growing, the need for alternative ports of call en route has focused attention on Prince Rupert's Northland Dock at Cow Bay. The city is in the process of extending and spiffing up the facility and, by the time the 2005 cruise season begins, a complex of a dozen retail stores will have opened alongside.

Last year, the city enjoyed a couple of dozen ship visits (Silversea Cruises, Norwegian Cruise Line) and expects this year to begin the process of attracting at least 60 a year by 2006. At press time, negotiations were underway between local officials and various cruise operators to reroute at least some of their ships into Prince Rupert during the summer.

The town was named in 1670 for the first governor of the Hudson's Bay Company. He was Rupert, the son of Frederick V, king of Bohemia, and Elizabeth Stuart, daughter of James I of England. Today, many of its 13,000 inhabitants work in commercial fishing. There is also a flourishing artists' colony, the results of whose efforts can be seen in the Cow Bay galleries right next to the passenger ship dock. The town has two shopping malls, a number of good quality stores, and some fine restaurants.

Prince Rupert's location makes it an ideal jumping-off point for visits to Southeast Alaska, the Queen Charlotte Islands, Vancouver Island, and the interior of British Columbia. The town is served year-round by both the B.C. Ferries system and the Alaska Marine Highway System. Both ferry systems offer up to five departures a week during the summer to a number of Alaskan Inland Passage ports. By road Prince Rupert is accessible via the Yellowhead Highway to Vancouver in the south, and to Dawson Creek, B.C. (not to be confused with Dawson City, the Yukon Territory gold-rush capital) and Alberta in the east.

VIA Rail operates daily between Prince Rupert and Jasper National Park, and Air Canada has two flights a day to Vancouver.

**COMING ASHORE**   The passenger pier is a very short distance from town, although there is a little uphill walking to be done.

**INFORMATION**   A walk of a few yards will get you from the ship to the **Prince Rupert Visitor Information Center,** 215 Cow Bay Rd. (© **800/667-1994** or 250/624-5637), open daily from 9am to 6pm (later if cruise ships are in town for evening stays). Try the website at www.TourismPrinceRupert.com.

### SHORE EXCURSIONS

**Bear Watching Adventure** (4 hr.; $350) Visit (by 43km/27-mile floatplane ride) the Khutzeymateen area, in which resides the largest concentration of grizzlies on the B.C. coast.

**Historic North Pacific Cannery** (3 hr.; $52): Declared a National Historic Site by the B.C. government on its 100th anniversary in 1989, the structure is an example of the kind of residential cannery—in which people both worked and lived—that was common in British Columbia a century and more ago.

**Whale-Watching** (4 hr.; $89): Orcas, humpbacks, grays, and minkes inhabit the waters off Prince Rupert in their season. Whales are the primary object of the search, but participants are likely also to see eagles, seals, sea lions, and an abundance of other kinds of wildlife.

## TOURING THROUGH LOCAL OPERATORS

**Ocean Adventures Charter Company** (© 604/815-8382) offers whale-watching, fishing, and kayaking opportunities at widely varying prices depending on the vessel chosen and the number of people in the group. Bear- and whale-watching outings and boat tours around nearby Kaien Island are available from **West Coast Launch** (© 800/201-8377 or 250/627-9166).

## ON YOUR OWN: WITHIN WALKING DISTANCE

**The Museum of Northern B.C.**   This well-laid-out facility traces the cultures and development of the aboriginal peoples of B.C. (Tsimshian, Haida, Nisga'a, and others). The historic ambience begins in the impressive longhouse lobby, with its cedar timbers and glass artworks. It continues through the Great Hall, the Hall of Nations, and the Treasures Gallery, which among them contain a striking collection of archaeological artifacts, ceremonial art and dress, weaponry from Indian wars, canoes, and much more. Television monitors in these rooms run oral histories of the area from its Indian origins right up to the modern-day commercial fishing and the creation of the city itself. At frequent intervals during the day, live performances by Indian dancers and musicians take place. The museum—a must-see for visitors to Prince Rupert—is located only a few hundred yards from the passenger terminal. But it should be noted that the first half of the road is steeply uphill.

100 1st Ave. W. © **250/624-3207.** Admission $5 adults, $1 children. Mon–Sat 9am–8pm; Sun 9am–5pm.

**The Kwinitsa Railway Museum**   Located in the city's Waterfront Park, very close to the Prince Rupert Museum, the facility traces the evolution of Prince Rupert from a tent town terminus for the Grand Trunk Railway, through incorporation as a city in the 1920s.

110 Bill Murray Way. Free admission. Daily 9am–noon and 1–5pm.

**The Firehall Museum**   This attraction is highlighted by the display of a rebuilt R.E.O. Speedwagon (ca. 1925) and the history of the Prince Rupert Fire Department in pictures and artifacts.

200 1st Ave. W. Free admission. Mon–Sat 1–5pm.

## 4 Ketchikan

Ketchikan is the southernmost port of call in Southeast Alaska, and its residents sometimes refer to it as "the first city." That's not because it's the most important city to the region's economy, or that it's the biggest, or even that it was literally the first built. It's just that it's usually the first city visited by cruise ships on the Inside Passage when ships are running northbound out of Vancouver or Seattle.

Just about the first thing that greets arriving cruise passengers on the dock at Ketchikan is a "Liquid Sunshine Gauge" put up by the city several years ago, on which is marked the cumulative rainfall for the year, day by day. We once checked and saw that the mark showed over 36 inches—and it was only June. Even at that, the gauge had a long way to go. The average annual rainfall is about 160 inches (more than 13 ft.!) and has topped 200 inches in the rainiest years. Precipitation is so predictable here that the locals joke that if you can't see the top of nearby Deer Mountain, it's raining; if you *can* see it, it's *going* to rain!

But here's a strange thing. Through the years, we've been in Ketchikan at least once in every month of the season, and we can recall only two real downpours. Go figure.

# Prince Rupert, British Columbia

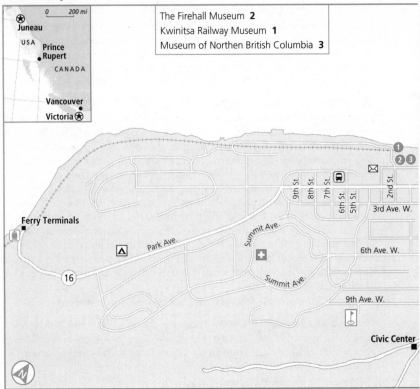

The Firehall Museum **2**
Kwinitsa Railway Museum **1**
Museum of Northen British Columbia **3**

    Maybe it's because the weather gods have been kind to us that we have a soft spot for this place. But it's not the only reason. Climate notwithstanding, this is a really fun port to visit—a glorified fishing village with quaint architecture, history, salmon fishing, the great scenery that is to be found in just about every Inside Passage community, and **totem poles**—lots and lots of totem poles.

    Ketchikan is a strong center of the Tlingit, Tsimshian, and Haida cultures. These proud Southeast Alaska Native peoples have preserved their traditions and kept their icons intact over the centuries, and have re-created **clan houses** and made replicas of totem poles that were irretrievably damaged by decades of exposure to the elements. The tall, hand-carved poles are everywhere—in parks, in the lobbies of buildings, in the street. It should be no surprise to anyone that there are more totems in Ketchikan than in any city in the world.

    *A word of caution about that:* Unless you're really, really interested in the origins and the meaning of totem poles, choose your shore excursion very carefully. It was a cold day the last time we did the **Totem Bight State Historical Park** tour, but the guide, oblivious to the group's discomfort, seemed intent on sharing with us every fact he'd ever learned about Alaska Native cultures and relating, in infinite detail, the story behind pole after pole after pole. (They're not merely decorative, and each tells the story of an incident in a tribe's life—a battle, a birth, and so on.) The first half dozen were fine, but then, frankly, the time began to drag. We're as curious as anyone else about other cultures, but by the time we

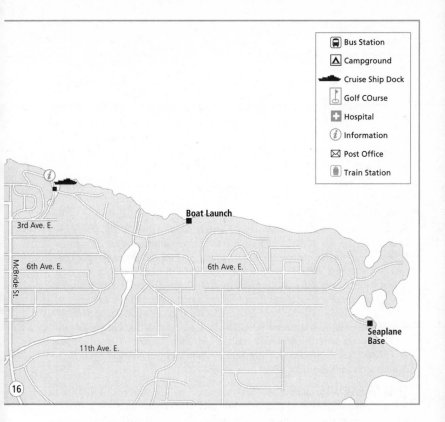

Legend:

- Bus Station
- Campground
- Cruise Ship Dock
- Golf COurse
- Hospital
- Information
- Post Office
- Train Station

Boat Launch

3rd Ave. E.

McBride St.

6th Ave. E.

6th Ave. E.

Seaplane Base

11th Ave. E.

climbed back on the coach more than 3 hours later to return to the ship, our teeth were chattering and our eyes were glassy from information overload.

The centerpiece of downtown Ketchikan is **Creek Street,** a row of buildings on pilings over a stream that the salmon swim up in their spawning season. Today the narrow, wood-sidewalk street is filled mainly with funky restaurants, such as the Creek Street Café, and boutiques and galleries specializing in offbeat pieces by local artists. But it's what used to be there that gives Creek Street its special place in history. In the early 1900s this was Ketchikan's red-light district, with more than 30 brothels lining the waterway. It was, according to the little history sign at the head of the street, the place where both the fishermen and the fish went up the stream to spawn. For reasons that don't seem to be entirely clear to anybody, the most famous of the courtesans (or at least the most enduring) was a woman who went by the name of Dolly Arthur (her real name was Thelma Copeland). She wasn't necessarily the most financially successful of the ladies of the night, and if the photographs of her are any indication, she probably wasn't the prettiest. But somehow, her name outlived the rest. Most people can tell you who Dolly Arthur was, but it's doubtful if many could name another Creek Street madam. **Dolly's House,** on Creek Street (© **907/225-2279**), is now a small museum. Like the house's old clientele, you have to pay to get inside. We don't know what they used to pay, but today it'll cost you $4. It's open daily from 8am to 4pm during the summer and when cruise ships are in town.

One of our favorite things to do in Ketchikan is to walk the short distance from the ship, by way of Creek Street, and take the **funicular railway to the Westmark Cape Fox Lodge** for lunch. The lunch is satisfying (if hardly gourmet), and the Alaskan Amber Ale is refreshing, but it's the views of the city and of the Tongass Narrows and Deer Mountain, both from the funicular and from parts of the lodge and its grounds, that make the trip worthwhile.

It's also an easy walk from here to the **Deer Mountain Tribal Hatchery & Eagle Center,** at 1158 Salmon Rd. (admission $6.95), a Native-run operation where you can learn where salmon come from and see some rescued and healing eagles. It's open May through September daily 8am to 4:30pm. Also nearby is the Totem Heritage Center (see information later in this section).

**COMING ASHORE**   Ships dock right at the pier in Ketchikan's downtown area.

**INFORMATION**   The first two places we usually drop in upon arrival in Ketchikan are the **Ketchikan Visitors Center,** at 131 Front St. (© **907/225-6166**), right on the dock, to pick up literature and information on what's new in town (and discount coupons for attractions), and the **Southeast Alaska Discovery Center,** at nearby 50 Main St. (© **907/228-6220**), one of the four Alaska Public Lands Information facilities in the state. The latter is more than a mere dispenser of information: It also houses a museum in which a number of exhibits and dioramas depict both Native Alaskan cultures and the modern business development of Ketchikan. Admission to the exhibits is $5. The visitor center is open whenever a cruise ship has docked. The Discovery Center is open May through September daily from 8am to 5pm, October through April Tuesday through Saturday from 10am to 4:30pm.

## SHORE EXCURSIONS
**Misty Fjords Flightseeing** (2 hr.; $209): Everyone gets a window seat aboard the floatplanes that run these quick flightseeing jaunts over Misty Fjords National Monument. No ice fields and glaciers on this trip, but Misty Fjords has another kind of majesty: You'll see sparkling fjords, cascading waterfalls, thick forests, and rugged mountains dotted with wildlife, then come in for a landing on a serene wilderness lake.

**Mountain Point Snorkeling Adventure** (3 hr.; $89): Believe it or not, you can snorkel around Ketchikan, where the climate is warm for Alaska. Still, it's not the Caribbean, and insulating wetsuits are provided on this excursion, as well as hot beverages for when you get out of the water. Undersea are fish, starfish, sea urchins, sea cucumbers, and more.

**Saxman Native Village and Ketchikan City Tour** (2½ hr.; $48): This modern-day Native village, situated about 3 miles outside Ketchikan, is a center for the revival of Native arts and culture. The tour includes either the telling of a Native legend or a performance by the Cape Fox dancers in the park theater, plus a guided walk through the grounds to see the totem poles and learn their stories. Craftspeople are sometimes on hand in the working sheds to demonstrate totem-pole carving.

**Tatoosh Island Sea Kayaking** (4 hr.; $120 adults, $86 children 12 and under): There are typically two kayaking excursions offered in Ketchikan: this one (which requires you to take a van and motorized boat to the island before starting your 90-min. paddle) and a trip that starts from right beside the cruise ship docks. Of the two, this one is far more enjoyable, getting you out into a wilder

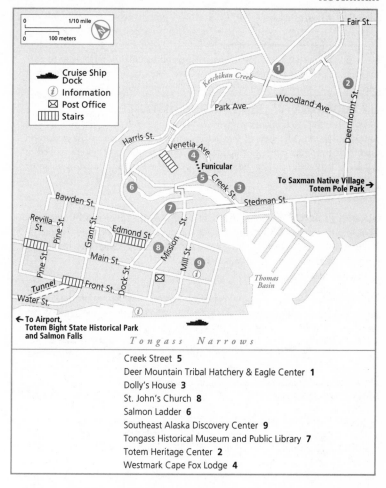

Creek Street **5**
Deer Mountain Tribal Hatchery & Eagle Center **1**
Dolly's House **3**
St. John's Church **8**
Salmon Ladder **6**
Southeast Alaska Discovery Center **9**
Tongass Historical Museum and Public Library **7**
Totem Heritage Center **2**
Westmark Cape Fox Lodge **4**

area rather than just sticking to the busy port waters. The scenery is incredible, and you have a good chance of spotting bald eagles, seals (whether swimming around your boat or basking on the rocks), and leaping salmon.

**Clover Passage by Kayak** (3 hr; $89 adults, $65 children ages 8–12): This is the other kayak excursion. Unlike the Tatoosh Island adventure, participants on this one leave directly from the dock downtown and paddle out to Clover Island. The waters are protected and, of the two, this is likely to be the less strenuous one.

**Totem Bight Historical Park and City Tour** (2–2½ hr.; $36 adults,$19 children 12 and under): This tour takes you by bus around Ketchikan and through the Tongass National Forest to see the historic Native fish camp where a ceremonial clan house and totem poles sit amid the rainforest. There's a fair amount of walking involved, making the tour a poor choice for anyone with mobility problems.

## TOURING THROUGH LOCAL OPERATORS

A bevy of tour operators sell their offerings at the **Ketchikan Visitors Center,** on 131 Front St. (© **907/225-6166**), right at the dock. Schoolteacher Lois

Munch of **Classic Tours** (*©* **907/225-3091;** www.classictours.com) makes her tours fun: She wears a poodle skirt to drive visitors around in her '55 Chevy. A 2-hour tour to the Saxman totem poles is $70; a 3-hour tour adds a natural-history stop and costs $90. Rates are per person and include the admission to Saxman and tax. The maximum group size is five. Other residents offer tours, too; check at the town visitor center (see above) for many more choices.

## ON YOUR OWN: WITHIN WALKING DISTANCE

**Creek Street** Ketchikan's former red-light district is now its number-one tourist attraction. The view of Creek Street from the bridge over the stream on Stedman Street (the main thoroughfare) is said to be the most photographed in Alaska. It may well be. (See the introduction to the Ketchikan section for more lore and legend.)

Off Stedman St., along Ketchikan Creek.

**St. John's Church** St. John's Church is the oldest place of worship in town. Both the church (Episcopal, by the way) and its adjacent Seaman's Center—built in 1904 as a hospital and now a commercial building—are interesting examples of local early 1900s architecture.

On Bawden St., at Mission St.

**The Salmon Ladder** We could spend hours on the observation deck at the artificial salmon ladder just off Park Avenue watching these determined fish make their way from the sea up to the spawning grounds at the top of Ketchikan Creek. How these creatures can keep throwing their exhausted bodies up the ladder at the end of their long journey from the ocean, never giving up though they fail in three out of four leaps, is one of those mysteries of nature that we will never understand—and never tire of observing.

Off Park Ave., in Ketchikan Creek.

**Tongass Historical Museum and Public Library** This museum offers Native cultural displays and other fine exhibits. It also contains one of the city's grizzlier relics: the bullet-riddled skull of Old Groaner, a brown bear that took to attacking humans and was shot for its troubles. In the same building, the attractive Ketchikan Public Library is a great place to recharge, especially in the children's section downstairs, where big windows look out on Ketchikan Creek's falls.

In the Centennial Building, 629 Dock St. *©* **907/225-5600.** Admission $2 summer. Summer daily 8am–5pm.

**Totem Heritage Center** The Totem Heritage Center, built by the city of Ketchikan in 1976, has the virtue of being indoors, so weather isn't a factor. The museum houses a fine collection of 33 original totem poles from the 19th century, retrieved from the Tlingit Indian villages on Tongass and Village islands and the Haida village of Old Kasaan. The Tsimshian people are also represented in some exhibits. There's a nice nature path outdoors. Be aware it's a long walk to the museum unless you take the funicular, which allows you to avoid some of the uphill hike.

601 Deermount St. *©* **907/225-5900.** Admission $5 summer. Summer daily 8am–5pm.

## ON YOUR OWN: BEYOND WALKING DISTANCE

**Saxman Native Village Totem Pole Park** This modern Native village is a center for the revival of Native arts and culture. There's a totem pole park (and artists at work on new poles) and a theater that showcases Native dance, and the 2-hour tours are timed to coincide with cruise ship arrivals.

South of town on the S. Tongass Hwy. ✆ **907/225-4846.** Tour admission $38 adults, $18 children 12 and under; unguided visits free. The village is mostly sold as a shore excursion for cruise passengers, at about $48 a head. If you want to do it independently (frankly, we don't advise it), you can take a cab from the ship for about $12 or $13. Closed Oct–Apr.

**Totem Bight State Historical Park**    This park presents poles and a clan house carved beginning in 1938 by Natives working with traditional tools to copy fragments of historic poles that had mostly rotted away. Visits to the facility are available from **Ketchikan City Tours** (✆ **800/652-8687** or 907/225-9465) for $29 for adults, $13 for kids. We do not recommend taking a cab to Totem Bight State Park. It's a long way out, and the fare is hefty. See the introduction to Ketchikan for details on our visit. This is another attraction that we recommend visiting as part of a shore-excursion group.

On the edge of Tongass Narrows, 10 miles outside town. ✆ **907/247-8574.** www.alaskastateparks.org (click on "Individual Parks"). Free admission. Park daily 24 hr.

## 5 Misty Fjords National Monument

The 2.3-million-acre, Connecticut-size area of Misty Fjords starts at the Canadian border in the south and runs along the eastern side of the Behm Canal. Revillagigedo Island, where Ketchikan is located, is on the western side of the canal. It is topography, not wildlife, that makes a visit to Misty Fjords worthwhile. Among the prime features of Misty Fjords are New Eddystone Rock, jutting 237 feet out of the canal, and the Walker Cove/Rudyerd Bay area, a prime viewing spot for marine life, eagles, and other wildlife. Volcanic cliffs (up to 3,150 ft. high), coves (some as deep as 900 ft.), and peace and serenity are the stock in trade of the place.

Only passengers on small ships will see Misty Fjords close up, as its waterway is too narrow in most places for big ships. The bigger ships pass the southern tip of the Misty Fjords National Monument and then veer away northwest to dock at Ketchikan. Unfortunately, this means that large-ship passengers miss one of the least spoiled of all wilderness areas.

Archaeologists believe that Misty Fjords was inhabited by the local Indian tribes (Haida, Tlingit, and Tsimshian primarily) as far back as 10,000 years ago. The only way you are likely to see any trace of their existence now, though, is from a kayak or a very small boat which can get close enough to the rock face that you can discern the few remaining pictographs etched into the stone along the shoreline.

Anglers in Misty Fjords are liable to think they've died and gone to heaven. The pristine waters yield a rich harvest of enormous Dolly Varden, grayling, and lake trout. It is possible to walk in the park but only the hardy and the experienced are advised to do that. And it is necessary to follow some simple rules. Let somebody know where you are going and when you expect to return. Keep to the trails. (The wildlife—especially bears—doesn't always appreciate intruders.) And carry out everything you carried in. (That's the law.)

By the way, the name Misty Fjords comes from the climatic conditions. Precipitation tends to leave the place looking as though it was under a steady mist much of the time. It was named a protected national treasure by President Jimmy Carter in 1978.

## 6 Admiralty Island National Monument

Situated about 15 miles due west of Juneau (see the Juneau section starting on p. 200), this monument comprises almost a million acres and covers about 90% of Admiralty Island. It's another of those Alaska areas that cruise passengers on the bigger ships will never set foot on, but whose villages, some of them Native, have recently begun to attract some small-ship operators. The Tlingit village of Angoon, for example, welcomes small groups of visitors off ships. Small ships (such as those operated by Alaska's Glacier Bay Cruiseline) may also ferry passengers ashore in a more remote area of the island for a hike. Admiralty Island is said to have the highest concentration of bears on earth. Naturalists estimate that there may be as many as four of these creatures per square mile.

Bears, though, don't have a monopoly on the island. Also plentiful are Sitka black-tailed deer and bald eagles, and the waters around teem with sea lions, harbor seals, and whales. One of the largest concentrations of bald eagles in Southeast (second, perhaps, only to that in Haines in the fall) is to be found in the bays and inlets on the east side of the island. An estimated 4,000 of the eagles congregate there because the food supply is more abundant and is easier to get at.

A 25-mile-long trail system links the major lakes on the island, with some overland portions where visitors must carry their canoes. But those who are willing to work at it are rewarded by magnificent scenery and deep peace and quiet.

Angoon itself is not particularly close to the natural wonders of Admiralty Island. There's not much to do there except walk along the beach to an old cemetery that houses some interesting headstones.

## 7 Tracy Arm & Endicott Arm

Located about 50 miles due south of Juneau, these long, deep, and almost claustrophobically narrow fjords are a striking feature of a pristine forest and mountain expanse with a sinister name: **Tracy Arm–Ford's Terror Wilderness.** The place gets its name from the 1889 incident in which a crewman from a U.S. naval vessel (name: Ford; rank: unknown) rowed into an inlet off Endicott Arm and found himself trapped for 6 hours in a heaving sea as huge ice floes bumped and ground around and against his flimsy craft. He survived, but the finger of water in which he endured his ordeal was forever after known as Ford's Terror.

The Tracy and Endicott arms, which reach back from Stephens Passage into the Coastal Mountain Range, are steep-sided waterways, each with an active glacier at its head—the **Sawyer Glacier** in Tracy Arm and **Dawes Glacier** in Endicott. These calve constantly, sometimes discarding ice blocks of such size that they clog the narrow fjord passages, making navigation difficult. When the passage is not clogged, ships can get close enough for amazing viewing of and listening to the calving glaciers (the sound of white thunder is amazing!). And on a Radisson ship recently, we were thrilled to find the captain ordering out the tenders at Sawyer Glacier to provide us lucky passengers optimum viewing and a great photo op.

A passage up either fjord offers eye-catching views of high, cascading waterfalls, tree- and snow-covered mountain valleys, and wildlife that might include **Sitka black-tailed deer, bald eagles,** and possibly even the odd **black bear.** Around the ship, the animals you're most likely to see are whales, sea lions, and harbor seals.

## 8 Baranof Island

Named after the Russian trader Alexander Baranof, Russian America's first appointed honcho, the island's main claim to fame is **Sitka,** on the western coast, the center of Russian-era culture and the seat of the Russian Orthodox Church in Alaska. (The island name, by the way, is often spelled "Baranov," which some people contend is the way Alexander himself spelled it.) **Peril Straits,** off the northern end of the island, separating Baranof from Chichagof Island, is a scenic passageway too narrow for big cruise ships. Some of the smaller ones can manage the passage.

## 9 Sitka

Sitka differs from most ports of call on the Inside Passage cruises in that, geographically speaking, it's not on the Inside Passage at all. Rather, it stands on the outside (or western) coast of Baranof Island. Its name, in fact, comes from the Tlingit Indian *Shee Atika,* which means "people on the outside." For the relatively short time it takes ships to get to Sitka, they must leave the protected waters of the passage and sail with nothing between them and Japan but the sometimes turbulent Pacific Ocean. If you're going to run into heavy seas at any point on an Inside Passage cruise, this is where you're most likely to find them. And this is one of the ports in Alaska where you're more likely to have to tender to shore (in small boats) rather than dock at the harbor. Be that as it may, the idea of missing this delightful port of call is unthinkable to many people.

Step off your cruise ship here, and you step into Russian Alaska, the Alaska of yesteryear. This is where, in 1799, trader Alexander Baranof established a fort in what became known as New Archangel. Today Sitka has two main attractions that reflect its Russian heritage. **St. Michael's Cathedral,** with its striking onion-shaped dome and its ornate gilt interior, is one. Located on Lincoln Street, and standing as the focal point of the downtown thoroughfare, it's the official seat of the Russian Orthodox Church in Alaska. The other attraction that illustrates Sitka's Russian background is the **New Archangel Dancers,** who perform during the cruise season in **Harrigan Centennial Hall,** just a stone's throw from the pier. The colorfully costumed, 30-strong troupe performs a program of energetic Russian folk dances several times a day. Once a week, the New Archangel Dancers get together with a Tlingit dance troupe for a joint performance in the Sheet'ka Kwaan Naa Kahidi Community House on Katlian Street. (See "On Your Own: Within Walking Distance," later in the Sitka section, for more information.)

Most attractions in Sitka are within walking distance of the passenger docks. The **Sitka National Historical Park,** a must-do attraction with its impressive (mostly reproduction) totem poles and excellent views, is about a 10-minute walk from the passenger docks. One attraction that is too far to walk to but ought not to be missed is the **Alaska Raptor Rehabilitation Center** (see the description later under "On Your Own: Beyond Walking Distance"). A non-profit venture supported by tour companies, cruise lines, and public donations, the center was opened in 1980 to treat sick or injured birds of prey (primarily eagles) and to provide an educational experience for visitors. We don't mind admitting that the sight of our majestic national bird close up, with its snowy white head and curved beak, gives us goose bumps. We often wonder what they're thinking about when they fix you with that unblinking, disdainful eye.

You almost get the feeling that they're asking, "What do you think you're gaping at, Buster?"

Chamber music fans, listen up. Every year in June, Sitka hosts a celebration of chamber music, performed by world-class practitioners of the art in various halls throughout the town. Called the Sitka Summer Music Festival, the event has been held every year since 1972 under the guidance of renowned violinist Paul Rosenthal. Performances are on Tuesday and Friday evenings and the admission prices vary. Having sat in on one of the festival's presentations a year or so ago, we recommend it as a perfect complement to the more frenzied latter-day music ("Broadway in Rhythm," "Hits of the '60s") to be found on cruise ships. Of course, not every cruise includes a Tuesday or Friday evening stop in Sitka, but if yours does . . . . If you get the munchies while in town, stop at the Sitka Bowling Center (no, we're not kidding) on Lincoln Street, a stone's throw from the passenger pier, where you'll find good burgers and shakes. Nearby, at the **Westmark Shee Atika,** at 360 Seward St., you can get a fancier restaurant meal with fine service by a bunch of energetic and friendly young people. Highliner Coffee, in Seward Square Mall (behind the Subway shop, which is next to the lodge), offers lattes and other coffee drinks and excellent baked goods (try the giant oatmeal cookies), and has computers you can use (for a fee) to e-mail your friends back home.

**COMING ASHORE**   Most passengers will arrive in Sitka by tender because the harbor is too small to accommodate large ships. Tenders drop you right by the downtown area, but shuttle buses are also available to ferry you to local sights ($7 for an all-day pass or $3 for a one-way pass). They meet arrivals at the docks. Cabs are also available for a $3 ride downtown. Frankly, unless you have a very specific, distant destination in mind (the Raptor Center, for instance), we don't recommend taking a taxi or bus. Sitka is so small and the heart of town so close to the passenger pier that it's an ideal place to walk, rather than ride, around.

**INFORMATION**   A kiosk in the city-operated **Harrigan Centennial Hall Visitor Center,** 330 Harbor Dr., next to the Crescent Boat Harbor (© **907/ 747-3225**), is the only walk-in information stop. It is staffed by volunteers only when cruise ships are in town. The hall is open Monday through Friday from 8am to 10pm, Saturday 8am to 5pm, and sometimes Sunday.

## SHORE EXCURSIONS

**Russian America History Tour** (3 hr.; $39 adults, $19 children 12 and under): This motorcoach excursion hits all the historic sights, including St. Michael's Cathedral, the Russian Cemetery, Castle Hill, and Sitka's National Historical Park with its totem poles and forest trails.

**Sea Otter & Wildlife Quest** (3 hr.; $105 adults, $77 children 12 and under): A naturalist accompanies passengers on this jet-boat tour to point out the various animals you'll encounter and explain the delicate balance of the region's marine ecosystem. They're so sure you'll see a whale, bear, or otter that they offer a partial cash refund if you don't.

**Silver Bay Nature Cruise and Hatchery Tour** (2 hr.; $47 adults, $23 children 12 and under): An excursion vessel takes you through beautiful Silver Bay to view wildlife, scenery, the ruins of the Liberty Prospect Gold Mine, and a salmon hatchery.

**Sport Fishing** (4 hr.; $169): An experienced captain will guide your fully equipped boat to a good spot for halibut and salmon; the rest is up to you. Your

# Sitka

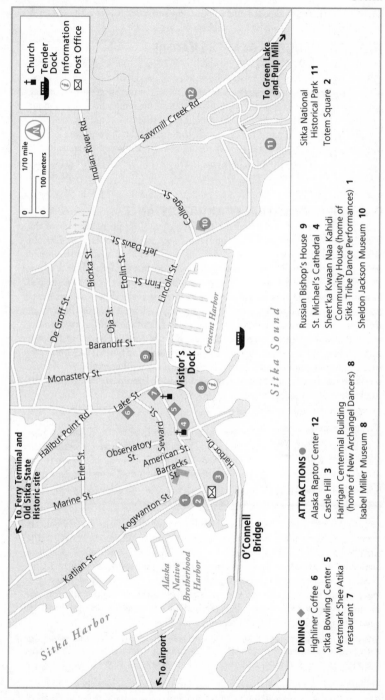

**Legend:**
- † Church
- 🚢 Tender Dock
- ⓘ Information
- ⊠ Post Office

N

1/10 mile
100 meters

To Green Lake
and Pulp Mill

Sawmill Creek Rd.

Indian River Rd.

College St.

Jeff Davis St.

De Groff St.

Biorka St.

Etolin St.

Finn St.

Oja St.

Lincoln St.

Baranoff St.

Monastery St.

Halibut Point Rd.

Lake St.

Seward St.

Observatory St.

American St.

Barracks St.

Erler St.

Marine St.

Kogwanton St.

Katlian St.

Crescent Harbor

Sitka Sound

Visitor's Dock

Harbor Dr.

O'Connell Bridge

Alaska Native Brotherhood Harbor

Sitka Harbor

To Ferry Terminal and
Old Sitka State
Historic site

To Airport

**ATTRACTIONS** ●

Alaska Raptor Center **12**
Castle Hill **3**
Harrigan Centennial Building
(home of New Archangel Dancers) **8**
Isabel Miller Museum **8**
Russian Bishop's House **9**
St. Michael's Cathedral **4**
Sheet'ka Kwaan Naa Kahidi
Community House (home of
Sitka Tribe Dance Performances) **1**
Sheldon Jackson Museum **10**
Sitka National
Historical Park **11**
Totem Square **2**

**DINING** ◆

Highliner Coffee **6**
Sitka Bowling Center **5**
Westmark Shee Atika
restaurant **7**

catch can be frozen or smoked and shipped to your home if you wish. (***Note:*** A $10 fishing license and a $10 king-salmon tag are extra.)

## TOURING THROUGH LOCAL OPERATORS

**Tribal Tours** (© 907/747-7290), owned by the Sitka Tribe of Alaska, offers a cultural tour program that relates the history of Sitka, with an emphasis on Native history and culture. Tickets can be purchased at the Sheet'ka Kwaan Naa Kahidi Community House at 200 Katlian St. (near the tender docks). A 1-hour city tour by bus is $10 per person. A 2½-hour comprehensive tour, priced at $29, includes a 45-minute narrative drive, a half-hour stop at the Sheldon Jackson Museum, a stop at the Sitka National Historical Park, and a performance by the Tlingit Indian Dance Troupe. (This tour is $39–$45 per person if the group size is below 10—but if you have a group below 10, you also get to visit the Alaska Raptor Rehabilitation Center.)

## ON YOUR OWN: WITHIN WALKING DISTANCE

**Castle Hill** At first, we found the prospect of a climb up to the top of the hill—by way of a lengthy flight of stairs from the western end of Lincoln Street—a little daunting, but after climbing to the top, we have two words of advice: Do it. The reward is panoramic views of downtown Sitka. This is where the first post–Alaska Purchase U.S. flag was raised, in 1867. The place is steeped in history. It was on this site, in the 1830s, that the marauding Russians drove off the resident Kiksadi clan of Tlingit Indians and built a stronghold from which to conduct their fur-trading business. The last of the buildings within the walls of the stronghold was used by the first Russian America governor and was called Baranof's Castle (hence: Castle Hill). The structure burned some 60 years later and its remains can still be seen, along with a lot of other reminders of those pre-Purchase days. Castle Hill is a National Historic Landmark, managed by the Alaska State Parks Department.

Climb stairs near intersection of Lincoln and Katlian sts.

**Isabel Miller Museum** Sharing a building with the Archangel dance troupe (see below), this museum, operated by the Sitka Historical Society, illustrates the city's history with art and artifacts. There's also a large diorama of Sitka as it was in 1867 when the land was transferred from Russia to the United States.

In the Harrigan Centennial Building, 330 Harbor Dr., near the tender docks. Free admission, but donations are accepted. May 4–Sept 22 daily 8am–5pm; off season Tues–Sun 10am–4pm.

**New Archangel Dancers** Just watching the way these Russian folk dancers throw themselves around the stage makes us tired. Where do they get the energy? The dancers are all women—they even play the men's parts, complete with false beards if the dance requires it. When the troupe was organized in 1969, the men of the town pooh-poohed the idea. It'll never work, they said. Later, when the original handful of women proved that it could work, some of the men expressed the feeling that they might not mind joining in. Too late, guys. The founders decided to keep the show all female.

Performances (on most days that a cruise ship is in port) are held in the Harrigan Centennial Building, 330 Harbor Dr., near the tender docks. © 907/747-5516. Admission $6. Call to find out when performances are, as times change daily. Tickets must be purchased at least half-hour before the show.

**The Russian Bishop's House** Bishop Innocent Veniaminov, born in 1797, translated scriptures into Tlingit and trained deacons to carry Russian Orthodoxy back to their Native villages. Unlike most of the later Protestant missionaries led by Sitka's other historic religious figure, Sheldon Jackson, Veniaminov and his followers allowed parishioners to use their own language, a key element to saving Native cultures. The house was built in 1842 for Veniaminov, and is now owned and operated by the National Parks Service. Ranger-led tours include the bishop's furnished quarters and an impressive chapel. Exhibits downstairs trace the development of New Archangel into Sitka.

Lincoln and Monastery sts. No phone; call Sitka National Historical Park Visitor Center (② **907/747-0110**). Admission $3 per person or $15 per family. Summer daily 9am–5pm.

**St. Michael's Cathedral**   Even if you're not a fan of religious shrines, you'll probably be impressed by the architecture and the finery of this rather small place of worship. One of the 49th state's most striking and photogenic structures, the current church is actually a replica; the original burned to the ground one night in 1966. So revered was the cathedral that Sitkans, whether Russian Orthodox or not, formed a human chain and carried many of the cathedral's precious icons, paintings, vestments, and jeweled crowns from the flames. Later, with contributions of cash and labor from throughout the land, St. Michael's was lovingly re-created on the same site and rededicated in 1976. It still contains those religious symbols that the citizens worked so hard to rescue from the inferno. A knowledgeable guide is on hand to answer questions or give talks when large groups congregate. Sunday services are sung in English, Slavonic, Tlingit, Aleut, and Yupik.

At Lincoln and Cathedral sts. ② **907/747-8120.** Suggested donation $2. Summer Mon–Fri 9am–4pm, Sat–Sun varies (call in advance).

**The Sheldon Jackson Museum**   Located on the grounds of a college founded by Presbyterian missionary Sheldon Jackson as a vocational school for young Tlingits (founded in 1878, it was the first educational institution in Alaska), the museum contains a fine collection of Native artifacts—not just those of the Tlingits, but also those of the Aleut, Athabascan, Haida, and Tsimshian peoples, as well as the Native peoples of the Arctic. The museum has a decent gift shop.

104 College Dr. (at Lincoln St.). ② **907/747-8981.** Admission $4, free for ages 18 and under. Mid-May to mid-Sept daily 9am–5pm; mid-Sept to mid-May Tues–Sat 10am–4pm.

**Sitka National Historical Park**   At just 107 acres, this is the smallest national park in Alaska, but don't let that discourage you because the place breathes history. This is where the Russians and the Tlingits fought a fierce battle in 1804. Within the park are a beautiful totem-pole trail (which you can tour on a ranger-led tour or on your own) and a visitor center where exhibits explain the art of totem carving, and Native artisans from the Southeast Alaska Indian Cultural Center create totems, jewelry, and Native drums.

106 Metlakatla St. (about a 10-min. walk from the tender pier). ② **907/747-6281.** Admission $3. Visitor center summer daily 8am–5pm. Park summer daily 6am–10pm.

**Sitka Tribe Dance Performances**   The Sheet'ka Kwaan Naa Kahidi, Sitka's community house, standing on the north side of the downtown parade ground, is a modern version of a Tlingit clan house, with an air-handling system that pulls smoke from the central fire pit straight up to the chimney. The magnificent house screen at the front of the hall, installed in 2000, is the largest in the Pacific Northwest. Performances last 30 minutes, including three dances and a story. It's entirely traditional and put on by members of the tribe. You can also sign up for tours and activities in the lobby.

200 Katlian St. ℂ **888/270-8687** or 907/747-7290. www.sitkatribal.com. $6 adults, $4 children. Call for times.

**Totem Square**   This area was originally underwater. It was the Russian ship-yard, which was reclaimed from the sea from 1940 to 1941 and now contains Russian cannons, huge anchors believed to have come from ships lost in Sitka Harbor in the 1700s, and other historical memorabilia.

Katlian St., at the west end of Lincoln St. Free admission. Daily 24 hr.

## ON YOUR OWN: BEYOND WALKING DISTANCE

**Alaska Raptor Rehabilitation Center**   Local informational literature claims that the center is 20 minutes on foot from town, but these must be some kind of special Chamber of Commerce minutes because it seems to take at least that long by bus. However you get there, though (and every cruise line offers it as a shore excursion), the center is well worth seeing. It's not a performing-ani-mal show with stunts and flying action, but rather a place where injured raptors (birds of prey) are brought and, with luck, healed to the point where they can be returned to the wild. Some eventually can; those that cannot are housed per-manently at the center or sent to zoos. Very few are euthanized. A new flight-training center, completed in 2003, is a little rainforest in an aviary where recuperating birds learn to fly again. Visitors walk through in a tube with one-way glass so they can watch the birds without disturbing them. The tour through the center and on a wheelchair-accessible nature trail in the surround-ing rainforest takes about an hour.

1101 Sawmill Creek Rd. (milepost .9), just across Indian River. ℂ **907/747-8662**. Admission $12 adults, $6 ages 3–12. Summer Sun–Fri 8am–4pm.

## 10 Juneau

Quick quiz: Can you name a state capital that cannot be reached by road from anywhere else in the state? The answer is Juneau. Fronted by the bustling Gastineau Channel and backed by Mount Juneau (elevation 3,819 ft.) and Mount Roberts (elevation 3,576 ft.), the city is on the mainland of Alaska but is cut off by the Juneau Icefield to the east and wilderness to the north and south. To be sure, there are roads—150 miles of them, in fact—but they all dead-end against an impenetrable forest or ice wall.

In 1900 Congress moved the territorial capital to Juneau from Sitka, which had fallen behind in the flurry of gold-rush development. Not all Alaskans believe Juneau is the right and logical place for a legislative center. Its inaccessi-bility, some argue, disenfranchises many voters, and every few years somebody puts a "move the capital" initiative on the ballot. Like all the rest (so far), the most recent proposal was defeated, which is good news for Juneau's 12,500 civil servants. In Juneau, government is the city's biggest industry. However, tourism is not far behind: Besides the thousands of independent visitors who arrive by air and ferry, many thousands more come ashore during the 450-plus passenger-ship port calls made here each summer.

On any given day, four or five cruise ships might be in port, ranging from the biggest in the fleets of Princess, Celebrity, Holland America, and the rest, to the small ships of Cruise West, Glacier Bay Cruiseline, Clipper, and others. The small ships and most of the large ships usually find a dock, but depending on how many large ships are in port that day, some might have to anchor in the channel and tender their guests ashore.

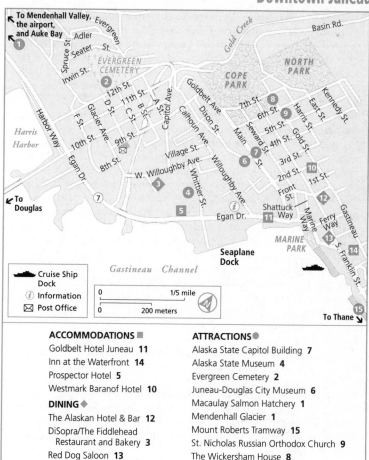

## ACCOMMODATIONS ■
Goldbelt Hotel Juneau **11**
Inn at the Waterfront **14**
Prospector Hotel **5**
Westmark Baranof Hotel **10**

### DINING ◆
The Alaskan Hotel & Bar **12**
DiSopra/The Fiddlehead
Restaurant and Bakery **3**
Red Dog Saloon **13**

## ATTRACTIONS ●
Alaska State Capitol Building **7**
Alaska State Museum **4**
Evergreen Cemetery **2**
Juneau-Douglas City Museum **6**
Macaulay Salmon Hatchery **1**
Mendenhall Glacier **1**
Mount Roberts Tramway **15**
St. Nicholas Russian Orthodox Church **9**
The Wickersham House **8**

It surprises some people to think that a city so dependent on the revenue generated by tourism, and cruises in particular, should think of imposing additional taxes on visitors, but that's just what Juneau did 4 years ago. Some movers and shakers there decided that they didn't like having their turf invaded by so many outsiders, and so they imposed a $5 head tax on each arriving cruise passenger, ostensibly to cover the cost of the vital services they use—roads, police, sewers, and so on. It's easier to grasp the residents' unhappiness when you think of the number of cruise passengers who pour into the city. We were recently in Juneau on a day when three large ships were docked and another was anchored in the channel. That meant that more than 7,000 visitors—counting crews—might be coming ashore that day, a crowd equal to almost one-fifth of the total population of Juneau. On some days there might be as many as 10,000 cruise visitors in town!

Juneau is a product of Alaska's golden past. It was no more than a fishing outpost for local Tlingit Indians until 1880, when gold was discovered in a creek off the Gastineau Channel by two prospectors, Joe Juneau and Richard (Dick) Harris. To be accurate, the gold was discovered first by Chief Kowee of the Auk

Tlingit clan who, in return for 100 warm blankets (more important to him than gold), passed the information on to a German engineer named George Pilz. Pilz, then surveying sites around the Inside Passage for mineral deposits, gave the hitherto unsuccessful Juneau and Harris directions to the spot described by Chief Kowee—and they couldn't find it! Only when Kowee accompanied them on a second expedition did they succeed in pinpointing the source of the precious metal. And the rush was on.

Mines sprang up on both sides of the channel. So rich was the area's gold yield that mines continued to open for the next 3 decades, including the most successful of them all, the **Alaska-Juneau Mine,** known locally simply as the A-J, which produced a whopping 3.5 million ounces of gold before it closed in 1944.

Today Juneau is arguably the most handsome of the 50 state capitals, despite a glut of souvenir shops near the pier (where you can buy anything from "I Love Alaska" backscratchers to fur coats). The city runs with a mix of quiet business efficiency and easygoing informality. It has a good deal more sophistication to it than any city in Alaska outside of Anchorage, and yet it also has the frontier-style **Red Dog Saloon,** 278 S. Franklin St., a sawdust-floored, swing-door, memorabilia-filled pub (offering food and drink) whose old-time raucousness may be tempered by its pursuit of the tourist buck (and by its location adjacent to the Juneau Police headquarters) but whose appeal is undeniable. Another place to enjoy a not-so-quiet drink is the bar of the **Alaskan Hotel,** nearby at 167 S. Franklin St., built in 1913. On the National Register of Historic Sites, the Alaskan is Juneau's oldest operating hotel.

For those who can tear themselves away from that cool drink, Juneau offers another major attraction: the **Mendenhall Glacier,** at the head of a valley a dozen miles away. The glacier is one of Alaska's most accessible and most photographed ice faces.

All of you smokers . . . beware! The Juneau Council enacted a law, effective January 1, 2005, banning smoking in certain bars and lounges. Over the next few years, the plan is to make it illegal to light up indoors in any public place. Right now, though, watch for the signs that tell you if it's safe to satisfy your nicotine craving.

**COMING ASHORE**   Unless you arrive on one of the busiest days of the year, your ship will dock right in the downtown area, along Marine Way. The pier is directly adjacent to the downtown area, but there is also shuttle bus service available that travels back and forth along the waterfront road.

**INFORMATION**   Midway down the cruise ship wharf a blue building houses the visitor information center; stop in to pick up a walking-tour map and visitors guide before striking out to see the sights. Another **Visitor Information Center** is in Centennial Hall at 101 Egan Dr., near the State Museum (© **888/ 581-2201** or 907/586-2201; fax 907/586-6304; www.traveljuneau.com). It's open May through September daily from 8:30am to 5pm, and October through April Monday through Friday from 9am to 4:30pm. The visitor center at the cruise ship dock is open during the summer when the ships come in.

## SHORE EXCURSIONS

**Deluxe Mendenhall Glacier & City Highlights Tour** (4 hr.; $79 adults, $45 children 12 and under): Twelve miles long and 1½ miles wide, Mendenhall is the most visited glacier in the world and the most popular sight in Juneau. This trip will take you by bus to the U.S. Forest Service Observatory, from which you can walk up a trail to within ½ mile of the glacier (which feels a lot closer) or take one of the nature trails if time allows. After this, you will visit Juneau's historic highlights and you might, on some tours, also visit the Macaulay Salmon Hatchery, the Alaska State Museum, and other local attractions.

**Extended Helicopter Glacier Trek** (6½ hr.; $419): This is definitely not an excursion for the faint of heart or the sedentary. The excursion involves a flight to the Juneau Icefield, followed by 4 hours of hiking and climbing on rugged terrain, descending ice walls, and exploring glacial pools and ice caves along the way, always in the company, of course, of a trained mountain guide. All necessary equipment is included in the hefty price and the minimum age for participation is 16. Unless you're in pretty good shape, we suggest that you choose something else for your Juneau adventure.

**Glacier Helicopter Trek** (4 hr.; $359): Here's your chance to walk on the face of a glacier. After transferring to the airport by bus, guests board helicopters bound for Mendenhall, Norris Glacier, or other glacier areas. The tour may include one or two stops on a glacier, and you will soar over the jagged peaks carved by the massive Juneau Icefield. If special equipment (boots, rain slickers, and so on) is required, it will be provided.

**Gold Mine History Tour** (4 hr.; $59 adults, $25 children 12 and under): Juneau's gold-rush history comes to life (especially for kids) as you visit the ruins of the Alaska Gastineau mine and don a hard hat for a walk along a 360-foot tunnel for a demonstration of early-20th-century mining equipment and methods.

**Mendenhall Glacier Float Trip** (3½ hr.; $99 adults, $66 children under 12): You'll board 10-person rafts on the shore of Mendenhall Lake, and an experienced oarsman will guide you out past icebergs and into the Mendenhall River. You'll encounter moderate rapids and stunning views, and be treated to a snack of smoked salmon and reindeer sausage somewhere along the way.

**Wilderness Lodge Flightseeing Adventure** (3 hr.; $235 adults, $165 children 12 and under): This trip combines flightseeing over glaciers and an ice field with a stop at the Taku Glacier Lodge for a traditional all-you-can-eat salmon bake. After a hearty lunch, you can hike the nature trails around the wilderness lodge before reboarding the floatplane for the flight back to Juneau.

## TOURING THROUGH LOCAL OPERATORS

**The Juneau Trolley Car Company** (© 907/789-4342) provides narrated tours around the downtown area. Pickup is at the Tram Center at the pier. You can get off and on as you like at sites including the Alaska State Capitol and the Alaska State Museum. Fares are $12 for adults, $8.50 for kids. Also at the pier you'll find booths operated by various independent tour operators selling city and glacier tours starting at about $15 to $20 a head.

## ON YOUR OWN: WITHIN WALKING DISTANCE

**Alaska State Capitol Building**   We've often wondered how so lovely a capital city could come up with such an unprepossessing legislative home. The interior is worth a visit, though, to see the old-fashioned woodwork and interesting decorative details.

4th St., between Main and Seward sts. © 907/465-3800. Free admission. Tours during the summer start every half-hour Mon–Fri 9am–4:30pm.

**Alaska State Museum**   This place opened as a territorial museum in 1900 and has a wildlife exhibit, a first-class collection of artifacts reflecting the state's

Russian history and Native cultures, and exhibits illustrating the history of the city's mining and fishery industries.

395 Whittier St. ℂ **907/465-2901**. Admission $5 adults, free for ages 18 and under. Summer daily 8:30am–5:30pm.

**Evergreen Cemetery**   At this beautiful cemetery, which slopes toward the ocean, you can view the gravesites of Joe Juneau, Richard Harris, and other pioneers. The old Alaska Native graves are located in the wooded area on the far side of the cemetery.

12th St., just west of the downtown area.

**Juneau-Douglas City Museum**   This museum highlights the development of the city from its golden beginnings to statehood, and also has exhibits on Tlingit culture. The facility specializes in programs and displays geared toward youngsters.

Corner of 4th and Main sts. ℂ **907/586-3572**. Admission $3 adults, free for ages 18 and under. Summer Mon–Fri 9am–5pm, Sat–Sun 10am–5pm.

**Mount Roberts Tramway**   The best place to take in Juneau's lovely position on the Gastineau Channel is from high up on Mount Roberts. The ascent of the mountain used to entail a strenuous hike but is now an easy 6-minute ride in the comfortable, 60-passenger cars of the Mount Roberts Tramway. Operated by Goldbelt, a Tlingit corporation, the tramway rises from a base alongside the cruise ship docks and whisks sightseers 2,000 feet up to a center with a restaurant/bar, a gift shop, a museum, cultural film shows, a series of nature trails (bring mosquito repellent!), and a fabulous panorama. Don't miss it, but on the other hand, don't bother if the day is overcast: Many visitors have paid their $22 ($14 for kids) for an all-day pass, reached the top, and been faced with a solid wall of white mist.

At the cruise ship docks. ℂ **888/461-TRAM** or 907/463-3412. All-day pass $22 adults, $14 children 12 and under. Mar–Nov daily 9am–9pm.

**Red Dog Saloon**   This is the place to go for a taste of frontier Alaska—and of the scrumptious locally brewed Alaskan Amber Ale. Look up on the wall behind the bar, where, among other things (many other things), they've got one of Wyatt Earp's pistols. Also look at the rest of the walls, where you'll see scrawled messages from legions of cruise ship passengers who came before you.

278 S. Franklin St., right by the cruise ship docks. Main courses $7.50–$11. AE, DISC, MC, V. Summer daily 11am–11pm.

**St. Nicholas Russian Orthodox Church**   This tiny, ornate, octagonal structure is altogether captivating. It was built in 1893 by local Tlingits who, under pressure from the government to convert to Christianity, chose the only faith that allowed them to keep their language. Father Ivan Veniaminov (p. 198) had translated the Bible into Tlingit 50 years earlier, when the Russians were still in Sitka.

5th and Gold sts. $2 donation requested. Lengthy services are sung in English, Tlingit, and Slavic for Sat vespers at 6pm and on Sun at 9am; the congregation stands throughout the service. Otherwise, the church is open for visitors during the summer Mon–Sat 9am–5pm, Sun noon–5pm.

**The Wickersham House**   This house was built in 1899 and bought in 1928 by Judge James Wickersham, who did much to shape the face of Alaska. Wickersham was the first territorial delegate to the U.S. Congress, was in the vanguard of the fight for statehood, and founded the University of Alaska. The house was in the family from 1928 until the state bought it in 1984, so it still contains Wickersham's belongings, including an Edison cylinder gramophone he took to Fairbanks, and his assignment to go to Alaska, which is signed by Theodore Roosevelt. *Note:* The house is at the top of a very steep hill.

7th St. ℭ **907/586-9001.** A live-in guide requests a $2 donation. Mid-May to late Sept 10am–noon and 1–5pm.

## ON YOUR OWN: BEYOND WALKING DISTANCE

**Macaulay Salmon Hatchery**    From the well-designed outdoor decks at this hatchery, visitors can watch the whole process of harvesting and fertilizing salmon eggs. Guides and exhibits explain what's happening. The Capital Transit bus stops at the hatchery on its way from downtown to the airport. Pick up a route map and schedule at the visitor information center at the cruise ship dock.

2697 Channel Dr., about 3 miles from downtown. ℭ **877/463-2486** or 907/463-4810. Admission $3 adults, $1.50 children ages 12 and under. Summer Mon–Fri 10am–6pm, Sat–Sun 10am–5pm; off season call ahead.

**Mendenhall Glacier**    Mendenhall is the easiest glacier to get to in Alaska and the most visited glacier in the world. Its U.S. Forest Service visitor center has glacier exhibits, a video, and rangers who can answer questions, and there are several trails that'll take you close to the glacier, the easiest being a .5-mile nature trail. Mendenhall is located about 13 miles from downtown, and taxis and local bus services are readily available in town (the bus costs $1.50 each way; taxis about $15) for those who want to visit independent of a tour. If you take a taxi out, make arrangements with the driver to also pick you up—and negotiate a round-trip price before you leave. One highly economical way to get out there is to use the services of Mendenhall Glacier Bus Company, which will carry you from the pier to the door of the glacier visitor center and back for $10. No reservation is needed; just walk off the ship and get on one of the buses parked 50 yards away. The equipment used is a school bus—not necessarily the most comfortable way to go—but the advantage over the city transportation is that this one really takes you to Mendenhall Glacier, as opposed to dropping you off at the bus stop more than a mile away. Since it doesn't stop to embark and disembark riders along the way, the Mendenhall Glacier Bus Company gets you there in 20 minutes; although the city bus is cheaper, the ride takes closer to an hour.

Off Mendenhall Loop Rd. Visitor center ℭ **907/789-0097.** Admission to the visitor center $3 adults, free for children under 12. Summer daily 8am–6pm.

## 11 Icy Strait, Point Adolphus & Gustavus

The strait, the promontory, and the town all lie at or near the mouth of Glacier Bay, in prime **whale-watching** waters. The whales, which migrate to the bay each year to feed in preparation for their winter breeding in Mexico, must pass through the strait to get in or out of the bay. Passengers aboard large ships may well be fortunate enough to see them on their journey, and those in small ships will likely have an even better chance, since the small ships have the luxury of going places the bigger vessels can't, and their size and maneuverability make it possible for them to get closer to the whales.

The big ships don't visit **Gustavus,** which isn't too much of a town anyway (it has just 400 residents) and is interesting more as an anthropological exercise ("What on earth makes people live here?") than anything else. It should be noted, though, that the area has assumed increased importance in the cruise business this year with the opening of Icy Strait Point, a fancy name for a private dock built by a Tlingit Indian corporation that will be visited on regular basis by some ships of Royal Caribbean and its affiliate, Celebrity. There's no town there, only wilderness. The idea is to give passengers easier access to another part of Alaska's hitherto untouched wilderness. The two cruise lines experimented with the concept last year on a very limited basis. (See "What's New in Alaska Cruising in 2005" for more details.)

## 12 Glacier Bay National Park & Preserve

There are about 5,000 glaciers in Alaska, so what's all the fuss about Glacier Bay? Everybody has a theory about that, of course. Some think it's the wildlife, which includes humpback whales, bears, Dall sheep, seals, and more. Some think it's the history of the place, which was frozen behind a mile-wide wall of ice until about 1870. A mere 55 years later, it was designated as a national park, along with its 3.3 million surrounding acres. Those with an interest in geology and glaciology might argue that it's the receding ice faces at the ends of Glacier Bay's various inlets. Thought to be the fastest-moving glaciers in the world, they retreat at some 1½ inches a year. Whatever the reason, Glacier Bay has taken on an allure unachieved by other glacier areas.

The first white man to enter the vast (60-plus miles) Glacier Bay inlet was naturalist **John Muir** in 1879. Just 100 years earlier, when Capt. James Cook and, later, George Vancouver sailed there, the mouth was still a wall of ice. Today, all that ice has ebbed back, leaving behind a series of glaciers and inlets (**Margerie, Johns Hopkins, Muir,** and others) whose calving activity provides entertainment for hundreds of cruisers lining the rails as their ships sit, becalmed, for several hours. Watching massive slabs of ice break away and crash with a roar into the ice-strewn waters is one of our favorite experiences.

Each ship that enters the bay takes aboard a park ranger who provides commentary over the ship's PA throughout the day about glaciers, wildlife, and the bay's history. On large ships, the ranger may also give a presentation in the show lounge about conservation; on small ships, he or she will often be on deck throughout the day and available for questions.

Glacier Bay is the world's largest protected marine sanctuary. The bay is so vast that the water contained within its boundaries would cover the state of Connecticut, the third smallest in the U.S. (Don't even think about what it would do to Rhode Island or Delaware!) The ecological sensitivity of the bay is a source of concern for environmentalists, who would like to see cruise ships banned from entering, or at least have their access severely curtailed. The ship operators, on the other hand, argue that no evidence shows that their vessels have any negative impact on the wildlife of the bay. In fact, they note that they provide an excellent opportunity for the maximum number of people to enjoy the natural wonders of the park at one time with the minimum of damage to the water's denizens.

The subject has been a political hot potato for many years and it's likely to go on being one for years to come. The lines find some reason for hope in recent pronouncements of officials of the U.S. Department of the Interior that the number of access permits may be raised from its current 139 to as many as 170. But it's not going to happen without a fight by environmentalists. And it won't happen quickly. Look to 2006 at the very earliest.

The glaciers, which form the basis of the park's appeal, are numerous. There are 16 major tidewater glaciers (those that go all the way to the water), and 30 valley or alpine glaciers (those that compress between two hills but don't extend all the way to the water). In Tarr Inlet, at the Alaska/Canada border, two notable

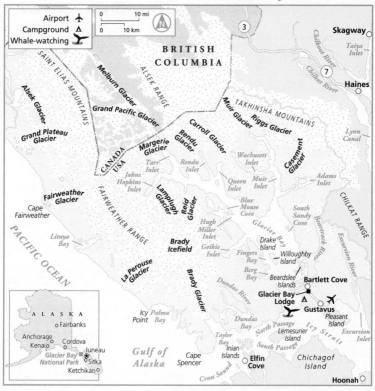

glaciers meet—Margerie and Grand Pacific. Margerie, on the Alaskan side, is pristine white and very active, calving frequently; Grand Pacific, on the Canadian side of the line, is black, gritty, and not particularly active. The widely differing coloration of the two is caused by the terrain through which each glacier pushes its way to the sea. Margerie cuts through a relatively clean path, while Grand Pacific picks up rocks and dirt along the way. It makes for an interesting contrast for cruise ship passengers in the inlet.

Visible from much of the bay (on a clear day) is the massive Mount Fairweather (elevation 15,320 ft.). Although Fairweather is taller than any mountain in the Lower 48, and second only to Mont Blanc in the Alps, it ranks no higher than 19th among Alaska's peaks.

Incidentally, if you want to appear smart, ask your friends if they know how long it takes for the ice that falls off the face of a glacier to reach that point. Chances are they won't know that it is estimated that the process takes as long as 200 years!

## 13 Haines

This pretty, laid-back port is an example of Alaska the way you probably thought it would be. It's a small, scenic town with wilderness at its doorstep. If you are not on one of the few ships that regularly visit Haines (pop. 2,250), you can easily reach the port on a day excursion from **Skagway.** The two communities lie at the northern end of the Lynn Canal, just a stone's throw apart. The trip is worth the $35 round-trip water-taxi fare, especially for those who have "done" Skagway before.

The thing that's immediately striking about Haines is its setting, arguably one of the prettiest in Alaska. The village lies in the shadow of the Fairweather Mountain Range, about 80 or so miles north of Juneau and on the same line of latitude as the lower reaches of Norway. Framed by high hills, it is more protected from the elements than many other Inside Passage ports. Ketchikan, for instance, gets up to 200 inches of rain in a wet year; Haines a mere 60 inches. That's positively arid by some Southeast Alaska standards!

Haines was established in 1879 by Presbyterian missionary S. Hall Young and naturalist John Muir as a base for converting the Chilkoot and Chilkat Tlingit tribes to Christianity. They named the town for Mrs. F. E. Haines, secretary of the Presbyterian National Committee, who raised the funds for the exploration. The natives called it *Da-Shu,* the Tlingit word for "end of the trail." Traders knew the place as Chilkoot. The military, which came later and built a fort here in 1903, knew it as Fort Seward or Chilkoot Barracks. In 1897 and 1898, the town became one of the lesser-known access points (it was less popular than Skagway and Dyea) to a route to the Klondike; it was located at the head of what became known as the Jack Dalton Trail into Canada. At about the same time, gold was discovered much closer to home—in Porcupine, just 36 miles away—and that strike drew even more prospectors to Haines. The gold quickly petered out, though, and Porcupine is no more.

The **old fort** still stands, although it was touch and go for a while whether it would survive. After World War II, and after 42 years of service, it was decommissioned and the future of the place—and of Haines itself, to some extent—was in doubt. So much of the local economy had depended on the spending of the military personnel stationed there. A group of veterans once stationed at Chilkoot Barracks, however, would not let the fort die. In 1947, they bought the 85 buildings standing on 400 acres. They built a salmon smokehouse, a furniture-making plant, and other cooperative business ventures that they hoped would keep alive the place that held such a special place in their hearts. They agitated to have Haines included on the Alaska Marine Highway System. They built the Hotel Halsingsland, established art galleries, and funded Indian arts training programs for local youngsters.

The **Officers' Club Lounge** in the Halsingsland Hotel is a dandy place to stop for a libation. It features Alaskan and Yukon beers and a house special known as "The Fort Seward Howitzer." What's in it? If you have to ask, you can't handle it!

The descendants of some of these modern-day pioneers still live in homes their fathers and grandfathers built on the fort grounds. Designated a National Historic Site by the U.S. government in 1972, **Fort William Seward** is a must see for visitors, including cruise passengers. All lines invariably include a fort shore excursion in their brochure.

Haines is so small that it can be absorbed on foot. Depending on how long you want to walk, you can probably see most everything in 1 to 2 hours of reasonably flat walking. Start at **Steve Sheldon's museum,** a stone's throw from the pier, turn west up Main Street (the only uphill part of the journey), which allows some beautiful views of the Chilkat Mountains. The next point of interest is the **Hammer Museum.** No, it's not a facility established by Armand Hammer! It is literally a museum dedicated to hammers—and it's free of charge. Haines' tallest building—all of four stories high—is a little farther on. Turn right onto Second

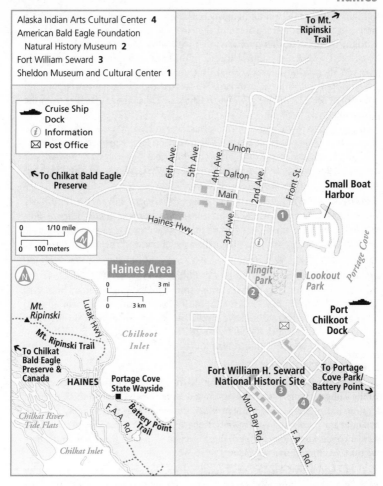

Alaska Indian Arts Cultural Center **4**
American Bald Eagle Foundation
  Natural History Museum **2**
Fort William Seward **3**
Sheldon Museum and Cultural Center **1**

Cruise Ship Dock
(i) Information
⊠ Post Office

←To Chilkat Bald Eagle Preserve

0 — 1/10 mile
0 — 100 meters

To Mt. Ripinski Trail

6th Ave.  5th Ave.  4th Ave.  2nd Ave.  Front St.

Union
Dalton
Main
Haines Hwy.  3rd Ave.

Small Boat Harbor

Portage Cove

Tlingit Park
Lookout Park

Port Chilkoot Dock

**Haines Area**

0 — 3 mi
0 — 3 km

Mt. Ripinski
Mt. Ripinski Trail
←To Chilkat Bald Eagle Preserve & Canada
HAINES
Chilkat River Tide Flats
Chilkat Inlet
Chilkoot Inlet
Lutak Hwy.
Portage Cove State Wayside
F.A.A. Rd.
Battery Point Trail

Fort William H. Seward National Historic Site **3**
Alaska Indian Arts Cultural Center **4**
To Portage Cove Park/Battery Point →
Mud Bay Rd.
F.A.A. Rd.

Avenue and have a drink or a meal at the **Pioneer Bar & Bamboo Room Restaurant,** or visit the nearby **Old City Hall and Fire Station.** Turn left onto Union Street, past the **Lindholm House** (built in 1912), left onto Third Avenue, and right onto Dalton Street, named for Jack Dalton, a turn-of-the-century entrepreneur who helped put Haines on the map. A few blocks later, turn left onto Fifth Avenue and then left again onto Main Street toward the Lynn Canal. In no time at all, you're back at the ship, having seen much of what Haines has to offer.

The town's gold history, its military background, and its Native heritage are the significant draws for travelers to Haines. So are **eagles.** The area is a magnet for these magnificent creatures—a couple hundred are year-round residents. Unfortunately, cruise passengers are unable to experience one of Haines's most spectacular avian events: the annual **Gathering of the Eagles,** which occurs in winter (usually Oct until mid-Feb), after the cruise season, and which brings as many as 4,000 birds from all over the Pacific Northwest to the area in search of salmon, which can't be found anywhere else during these months. During this time, trees along a 5-mile stretch of the river (in an area known as the **Alaska Chilkat Bald Eagle Preserve**) are thick with rows of these snow-headed raptors—often a dozen or more sharing a limb, from which they swoop down to carry off their favorite takeout food. But even during the cruise season, you're likely to spot at least an eagle or two. We spotted eight in various swooping and tree-sitting poses on a bike ride out to Chilkoot Lake (about 10 miles from the cruise ship pier) last May.

For ages, one of the most popular attractions in Haines was a performance by the **Chilkat Dancers** dance troupe. The troupe no longer performs, but there is a Chilkat Dancers Storytelling Show in the tribal house at Fort Seward (see below) throughout the summer. Admission is $10 adults, $5 for kids. For updated information, call ℂ/fax **907/766-2160**.

**COMING ASHORE**  Ships either dock at the Port Chilkoot Dock, directly opposite Fort Seward, or tender passengers in, dropping them either at Port Chilkoot or at the small-boat harbor in the downtown area, less than a mile away. Both docks are within walking distance of many of the main attractions.

**INFORMATION**  Pick up some walking-tour information on Haines at the **visitor center,** on Second Avenue (ℂ **800/458-3579** or 907/766-2234). It's open in summer Monday through Friday from 8am to 7pm, Saturday from 9am to 5pm, and Sunday from 11am to 5pm. It's easy to explore the town on foot, or you can rent a bike at **Sockeye Cycle,** on Portage Street right up the street from the cruise ship dock (ℂ **907/766-2869**), for $12 for 2 hours or $30 a day. The company also offers guided bike tours.

## SHORE EXCURSIONS

**Klukwan Native Tlingit Village** (5 hr.; $189): Klukwan is the "mother village" of the Tlingit people in the Haines/Chilkat Valley area. Although the settlement is poor, it contains a tribal house in which the locals share their stories. The tour includes a drive through some pretty scenery and ends with a visit to the superb Chilkat Bald Eagle Preserve near the passenger-ship pier. (See "On Your Own: Within Walking Distance," below.)

**Best of Haines by Classic Car** (1 hr.; $52): Explore Haines in style in a 1930s or 1940s vintage automobile. The entertaining guides share the history of the area, and you'll get an insight into how Hainesians live and work.

**Chilkat Nature Hike** (4 hr.; $65): This hike takes you through a rainforest and includes a narrative on forest flora and fauna by a naturalist. You might spot a bald eagle or two. Moderately difficult hiking.

**Chilkat Bald Eagle Preserve Jet-Boat Tour** (3½ hr.; $99): A bus takes you to the world-famous Bald Eagle Preserve, where you board small boats specially designed to traverse the narrows of the Chilkat River into the Alaskan wilderness. Eagle spotting is the thing on this excursion, and you may also see bears, moose, and beavers.

**Chilkat Bicycle Adventure** (4 hr.; $89): Tour the Fort Seward area and then travel along the Chilkat River estuary by bicycle. You'll hit some minor hills, but nothing too challenging. And you may even spot a few eagles. Bike, helmet, and rain gear provided.

**Horse-Drawn Carriage Tour** (1½ hr; $35): A carriage tour is a leisurely, fun way to see this quaint little Lynn Canal community.

**A Taste of Haines** (4½ hr.; $139): Accompanied by a local guide, the tour takes in Fort Seward followed by a 10-mile drive along the banks of the Chilkat River and a photo stop at the picturesque and historic Letnikof Cove Cannery, a vantage point for spotting seals, sea lions, bald eagles, and other aquatic wildlife. The tour includes visits to an artist colony and a working smokehouse to sample the freshly smoked salmon.

## TOURING THROUGH LOCAL OPERATORS

**Chiliast Guides,** on Portage Street (*✆* **907/766-2491**), offers a rafting trip twice a day during the summer down the Chiliast to watch eagles. The rapids are pretty easy—there's a chance you may be asked to get out and push—and you'll see lots of eagles. The 4-hour trip, with a snack, costs $79 for adults and $53 for children. **Alaska Nature Tours** (*✆* **907/766-2876**) offers a variety of escorted tours, including a 3-hour bus and walking tour of the Chiliast Bald Eagle Preserve for $50 per person ($60 with lunch).

## ON YOUR OWN: WITHIN WALKING DISTANCE

**Alaska Indian Arts Cultural Center**    Located in the old fort hospital on the south side of the parade grounds, the center has a small gallery and a carvers' workshop where you may be able to see totem carving in progress.

On the south side of the parade grounds. Mon–Fri 9am–5pm and evenings when cruise ships are in town.

**The American Bald Eagle Foundation Natural History Museum**    This foundation celebrates Haines's location in the "Valley of the Eagles" with a huge diorama depicting more than a hundred eagles.

At Second Ave. and Haines Hwy. *✆* **907/766-3094**. Admission $3 adults, $1 kids 8–12, free for kids under 8. Mon–Fri 9am–5pm and evenings when cruise ships are in town.

**Fort William Seward**    The central feature of the town, rising right above the docks, Fort Seward was retired after World War II and redone by a group of returning veterans. It's not the kind of place one thinks of when envisioning a fort. It has no parapets, no walls, no nothing—just an open parade ground surrounded by large, wood-frame former barracks and officers' quarters that have today been converted into private homes, the Halsingsland Hotel, a gallery and studio, and the Alaska Indian Arts Cultural Center (see above). In the center of the sloping parade ground you'll find a replica of a Tlingit tribal house.

The area is just inland from the cruise ship dock.

**The Sheldon Museum and Cultural Center**    Not to be confused with the Sheldon Jackson Museum in Sitka, this place was established by a local man, Steve Sheldon. Small by some museum standards, it nevertheless has a wonderful collection of Hainesiana: Tlingit artifacts, gold-rush-era weaponry, military memorabilia, and so on.

Corner of Main and Front sts. *✆* **907/766-2366**. Admission $3, free for children under 12. Summer Mon–Fri 11am–6pm, Sat–Sun 2–6pm.

## 14  Skagway

No port in Alaska is more historically significant than this small town at the northern end of the picturesque Lynn Canal. In the late 19th century, a steady stream of prospectors began the long trek into Canada's Yukon Territory, seeking the vast quantities of Klondike gold that had been reported in Rabbit Creek (later renamed Bonanza Creek). Not many of them realized the unspeakable hardships they'd have to endure before they could get close to the stuff. They first had to negotiate either the **White Pass** or the **Chilkoot Pass** through the coastal mountain range to the Canadian border. To do so, they had to hike 20 miles, climbing nearly 3,000 feet in the process. And, by order of Canada's North West Mounted Police, they had to have at least a year's supply of provisions with them before they could enter the country. Numbed by temperatures that fell at times into the –50s (–40s Celsius), and often blinded by driving snow or stinging hail (they were, after all, hiking through the mountain passes that gave Skagway its name—in Tlingit, *Skagua* means "home of the North Wind"), they plodded upward, ferrying part of their supplies up part of the way, stashing them, and returning to Skagway to repeat the process with another load, always inching their way closer to the summit. The process took as many as 20 trips for some, and often enough, their stashes were stolen by unscrupulous rivals or opportunistic locals. Prospectors who thought themselves lucky enough to be able to afford horses or mules found their pack animals to be less than sound of limb. Not for nothing is one stretch of the trail through the White Pass (the more popular of the two routes through the mountains) called **Dead Horse Gulch.**

Arduous as it was, that first leg was just the beginning. From the Canadian border, their golden goal lay a long and dangerous water journey away, part of the way by lake (and thus relatively easy), but most of it down the mighty Yukon River and decidedly perilous.

The gold rush brought to Skagway a way of life as violent and as lawless as any to be found in the frontier West. The Mounties (the law in Canada) had no jurisdiction in Skagway. In fact, there was no law whatsoever in Skagway. Peace depended entirely on the consciences of the inhabitants, and the smell of gold and the realization that there were opportunities for profit without ever setting foot in the Klondike drew to the town many for whom conscience would never be a factor—saloonkeepers, gamblers, prostitutes, and desperadoes of every stripe.

The most notorious of the Skagway bad men was Jefferson Randolph "Soapy" Smith, a thug and an accomplished con man. He earned his nickname in Denver, Colorado, by persuading large numbers of people to buy bars of cheap soap for $1 in the belief that some of the bars were wrapped in larger denomination bills. They weren't, of course, but the scam made Smith a lot of money. In Skagway he and his gang engaged in all kinds of nastiness, charging local businesses large fees for "protection"; exacting exorbitant sums to "store" prospectors' gear (and then selling the equipment to others); setting up a telegraph station and charging prospectors to send messages home (though the telegraph wire went no farther than the next room); and generally practicing all kinds of nefarious activities designed to separate the starry-eyed gold seekers from their cash.

The gold-rush days of Skagway had their heroes as well. One of them was the man who finally put an end to Soapy's reign of terror. He was city surveyor Frank Reid, who shot Smith dead and was himself mortally wounded in the gunfight. In his honor, the local citizenry erected an impressive granite monument (which reads, in part, "He gave his life for the honor of Skagway") over his grave in the Gold Rush Cemetery; Smith's marker, on the other hand, is very simple, and his remains aren't even underneath it (they're 3 ft. to the left, outside consecrated ground). Perversely, though, perhaps because he was the more colorful character, it is the villain Smith whose life is commemorated each July 8, with songs and entertainment.

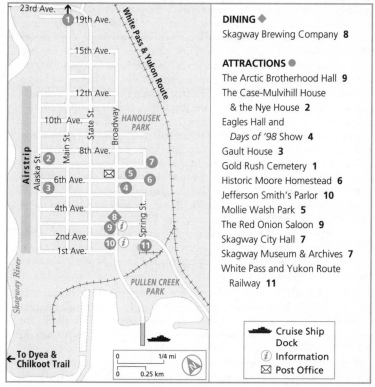

**DINING** ◆
Skagway Brewing Company **8**

**ATTRACTIONS** ●
The Arctic Brotherhood Hall **9**
The Case-Mulvihill House
& the Nye House **2**
Eagles Hall and
*Days of '98 Show* **4**
Gault House **3**
Gold Rush Cemetery **1**
Historic Moore Homestead **6**
Jefferson Smith's Parlor **10**
Mollie Walsh Park **5**
The Red Onion Saloon **9**
Skagway City Hall **7**
Skagway Museum & Archives **7**
White Pass and Yukon Route
Railway **11**

🚢 Cruise Ship Dock
ⓘ Information
✉ Post Office

Another memorable figure of the day was Mollie Walsh, "The Angel of the White Pass." Moved by the suffering of the prospectors trekking into Canada, the pious Walsh opened an eatery in a tent at the summit of the White Pass, from which she dispensed hot soup and coffee to the often frozen gold seekers. Her life is commemorated by a bronze bust in Mollie Walsh Park at 6th Avenue and Spring Street downtown. It says much about the nature of Skagway and the kind of people it attracted at the turn of the century that the man Walsh met and married there murdered her in 1902 and then committed suicide.

Unlike many other Alaska frontier towns, Skagway has been spared the ravages of major fires and earthquakes. Some of the original buildings still stand, protected by the National Park Service. The Klondike Gold Rush National Historic District, which comprises much of the downtown area, contains some striking examples of these buildings. Other little touches of history are preserved around town, such as the huge watch painted on the mountainside above town—it was an early billboard for the long-gone Herman Kirmse's watch-repair shop. Also remaining from the old days is the White Pass and Yukon Route narrow-gauge railroad, opened in 1900 to carry late stampeders in and gold out. Now, a ride on the train is a must for visitors. The round-trip to the summit of the pass, following a route carved out of the side of the mountain by an American/Canadian engineering team backed by British money, takes 3 hours from a departure site conveniently located a short walk (or an even shorter shuttle bus ride) from the cruise ship piers.

Having a sweet little historic town is nice for Skagway's 860 or so year-round residents, of course, but by itself, history doesn't pay the bills. So, though Skagway is trying to hang on to its gold-rush heritage, it's also trying to make money off it—so much so, and so successfully, that on any given day in the summer, thousands of seasonal workers will be around to reap the profits from the summer influx of visitors, principally from cruise ships. New businesses, including restaurants and jewelry stores, are sprouting up as well, many of which have gold-rush connotations only in the sense that they've opened to cash in on visitor's gold.

A few years back, we were struck that one of the first things that greeted us as we walked from the ship, on the wall of the Mercantile Building on 2nd Avenue, was the most 21st century of all logos: Starbucks coffee! Then last year, we were actually given a verbal invite by a clerk at one of those fancy jewelry stores that have followed cruise passengers here from the Caribbean. We know he was only doing his job, but really, you used to be able to window-shop in Skagway in peace without having to worry about being lured in.

For a respite from shopping, check out the $3 beer specials at the 1898 Red Onion Saloon (at Broadway and 2nd Ave.), or down Broadway, test the product at the **Skagway Brewing Company,** where you can have a beer and also check your e-mail.

**COMING ASHORE**    Ships dock at the cruise pier, at the foot of Broadway or off Congress Way. From the farthest point, it's about a 5-minute walk from the pier across the train tracks to downtown, but shuttle buses are also offered. The only street you really need to know about is Broadway, which runs through the center of town and off which everything branches.

After you've docked, take a few minutes to study the painting of ships' and captains' names and dates that blankets the 400-foot-high cliffs alongside the pier. It's not graffiti; it is a genuine history of the development of the cruise industry in Skagway over the last 4 decades or more. Each of the paintings, mostly of shipline logos, were done by members of the crews of visiting ships. Some of the pictures are placed hundreds of feet up the cliffs. If you're interested in how it was done, cruise officials tell us that some of the artists climbed halfway up the sheer wall face to make their marks; others lowered themselves on rope pulleys from the top. Either way, it must have been a nerve-wracking process—so much so that the local authorities have put a stop to it. For several years past it's been a case of "Paint a rock, go to jail."

**INFORMATION**    Walking maps are available at the **Skagway Visitor Information Center,** at the Arctic Brotherhood Hall, 245 Broadway, between 2nd and 3rd avenues (© **907/983-2854**). Located in the restored railroad depot, the **National Park Service Visitor Center,** 2nd Avenue and Broadway (P.O. Box 517), Skagway, AK 99840 (© **907/983-2921;** www.nps.gov/klgo), is the focal point for activities in Skagway. Rangers answer questions, give lectures, and show films, and five times a day lead an excellent guided walking tour. The building houses a small museum that lays the groundwork for the rest of what you'll see. The park service's programs are free. The visitor center is open May through September daily from 8am to 6pm, the rest of the year Monday through Friday from 8am to 5pm.

## SHORE EXCURSIONS

**Dyea Bicycle Adventure** (3 hr.; $69): A 20-minute van ride to Dyea, once a bustling gold-rush community, followed by a 6-mile cycle ride through the area. Not strenuous for anybody in reasonably good health.

**Eagle Preserve Float Adventure** (6 ½ hr.; $169): Combines a fjord cruise (30 min. to Haines) with a leisurely raft float (no white-water rapids here) through the Chiliast Bald Eagle Preserve. Essential equipment (boots and life jackets, rain poncho if needed) is provided.

**Glacier Flight & Bald Eagle Float** (4½–5½ hr.; $164–$215): Board a plane in Skagway for a scenic flight over peaks and glaciers, then hop a raft in Haines for a gentle float trip through the Chiliast Bald Eagle Preserve to see eagles, wolves, moose, and bears. You rejoin your ship in Haines. There are also less expensive options that involve a cruise to Haines, but you miss the aerial view of the peaks.

**Horseback Riding** (3½ hr; $149): Giddy-up on horseback to see the remnants of Dyea, once a booming gold-rush town, and explore the scenic Dyea Valley. Participants must, of course, be able to mount a horse and maintain balance in a saddle.

**Skagway by Streetcar** (2 hr.; $37 adults, $22 children under 12): This is as much performance art as historical tour. Guides in period costume relate tales of the boomtown days as you tour the sights both in and outside of town aboard vintage 1930s Kenworth, Dodge, and White sightseeing limousines. Though theatrical, it's all done in a homey style, as if you're getting a tour from your cousin Martha. The guide is as likely to point out funky small-town oddities as major historical sights (example: "And that's Buckwheat's old truck; his niece Kelly's husband uses it," said while pointing to an old blue pickup belonging to local performer/tourism booster Buckwheat Donahue). After seeing the Historic District, the Lookout, the Gold Rush Cemetery, and other sights, guests see a little song-and-dance and film presentation about Skagway history and become honorary members of the Arctic Brotherhood. This part is very hokey.

**White Pass & Yukon Route Railway** (3 hr.; $95): The sturdy engines and vintage parlor cars of this famous narrow-gauge railway take you from the dock past waterfalls and parts of the famous "Trail of '98" to the White Pass Summit, the boundary between Canada and the United States. Don't take this trip on an overcast day—you won't see anything. If you're lucky and have a clear day, though, you'll be able to see all the way down to the harbor, and you might spot the occasional hoary marmot or other critter fleeing from the train's racket.

**White Pass Railway & Heli-Hike** (5½ hr.: $305): A ride on the historic narrow-gauge railroad and a helicopter flight over the Juneau Icefield. The hike—a 4-mile round-trip stride along the banks of the rushing Skagway River—is not to be undertaken by the aged or infirm.

**Yukon Jeep Adventure** (6 hr.; $129 adults, $89 children 12 and under): Retrace the steps of the gold miners along the Trail of '98 from the comfort of a four-wheel-drive Jeep Wrangler. Interactive headphones permit drivers in the convoy to keep in touch with guides as they describe the events of '98.

## TOURING THROUGH LOCAL OPERATORS

There are independent tours sold at a tour center at 7th Avenue and Broadway. Tours are offered here by a number of operators and are priced in the $35 range for a 2½-hour city and White Pass Summit tour by van. **Haines-Skagway Water Taxi** (✆ **888/766-3395**) operates Lynn Canal sightseeing cruises that take you to Haines, about an hour away, for $35 round-trip for adults and $18 for kids 12 and under. The cruises leave Skagway at 10:45am and return at 3:45pm. There is also **Chiliast Cruises** (✆ **888/766-2103**), which offers a fast ferry that takes you to Haines in about 35 minutes. They run several trips a day, costing $48 round-trip for adults and $24 round-trip for kids 12 and under.

## ON YOUR OWN: WITHIN WALKING DISTANCE

**The Case-Mulvihill House, the Gault House, and the Nye House**    All within a block of one another, these three buildings are striking examples of gold-rush-era Skagway architecture.

The Case-Mulvihill House and the Nye House are on Alaska St., between 7th and 8th aves. The Gault House is on Alaska St., between 5th and 6th aves.

**Eagles Hall and Days of '98 Show**    This is the venue for Skagway's long-running (since 1927) *Days of '98* show, a live melodrama of the Gay '90s featuring dancing girls, ragtime music, Smith and Reid in their historic shootout (naturally), and more. Daytime performances are offered at 10:30am and 2:30pm, timed so cruise passengers can attend. (Mon there is only a 2:30pm show, and Sat there is only a nighttime show.)

Southeast corner of 6th Ave. and Broadway. ✆ 907/983-2234. Daytime performances $14, kids $7.

**Historic Moore Homestead**    The Moore Cabin was built in 1887 as the home of Capt. William Moore, the founder of Skagway. The cabin was restored recently by the National Park Service.

5th Ave. and Spring St. Free tours offered 10am–5pm during the summer.

**Jefferson Smith's Parlor**    Also known as Soapy's Parlor, Jefferson Smith's Parlor was a saloon and gambling joint operated by the notorious bandit in the late 1890s. The building, which tourists can inspect only from the outside, has been relocated twice over the decades but looks pretty much as it did at the time of Smith's death.

2nd Ave., just off Broadway.

**Red Onion Saloon**    Located near the Arctic Brotherhood Hall, whose eye-catching facade is constructed of thousands of pieces of driftwood, the Red Onion was originally a dance hall and honky-tonk bar (ca. 1898) with the obligatory bordello upstairs. The bartenders still serve drinks over the same mahogany counter as their turn-of-the-century predecessors did. The waitresses wear dance-hall outfits, and there's often live entertainment.

205 Broadway, at the corner of 2nd Ave. ✆ 907/983-2222. Summer daily 11am–11pm.

**Skagway City Hall**    This is not, strictly speaking, a tourist site, but as the town's only stone building, it's worth eyeballing.

Spring St. and 7th Ave.

**Skagway Museum & Archives**    Now back in its original and newly renovated location at the historic McCabe College building (built 1899–1900), this museum offers a look at Skagway's history through artifacts, photographs, and historical records. Items on display include a Tlingit canoe and Bering Sea kayaks, as well as a collection of gold-rush supplies and tools, and Native American items including baskets and beadwork. There's also a big, stuffed, and standing brown bear.

7th and Spring sts. © **907/983-2420.** Admission $2 adults, $1 students, free for children 12 and under. Summer Mon–Fri 9am–5pm, Sat–Sun 1–5pm.

## ON YOUR OWN: BEYOND WALKING DISTANCE

**The Gold Rush Cemetery**    This is the permanent resting place of Messrs Smith and Reid. The cemetery is small and lies a short walk from the scenic Reid Falls, named after the heroic one-time surveyor. Aside from Reid's impressive monument, most of the headstones at the cemetery are whitewashed wood and are replaced by the park service when they get too worn.

About 1½ miles away from the center of downtown, up State St. (Walkable if you have the time and inclination.)

# 9

# Ports & Wilderness Areas along the Gulf Route

Remember what we said back in chapter 2: Going on a Gulf cruise does not mean that you miss out on the ports and natural areas of the Inside Passage. It just means that, whereas Inside Passage cruise itineraries typically begin and end in Vancouver or more recently, Seattle, the Gulf routing is one-way—from Vancouver to Whittier/Seward (ports for Anchorage) or the reverse—and may sail an itinerary that includes Inside Passage stops and attractions like Ketchikan, Juneau, Skagway, and Glacier Bay, plus Gulf ports and attractions like Hubbard Glacier, College Fjord, and Seward.

See chapter 4 for information on shore excursions and a few tips on debarkation, what to bring along with you while ashore, and little matters such as not missing the boat.

## 1 Hubbard Glacier

Said to be Alaska's longest cruise ship–accessible ice face—it's about 6 miles across—Hubbard lies at the northern end of **Yakutat Bay.** The glacier has a rather odd claim to fame: It is one of the fastest moving in Alaska. So fast and far did it move about a dozen years ago that it quickly created a wall across the mouth of **Russell Fjord,** one of the inlets lining Yakutat Bay. That turned the fjord into a lake and trapped hundreds of migratory marine creatures inside. Scientists still can't tell us why Hubbard chose to act the way it did, or why it receded to its original position several months later, reopening Russell Fjord.

Cruise ships in Yakutat Bay get spectacular views of the glacier, which, because of the riptides and currents, is always in motion, calving into the ocean and producing lots of white thunder. It should be noted, however, that only one ship can get close to the glacier at a time, and if another ship is hogging the space, your ship may have to wait or may not get close at all.

There is one footnote to the Yakutat Bay cruise experience: Some Alaska residents wish to make visitors pay for the privilege of viewing the glacier. Some residents of the **village of Yakutat,** at the mouth of the bay, tried to impose a $1.50 head tax on all ship passengers visiting Hubbard Glacier—even though ships *never* call at Yakutat! Ultimately, the ship operators and the villagers reached a compromise. Instead of paying a tax on passengers carried into the bay, the lines now buy fish and other area products for use in the dining room, thereby enriching the locals without having to add to the cost of a cruise berth.

## 2 Prince William Sound

Located at the northern end of the underside of the Kenai Peninsula, this is truly one of Alaska's most appealing wilderness areas, though it suffered mightily following the *Exxon Valdez* oil spill in 1989. The area has recovered nicely from the

# The Kenai Peninsula & Prince William Sound

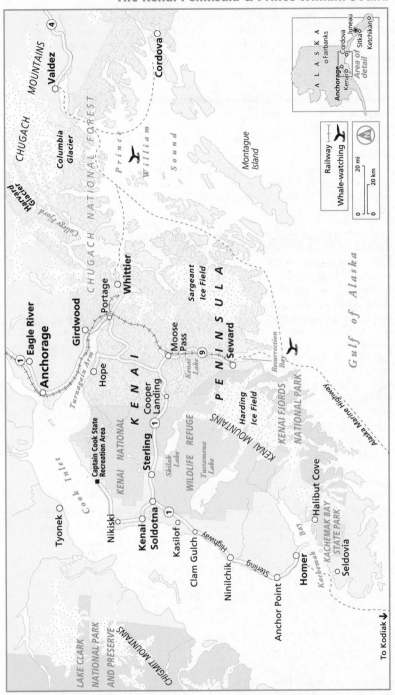

ravages of that infamous spill, and today visitors are absolutely guaranteed wildlife—whales, harbor seals, eagles, sea lions, sea otters, puffins, and more.

If your cruise doesn't spend enough time on the sound for your taste, day cruises are available out of Whittier and Seward. One company, **Phillips' Cruises and Tours,** 519 W. 4th Ave., Suite 100, Anchorage, AK 99501 (© **800/ 544-0529** or 907/276-8023; www.26glaciers.com), markets what it calls a "26 Glaciers Cruise." All in 1 day! That tells you just about as much as you need to know about the scenic beauty of the sound. The cruise—$129 per adult and $69 per child—is well worth taking.

Perhaps the most spectacular of the sound's ice faces is **Columbia Glacier,** whose surface spreads over more than 400 square miles and whose tidewater frontage is more than 5 miles across. Columbia is receding faster than most of its Alaska counterparts. Scientists reckon it will retreat more than 20 miles in the next 20 to 50 years, leaving behind nothing but another deep fjord—just what Prince William Sound needs.

## 3 Valdez

Until one miserable, overcast day in 1989, probably not many people could have located Valdez (pronounced val-*deez*) on a map. The town seldom appeared on tourist agendas, even though its interesting history includes both gold-rush action and a devastating earthquake in 1964 (registering 9.2 on the Richter scale). Then, with a grinding and a gurgling, the supertanker *Exxon Valdez,* having just left the harbor there, grounded on Bligh Rock and disgorged 11 million gallons of crude oil into the hitherto pristine waters of Prince William Sound. Suddenly, the eyes of the world were on Valdez. Newspapers carried stories, invariably illustrated with a map insert showing the affected region, and all at once everybody knew where Valdez was.

Nowadays you can take a boat into the sound without seeing much evidence of the oil spill, unless you're in a canoe or similar small craft and get close to the walls of the surrounding fjords. In some of them, you can still see faint scum marks on the rocks and shoreline—like a bathtub that's been used and not cleaned afterward.

A town's tourism image could be seriously damaged by a catastrophic event like the *Exxon Valdez* grounding. Valdez, though, didn't have much of a tourism image to start with. It still doesn't, to be perfectly frank. The town's position as the southern terminal of the 800-mile-long **Trans-Alaska Pipeline** conjures up all kinds of negative visions in people's minds—storage tanks, pipes, heavy equipment, tankers lined up waiting to get into the always ice-free, deep-water harbor. The reality is not as bad as that, but there's no doubt that Valdez is an industrial center. And even though it has about 4,000 inhabitants, a great many of them are there to work for the oil companies and have no intention of remaining beyond the period of their contracts. Consequently, the sense of community that you get in places like Juneau, Sitka, and the rest just doesn't seem to exist here.

It used to be possible to visit the pipeline terminal on shore excursions. But that was stopped after the events of 9/11.

Downtown, there are a few shops selling T-shirts, jewelry, and other souvenirs, and you'll also find a couple of places where you can get a latte (including a booth at the grocery store).

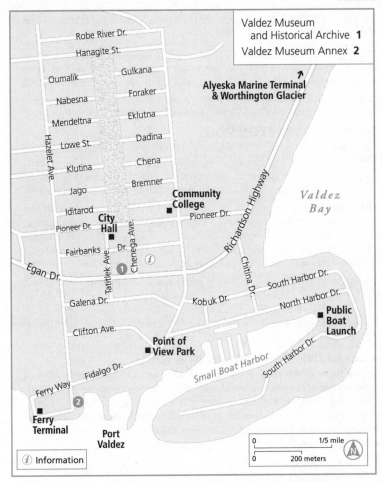

Valdez Museum and Historical Archive **1**
Valdez Museum Annex **2**

Alyeska Marine Terminal & Worthington Glacier

Valdez Bay

Community College
City Hall
Information
Public Boat Launch
Point of View Park
Small Boat Harbor
Ferry Terminal
Port Valdez

0 — 1/5 mile
0 — 200 meters

*(i) Information*

## ESSENTIALS

**ARRIVING**   Ships dock at a huge commercial facility a couple miles from the town center. Shuttle buses transport visitors to the information center in town.

**VISITOR INFORMATION**   The Valdez Convention and Visitors Bureau maintains a **Visitor Information Center,** 200 Fairbanks St., a block off Egan Drive (P.O. Box 1603), Valdez, AK 99686 (© **800/770-5954,** 907/835-4636, or 907/835-2984; www.valdezalaska.org). Pick up the free town map and useful *Vacation Planner.* They're open in summer daily from 8am to 8pm, and in the winter from 9am to 5pm.

## ATTRACTIONS WITHIN WALKING DISTANCE

The Valdez Museum and Historical Archive   This museum contains an exceptional display that reveals the history of the area, from early white exploration through the oil spill, and includes such unusual items as parkas made of bear and seal gut.

217 Egan Ave. ✆ **907/835-2764**. Admission $3 adults, $2.50 seniors, $2 ages 14–18, free for children under 14. Summer Mon–Sat 9am–6pm, Sun 8am–5pm.

**The Valdez Museum Annex**   The museum annex, located about 4 blocks from the main museum (near the ferry terminal), has the **Historical Old Town Valdez Model,** a 1:20 scale replica of Valdez as it appeared before the 1964 earthquake destroyed much of the town.

Hazelet Ave. (at the ferry dock). ✆ **907/835-5407**. Admission $1.50. Summer daily 9am–4pm.

## THE BEST SHORE EXCURSIONS

**Canyon Rafting** (2¼ hr.; $79): You can't beat the rafting in Keystone Canyon. There are a few thrilling hiccups along the 4½-mile, Class III run, but it's mild for the most part, and the sheer canyon walls and waterfalls pounding into the Lowe River are stunning. Knowledgeable guides and all equipment are provided.

**Helicopter Flightseeing** (1½–3¾ hr.; $220): This quick helicopter adventure zips you over old Valdez (destroyed in the 1964 earthquake), the Trans-Alaska Pipeline, and the crevasses of the Columbia Glacier, Prince William Sound, and Anderson Pass, then lands on the beach at the face of Shoup Glacier for a little ground-level gawking. Some tours, billed as heli-hiking, include a wilderness hike.

**Valdez Sport Fishing** (4 hr; $210): It might sound odd given the oil spill and all, but Valdez is a wonderful fishing destination, especially for coho salmon. The excursion, which is offered mid-July to early September only, is designed for beginners and experienced fishermen alike. Equipment, tackle, and bait are provided. You need to buy a $10 fishing license on the boat.

## ALTERNATIVE TRANSPORTATION & TOURS

**Valdez Tours** (✆ **907/835-2686**) operates 2-hour coach tours with narrative en route explaining the history of the city, with emphasis on its pipeline significance. The tour costs $18. Unfortunately, as this book was going to press, visitors could no longer go into the pipeline marine terminal itself. Heightened security following September 11, 2001, put the facility off-limits and authorities have no immediate plans to reopen it to tourists.

## 4 College Fjord

College Fjord is in the northern sector of Prince William Sound, roughly midway between Whittier and Valdez. It's not one of the more spectacular Alaska glacier areas, being very much overshadowed by Glacier Bay, Yakutat Bay (for Hubbard Glacier), and others, but it's scenic enough to merit a place on a lot of cruise itineraries, mostly for **Harvard Glacier,** which sits at its head.

The fjord was named in 1898 by an expedition team that opted to give the glaciers lining College Fjord and their neighbor, Harriman Glacier, the names of Ivy League and other prominent Eastern universities—hence, Harvard, Vassar, Williams, Yale, and so on.

## 5 Seward

Seward is the main northern embarkation/debarkation port for north- and southbound Alaska cruises. For information on attractions, shore excursions, tours, accommodations, and dining, see chapter 7, "The Ports of Embarkation."

# 10

# Cruisetour Destinations

No matter how powerful your binoculars, you can't see all of Alaska from a cruise ship, and that's why the cruise lines invented the cruisetour. In this chapter we'll give you info on the most popular cruisetour destinations.

(See "Cruisetours: The Best of Land & Sea," in chapter 2, for a discussion of the various cruisetour packages offered; for much more in-depth information on these destinations, pick up a copy of *Frommer's Alaska*.)

## 1 Denali National Park & Preserve

This is Alaska's most visited—environmentalists say overvisited—wilderness area, with almost one million people a year entering by bus and train to soak up the park's scenic splendor. It used to be difficult to overnight anywhere in or near the park, but it's getting easier. The opening in the last couple of years of the Talkeetna Alaskan Lodge and the Princess McKinley Lodge—both with spectacular views of the Alaska Range and Mount McKinley—added valuable new accommodations. An addition to the McKinley Chalet Resort last year brought the room count in the area around the mountain to 345. That's not by any means a lot, but it has made stopping over by the park much easier. There are, however, times when demand outstrips supply, so book early.

**Wildlife** is the thing in Denali—somewhere in the realm of 161 bird species, 37 mammal species, and no fewer than 450 plant species are to be found there.

The **Alaska Railroad** operates daily service from Anchorage and Fairbanks alongside the park, towing the private rail cars of Holland America Line and Princess, as well as those of Royal Celebrity Tours (Royal Caribbean and Celebrity Cruises' tour product), in addition to its own more basic (but less expensive and perfectly adequate) carriages.

Besides the wildlife, the focal point of the park is North America's highest peak, **Mount McKinley** (commonly known to Alaskans by its original Native name, Denali, which means "the great one"). In fact, you could argue that McKinley is the two highest peaks in North America: Its north face towers over the Alaska Range at 20,320 feet, while its south face rises to 19,470 feet. As far as the eye can see in either direction are impressive, permanently snow-covered mountains. Besides McKinley, there's Mount Foraker, which stands a mere 17,400 feet; Mount Silverthrone, at 13,320 feet; Mount Crosson, at 12,800 feet; and many, many more giant heaps. It's an awesome sight, viewed from the grounds of one of the nearby lodges. You just have to hope you can see it.

As with all enormous mountains, The Great One creates its own weather system, and foggy seems to be its favorite flavor. Sadly, it's possible to be in the area for days on end and never catch a glimpse of the Alaska Range. Trust us, though: When you do get to study it in all its splendor, you'll find that the wait was well worthwhile.

## A Mountain by Any Other Name . . .

We've long been taught that the Athabascans of Interior Alaska named the mountain *Denali*, meaning "the high one" or "the great one." But at least one historian contends that the word *Denal'iy* actually referred to a mountain near Anchorage, now known as Pioneer Peak, and means "one that watches," and that the Native word for McKinley, "the high one," is actually *Doleika*. In any event, Alaska Natives seldom made use of the area, as it produced little fish or game, and white men came only in search of gold. In 1896, a prospector named the mountain after William McKinley of Ohio, who was elected president of the United States that year.

All well and good, except that most Alaskans prefer the name Denali and since 1975 have petitioned to change it officially back. Ohio won't allow it. Although congressmen from Alaska and Ohio compromised on the issue in 1980, changing the name of the national park to Denali and leaving the mountain named McKinley, Alaskans have kept pushing for Denali. But the U.S. Board on Geographical Names has refused to take up the issue. It seems that the board has a rule against considering an issue that is also before Congress, and Rep. Ralph Regula of Ohio repeatedly introduces a one-paragraph bill stating that the name should stay the same. His bill never goes anywhere, but just having it introduced has been enough to stop the name board. In 1999, Alaska representative Don Young brought the issue back to life with an opposing bill to change the mountain's name to Denali, saying that Regula should name something in Ohio for McKinley. Young's bill also died quietly.

You are unlikely, unfortunately, to be able to drive very far into the park by yourself. Private vehicles are tightly restricted, for environmental reasons, and are allowed only to about Mile 15 on the park road. That cuts down on your wildlife-viewing chances. The thing to do is to take the park concessionaire's coach (a school bus), which is allowed to penetrate much more deeply into the park. The buses leave from the few local hotels. The drivers of these buses are all expert in the flora and fauna of the area. They always seem to be able to spot Dall sheep on the hillside, or caribou in the tall grass—even bears. When that wildlife is close enough, the driver/guide will ask for quiet so as not to startle the animals. And you'd better be quiet! The tour demands a long day—about 8 hours—but, if the weather holds and the viewing is good, it'll be the best 30 bucks you ever spent.

## 2 Fairbanks

Alaska's second-largest city (after Anchorage) is friendly, unpretentious, and easygoing in the Alaska tradition, although its downtown area is drab and, frankly, sort of depressing. The major attraction in Fairbanks is the **Riverboat Discovery**, 1975 Discovery Dr. (© **866/479-6673** or 907/479-6673), a three-deck stern-wheeler that operates 3½-hour cruises twice a day throughout the summer on the Chena (*chee*-nah) and Tanana (tana-*naw*) rivers. The trip features visits to a re-created Indian village and a sled-dog training school, a viewing (with narration) of an Athabascan Indian fish camp, and a flyby performed by a genuine Alaskan bush pilot. The cruise costs $50 for adults, $30 for kids ages 3 to 12, and is free for kids under 3. Sailings are mid-May to mid-September. The Binkleys, the family that owns the stern-wheeler, also own **El Dorado Gold Mine,** off the Elliott Highway, 9 miles north of town (© 866/479-6673 or 907/479-6673). Here visitors can pan for gold and, while riding on the open-sided Tanana Valley Railroad, study the workings of the mine just as it was a century ago. It's hokey, of course, but it's good fun, especially for youngsters. Tours, which run daily (call for times), are $30 for adults, $20 for ages 3 to 12, and free for kids under 3.

**Pioneer Park** (formerly **Alaskaland**), at the intersection of Airport Way and Peger Road (© 907/459-1087), is a low-key Native culture–themed park with a couple of small museums, a playground, and a little tour train. The park is open year-round, but the attractions operate only Memorial Day weekend to Labor Day daily from 11am to 9pm. And the best part of all? Admission is free.

Your cruisetour may include a tour of the gold mine or a visit to **Gold Dredge No. 8,** a huge monster of a machine that dug gold out of the hills until 1959

---

**Tips  Denali Changes**

Massive changes to the main Denali National Park visitor area underway for several years should be nearing completion for the 2005 season, but other changes farther inside the park are just getting started. Here are the major changes pending as we went to press.

- The Eielson Visitor Center, 66 miles within the park, is scheduled to be demolished and rebuilt in a new version four times larger than the original. The project is planned to start in 2005 and continue for 2 years. Shuttle buses that formerly turned around at Eielson will probably turn around a few miles short of there, at Stony Overlook. Pricing details were not yet available for that shorter ride at press time.

- The new Murie Science and Learning Center is due to open by the time this edition is published. It will add an educational resource in the easily accessible front-country area.

- The Visitor Center Campus is scheduled for completion during the 2005 season. The campus as a whole will have programs, exhibits, a theater, food courts, a bookstore, parking, and so on.

- The existing Visitor Access Center will become a transit center, just for boarding buses and getting tickets and permits for the buses, campgrounds, and backcountry.

- If you've been to Denali before, you will be pleased to see the improvements along the highway in the commercial Glitter Gulch area. New lighting, streetlights, and pathways make it more pleasing to the eye and, more important, much safer for pedestrians. A pedestrian bridge over the Nenana River is due to be completed by 2005.

and is now open for visitors. Shore excursions and cruisetours almost always include the *Riverboat Discovery.*

## 3 Prudhoe Bay

Prudhoe Bay is located at the very end of the Dalton Highway, also known locally as the Haul Road, a 414-mile stretch built to service the Trans-Alaska Pipeline. The road connects the Arctic coast with Interior Alaska, and passes through wilderness areas that include all sorts of scenic terrain—forested rounded hills, the rugged peaks of the Brooks Range, and the treeless plains of the North Slope. The route offers lots of wildlife-spotting opportunities, with strong chances of seeing caribou, Dall sheep, moose, and bear.

But the real reason to come way up here is the **Prudhoe Bay Oilfield.** Although touring an oil field may not be high on your vacation must-do list, the bay complex is no ordinary oil field. It's a historic and strategic site of great importance and a great technological achievement. The industry coexists here with migrating caribou and waterfowl on wet, fragile tundra that permanently shows any mark made by vehicles. (Visits to the oil field were curtailed following the Sept 11, 2001, terrorist attacks, but a modified version has since been resumed under stricter security rules.) Tours (2 hr. long and costing $37 a head) are operated by the **Arctic Caribou Inn,** P.O. Box 340111, Prudhoe Bay, AK 99734 (© **877/658-2368** or 907/659-2368; www.arcticcaribouinn.com). They will need your name and an identification number that British Petroleum can use to run a background check before allowing you on the oil field: A driver's license, passport, or Social Security number will work.

To get here, you usually drive the Dalton Highway in buses one way and fly the other, with either **Fairbanks** or **Anchorage** being the other connecting point. The trip includes an overnight in **Coldfoot.**

*Be aware:* The bus trip is a long one and not always terribly comfortable.

## 4 Nome & Kotzebue

There's no place like Nome. Well, we had to say it. But, really, this Arctic frontier town is a special place, combining a sense of history, a hospitable and silly attitude (we're talking about a place that holds an annual Labor Day bathtub race), and an exceptional location on the water in front of a tundra wilderness.

What it does not have is anything that remotely resembles a tourist destination. Anthropological, yes. Touristy, no! It's little more than a collection of beat-up residences and low-rise commercial buildings. It looks like the popular conception of a century-old gold-rush town—which isn't really surprising, since that's what it is. But if it seems to be in need of a face-lift—and how!—the inhabitants make up for all that by the warmth of their welcome. Probably they're glad to see a strange face in the summer because they know they'll see precious few in the winter when the weather turns ugly and the sun disappears for 3 or 4 months. There are local roads, but no highway link with the rest of the state.

The name Nome is believed to have been an error by a British naval officer in 1850, who wrote "? Name" on a diagram. The scrawl was misinterpreted by a mapmaker as "Nome." The population boom here in 1899 also happened by chance, when a prospector from the 1898 gold rush was left behind on the beach due to an injury. He panned the sand outside his tent and found that it was full of gold dust.

Undoubtedly, on your visit, you'll find time to try your own hand at gold panning. The city also offers a still sloppy, gold-rush-era-style saloon scene, and bargains on **Inupiat Eskimo** arts and crafts.

Your tour will also visit **Kotzebue** (pronounced *kotz*-eh-biew) to the north, one of Alaska's largest and oldest Inupiat Eskimo villages. Here you'll tour the **NANA Museum of the Arctic,** run by a regional Native corporation representing the 7,000 Inupiat people who live in the northwest Arctic region.

To get here, you fly from Anchorage, fly between Nome and Kotzebue, and fly back to Anchorage, as part of itineraries that typically include an overnight in Anchorage and a visit to Denali and Fairbanks. Cruise West has a couple of sailings each year between Anchorage and Nome, by way of the Aleutians and the Russian Far East.

## 5 The Kenai Peninsula

The Kenai (*kee*-nye) Peninsula, which divides Prince William Sound and Cook Inlet, offers glaciers, whales, legendary sport fishing, spectacular hiking trails, bear, moose, and high mountains. And it's easy to get to, to boot. At least, it's not a long ways away and there's a good road to help you get there. The trouble is, there's an awful lot of traffic on it. The traffic jams on Friday evenings and Saturday morning especially can make the most jaded Los Angelenos forget crush on the I-405 at rush hour, or New Yorkers the Lincoln Tunnel. But try to get to Anchorage a day or two before your cruise begins (or stay a day or two afterward) and make the trip in midweek. The scenery alone is well worth the effort. There are two main towns on the peninsula, Kenai and Soldotna, the former slightly bigger than the latter, but neither by any stretch of the imagination a major metropolis.

People from Anchorage come here for the weekend to hike, dig clams, paddle kayaks, and, particularly, to fish. There's a special phrase for what happens when the red salmon are running in July on the Kenai and Russian rivers: **combat fishing.** Anglers stand elbow to elbow on a bank, each casting into his or her yardwide slice of river, and still catch plenty of fish.

Cruisetours to the Kenai Peninsula include options for fishing, **river rafting,** and other soft-adventure activities.

You typically travel here by bus or rail from **Seward.** Princess includes an overnight at its own Kenai Princess Lodge, a wilderness resort with a gorgeous setting on a bluff overlooking the river, and other cruise lines offer overnights at other properties. Some tours combine a visit to Kenai Peninsula with an overnight in **Anchorage.**

## 6 The Yukon Territory

You'll pass plenty of beautiful scenery along the way, but today the real reason to cross the Canadian border into this region is the same as it was 100 years ago: **gold** (or, rather, gold-rush history).

Gold was discovered in the Canadian Klondike's Rabbit Creek (later renamed Bonanza Creek—for fairly obvious reasons) in 1896. In a matter of months, tens of thousands of people descended into the Yukon for the greatest gold rush in history, giving birth to Dawson City, Whitehorse, and a dozen other tent communities. By 1898, the gold rush was on in earnest and the following year, the White Pass Yukon Rail Route was opened from Skagway to the Canadian border to carry prospectors and their goods.

Once part of the Northwest Territories, the Yukon is now a separate Canadian territory bordered by British Columbia and Alaska. The entire territory has a population of just over 33,000, two-thirds of them living in **Whitehorse,** the capital of the region since 1953. Located on the banks of the Yukon River, Whitehorse was established in 1900, 2 full years after the stampeders swarmed into Dawson City. Today the city serves as a frontier outpost, its tourism influx also giving it a cosmopolitan tinge complete with nightlife, good shopping opportunities (with some smart boutiques and great outdoor shops), fine restaurants, and comfortable hotels.

**Dawson City** was once the biggest Canadian city west of Winnipeg, with a population of 30,000, but it withered to practically a ghost town after the gold-rush stampeders stopped stampeding. Dawson today is the nearest thing to an authentic gold-rush town the world has to offer, with old buildings, vintage watering holes, dirt streets flanked with raised boardwalks, shops (naturally), and some particularly good restaurants (such as Marina's, a fine Italian place on 5th Ave., and Klondike Kate's, at 3rd and King St.). Diamond Tooth Gertie's Gambling Hall (full service bar, poker, blackjack, roulette, and slots) is open to adults for a $5 admission charge. The place is operated by the Klondike Visitors Association and it's all in fun. The proceeds go to maintain the gold-rush-style architecture and ambience of the town.

If you're on a Holland America cruisetour—highly likely, since that company operates more Yukon cruisetours than any other—you'll travel between Dawson City and the tiny Alaskan town of Eagle via the MV *Yukon Queen II,* a high-speed, 115-passenger catamaran that makes the trip along the Yukon River in 5 hours, passing through incredibly beautiful wilderness scenery, where the only sign of civilization is the occasional fisherman.

Holland America recently added another Yukon string to its bow—exclusive rights to enter the UNESCO World Heritage Site known as **Kluane National Park,** a protected Canadian wilderness area that was hitherto all but inaccessible (a few backpackers, campers, and cyclists made up just about the only traffic into the park). Holland America has permission to include the park in a number of its cruisetours in 2005. This year, the company adds another Yukon wilderness—Tombstone Territorial Park, about a 90-minute drive from Dawson City.

## 7 The Canadian Rockies

Canadian Rockies cruisetours typically include travel by bus and/or train between Vancouver and either Seattle or Calgary.

Highlights of the tour include a visit to the parks at **Jasper** and **Banff,** which together comprise 17,518 sq. km (6,764 sq. miles). The parks are teeming with wildlife, with some animals—like bighorn sheep, mountain goats, deer, and moose—meandering along and across highways and hiking trails. There are also coyotes, lynx, and occasional wolves (though they tend to give humans a wide berth), as well as grizzlies and black bears, both of which are unpredictable and best photographed with a telephoto lens.

The two "capitals," Banff and Jasper, are 287km (178 miles) apart and connected by scenic Highway 93. **Banff** is in a stunningly beautiful setting, with the mighty Bow River, murky with glacial till, coursing through town.

The **Banff Springs Hotel** (© **403/762-2211**) was built in 1888 as a destination resort by the Canadian Pacific Railroad. Ever since then, tourists have been visiting this area for its scenery and hot springs, plus nearby fishing, hiking, and other outdoor activities. Today the streets of Banff are also an attraction, lined with trendy cafes and exclusive boutiques offering international fashion.

**Lake Louise** is located 56km (35 miles) north of Banff and is a famed beauty spot, deep green from the minerals it contains (ground by the glaciers above the lake) and surrounded by forest-clad snowcapped mountains. The village near the lake is a resort destination in its own right. Nearly as spectacular as the lake is **Chateau Lake Louise,** 111 Lake Louise Dr., Lake Louise (✆ **800/441-1414** or 403/522-3511), built by the Canadian Pacific Railroad and one of the most celebrated hotels in Canada.

Between Lake Louise and Jasper is the **Icefields Parkway,** a spectacular mountain road that climbs through three deep-river valleys, beneath soaring, glacier-notched mountains, and past dozens of hornlike peaks. Capping the route is the **Columbia Icefields,** a massive dome of glacial ice and snow that is the largest nonpolar ice cap in the world.

**Jasper** isn't Banff. It was born as a railroad division point, and the town does not offer the glitz of its southern neighbor. **Jasper National Park** is Canada's largest mountain park and offers an outdoor-oriented experience with opportunities to hike, ride horses, fish, or even climb mountains.

# Appendix A:
# Alaska in Depth

*by Charles Wohlforth*

**A**n old photo album opens, emitting a scent of dust and dried glue. Inside, pale images speak wanly of shrunken mountains and glaciers, a huge blue sky, water and trees, a moose standing way off in the background. No family photographer can resist the urge to capture Alaska's vastness in the little box of a camera, and none, it seems, has ever managed it. Then, turning the page, there it is—not in another picture of the landscape, but reflected in a small face at the bottom of the frame: my own face, as a child. For anyone who hasn't experienced that kind of moment, the expression is merely enigmatic—slightly dazed, happy but abstracted. But if you've been to Alaska, that photograph captures something familiar: It's an image of discovery. I've seen it on the fresh, pale faces in photographs stamped with the dates of my family's first explorations of Alaska 36 years ago. And then, researching this book, I got to see it once again, on my own young son's face. And I knew that, like me, he had discovered something important.

So, what exactly am I talking about? Like anything worth experiencing, it's not simple to explain.

Tour guides try to get it across with statistics. Not much hope of that, although some of the numbers do give you a general idea of scale. Once you've driven across the continental United States and know how big that is, seeing a map of Alaska placed on top of the area you crossed, just about spanning it, provides some notion of size. Alaskans always like to threaten that we'll split in half and make Texas the third-largest state. Alaska has fewer than 650,000 residents. If you placed them an equal distance apart, each would be almost a mile from any other. Of course, that couldn't happen. No one has ever been to some parts of Alaska.

But none of that expresses what really matters. It's not just a matter of how big Alaska is or how few people it contains. It's not an intellectual concept at all. None of that crosses your mind when you see a chunk of ice the size of a building fall from a glacier and send a huge splash and wave surging outward, or when you feel your sea kayak lift on a wave caused by the fall of a breaching humpback whale. Or when you hike for a couple of days to stand on top of a mountain, and from there see more mountaintops, layered off as far as the horizon in unnamed, seemingly infinite multiplicity. A realization of what Alaska means can also come in a simple little moment. It can come at the end of a long day driving an Interior Alaska highway, as your car climbs into yet another mountain range, the sun still hanging high in what should be night, storm systems arranged before you across the landscape, when you realize that you haven't seen another car in an hour. Or standing on an Arctic Ocean beach, it could happen when you look around at the sea of empty tundra behind you, the sea of green water before you, and your own place on what seems to be the edge of the world. Or you might simply be sitting on the sun-warmed rocks of a beach in Southeast or Southcentral Alaska when you discover that you're occupying only one of many worlds—a world of intermediate size, lying in magnitude between the tiny tide-pool universes of life all around you and the larger world as seen by an eagle gliding through the air high above.

What's the soul alchemy of such a moment? I suppose it's different for each person, but for me it has something to do with realizing my actual size in the world, how I fit in, what it means to be just another medium-size mammal, no longer armed with the illusions supplied by civilization. On returning to the city from the wilderness, there's a reentry process, like walking from a vivid movie onto the mundane, gray street outside—it's the movie that seems more real. For a while, it's hard to take human institutions seriously after you've been deep into Alaska.

Some people never do step back across that boundary. They live their lives out in the wilderness, away from people. Others compromise, living in Alaskan cities and walking out into the mountains when they can, the rest of the time just maintaining a prickly notion of their own independence. But anyone with the courage to come to Alaska—and the time to let the place sink in—can make the same discovery. You don't have to be an outdoors enthusiast or a young person. You only have to be open to wonder and able to slow down long enough to see it. Then, in a quiet moment when you least expect it, things may suddenly seem very clear and all that you left behind, oddly irrelevant.

How you find your way back to where you started is your affair.

## 1 Natural History: Rough Drafts & Erasures

### THE SURGING ICE

In 1986 Hubbard Glacier, north of Yakutat, suddenly decided to surge forward, cutting off Russell Fjord from the rest of the Pacific Ocean. A group of warm-hearted but ill-advised wildlife lovers set out to save the marine mammals that had been trapped behind the glacier. Catching a dolphin from an inflatable boat isn't that easy—they didn't accomplish much, but they provided a lot of entertainment for the locals. Then the water burst through the dam of ice, and the lake became a fjord again, releasing the animals anyway. In 2002 it happened again (no rescue this time). Ships were warned away as the 70-square-mile lake, having risen 61 feet above sea level, quickly drained through a 300-foot-wide channel with a whoosh.

Bering Glacier, the largest in North America (about 30×145 miles in area), can't decide which way to go. Surging and retreating on a 20-year cycle, it reversed course in 1995 after bulldozing a wetland migratory bird stopover, and speedily contracted back up toward the mountains. Yanert Glacier surged 100 yards a day in 2000 after moving 100 yards a year since 1942. The next year Tokositna Glacier started galloping after 50 years of quiet. In 1937 surging Black Rapids Glacier almost ate the Richardson Highway. In Prince William Sound, Meares Glacier has plowed through old-growth forest. On the other hand, some glaciers are so stable that they gather a layer of dirt where trees and brush grow to maturity. When Malspina Glacier retreated, the trees on its back toppled. And on a larger scale, all the land of Glacier Bay—mountains, forests, sea floor—is rising 1½ inches a year as it rebounds from the weight of melted glaciers that 100 years ago were a mile thick and 65 miles longer.

Yet these new and erased lands are just small corrections around the margins compared to all the earth has done in setting down, wiping out, and rewriting the natural history of Alaska. In the last ice age, 15,000 years ago, much of what is Alaska today was one huge glacier. Looking up at the tops of granite mountains in Southeast Alaska, especially in the Lynn Canal, you can see a sort of high-water mark—the highest point to which the glaciers came in the ice age. Even looking from the deck of a boat, thousands of feet below the upper reaches of the mountains, you can see that many mountain shoulders were rounded by the passage of ice, and thus are much smoother than the sharp, craggy peaks just above, which stuck out of that incredible sheet of ice.

Some 7-year-old children worry about the bogeyman or being caught in a house fire. When I was that age, living with my family in Juneau, I was worried about glacier ice. I had learned how Gastineau Channel was formed, I had seen Mendenhall Glacier, I had heard how it was really a river of ice, advancing and retreating. I came to fear that while I slept, another ice age would come and grind away the city of Juneau.

It's possible that a glacier *could* get Juneau—the city fronts on the huge Juneau Ice Field—but there would be at least a few centuries' warning before it hit. Glaciers are essentially just snow that doesn't get a chance to melt. It accumulates at higher altitudes until it gets deep enough to compress into ice and starts oozing down the sides of the mountain. When the ice reaches the ocean, or before, the melt and calving of icebergs at the leading edge reaches a point of equilibrium with the snow that's still being added at the top. The glacier stops advancing, becoming a true river of ice, moving a snowflake from the top of the mountain to the bottom in a few hundred years. When conditions change— more snow or colder long-term weather, for example—the glacier gets bigger, which is called "advancing"; when there is less snow and warmer weather, the glacier gets smaller, which is known as "retreating." Sometimes, something strange will happen under the glacier and it will surge. Bering Glacier started to float on a cushion of water, and Yanert Glacier slid on a cushion of mud. But most of the time, the advance or retreat is measured in inches or feet per year.

It took some time to figure out how glaciers work. The living glaciers of Alaska, like living fossils from the last ice age, helped show the way. In the 1830s scientists in Switzerland found huge rocks (now called glacial erratics) that appeared to have moved miles from where they had once been a part of similar bedrock. Scientists theorized that ancient glaciers shaping the Alps must have moved the rocks. **John Muir,** the famous writer and naturalist, maintained in the 1870s that the granite mountains of Yosemite National Park had been rounded and polished by the passing of glaciers that melted long ago (he was only part right). He traveled to Alaska to prove it. Here, glaciers were still carving the land—they had never finished melting at the end of the last glacial period—and Muir could see shapes like those at Yosemite in the act of being created. Glacier Bay, which Muir "discovered" when guided there by his Alaska Native friends, was a glacial work in progress, as it still is today.

When you visit, you can see for yourself how the heavy blue ice and white snow are streaked with black rock and dust that were obviously gouged from mountains and left in hills at the faces and along the flanks of the glaciers, in debris piles called moraines. At Exit Glacier, in Kenai Fjords National Park, you can stand on a moraine that wraps the leading edge of the glacier like a scarf, and feel the cold streaming off spires of clicking ice—like standing in front of a freezer with the door open. Find another hill like that, no matter where it is, and you can be pretty sure a glacier once came that way. Likewise, you can see today's glaciers scooping out valleys in the mountains.

## An Iceberg by Any Other Name

When a glacier calves, the icebergs formed are classified differently depending on their size, a system that allows one ship's captain to warn another of the relative ice hazard. Very large chunks are officially called **icebergs;** pieces of moderate size (usually 7–15 ft. across) are known as **bergy bits; growlers** are slightly smaller still, at less than 7 feet across, with less than 3 feet showing above water; and **brash ice** is any random smaller chunks. And remember the old adage: What you're seeing is only the tip—most of the berg is below the water.

Today Alaska's 100,000 glaciers cover about 5% of its landmass, mostly on the southern coast. There are no glaciers in the Arctic—the climate is too dry to produce enough snow. The northernmost large glaciers are in the Alaska Range, such as those carving great chasms in the side of Mount McKinley. At that height, the mountain creates its own weather, wringing moisture out of the atmosphere and feeding its glaciers. The Kahiltna Glacier flows 45 miles from the mountain, going 15,000 feet downhill over its course. The Ruth Glacier has dug a canyon twice as deep as the Grand Canyon, half-filled with mile-deep ice. The glaciers of the 50 ice ages that have covered North America in the last 2.5 million years are the most likely explanation for the fjords and valleys that appear all over Alaska.

Glaciers come in several different varieties. **Tidewater glaciers** are the kind most often seen on postcards; they spill down out of the mountains and run all the way to the sea. **Piedmont glaciers** are two glaciers that have run together into one. When seen from above, piedmonts resemble a highway interchange, edged by road slush, with the median moraine looking like lane dividers. **Hanging glaciers** are glaciers that are draped over hillsides but don't come all the way down to the bottom of the hill. They "hang" up there, resting against the hillside, a few hundred feet or more above the foot of the hill. There are also **mountain glaciers** (also known as alpine glaciers), which are confined by surrounding mountain terrain; **valley glaciers,** which are mountain glaciers confined by valley walls; and **cirque glaciers,** which sit in basins near ridge crests and are usually circular (as opposed to the typical river shape).

It's still not known exactly why glacial periods come and go. The best theory to date holds that the wobbles and imperfections in the earth's spin and orbit around the sun alter energy flow into the global ecosystem, which in turn changes the balance of carbon dioxide in the atmosphere. Carbon dioxide traps heat on the earth. The earth is warming today in time with its normal cycles of cold and warm, but the warmth may also be accelerated by human release of carbon dioxide into the atmosphere from the burning of fossil fuels. Those effects are felt more strongly in the Arctic than anywhere else on earth. Forests are moving north, wetlands are drying, sea ice is thinning and withdrawing, and permanently frozen ground is warming. Glaciers are shrinking.

Some of the most visited glaciers on the various cruise itineraries include **Glacier Bay National Park and Preserve** and its 16 tidewater glaciers (p. 206), **Hubbard Glacier** in Yakutat Bay (p. 218), **Mendenhall Glacier** outside Juneau (p. 205), **North and South Sawyer Glaciers** in Tracy Arm (p. 194), and the many glaciers of **College Fjord** (p. 222).

## THE TREMBLING EARTH

Despite my early glacier phobia, I never had a similar fear of earthquakes. Living in Anchorage, I'd been through enough of them that, as early as I can remember, I generally didn't bother to get out of bed when they hit. Alaska has an average of 13 earthquakes a day, or 11% of all the earthquakes in the world, including three of the six largest ever recorded. On November 3, 2002, Alaska felt the world's largest earthquake of the year and one of the largest ever in the United States. My car rocked as I drove the streets of Anchorage. No one died and few people were injured because the quake occurred in such a sparsely populated area, the region between Anchorage and Fairbanks in the Alaska Range east of Mount McKinley. A 140-mile-long crack appeared right across the middle of Alaska, running over mountains and through glaciers. The land on each side moved laterally as much as 22 feet and vertically up to 6 feet. The Glenn Highway section known as the Tok Cut-Off, between Glennallen and Tok, broke into many deep cracks. A tractor-trailer fell into one of them. Where the Interior highways crossed the big fault-line crack, lanes no longer line up; now the road jogs where it used to be straight.

It's all part of living in a place that isn't quite done yet. Any part of Alaska could have an earthquake, but the Pacific Rim from Southcentral Alaska to the Aleutians is the shakiest. This is where Alaska is still under construction. The very rocks that make up the state are something of an ad hoc conglomeration, still in the process of being assembled. The floor of the Pacific Ocean is moving north, and as it moves, it carries islands and mountains with it. When they hit the Alaska plate, these pieces of land, called **terranes,** dock like ships arriving, but slowly—an island moving an inch a year takes a long time to travel thousands of miles. Geologists studying rocks near Mount McKinley have found a terrane that used to be tropical islands. In Kenai Fjords National Park, fossils have turned up that are otherwise found only in Afghanistan and China. The slowly moving crust of the earth brought them here on a terrane that makes up a large part of the south coast of Alaska.

The earth's crust is paper thin compared to the globe's forces, and, like paper, it folds where the two edges meet. Alaska's coast is bending down; and farther inshore, where McKinley stands, it is bowing up. At Kenai Fjords National Park, you can see steep little rock islands filled with birds: They are old mountaintops, shrinking down into the earth. The monolith of McKinley is a brand-new one growing higher.

Here's how it works: Near the center of the Pacific, underwater volcanoes and cracks that constantly ooze molten new rock are adding to the tectonic plate that forms the ocean floor. As it grows from the middle, the existing sea floor spreads at a rate of perhaps an inch a year. At the other side of the Pacific plate, where it bumps up against Alaska, there's not enough room for more crust, so it's forced, bending and cracking, downward into the planet's great, molten, recycling mill of magma. Landmasses that are along for the ride smash into the continent that's already there. When one hits—the so-called Yakutat block is still in the process of docking—a mountain range gets shoved up. Earthquakes and volcanoes are a byproduct.

Living in such an unsettled land is a matter of more than abstract interest. The Mount Spurr volcano, which erupted most recently in 1992, turned day to night in Anchorage, dropping a blanket of ash all over the region. A Boeing 747 full of passengers flew into the plume and lost power in all its engines, falling in darkness for several minutes before pilots were able to restart the clogged jets.

After that incident, the airport was closed until aviation authorities could find a way to keep volcanic plumes and planes apart. More than 80 volcanoes have been active in Alaska in the last 200 years. Earthquakes between 7 and 8 on the Richter scale occur once a year on average, and huge quakes over 8 averaged every 13 years over the last century. The worst of the quakes, on March 27, 1964, was the strongest ever to hit North America. It ranked 9.2 on the Richter scale, lowering an entire region of the state some 10 feet and moving it even farther laterally. No other earthquake has ever moved so much land.

The earthquake destroyed much of Anchorage and several smaller towns, and killed about 131 people, mostly in sea waves created by underwater landslides. In Valdez the waterfront was swept clean of people. In the Prince William Sound village of Chenega, built on a hill along the water, people started running for higher ground when the wave came. About half made it. But the earthquake could have been much worse. It occurred in the early evening, on Good Friday, when most public buildings were empty. An elementary school in Anchorage that broke in half and fell into a hole had no one inside at the time.

But even that huge earthquake wasn't an unusual occurrence, at least in the earth's terms. Geologists believe the same Alaska coast sank 6 feet in an earthquake in the year 1090.

## THE FROZEN TUNDRA

The northern Interior and Arctic parts of the state are less susceptible to earthquakes and, since they receive little precipitation, they don't have glaciers, either. But there's still a sense of living on a land that's not permanent, since most of northern Alaska is solid only by virtue of being frozen. When it thaws, it turns to mush. The phenomenon is caused by **permafrost,** a layer of earth a little below the surface that never thaws—or at least, you'd better hope it doesn't. Buildings erected on permafrost without some mechanism for dispersing their own heat—pilings, a gravel pad, or even refrigerator coils—thaw the ground below and sink into a self-made quicksand. You occasionally run across such structures. There's one in Dawson City, Yukon Territory, still left from the gold rush, that leans at an alarming angle with thresholds and lower tiers of siding disappearing into the ground.

Building sewer and water systems in such conditions is a challenge still unmet in much of Alaska's bush, where village toilets are often "honey buckets" and the septic systems are sewage lagoons on the edge of town where the buckets are dumped. Disease caused by the unsanitary conditions sweeps the villages as if rural Alaska were a Third World country. Large state and federal appropriations are resolving the problem one village at a time, but years of work are left.

Permafrost makes the land do other strange things. On a steep slope, the thawed earth on top of the ice can begin to slowly slide downhill like a blanket over a pile of pillows, setting the trees at crazy angles. These groves of black spruce—the only conifer that grows on this kind of ground—are called drunken forests, and you can see them in Denali National Park and elsewhere in the Interior. Permafrost also can create weird ground with shaky tussocks the size of basketballs that sit a foot or two apart on a wet, muddy flat. From a distance, it looks smooth, but walking on real basketballs would be easier.

The Arctic and much of the Interior are a swampy desert. Annual precipitation measured in Barrow is the same as in Las Vegas. Most of the time, the tundra is frozen in white; snow blows around, but not much falls. It melts in the summer, but it can't sink into the ground, which remains frozen. Liquid water on top of the permafrost layer creates huge, shallow ponds. Alaska is a land of 10 million lakes, with 3 million larger than 20 acres. Birds arrive to feed and paddle around those circles and polygons of deep green and sky blue. Flying over the Arctic in a small plane is disorienting, for little pattern emerges from the flat green tundra and the irregularly shaped patches of water that stretch as far as the eye can see. Pilots can find their way by following landmarks like tractor tracks etched into the tundra. Although few and far between, the tracks remain clearly delineated for decades after they're made, appearing as narrow, parallel ponds reaching from one horizon to the other.

The permafrost also preserves much older things. The meat of prehistoric mastodons, still intact, has been unearthed from the frozen ground. On the Arctic Coast, the sea eroded ground near Barrow that contained ancient ancestors of the Eskimos who still inhabit the same neighborhood. In 1982 a family was found that apparently had been crushed by sea ice up to 500 years ago. Two of the bodies were well preserved, sitting in the home they had occupied and wearing the clothes they had worn the day of the disaster, perhaps around the time Columbus was sailing to America.

**Sea ice** is the frozen ocean that extends from northern Alaska to the other side of the world. For a few months of summer, it pulls away from the shore. Then, in September or October, icebergs float in toward land, cemented by new ice forming along the beach. But even when the ice covers the whole ocean, it still moves under the immense pressure of wind and current. The clash creates towering pressure ridges—piles of broken ice that look like small mountain ranges and are about as difficult to cross. At its extreme, in March, the ice normally extends all the way south to the Pribilof Islands. Then it is possible to drive a dog team across the Bering Sea to Siberia. The National Weather Service keeps track of the ice pack and issues maps and predictions you can find on the Internet (www.arh.noaa.gov). Crab boats like to tempt the south-moving edge of the ice in the fall and shippers look for the right moment in the summer to venture north with barges of fuel and other supplies for the coast of the Arctic Ocean—they barely have time to get there and back before the ice closes in again in the fall.

The land of the Arctic and Interior are relatively barren biologically compared with the southern coastal areas of the state. Polar bears wander the Arctic ice pack, but they, like the Eskimos, feed more on marine mammals than on anything found on the shore. A 1,200-pound adult polar bear can make a meal of a walrus, and they're expert at hunting seal. The Inupiat diet includes those foods, plus polar bear and bowhead whale, which they still hunt from small open boats. The people of this region also eat fish and waterfowl from the streams and lakes, as well as caribou that graze the tundra. In the summer, herds of caribou in the tens of thousands come north to their Arctic calving grounds.

In Barrow the sun doesn't rise for more than 65 days in the winter. In February the average daily high temperature is –12°F (–24°C), and the average low is –24°F (–31°C). The Inupiat people learned to survive in this climate for millennia, but life was short and terribly hard. Today they've made some sensible allowances

### Higher, Higher

The Eskimo blanket toss—the game of placing a person in the center of a walrus-skin blanket and bouncing him or her high in the air—was traditionally used to get hunters high enough to see over the pressure ridges so they could spot game.

while holding on to many cultural traditions. For example, Ipalook Elementary School, in Barrow, has wide, light hallways and a large indoor playground.

## THE RAINFOREST

By comparison, southern coastal Alaska is warm and biologically rich. Temperate rainforest ranges up the coast from Southeast Alaska into Prince William Sound, with bears, deer, moose, wolves, and even big cats living among the massive western hemlock, Sitka spruce, and cedar. This old-growth forest, too wet to burn in forest fires, is the last vestige of the virgin, primeval woods that seemed so limitless to the first white settlers who arrived on the east coast of the continent in the 17th century. The trees grow on and on, sometimes rising more than 200 feet high, with diameters of 10 feet, and falling only after hundreds or even thousands of years. When they fall, the trees rot on the damp moss of the forest floor and return to soil to feed more trees, which grow in rows upon their nursery trunks.

Here at least, Alaska *does* seem permanent. That sense helps explain why logging the rainforest is so controversial. Just one of these trees contains thousands of dollars' worth of wood, a prize that drives logging only as voraciously as the federal government allows. Already, vast Southeast lands owned by Alaska Native corporations have been stripped of their old trees.

The rivers of the great coastal forests bring home runs of big **salmon** that clog the rivers in spawning season like a busy sidewalk at rush hour. The fish spawn only once, returning by a precisely tuned sense of smell to the streams where they were hatched as many as 7 years before. When the fertilized eggs have been left in the stream gravel, the fish conveniently die on the beach, making a smorgasbord for bears and other forest animals. The huge **Kodiak brown bear,** topping 1,000 pounds, owes everything to the millions of salmon that return to Kodiak Island each summer. By comparison, the grizzly bears of the Interior— the same species as browns, but living on grass, berries, and an occasional ground squirrel—are mere midgets, their weight counted in the hundreds of pounds. Forest-dwelling black bears grow to only a few hundred pounds.

## TAIGA & FIRE

Rainforest covers only a small fraction of Alaska. In fact, only a third of Alaska is forested at all, and most of the forests are the boreal forests that cover the central part of the state, behind the rain shadow of coastal mountains that intercept moist clouds off the oceans. Ranging from the Kenai Peninsula, south of Anchorage, to the Brooks Range, where the Arctic begins, you'll find **taiga**—a moist, subarctic forest of smaller, slower-growing, hardier trees that leave plenty of open sky between their branches. In well-drained areas, on hillsides, and on southern land (which is less susceptible to permafrost), the boreal forest is a lovely, broadly spaced combination of straight, proud white spruce and pale, spectral paper birch. Along the rivers, cottonwoods grow, with deep-grained bark and branches that spread in an oaklike matrix—if they could speak, it would be as wise old men. Where it's wet and swampy, over more and more land as you go north, all that will grow are low, brushy willow and the glum black spruce, which struggles to become a gnarled stick a mere 3 inches thick in 100 years, if it doesn't burn first. As the elevation grows, the spruce shrink, turning into weirdly bent, ancient shrubs just before the tree line and the open alpine tundra.

**Forest fires** tear through as much as a million acres of Alaska's boreal forest each summer. In most cases, forest managers do no more than note the occurrence on a map. There's little commercially valuable timber in these thin stands, and, anyway, it isn't possible to halt the process of nature's self-immolation over the broad expanse of Alaska. The boreal forest regenerates through fire—it was made to burn. The wildlife that lives and eats in these woods needs new growth from the burns as well as the shelter of older trees. When the forest is healthiest and most productive, streaks and patches of light-green new brush break up the dark green of the spruce in an ever-changing succession.

This is the land of the **moose.** They're as big as large horses, with long, bulbous noses and huge eyes that seem to know, somehow, just how ugly they are. Their flanks look like a worn-out shag carpet draped over a sawhorse. But moose are survivors. They thrive in land that no one else wants. In the summer they wade out into the swampy tundra ponds to eat green muck. In the winter they like nothing better than an old burn, where summer lightning has peeled back the forest and allowed a tangle of willows to grow—a moose's all-time favorite food. Eaten by wolves, hunted and run over by man, stranded in the snows of a hard winter, the moose always come back. In the summer the moose disperse and are not easily seen in thick vegetation. In the winter they gather where walking is easy, along roads and in lowlands where people also like to live. Encounters happen often in the city, until, as a resident, you begin to take the moose for granted. Then, skiing on a Nordic trail one day, you round a corner and come face to face with an animal that stands 2 feet over you. You can smell the beast's foul scent and see his stress, the ears pulled back on the head and the whites of the eyes showing, and you know that this wild creature, fighting to live until summer, can easily kill you.

## THE LIGHT & THE DARKNESS

There's no escaping the stress of winter in Alaska—not for moose or people—nor any shield from the exhilaration of the summer. In summer it never really gets dark at night. In Fairbanks in June, the sun sets in the north around midnight, but it doesn't go down far enough for real darkness to settle, instead rising again 2 hours later. It's always light enough to keep hiking or fishing, and, in clear weather, always light enough to read by. You may not see the stars from early May until sometime in August (the climate chart in chapter 4, "The Cruise Experience," gives seasonal daylight for Anchorage and Juneau). Visitors have trouble getting used to it: Falling asleep in broad daylight is hard. Alaskans deal with it by staying up late and being active outdoors. In the winter, on the other hand, Alaskans forget what the sun looks like. Kids go to school in the dark and come home in the dark. The sun rises in the middle of the morning and sets after lunch. At high noon in December, the sun hangs just above the southern horizon with a weak, orange light—a constant sunset. Animals and people go into hibernation.

As you go north, the changes in the length of the days throughout the year get larger. In Ketchikan, on the summer solstice (the longest day of the year), direct sunlight lasts 17 hours, 28 minutes; in Fairbanks, 21 hours, 48 minutes; and in Barrow, the longest day is more than 2 months. In contrast, in Seattle the longest day is 16 hours, and in Los Angeles, 14 hours, 26 minutes. On the equator, days are always the same length: 12 hours. At the North and South poles, the sun is up half the year and down the other half.

In the north, on a long, summer evening, you can almost feel the planet leaning toward the sun. Come feel it for yourself.

## THE AURORA BOREALIS

Many Alaska cruise visitors have thrilled to the vivid splashes and streaks of color in the night sky that are the aurora borealis, otherwise known as the northern lights. The streamers of pale green, pink, white, and blue bathe the night skies in a spectacular, moving display that elicits choruses of "Ooohs" and "Aaahs" from observers. There are even those who say they can hear the crackling as the flashes shoot across the heavens. So what causes the phenomenon? Well, we'll tell you. (And if you understand it, you're smarter than we are!) The explanation given by many scientists is this:

Solar dust particles enter the earth's magnetic field somewhere around the northern polar regions, where they encounter gases that are ever present in our upper atmosphere. These particles combine to alter the molecular structure of the gases and turn them, in effect, into virtual neon lights. Got that?

But you don't have to fully grasp the scientific forces at work here to appreciate the awesome, if sometimes spooky, late-night occurrence. Usually, the lights go on at or soon after midnight. And the best chance of catching them is late in the cruise season, when the nights begin to draw in. Darkness, you see, is essential if you're to have the full effect. Late August and early September is the likeliest period to run into them. And the less ambient light around you, the better. You have more chance of getting a good eyeful on a darkened deck in the Gulf of Alaska than you do in, say, the streets of Anchorage.

## 2  A Short Gold-Rush History

The biggest event in Alaska history happened 107 years ago: the 1898 Klondike gold rush. If you're coming to Alaska, you'll be hearing a lot about it. Here's some context for the barrage of anecdotes you can expect.

Prospectors sought gold in small numbers even before Russia sold Alaska to the United States in 1867. However, the Russians' main interest in Alaska was sea otter pelts. They made few forays beyond the coast, leaving the great mass of the North and Interior unexplored. When the United States took over, Alaska had virtually no white population and what it had was concentrated in the Southeast—in Sitka, the Russian capital; in a few other Russian settlements; and at the trading post of Wrangell, which miners used as a jumping off point for gold fields up the Stikine River in British Columbia.

After the American flag went up over Sitka, prospectors slowly worked their way into Alaska's vastness, often led by or in partnership with Natives, who knew the country. Called **sourdoughs** for the yeast and flour mixture they carried to make their bread, these were tough wilderness men, living way beyond the law or communications with the outside world. A few of them struck it rich. In 1880, a major find on the Gastineau Channel started the city called Juneau and decades of industrial, hard-rock mining there. Finds followed on the Fortymile River in 1886 (on the Taylor Hwy.), near Circle in 1893 (on the Steese Hwy.), and near Hope on the Kenai Peninsula in 1895 (on the Seward Hwy.). Gold slowly brought more people to Alaska, but not enough to catch the nation's attention.

In 1896, white prospector George Carmack and his Native partners, Tagish Charlie and Skookum Jim, found gold on the Klondike River, a tributary of the Yukon in Canada. Word traveled downriver to the goldfields in Fortymile country, and within 48 hours, that area was empty and claims on the Klondike were being staked. The miners dug gravel from the creek that winter and when they washed it, it yielded big chunks of solid gold, a massive discovery. They were instant millionaires at a time when a million dollars meant something.

It's hard to imagine today the impact of the news on the outside world. The U.S. economy was in a deep depression. The dollar was on the gold standard and the scarcity of that precious metal had caused a deflationary vise that in 1893 brought a banking collapse and unemployment of 18%. Suddenly, in 1897, a steamer arrived in Seattle bearing men from a place called the Klondike with trunks and gunnysacks full of gold. The supply of money suddenly grew and economic confidence returned. The national economy turned around on the news and some 100,000 people set off for Alaska (the jumping-off point for the Canadian interior) in hopes of getting rich too, plunging off into a trackless wilderness for which they were completely unprepared.

The **Klondike gold rush** marks the start of contemporary Alaska. Before the gold rush, Alaska largely remained as it had been for thousands of years, ruled and inhabited by indigenous people. As late as the 1880 census, the territory had fewer than 500 white residents and only 4,000 by 1890. In 1898, the gold stampede began, bringing an instant population. Even the mayor of Seattle left for Alaska. Within a few years, Alaska had cities, telegraph lines, riverboats, and sled-dog mail routes. About 30,000 made it all the way to Dawson City in the Yukon Territory. Few of the miners struck it rich, but those entrepreneurs who built the towns and business to serve them did. Suddenly there were saloons and brothels, dress shops and photo studios. Promoters sold a credulous public newly laid-out towns on supposed routes to the gold mines, including many that were virtually impassable.

The **White Pass** above Skagway and the **Chilkoot Pass** above Dyea carried the most stampeders. Gold seekers arrived in the crazily lawless settlements by steamer from Seattle, got robbed and cheated, and then ferried their goods over one or other of the passes to **Lake Bennett.** Upon completion of the railroad through the White Pass in 1901, Dyea and the Chilkoot Pass were abandoned, but Skagway lived on (see chapter 8). The Canadian authorities wisely required each stampeder to bring a ton of supplies, a rule that undoubtedly prevented famine but which made the single-file journey over the passes a miserable ordeal. Prospectors sometimes had to make dozens of trips up the trail to get their supplies over the pass. At Lake Bennett, the stampeders built boats and rafts, crossed the lake, and then floated down the Yukon River, through the dangerous Five Finger Rapids to **Dawson City**—a 500-mile journey from the sea. Many of them didn't make it.

Imagine the disappointment of those who did when they found, upon arrival, that the gold claims had all been staked and big companies were taking over. Prospectors looking to strike it rich had humbling choices. The smart ones started businesses to make money off the others and some of them did quite well. Others worked for wages or went home. But many continued their quest for the next big find. Their wild chase for gold drew the modern map of Alaska, founding dozens of towns. Many of them disappeared as soon as the frenzy cooled and now are entirely forgotten or live on only as place names in memory. But some became real cities. **Nome** came in 1899; **Fairbanks** in 1902; **Kantishna,** now within Denali National Park, in 1905; **Iditarod** in 1908; and many others until the rush finally ended with the start of World War I in 1914.

Even without a rush, there's still gold to be dug. Small-time prospectors are still looking all over Alaska and working their claims, and sometimes someone makes a significant strike. In 1987 a find north of Fairbanks produced as much as 1,000 ounces of the precious metal every day for years.

But there's a bigger, and safer, business: mining the tourist trade. The rush of visitors each summer dwarfs the number who came in 1898. In the true spirit of the event whose history they celebrate, the gold-rush towns of Skagway, Dawson City, Fairbanks, and Nome know there's more money to be made from people than from gold.

## 3 Politics & History: Living a Frontier Myth

The occupations of prospector, trapper, and homesteader—rugged individualists relying only on themselves in a limitless land—would dominate Alaska's economy if the state's image of itself were accurate. Alaskans talk a lot about the Alaskan spirit of independence, yearn for freedom from government, and declare that people from "Outside" just don't understand Alaskans when they insist on locking up Alaska's lands in parks and wilderness status. The bumper sticker says, simply, "We don't give a damn how they do it Outside." A state full of self-reliant frontiersmen can't be tied down and deterred from their manifest destiny by a bunch of Washington bureaucrats. At the extreme, there has even been a movement to declare independence as a separate nation so Alaskans can extend the frontier, extracting its natural resources unfettered by bunny-hugging Easterners.

But just because you wear a cowboy hat doesn't mean you know how to ride a horse. In Las Vegas you find a lot more hats than horsemen, and Alaska is full of self-reliant pioneers who spend rush hour in traffic jams and worry more about urban drug dealing and air pollution than where to catch their next meal or dig the mother lode. As for self-reliance and independence from government, Alaska has the highest per capita state spending of any state in the nation, with no state income or sales taxes and an annual payment that can reach as much as $1,700 a year to every man, woman, and child just for living here. The state government provides retirement homes; it owns various businesses, including a dairy, a railroad,

### Dateline

- Approximately 15,000 years ago First human explorers arrive in Alaska from Asia.
- 1741 Vitus Bering, on a mission originally chartered by Peter the Great, finds Alaska; ship's surgeon and naturalist Georg Steller goes ashore for a few hours on Kayak Island, the first white to set foot in Alaska.
- 1743 Russian fur traders enter the Aleutian Islands; Aleuts are either enslaved to hunt sea otter or massacred; when they try to revolt, Aleut cultural traditions are eliminated. Over the coming decades, Aleuts relocate as far south as California.
- 1772 Unalaska, in the Aleutian Islands, becomes a permanent Russian settlement.
- 1776–79 British Capt. James Cook makes voyages of exploration to Alaska, seeking the Northwest Passage from the Pacific to the Atlantic, and draws charts of the coast.
- 1784 Russians build a settlement at Kodiak.
- 1799 Russians establish a fort near present-day Sitka, which will later become their capital; Tlingits attack and destroy the fort, but are later driven off in a counterattack; the Russian-America Company receives a 20-year exclusive franchise to govern and exploit Alaska.
- 1821 Russian naval officers are placed in control of the Russian-America Company, which begins to decline in profitability.
- 1824 Boundaries roughly matching Alaska's current borders are set by treaty between Russia, Britain, and the United States.
- 1839 The British Hudson's Bay Company, surpassing Russia in trade, begins leasing parts of Southeast Alaska and

*continues*

and a subsidized mortgage lender; it has built schools in the smallest communities; it operates a state ferry system and a radio and television network; and it owns nearly a third of the landmass of Alaska. And although the oil production that funds state government has been in decline in recent years, forcing the legislature to dig into savings to balance its books, the independent, self-reliant citizens have successfully resisted having to pay any taxes.

That conflict between perception and reality grows out of the story of a century of development of Alaska. The state is a great storehouse of minerals, oil, timber, and fish. A lot of wealth has been extracted, and many people have gotten rich. But it has always been because the federal government let them do it. Every acre of Alaska belonged to the U.S. government from the day Secretary of State William Seward bought Alaska from Russia in 1867. Since then, the frontier has never been broader than Uncle Sam made it.

Yet the whole concept of ownership didn't fit Alaska well from the first. Did the Russians really own what they sold? Alaska Natives didn't think so. They'd been living on this land for more than 100 centuries, and at the time of the purchase, most had never seen a white face. How could Russia hold title to land that no Russian had so much as explored? As Americans flooded into Alaska to search for gold in the late 19th century, this conflict became obvious. Alaska Natives, never conquered by war or treaty, began their legal and political fight to recover their land—a fight they would eventually win.

The concept of ownership has changed in other ways, too. For the first 100 years after the United States bought Alaska, it maintained the vast majority of the territory as "public

subsequently extends trading outposts into the Interior.

■ 1843 First overtures are made by American officials interested in buying Alaska from the Russians so that U.S. instead of British power could expand there.

■ 1867 In need of money and fearful that Russia couldn't hold onto Alaska anyway, Czar Alexander II sells Alaska to the United States; Secretary of State William Seward negotiates the deal for a price of $7.2 million, roughly 2¢ an acre; the American flag is raised in Sitka, and the U.S. military assumes government of Alaska.

■ 1870 The Alaska Commercial Company receives a monopoly on harvesting seals in the Pribilof Islands and soon expands across the territory. (The company remains a presence in the Alaska bush today.)

■ 1879 Naturalist and writer John Muir explores Southeast Alaska by canoe, discovering Glacier Bay with Native guides.

■ 1880 Joe Juneau and Richard Harris, guided by local Natives, find gold on Gastineau Channel and found city of Juneau; gold strikes begin to come every few years across the state.

■ 1884 Military rule ends in Alaska, but residents still have no right to elect a legislature, governor, or congressional representative, or to make laws.

■ 1885 Protestant missionaries meet to divide up the territory, parceling out each region to a different religion; they begin to fan out across Alaska to convert Native peoples, largely suppressing their traditional ways.

■ 1898 After prospectors arrive in Seattle with a ton of gold, the Klondike gold rush begins; gold rushes in Nome and Fairbanks follow within a few years; Americans begin to populate Alaska.

■ 1906 Alaska's first (nonvoting) delegate in Congress takes office; the capital moves from Sitka to Juneau.

■ 1908 The Iditarod Trail, a sled-dog mail route, is completed, linking trails continuously from Seward to Nome.

■ 1913 The first territorial legislature convenes, although it has few powers;

domain," with federal land and its mineral resources free for the taking as in the Old West of frontier lore. Each piece of Alaska belonged to everyone until someone showed up to lay private claim. Today, amid deep conflict over whether to develop such areas as the Arctic National Wildlife Refuge (known as ANWR), federal control stands out far more clearly than it did during the gold rush, when the land's wealth was free to anyone with strength enough to take it. Alaskans who want to keep receiving the good things that a rich state government brings equate the frontier spirit of the past with their own financial well-being, whether that means working at a mining claim or at a desk in a glass office tower. But other Americans feel they own Alaska, too, and they don't necessarily believe in exploiting its resource treasures. They want the frontier to stay alive in another sense—unconquered and still wild.

White colonization of the territory came in boom-and-bust waves of migrants arriving with the goal of making a quick buck and then clearing out—without worrying about the people who already lived there. Although the gold-rush pioneers are celebrated today, the Klondike rush of 1898 that opened up and populated the territory was motivated by greed and was a mass importer of crime, inhumanity, and, for the Native people, terrible epidemics of new diseases that killed off whole villages. Like the Russians 150 years before who had made slaves of the Natives, the new white population behaved as if the indigenous people were less than human. Until Franklin Roosevelt became president, federal policy was to suppress Alaska Native cultures. Protestant missionaries had the authority of law to forbid Native people from telling their old stories or even speaking their own languages.

the first automobile drives the Richardson Highway route, from Valdez to Fairbanks.

- 1914 Federal construction of the Alaska Railroad begins; the first tents go up in the river bottom that will be Anchorage, along the rail line.
- 1917 Mount McKinley National Park is established.
- 1920 The first flights connect Alaska to the rest of the United States; aviation quickly becomes the most important means of transportation in the territory.
- 1923 Pres. Warren Harding drives the final spike on the Alaskan Railroad at Nenana, then dies on the way home, purportedly from eating bad Alaskan seafood.
- 1925 Leonhard Seppala and other dog mushers relay diphtheria serum on the Iditarod Trail to fight an epidemic in Nome; Seppala and his lead dog, Balto, become national heroes.
- 1934 Federal policy of forced assimilation of Native cultures is officially discarded and New Deal efforts to preserve Native cultures begin.
- 1935 New Deal "colonists," broke farmers from all over the United States, settle in the Matanuska Valley north of Anchorage.
- 1940 A military buildup begins in Alaska; bases built in Anchorage accelerate city's growth into a major population center.
- 1942 Japanese invade Aleutians, taking Attu and Kiska islands and bombing Dutch Harbor/Unalaska (a U.S. counterattack the next year drives out the Japanese); Alaska Highway links Alaska to the rest of the country overland for the first time, but is open to civilians only after the war.
- 1949 Massive Cold War military buildup feeds fast economic growth.
- 1957 Oil is found on Kenai Peninsula's Swanson River.
- 1959 Alaska becomes a state.
- 1964 The largest earthquake ever to strike North America shakes South-central Alaska, killing 131 people, primarily in tsunami waves.

*continues*

Segregation ended only after World War II. Meanwhile, the salmon that fed the people of the territory were overfished by a powerful, outside-owned canning industry with friends in Washington, D.C. Their abuses destroyed salmon runs. Formerly rich Native villages faced famine when their primary food source was taken away.

It was only with World War II, and the Japanese invasion of the Aleutian Islands, that Alaska developed an industry that was not based on exploitation of natural resources: the military industry. The war brought the construction of the territory's first road to the outside world, the Alaska Highway. After the war, military activity dropped off, but only briefly. By the late 1940s, Alaska was on the front line of the Cold War. Huge Air Force and Army bases were built and remote radar stations were installed to detect and repel Soviet bombers and missiles. To this day, the federal government remains a key industry whose removal would deal the economy a grievous blow.

The fight for Alaska statehood also began after World War II. Alaskans argued that they needed local, independent control of natural resources, pointing to the example of overfishing in the federally managed salmon industry. Opponents said that Alaska would never be able to support itself, that it would always require large subsidies from the federal government, and therefore should not be a state. But the advocates pointed out that Alaska's lack of self-sufficiency came about because its citizens did not control the resources—Alaska was a colony, with decisions and profits taken away by the mother country. If Alaskans could control their own land, they could use the resources to fund government. The discovery of oil on the Swanson River on the Kenai

1968 Oil is found at Prudhoe Bay, on Alaska's North Slope.

1970 Environmental lawsuits tie up work to build the Alaska pipeline, which is needed to link the North Slope oil field to markets.

1971 Congress acknowledges and pays the federal government's debt to Alaska's indigenous people with the Alaska Native Claims Settlement Act, which transfers 44 million acres of land and almost $1 billion to new Native-owned corporations.

1973 The first Iditarod Trail Sled Dog Race runs more than 1,000 miles from Anchorage to Nome.

1974 Congress clears away legal barriers to construction of the Trans-Alaska Pipeline; Vice Pres. Spiro Agnew casts the deciding vote in the U.S. Senate.

1977 The Trans-Alaska Pipeline is completed and begins providing up to 25% of the U.S. domestic supply of oil.

1980 Congress sets aside almost a third of Alaska in new parks and other land-conservation units; awash in new oil wealth, the state legislature abolishes all taxes paid by individuals to state government.

1982 Alaskans receive their first Alaska Permanent Fund dividends, interest paid on an oil-wealth savings account.

1985 Declining oil prices send the Alaska economy into a tailspin; tens of thousands leave the state and most of the banks collapse.

1989 The tanker *Exxon Valdez* hits Bligh Reef in Prince William Sound, spilling 11 million gallons of North Slope crude in the worst oil spill ever in North America.

1994 A federal jury in Anchorage awards $5 billion to 10,000 fishermen, Natives, and others hurt by the Exxon oil spill; Exxon appeals continue today.

1996 Wildfire rips through the Big Lake area, north of Anchorage, destroying 400 buildings.

1999 Alaskans vote 87% against a plan to use Permanent Fund earnings to cover a state budget shortfall.

Peninsula in 1957 helped win that argument. Here was real money that could fund a state government. In 1959 Alaska finally became the 49th state. Along with the rights of entering the Union, Alaska received a dowry—an endowment of land to develop and pay for future government. The Statehood Act gave the new state the right to select 103 million acres from a total landmass of 365 million acres. Indeed, that land does pay for state government in Alaska, in the form of oil royalties and taxes—but, to this day, the federal government still spends a lot more in Alaska than it receives.

Oil revenues supported the new state of Alaska as it began to extend services to its vast, undeveloped expanses. Anchorage boomed in the 1960s in a period of buoyant optimism. Leaders believed that the age-old problems of the wide-open frontier—poverty, lack of basic services, impenetrable remoteness—would be remedied under the new government and new money, while the land would remain wide open. The pace of change redoubled in 1968 with the discovery of the largest oil field in North America at Prudhoe Bay, on land that had been a wise state selection in the federal land-grant entitlement. The state government received as much money in a single oil lease sale auction as it had spent in total for the previous 6 years. This was going to be the boom of all booms.

The oil bonanza on the North Slope would change Alaska more than any other event since the gold rush. Once, opening the frontier meant letting a few prospectors scratch the dirt in search of a poke of gold. But getting this immense pool of oil to the markets from one of the most remote spots on the globe would require allowing the world's largest companies to build a pipeline across Alaska. When completed, the pipeline could credibly claim to be the largest privately financed construction project in world history. With the stakes suddenly so much higher, it came time to figure out exactly who owned which parts of Alaska. The land couldn't just be public domain any longer.

That division wouldn't be easy. Much of the state had never even been mapped, much less surveyed, and there were some large outstanding claims that had to be settled. Alaska Natives, who had lost land, culture, and health in 2 centuries of white invasion, finally saw their luck start to turn. It wouldn't be possible to resolve the land issues surrounding the pipeline until their claims to land and compensation were answered. Native leaders cannily used that leverage to assure that they got what they wanted.

In the early 1970s, America had a new awareness of the way its first people had been treated in the settlement of the West. When white frontiers expanded, Native traditional homelands were stolen. In Alaska, with the powerful lure of all that oil providing the impetus, Native people were able to insist on a fairer resolution. In 1971, with the support of white Alaskans, the oil companies, and Pres. Richard Nixon, who threatened to veto any settlement that Natives did not support, Congress passed the Alaska Native Claims Settlement Act, called ANCSA. The act transferred 44 million acres of land and $962.5 million to corporations whose shareholders were all the Native people of Alaska. The new Native corporations would be able to exploit their own land for their shareholders' profit. In later legislation, Natives also won guaranteed subsistence hunting and fishing rights on federal land. Some Natives complained that they'd received only an eighth of the land they had owned before white contact, but it was still by far the richest settlement any of the world's indigenous people had received at that time. Today, the Native corporations are Alaska's largest and most powerful homegrown businesses. Many have invested heavily in the

## An Alaska Glossary

If Alaska feels like a different country from the rest of the United States, one reason may be the odd local usage that makes English slightly different here—different enough, in fact, that the Associated Press publishes a separate stylebook dictionary just for Alaska. Here are some Alaskan words you may run into:

**breakup**   When God set up the seasons in Alaska, He forgot one: spring. While the rest of the United States enjoys new flowers and baseball, Alaskans are looking at melting snowbanks and mud. Then, in May, summer miraculously arrives. Breakup officially occurs when the ice goes out in the Interior's rivers, but it stands for the time period of winter's demise and summer's initiation.

**bunny boots**   If you see people wearing huge, bulbous, white rubber boots in Alaska's winter, it's not necessarily because they have enormous feet. Those are bunny boots, superinsulated footwear originally designed for Arctic air force operations—and they're the warmest things in the world.

**cheechako**   A newcomer or greenhorn. Not used much anymore because almost everyone is one.

**dry** or **damp**   Many towns and villages have invoked a state law that allows them to outlaw alcohol completely (to go dry) or to outlaw sale but not possession (to go damp).

**Lower 48**   The contiguous United States.

**Native**   When capitalized, the word refers to Alaska's indigenous people. "American Indian" isn't used much in Alaska, "Alaska Native" being the preferred term.

**Native corporation**   In 1971, Congress settled land claims with Alaska's Natives by turning over land and money; corporations were set up, with the Natives then alive as shareholders, to receive the property. Most of the corporations still thrive.

tourism industry, operating tour packagers, accommodations, ferries, and wildlife-viewing day boats.

It was a political deal on a grand scale. It's unlikely that Natives would have gotten their land at all if whites hadn't had such a desire to get at the oil and hadn't had such a need for Native support in the endeavor. Nor could the pipeline have overcome environmental challenges without the Natives' dropping their objections. Even with Native support in place, legislation authorizing the pipeline passed the U.S. Senate by only one vote, cast by Vice Pres. Spiro Agnew.

But there were other side effects of the deal that white Alaskans didn't like so much. The state still hadn't received a large portion of its land entitlement, and now the Native corporations had a right to select the land they wanted. There still remained the question of who would get what. At this time Congress, influenced by a strong new environmental movement, wanted to maintain some of the wild lands as national parks and wilderness rather than giving it away to the Alaskans.

**oosik**   The huge penile bone of a walrus. Knowing this word could save you from being the butt of any number of practical jokes people like to play on cheechakos.

**Outside**   Anywhere that isn't Alaska. This is a widely used term in print and is capitalized, like any other proper noun.

**PFD**   No, not personal floatation device; it stands for Permanent Fund Dividend. When Alaska's oil riches started flowing in the late 1970s, the voters set up a savings account called the Permanent Fund. Half the interest is paid annually to every man, woman, and child in the state. With more than $30 billion in investments, the fund now yields more than $1,700 in dividends to each Alaskan annually.

**pioneer**   A white settler of Alaska who has been here longer than most other people can remember—25 or 30 years usually does it.

**salmon**   There are five species of Pacific salmon, each with two names. The king, or Chinook, is the largest, growing up to 90 pounds in some areas; the silver, or coho, is next in size, a feisty sport fish; the red, or sockeye, has rich red flesh; and the pink, or humpy, and the chum, or dog, are smallish and not as tasty, mostly ending up in cans and dog lots.

**Southeast**   Most people don't bother to say "Southeast Alaska." The region may be to the northwest of everyone else in the country, but it's southeast of most Alaskans, and that's all we care about.

**tsunami**   Earthquake-caused sea waves are often called tidal waves, but that's a misnomer. The destructive waves of the 1964 Alaska earthquake were tsunamis caused by underwater upheavals like landslides.

**village**   A small, Alaska Native settlement in the bush, usually tightly bound by family and cultural tradition.

That issue wasn't settled until 1980, when the Alaska National Interest Lands Conservation Act passed, setting aside an additional 106 million acres for conservation, an area larger than California. Alaska's frontier-minded population screamed bloody murder over "the lockup of Alaska," but the act was only the last, tangible step in a process started by big oil and the need it created to draw lines on the map, tying up the frontier.

When construction of the $9-billion pipeline finally got underway in 1974, the huge influx of new residents chasing the high-paying jobs put any previous gold rush to shame. The newcomers were from a different part of the country than previously, too. Alaska had been a predominantly Democratic state, but oil workers from Texas, Oklahoma, and other Bible Belt states helped shift the balance of Alaska's politics, and now it's solidly Republican. In its frontier days, Alaska had a strong Libertarian streak, but now it became more influenced by fundamentalist Christian conservatism. A hippie-filled legislature of the early

1970s had legalized marijuana for home use. Conservatives at the time, who thought the government shouldn't butt into its citizens' private lives, went along with them. After the pipeline, times changed, and Alaska developed tough antidrug laws.

Growth also brought urban problems. As the pipeline construction boom waned in 1977, the boomtown atmosphere of gambling and street prostitution disappeared with it, but other big-city problems remained. No longer could residents of Anchorage and Fairbanks go to bed without locking their doors. Both cities were declared "nonattainment" areas by the Environmental Protection Agency because of air pollution near the ground in cold winter weather, when people leave their cars running during the day to keep them from freezing.

But the pipeline seemed to provide limitless wealth to solve these problems. For fear that too much money would be wasted, the voters altered the state constitution to bank a large portion of the new riches. The new Permanent Fund would be off-limits to the politicians in Juneau, with half the annual earnings paid out to citizens as dividends. As of 2004, the fund contains more than $30 billion in savings and has become one of the largest sectors of the economy simply by virtue of paying out $1 billion a year in dividends to everyone who lives at least a year in the state. All major state taxes on individuals were canceled at that time, and people got used to receiving everything free from the government.

Then, in 1985, oil prices dropped, deflating the overextended economy. Housing prices crashed and thousands of people simply walked away from their mortgages. All but a few of the banks in the state went broke. Condominiums that had sold for $100,000 went for $20,000 or less a year later. It was the bust that always goes with the boom, but it still came as a shock to many. The spending associated with the cleanup of the *Exxon Valdez* oil spill in 1989 restarted the economy, which continued on an even keel for a decade after, but the wealth of the earlier oil years never returned.

Meanwhile, the oil from Prudhoe Bay started running out. Oil revenues, an irreplaceable 85% of the state budget, started an inexorable downward trend in the early 1990s. The oil companies downsized. Without another boom on the horizon, the question became how to avoid, or at least soften, the next bust. At this writing, that question remains unanswered, even as state savings run out. Each year the legislature has deadlocked as some legislators call for taxes or cuts to the Permanent Fund Dividend and others, seeing that as political suicide, hope for a miracle. Meanwhile, government spending for visitor facilities such as state parks has been cut every year. The disadvantages of individualism now seem apparent. Some suggest that Alaskans have lost their capacity for collective sacrifice. More ask when the next big project will get the good times rolling again, such as a natural gas pipeline from the North Slope to middle America or oil development in ANWR. Economic barriers and resistance in Congress make either possibility increasingly remote.

Culture moves slower than politics or economics, and Alaskans still see themselves as gold-rush prospectors or wildcat oil drillers, adventuring in an open land and striking it rich by their own devices. Even as the economy blends ever more smoothly into the American corporate landscape, Alaskans' myth of themselves remains strong. Today, the state's future is as little in its own hands as it has ever been. Big petroleum projects will be decided in Congress and distant corporate boardrooms, not here. Ultimately, an economy based on exploiting natural resources is anything but independent.

## 4  An Introduction to Southeast Alaska's Native Cultures

*This essay was written for us by Jan Halliday, a former editor of* Alaska Airlines
Magazine *and author of* Native Peoples of the Northwest *(Sasquatch Books)
and* Native People of Alaska: A Traveler's Guide to Land, Art, and Culture
*(Sasquatch Books), both of which describe Native tours, interpretive centers, muse-
ums, art galleries, artists' studios, lodges, B&Bs, and restaurants in their area of
coverage, and provide detailed contact information.*

Welcome to the islands of the Inside Passage, the traditional and contemporary
home of the **Tlingit** (pronounced *klink*-get) Indians. Although the Tlingit's language is related to the language of the Athabascan of Interior Alaska and
Canada, and to the language of the Navajo of the American Southwest, no one
knows for sure when the group settled on this strip of Alaska coastline and
islands. The Tlingit may be descendants of the first wave of ice-age travelers who
crossed the Bering Sea from Asia into North America, or they may trace their
ancestry from a later wave of immigrants who returned to this fish-rich area
from the interior of the North American continent more than 10,000 years ago,
after ice-age glaciers retreated.

Until this century, Tlingits used channels between islands and river passage-
ways through barrier mountains as their highways. In the 1700s Tlingit paddlers, steering huge cargo canoes carved from cedar logs, were sighted as far
south as the Channel Islands off the coast of Los Angeles, reportedly to take
slaves. In the 18th and 19th centuries, before epidemics decimated their communities, the Tlingit people were trade partners with the Russians, British,
Americans, and interior tribes of Canada, controlling the waterways of Southeast Alaska and demanding tolls for their use. In the 1800s the Tlingits allowed
gold miners to travel over the rugged **Chilkoot Pass** between Skagway and the
Klondike gold fields, but only after they paid a substantial fee.

Newcomers to Southeast Alaska include the **Haida** and **Tsimshian** Indians,
who came into Tlingit territory from British Columbia in the last 2 centuries.
The Haida, from the Queen Charlotte Islands, settled on Prince of Wales Island
in the late 1700s; the Tsimshian Indians, from the Prince Rupert area, settled
Annette Island as a utopian Christian community in the late 1800s.

Today many Natives live in small villages on remote islands (such as **Angoon**
on Admiralty Island, **Hoonah** on Chichagof Island, and **Kake** on Kupreanof
Island) and in centers of commerce such as Juneau, Ketchikan, and Sitka. In
smaller villages, away from the bustle of larger towns, you may see Natives drying seaweed in front of their houses on a sheet of plywood or filleting and drying salmon—both of these are traditional foods. But visitors should not expect
people, villages, or towns to look as they did when photographers froze their
images 100 years ago, any more than you'd expect to see people in Oregon
dressed in pioneer garb, making soap over a wood fire. Although many Natives
do live traditional subsistence lifestyles, gathering and preserving fish and shellfish, beach greens, and berries, nowadays they also order bulk groceries from
Costco in Juneau. The primary source of income for villagers is logging and
commercial fishing. All small communities use fuel-burning generators for electrical power and have well-stocked stores, with larger items arriving by barge and
cargo jet, and fresh goods arriving daily by smaller planes.

It's important for visitors to remember that Native history and culture was
and is influenced by the cultural and economic impact of the Russian, British,

and American traders of the early 1800s; the gold miners of the late 1800s; and the timber, fishing, canning, and mining industries of the 20th century. Southeast Alaska clans led (and won) the fight for Native civil rights years before Martin Luther King, Jr., led the civil rights movement for blacks in the 1960s. Many clan members have served in the U.S. military, many own businesses, and several are Alaska state legislators.

In 1971, Natives gained economic clout when the **Alaska Native Claims Settlement Act** settled the 100-year-old question of aboriginal land rights. Under dispute were 375 million acres of land in Alaska. Under provisions of the act, Congress deeded title to 44 million acres, spread throughout the state, to Alaska Natives, and a payment of close to $1 billion was made to compensate for the loss of the remaining 331 million acres. The act created 13 regional corporations and more than 230 village corporations to receive federal money and manage land on behalf of Native shareholders. In Southeast Alaska, Native corporations such as Goldbelt, CIRI, Cape Fox, and Huna Totem have taken the lead in tourism development, investing in first-class hotels, cruise ships, air taxis, and passenger-ferry sightseeing boats. Huna Totem Corporation owns the *Alaskan Southeaster,* a magazine about the region. In Juneau, Goldbelt owns and operates the tram to the top of Mount Roberts and a modern hotel. CIRI owns hotels and sightseeing and tour operations. Sealaska Heritage Foundation, the nonprofit arm of Sealaska, another Juneau-based Native corporation, supports scholarly work, publishing videos, language-learning materials, and such books as *Haa Shuka, Our Ancestors: Tlingit Oral Narratives,* by poet Nora Marks Dauenhauer, written in both Tlingit and English. Even small corporations, such as the Organized Village of Kake, have built lovely little hotels for visitors, overlooking beautiful vistas of seacoast and snow-covered mountains.

Alaska Natives don ceremonial regalia (robes decorated with clan insignia and magnificent, carved headdresses inlaid with abalone shell) only during celebrations. (The largest of these traditional events, simply called **Celebration,** is held in Juneau every 2 years for 4 days in June, with clans gathering from throughout Southeast Alaska to celebrate their cultural heritage and perform traditional dances.) As in most of corporate America, Native Alaskans wear business suits when running their corporations, which are located in some of Juneau's finest office buildings.

Having said this, there are many facets of Native culture for you to enjoy in Southeast Alaska. Distinctive Tlingit, Haida, and Tsimshian **totemic art** is prevalent. In Ketchikan, for example, there are more than 70 standing **totem poles,** plus a museum dedicated entirely to the oldest poles collected from abandoned Tlingit villages. There are also two traditional **clan houses,** reminiscent of dozens of large houses that lined the waterfront in the last century, constructed from hand-hewn cedar and adorned with carved house posts and decorated house screens. Both houses are open to the public. You can observe Native carvers working on commissioned masks, canoes, and totem poles at places such as **Saxman Village,** 3 miles south of Ketchikan, and in private studios. Many Native artists, such as carvers Amos Wallace and Nathan Jackson, and Chilkat blanket weaver Delores Churchill, have their work in private and museum collections throughout the world.

Most towns in Southeast Alaska have fascinating museums filled with artifacts and traditional art. Those with the largest collections are the **Alaska State**

**Museum** in Juneau and the **Sheldon Jackson Museum** in Sitka, but smaller museums shouldn't be missed.

**Raven** and **Eagle** clan symbols, representing the two major clan divisions to which every Haida, Tsimshian, and Tlingit Native belongs, adorn everything from bags of fresh-roasted coffee to beach blankets and T-shirts. These clan symbols, plus other totem figures such as salmon, killer whales, frogs, and bears, represent the strong family ties that reach back far into the past and bind contemporary Native people in this region. Rather than describe complicated clan lineage systems in this guide, I suggest you learn firsthand about the clans from Native tour guides and at Native-based shore excursions designed especially for the time frame that cruise ship passengers have in port—**Saxman Village** in Ketchikan, **Metlakatla**'s tour and salmon bake, or one of **Sitka Tribal Tours**' bus or walking tours of the old Russian/Tlingit capital of Alaska.

When I researched my guidebook to the Native peoples of Alaska, I stayed at Native-owned hotels, visited with artists (one of the best places to meet carvers, weavers, painters, silversmiths, and bead workers while they work is at the **Southeast Alaska Indian Cultural Center** in Sitka), gazed in wonder at museum collections, saw the old Chilkat and Ravenstail woven robes come out from behind the glass windows to be worn, and danced to the resonant beat of box drums at Celebration. I watched the **Sheet'ka Kwaan Naa Kahidi Community House,** a gorgeous hall modeled after the old clan houses, being constructed in Sitka. I listened as Native guides explained how each totem pole tells a unique family story or honors a fallen clan member. I went fishing with Natives on their charter boats and toured canneries, fish-processing plants, and salmon hatcheries owned by Natives (one had a standing totem pole right in the center of the creek, with an opportunistic eagle perched on top, eyeing the spawning salmon below). In **Metlakatla,** I scaled Yellow Hill on the boardwalk and stairs that Terry Booth, a Tsimshian, built for his wife years ago, and watched the sun bathe the village in first morning light. They were all unforgettable experiences. I hope your trip will be an unforgettable experience as well.

# Appendix B:
# Alaska on the Wild Side

*by Charles Wohlforth*

The variety of wildlife found in our 49th state is mind-boggling, whether it rules on land or in the ocean or in the air. The one thing that Alaska cruises can guarantee is that passengers will see some of these creatures—from the decks of their ships, during organized shore excursions specifically planned to search for them, or even when just walking the streets of the communities their ships visit. Majestic bald eagles, the symbol of this nation, are all over the place and, thankfully, are now well and truly back, having been placed on the protected species list several years ago. Bears roam the woods, Dall sheep dot the hillsides, and caribou and moose inhabit parts of the interior of the state. The waters of the Inside Passage, Glacier Bay, and Prince William Sound teem with harbor seals, sea otters, sea lions, and—most spectacularly of all—whales. It is highly unlikely that you will ever take a cruise to Alaska without seeing the telltale flukes and condensation spouts in the vicinity of your vessel.

So that you can recognize what you're seeing, here's a short rundown on the creatures you may encounter along the way.

## 1 Whale-Watching 101

Imagine standing on the deck of a ship, looking out onto the calm silver waters of an Alaskan bay. Suddenly, the surface of the water pulls back and an immense yet graceful creature appears, moving silently, the curve of its back visible for a moment before the water closes over it again. You wait for it to reappear. And wait. And wait. Then, just as you're beginning to think it's gone forever, the creature leaps straight out of the water, twisting around in midair before falling back with a gigantic *kersploosh!* that's followed a half-second later by an equally distinctive sound: That of 1,000 cruise ship passengers saying "Oooh!," "Aaah!," and "Marty! Marty! Did you see *that?!*"

On most large cruise ships, the captain or officer on watch will make an announcement when he or she spots a whale, but due to its strict schedule, the ship probably won't be able to stop and linger. A few lines, though (mostly the small-ship lines), feature whale-watching as a major component of their cruises. Their ships visit areas favored by whales—for instance, waters near Petersburg or Sitka, near Gustavus and Glacier Bay National Park, and near Seward and Kenai Fjords National Park. Once in position, they will spend time waiting for an encounter, or will monitor marine-traffic radio broadcasts and deviate from course to go where whale sightings have been reported. Most ships, both large and small, will offer lectures about whales at some point during each cruise.

To get you ready for your whale encounters, we've prepared the following little whale primer. Study up so you'll know what you're looking at.

**THE HUMPBACK WHALE**    These migratory whales spend their summer in Alaska feeding, then swim to Mexican or Hawaiian waters for the winter, where they give birth to their young and then fast until going north again in spring. The cold northern waters produce the small fish and other tiny creatures that humpbacks filter through their baleen—the strips of stiff, fibrous material that humpbacks have instead of teeth. A humpback is easy to recognize by its huge, mottled tail; by the hump on its back, just forward of its dorsal fin; and by its armlike flippers, which can grow to be 14 feet long. Most humpback sightings are of the whales' humped backs as they cruise along the surface, resting, and of the flukes of their tails as they dive.

*The Humpback Whale. Maximum length: 53 ft.*

Humpbacks weave nets of bubbles around their prey, then swim upward through the schooled fish, mouths wide open, to eat them in a single swoop, sometimes finishing with a frothy lunge through the surface. Feeding dives can last a long time and often mean you won't see that particular whale again, but if you're lucky, the whale may just be dipping down for a few minutes to get ready to leap completely out of the water, a behavior called **breaching.** No one knows for sure why whales do this; it may simply be play. Breaching is thrilling for viewers and, if you happen to be in a small boat or kayak, a little scary (paddlers should group their boats and tap the decks to let the whales know where they are). Humpbacks are highly sensitive to noise, so keep quiet to see longer displays.

Humpbacks tend to congregate to feed, making certain spots with rich supplies of food reliable places to watch them. In Southeast Alaska the best humpback-watching spots include the waters of **Icy Strait,** just outside Glacier Bay; **Frederick Sound** outside Petersburg; and **Sitka Sound.** In Southcentral Alaska, **Resurrection Bay,** outside Seward near Kenai Fjords National Park, has the most reliable sightings.

**THE ORCA (KILLER WHALE)**    The starkly defined black-and-white patches of the orca, the ocean's top predator, recall the sharp, vivid look of the Native American art of the Pacific Northwest and Southeast Alaska. Moving like wolves in highly structured family groups called pods, and swimming at up to 25 knots (about 29 mph), orcas hunt salmon, porpoises, seals, sea lions, and even juvenile whales. There's never been a report of one attacking a human being. Like dolphins, orcas often pop above the surface in a flashing, graceful arc when they travel, giving viewers a glance at their sleek shape, markings, and tall dorsal fin.

*The Orca, or Killer Whale. Maximum length: 30 ft.*

Unlike humpbacks and other whales that rely on a predictable food supply, orcas' hunting patterns mean it's not easy to say exactly where you might find them—you need to be where their prey is that day. **Resurrection Bay** and **Prince William Sound** both have pods that are often sighted in the summer, and we saw a pod of orcas from the beach in Gustavus, but they could show up anywhere in Southeast Alaska waters. For cruisers coming to Alaska from Vancouver, a top spot to see orcas is **Robson Bight,** an area in Johnstone Strait (between Vancouver Island and mainland British Columbia).

**THE BELUGA WHALE**   This small white whale with a cute rounded beak is one of only three types that spend all their lives in cold water rather than heading south for the winter. (The other two are the narwhale and bowhead.) Belugas are more likely to be mistaken for dolphin than any other whales are. However, the beluga is larger and fatter than a dolphin and lacks the dolphin's dorsal fin. Adults are all white, while juveniles are gray. Belugas swim in large packs that can number in the dozens. The beluga is the only whale that can turn its head, and it's one of a few species with good eyesight.

*The Beluga Whale. Maximum length: 16 ft.*

Belugas feed on salmon, making the mouths of rivers with salmon runs the best places to see them. Occasionally, a group will strand itself chasing salmon on a falling tide, swimming away when the water returns. The Cook Inlet group of belugas is the most often seen: If you're in Anchorage after your cruise, head out the Seward Highway, just south of town, and keep your eyes on the waters of **Turnagain Arm,** or watch from the beach near the mouth of the **Kenai River** in Kenai.

**THE MINKE WHALE**   The smallest of the baleen whales, the minke is generally under 26 feet long and has a blackish-gray body with a white stomach; a narrow, triangular head; and white bands on its flippers. Along with the humpback and (occasionally) the gray whale, it is the only baleen whale commonly seen in Alaskan waters.

When breaching, minkes leap something like dolphins, gracefully reentering the water headfirst—unlike humpbacks, for instance, which smash down on their sides. Also unlike the humpbacks, they don't raise their flukes (the tips of their tails) clear of the water when they dive. Minkes are easy to confuse with dolphins: Watch for the dark skin color to tell the difference.

*The Minke Whale. Maximum length: 26 ft.*

**THE GRAY WHALE**    Here's one whale you'll probably see only if you take a shoulder-season cruise (in May or very late Sept), and then only if you're lucky. The grays spend their winter months off the coast of California and in the Sea of Cortez (between Baja and mainland Mexico) and their summer months off northern Alaska, meaning that cruise passengers sailing in the Inside Passage and Gulf of Alaska can only spot one while it's on its migration.

*The Gray Whale. Maximum length: 45 ft.*

Like the humpback, grays are baleen whales. They're also about the same size as the humpback, though they lack the humpback's huge flippers. Their heads are pointed, and they have no dorsal fin. Grays will often smack the water with their flukes and are very friendly—it's not uncommon for them to swim right up to a small boat and allow their heads to be patted.

## 2  Alaskan Wildlife

Large mammals other than humankind still rule most of Alaska—even in the urban areas, there sometimes remains a question of who's in charge. In this section we'll describe some of the more common forms of wildlife. For visitors, the chances of seeing the animals described below are excellent.

**BALD EAGLE**    Now making a comeback all over the United States, the bald eagle has always been extremely common in Alaska: In most coastal towns, a pigeon would be more unusual. Every fishing town is swarming with eagles, and they even soar over the high-rise buildings of downtown Anchorage. Only adult eagles have the familiar white head and tail; juveniles of a few years or less have mottled brown plumage and can be hard to tell from a hawk. Eagles are most often seen soaring on rising air currents over ocean or river waters, where they are likely looking for fish to swoop down and snatch, but you also can often see them perched on beach driftwood or in large trees. **Haines** is a prime eagle-spotting area, where thousands of birds congregate in the fall; **Sitka** and **Ketchikan** both have raptor centers where you can see eagles in enclosures.

The eagle represents one of the two main kinship groupings in the matrilineal Tlingit culture (the other group is represented by the raven), so eagles frequently appear on totem poles and in other Southeast Alaska Native art.

*Bald Eagle*

*Raven*

**RAVEN**    A member of the Corvidae family, which includes jays, crows, and magpies, the raven is found throughout the Northern Hemisphere and is extremely common in Southeast Alaska. You can tell a raven from a crow by its larger size, heavy bill, shaggy throat feathers, and unmistakable call, a deep and mysteriously evocative "kaw" that provides a constant soundtrack to the misty forests of Southeast. The raven figures importantly in Southeast Alaska Native stories and in the creation myths of many other Native American peoples. It is portrayed as a wily and resourceful protagonist with great magical powers, an understandable personality for this highly impressive and intelligent scavenger.

**BLACK BEAR**    Black bears live in forests all over Alaska, feeding on fish, berries, insects, and vegetation. In Southeast Alaska they can be so common that they are sometimes considered pests, and many communities have adjusted their handling of garbage to keep bears out of town. Although not typically dangerous, blackies still deserve caution and respect: They stand about a yard tall at the shoulders and measure 5 or 6 feet from nose to tail. Black bears are usually black, but can also be brown, blond, or even bluish—color is not the best way to tell a black bear from a brown bear. Instead, look for smaller size, a blunt face, and the shape of the back, which is straight and lacks the brown bear's large shoulder hump. You're liable to find black bears pretty much anywhere in Southeast Alaska where the popular Inside Passage ports are located. Mostly, you will spot them along riverbanks and near salmon streams. Four weeks before I updated this edition, on a cruise on the *Island Princess,* I saw one swimming across the mouth of Johns Hopkins Inlet in Glacier Bay. Quite a sight!

*Black Bear*

*Brown Bear*

**BROWN BEAR**    Also known as grizzly bears, brown bears are among the largest and most ferocious of all land mammals. Size depends on the bear's food source. In coastal areas where salmon are plentiful, such as Southeast Alaska and Katmai National Park (near King Salmon, Alaska), brown bears can grow well over 1,000 pounds and even approach the 1-ton mark. The largest bears are found on salmon-rich Kodiak Island. Inland, at Denali National Park and on similar tundra landscape (where they feed on rodents, berries, insects, and the like), brown bears top out closer to 500 pounds. Bears can also take larger prey, but that's less common. You can recognize brown bears by their prominent shoulder humps, long faces, and large sizes; color can range from almost black to blond. Among the best places to see brown bears are **Pack Creek** (on Admiralty Island near Juneau), at **Denali and Katmai national parks,** or on bear-viewing floatplane excursions from **Homer.** Of these, Denali is the only inexpensive option.

**MOOSE**    In winter, when they move to the lowlands, moose can be an absolute pest, blocking roadways and eating expensive shrubbery. In the summer they're a little more elusive, most often seen standing in forest ponds, eating the weeds from the bottom or pruning streamside willows. Even during the summer, though, gardeners can often be heard cursing these animals, which, despite their immense size, can oh-so-delicately and neatly chomp the blossom off each tulip in a flower bed. The largest member of the deer family, with males reaching 1,200 to 1,600 pounds, moose are found primarily in the boreal forest that covers Interior and Southcentral Alaska. You'll be likely to see one if you're on a pre- or post-cruise land package such as the Anchorage-Denali-Fairbanks route. They are unmistakable. As big as a large horse, with bristly, ragged brown hair; a long, bulbous nose; and huge, mournful eyes, moose seem to crave pity—though they get little from the wolves and people who hunt them or from the trains and cars that run them down, and they give little to anyone in their way when they're on the move. Males grow large antlers, which they shed after battling for a mate every fall. Females lack antlers, are smaller, and give birth to one to three calves each year.

*Moose*

*Caribou*

**CARIBOU**   Alaska's barren-ground caribou are genetically identical to reindeer but were never domesticated as reindeer were in Europe. For Inupiat and Athabascan people, they continue to be an essential source of food and hides, and caribou hunting remains a necessity. By law, nobody is allowed to kill caribou for sport or recreation in Alaska. Both males and females have antlers that they shed annually. Caribou travel the Arctic tundra and Interior foothills often in herds of thousands of animals, a stunning sight witnessed by only a lucky few, as the migration routes lie in remote regions. You can, however, often see caribou in smaller groups of a few dozen at Denali National Park, along the Dalton and Denali highways, and on other northern rural roads above tree line. They're skittish, so the best technique is to stop and let them approach you.

**SITKA BLACK-TAILED DEER**   The Sitka black-tailed deer is a relatively small deer found in the coastal rainforests of Alaska. Males typically weigh in at around 120 pounds and have small antlers. Both males and females sport a reddish-brown coat in summer. They can be found throughout Southeast, in Prince William Sound, and on Kodiak Island.

*Sitka Black-Tailed Deer*                    *Dall Sheep*

**DALL SHEEP**   Dall sheep resemble the more familiar bighorn sheep but are smaller, with males weighing up to 300 pounds and females topping out at 150 pounds. Like the bighorn, males have curling horns, which they butt against each other to establish dominance for mating. Their habitat is high, rocky places, where their incredible agility makes them safe from predators. Except in a few exceptional spots, such as on the **cliffs above the Seward Highway** just south of Anchorage on Turnagain Arm, you almost always need strong binoculars to see Dall sheep. **Denali National Park** is a good place to see them in the usual way: from a great distance. Scanning the mountains, pick out white spots, then focus in on them. The sheep often move in herds of a dozen or more.

**MOUNTAIN GOAT**   Another animal that you won't see unless you bring your binoculars, mountain goats inhabit the same craggy mountain habitat as Dall sheep, including the prime viewing area on **Turnagain Arm.** From a distance it's easy to confuse mountain goats with female Dall sheep, but mountain goats are shaggier; have short, straight black horns (which appear in both the male and female); have the typical goat beard; and have a much more pronounced hump at the shoulders.

Mountain Goat

Sea Otter

**SEA OTTER**   Possibly number one in Alaska's "cute critter" category, the sea otter is a member of the weasel family (as are minks and river otters) and spends almost all of its life in the water. Extensively hunted for its rich coat from the mid–18th century (when Russian explorer Vitus Bering brought back pelts from his voyage of discovery and initiated extensive Russian settlement of Alaska) until the early 20th century, the sea otter was almost driven to extinction—in 1911, there were probably fewer than 2,000 of them left in Alaska. But by the mid-1970s that number had risen above 150,000. Adult males weigh between 70 and 100 pounds, while females average 40 to 60 pounds. Adults average 4½ feet in length. Their fur is generally brown to black, often with a silvery or gray tinge, particularly in older animals. You typically see sea otters floating on their backs, sometimes cradling a rock on their stomachs (which they use to crack open shellfish), sometimes just watching the cruise ships float by.

**SEA LION**   You'll hear 'em—and smell 'em—before you see 'em. An argumentative honking, like cars stalled in traffic, mixes with a low undertone that sounds like elephants with sinus problems. Then the smell hits you: fishy

---

### Alaska's Animals: Did You Know ... ?

Here are some more fun animal facts compiled and shared by Holland America's Alaska marketing maven, Noel DeChambeau.

- **Bald Eagles**   Their eyesight is so good, they can spot a single fish a mile away. Their wingspan can reach 7 feet and they can weigh as much as 15 pounds.
- **Caribou**   There are as many as a million of them in Alaska, in 32 herds that travel distances of up to 3,000 miles.
- **Dall sheep**   The males of the species have a skull an inch thick to protect their brains during combat.
- **Moose**   The largest deer in the world, moose can run at up to 35 mph.
- **Musk ox**   Ever protective of their young, they form a fortresslike circle around them when they're threatened.
- **Wolf**   Wolves eat 20 pounds of meat at a time and then may go for a week without eating.

beyond belief. Still, when you get close enough to know what you're smelling, you won't mind because it's quite a sight: Sea lions typically haul out in the hundreds onto small islands, where they loll in the sun, argue, occasionally fight, go fishing, and breed—just like people on vacation. Their bodies are huge, blubbery, tubular affairs that are perfect for the cold northern waters but appear impossibly ungainly on land, over which they bounce and bound on perfectly inadequate-looking front flippers. Still, even on land you wouldn't want to mess with one: The average adult male weighs approximately 1,250 pounds and measures 10½ feet long, while adult females average 580 pounds and are 8½ feet long. Most adult females are brownish yellow, while males typically are a bit darker, some with a reddish coat.

*Sea Lion*

# Index

See also Accommodations and Restaurant indexes, below.

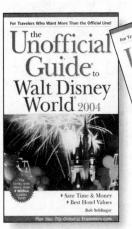
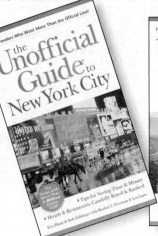
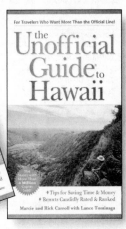
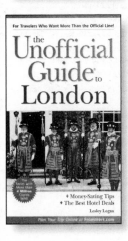
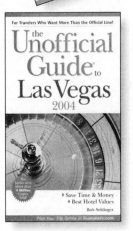
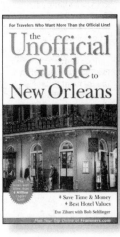

# *Frommer's* Portable Guides

## *Destinations in a Nutshell*

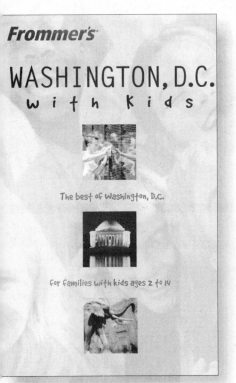 

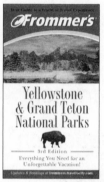

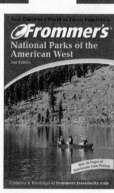
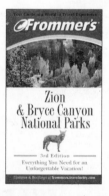

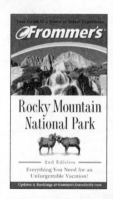

# FROMMER'S® COMPLETE TRAVEL GUIDES

Alaska
Alaska Cruises & Ports of Call
American Southwest
Amsterdam
Argentina & Chile
Arizona
Atlanta
Australia
Austria
Bahamas
Barcelona, Madrid & Seville
Beijing
Belgium, Holland & Luxembourg
Bermuda
Boston
Brazil
British Columbia & the Canadian Rockies
Brussels & Bruges
Budapest & the Best of Hungary
Calgary
California
Canada
Cancún, Cozumel & the Yucatán
Cape Cod, Nantucket & Martha's Vineyard
Caribbean
Caribbean Ports of Call
Carolinas & Georgia
Chicago
China
Colorado
Costa Rica
Cruises & Ports of Call
Cuba
Denmark
Denver, Boulder & Colorado Springs
England
Europe
Europe by Rail
European Cruises & Ports of Call

Florence, Tuscany & Umbria
Florida
France
Germany
Great Britain
Greece
Greek Islands
Halifax
Hawaii
Hong Kong
Honolulu, Waikiki & Oahu
India
Ireland
Italy
Jamaica
Japan
Kauai
Las Vegas
London
Los Angeles
Maryland & Delaware
Maui
Mexico
Montana & Wyoming
Montréal & Québec City
Munich & the Bavarian Alps
Nashville & Memphis
New England
Newfoundland & Labrador
New Mexico
New Orleans
New York City
New York State
New Zealand
Northern Italy
Norway
Nova Scotia, New Brunswick & Prince Edward Island
Oregon
Ottawa
Paris
Peru

Philadelphia & the Amish Country
Portugal
Prague & the Best of the Czech Republic
Provence & the Riviera
Puerto Rico
Rome
San Antonio & Austin
San Diego
San Francisco
Santa Fe, Taos & Albuquerque
Scandinavia
Scotland
Seattle
Shanghai
Sicily
Singapore & Malaysia
South Africa
South America
South Florida
South Pacific
Southeast Asia
Spain
Sweden
Switzerland
Texas
Thailand
Tokyo
Toronto
Turkey
USA
Utah
Vancouver & Victoria
Vermont, New Hampshire & Maine
Vienna & the Danube Valley
Virgin Islands
Virginia
Walt Disney World® & Orlando
Washington, D.C.
Washington State

# FROMMER'S® DOLLAR-A-DAY GUIDES

Australia from $50 a Day
California from $70 a Day
England from $75 a Day
Europe from $85 a Day
Florida from $70 a Day
Hawaii from $80 a Day

Ireland from $80 a Day
Italy from $70 a Day
London from $90 a Day
New York City from $90 a Day
Paris from $90 a Day
San Francisco from $70 a Day

Washington, D.C. from $80 a Day
Portable London from $90 a Day
Portable New York City from $90 a Day
Portable Paris from $90 a Day

# FROMMER'S® PORTABLE GUIDES

Acapulco, Ixtapa & Zihuatanejo
Amsterdam
Aruba
Australia's Great Barrier Reef
Bahamas
Berlin
Big Island of Hawaii
Boston
California Wine Country
Cancún
Cayman Islands
Charleston
Chicago
Disneyland®
Dominican Republic
Dublin

Florence
Frankfurt
Hong Kong
Las Vegas
Las Vegas for Non-Gamblers
London
Los Angeles
Los Cabos & Baja
Maine Coast
Maui
Miami
Nantucket & Martha's Vineyard
New Orleans
New York City
Paris

Phoenix & Scottsdale
Portland
Puerto Rico
Puerto Vallarta, Manzanillo & Guadalajara
Rio de Janeiro
San Diego
San Francisco
Savannah
Vancouver
Vancouver Island
Venice
Virgin Islands
Washington, D.C.
Whistler

## FROMMER'S® NATIONAL PARK GUIDES

Algonquin Provincial Park
Banff & Jasper
Family Vacations in the National
  Parks

Grand Canyon
National Parks of the American
  West
Rocky Mountain

Yellowstone & Grand Teton
Yosemite & Sequoia/Kings
  Canyon
Zion & Bryce Canyon

## FROMMER'S® MEMORABLE WALKS

Chicago
London

New York
Paris

San Francisco

## FROMMER'S® WITH KIDS GUIDES

Chicago
Las Vegas
New York City

Ottawa
San Francisco
Toronto

Vancouver
Walt Disney World® & Orlando
Washington, D.C.

## SUZY GERSHMAN'S BORN TO SHOP GUIDES

Born to Shop: France
Born to Shop: Hong Kong,
  Shanghai & Beijing

Born to Shop: Italy
Born to Shop: London

Born to Shop: New York
Born to Shop: Paris

## FROMMER'S® IRREVERENT GUIDES

Amsterdam
Boston
Chicago
Las Vegas
London

Los Angeles
Manhattan
New Orleans
Paris
Rome

San Francisco
Seattle & Portland
Vancouver
Walt Disney World®
Washington, D.C.

## FROMMER'S® BEST-LOVED DRIVING TOURS

Austria
Britain
California
France

Germany
Ireland
Italy
New England

Northern Italy
Scotland
Spain
Tuscany & Umbria

## THE UNOFFICIAL GUIDES®

Beyond Disney
California with Kids
Central Italy
Chicago
Cruises
Disneyland®
England
Florida
Florida with Kids
Inside Disney

Hawaii
Las Vegas
London
Maui
Mexico's Best Beach Resorts
Mini Las Vegas
Mini Mickey
New Orleans
New York City
Paris

San Francisco
Skiing & Snowboarding in the
  West
South Florida including Miami &
  the Keys
Walt Disney World®
Walt Disney World® for
  Grown-ups
Walt Disney World® with Kids
Washington, D.C.

## SPECIAL-INTEREST TITLES

Athens Past & Present
Cities Ranked & Rated
Frommer's Best Day Trips from London
Frommer's Best RV & Tent Campgrounds
  in the U.S.A.
Frommer's Caribbean Hideaways
Frommer's China: The 50 Most Memorable Trips
Frommer's Exploring America by RV
Frommer's Gay & Lesbian Europe
Frommer's NYC Free & Dirt Cheap

Frommer's Road Atlas Europe
Frommer's Road Atlas France
Frommer's Road Atlas Ireland
Frommer's Wonderful Weekends from
  New York City
The New York Times' Guide to Unforgettable
  Weekends
Retirement Places Rated
Rome Past & Present

Travel Tip: He who finds the best hotel deal has more to spend on facials involving knobbly vegetables.

Hello, the Roaming Gnome here. I've been nabbed from the garden and taken round the world. The people who took me are so terribly clever. They find the best offerings on Travelocity. For very little cha-ching. And that means I get to be pampered and exfoliated till I'm pink as a bunny's doodah.

**travelocity**®

Travel Tip: Make sure there's customer service for any change of plans — involving friendly natives, for example.

One can plan and plan, but if you don't book with the right people you can't seize le moment and canoodle with the poodle named Pansy. I, for one, am all for fraternizing with the locals. Better yet, if I need to extend my stay and my gnome nappers are willing, it can all be arranged through the 800 number at, oh look, how convenient, the lovely company coat of arms.